Jacob Harry Hollander

The Financial History of Baltimore

Jacob Harry Hollander

The Financial History of Baltimore

ISBN/EAN: 9783337338688

Printed in Europe, USA, Canada, Australia, Japan

Cover: Foto ©ninafisch / pixelio.de

More available books at **www.hansebooks.com**

JOHNS HOPKINS UNIVERSITY STUDIES

IN

HISTORICAL AND POLITICAL SCIENCE

HERBERT B. ADAMS, Editor

History is past Politics and Politics are present History.—*Freeman.*

EXTRA VOLUME

XX

The Financial History of Baltimore

BY

J. H. HOLLANDER, Ph. D.

ASSOCIATE IN ECONOMICS IN THE JOHNS HOPKINS UNIVERSITY

BALTIMORE
THE JOHNS HOPKINS PRESS
1899

The Lord Baltimore Press
THE FRIEDENWALD COMPANY
BALTIMORE, MD., U. S. A.

TO

MY MOTHER,

WHOSE INTEREST AND SYMPATHY HAVE ACCOMPANIED

ITS PROGRESS, THIS BOOK IS INSCRIBED

IN LOVE AND DEVOTION

PREFACE

The neglect of municipal economics by students of public finance is due in large part to the character of the subject-matter. The choice of the investigator is between crass and threadbare secondary materials, and crude and inaccessible primary sources. In both of these directions marked improvement is promised within the next few years. Yet it seems likely that until essential data have been digested and arranged in a series of detailed monographs tracing the financial development and describing the financial status of representative American cities, there can be no comprehensive study of many of the most important aspects of municipal finance.

The prime purpose of the present monograph is to contribute to this end. In many respects the financial history of Baltimore is typical of that of the ordinary American municipality, and details of local experience will be of value in subsequent generalizations. Where a distinctive municipal policy has been pursued, as with respect to works of internal improvement or street railway franchises, the results are interesting and instructive.

The investigation, although limited in scope, has been arduous. The absence of any detailed administrative study or even of any adequate municipal history of Baltimore has added much to the task. In crudeness of arrangement and in defectiveness of detail, the municipal reports of Baltimore are unsurpassed by those of any American city. The financial operations of the city have always been presented in the form of book-keeping accounts, instead of classified aggregates. This has made the mere determination of actual receipts and expenditures in any one year a matter of laborious compilation and arbitrary apportionment of several hundred items varying in amount from a few pennies to millions of dollars. An annual tabulation of receipts and expenditures has been attempted for each year up to 1835—thereafter, owing to the multiplication of entries, at quinquennial intervals. The assignment of contradictory and insufficiently described items has involved the exercise of personal judgment, and probably no two persons, proceeding independently, would have attained identical results. Yet the statistical tables, added as appendices, will serve the purpose of indicating the quantitative course of financial development, and have made it possible to confine the text proper to descriptive detail. The classification of public revenues proposed by Professor E. R. A. Seligman has been employed with no essential modification. In the case of expenditure, an empirical arrangement, corresponding in the main to the historical development of municipal functions, has been found more serviceable than the elaborate classifications suggested by recent writers as the basis of municipal accounting.

If the range of documentary materials has been limited, the number of persons who in one way or another have aided the study has been large. The financial officers of the city under successive administrations have spared no pains to make accessible the limited historical resources of their several departments. Suggestion and encouragement have been received at every stage of the inquiry from Professor Herbert B. Adams of the Johns Hopkins University.

Hon. Ferdinand C. Latrobe has discussed many phases of the work in the light of a long and intimate acquaintance with municipal affairs. Hon. Thomas G. Hayes has made repeated sacrifices of time and effort to elucidate legal aspects of municipal development. Hon. Alcaeus Hooper, Mr. Mendes Cohen, Mr. Theodore Marburg, Mr. E. Glenn Perine have read portions of the monograph in manuscript or in proof and have made helpful criticisms. Mr. N. Murray of the Johns Hopkins University has given valuable suggestions as to form and arrangement.

In a detailed investigation dealing with so large a body of specific facts, it seems inevitable that errors should creep in. Yet earnest effort has been made to secure accuracy, and it is hoped that few essential misstatements have been made. Critical comment and constructive suggestion have been freely introduced, but always in the objective spirit of the student and the investigator.

The monograph appears at a critical time in the municipal history of Baltimore. The early years of a second century of corporate existence are to be signalized by the practical operation of a reform city charter. In addition to whatever interest this study may possess for general students of finance, it is sent forth in the hope that it may contribute to the development of the new municipal spirit, strikingly manifest in Baltimore and evident in some degree throughout the United States.

TABLE OF CONTENTS

PART I.

THE FINANCES OF BALTIMORE TOWN, 1729–1796.

PART II.

THE FINANCES OF BALTIMORE CITY FROM 1797 TO 1816.

PART III.

THE FINANCES OF BALTIMORE CITY FROM 1817 TO 1856.

PART IV.

THE FINANCES OF BALTIMORE CITY FROM 1857 TO 1897.

PART V.

THE PRESENT FINANCIAL CONDITION OF BALTIMORE.

THE FINANCIAL HISTORY OF BALTIMORE

PRELIMINARY STATEMENT.

The financial history of Baltimore reflects with exactness the course of its material growth and of its administrative development. At no time has there been any important change in the organization of the city government or in the essential features of its economic life, without corresponding effect upon municipal finances. Similarly, each succeeding phase in fiscal life has left an enduring impress upon local administration, and to a less marked degree upon material development.

The first period in the fiscal history of Baltimore is the pre-corporate era from 1729, when Baltimore Town was created by legislative fiat as a market place and port of entry near the head of Chesapeake Bay, to 1796, when the original administrative shell, long since outgrown, was cast off and Baltimore was incorporated as a city.

Financial development within this period of fifty-seven years may be conveniently divided into three stages. The first, extending from the erection of the Town in 1729 to consolidation with Jones' Town in 1745, was characterized by slight independent financial activity; in financial as in administrative matters Baltimore Town was an integral part of Baltimore County. The second stage, from 1745 to the genesis of local self-government in 1781, was marked by the slow emergence of local life in financial matters, incident to territorial expansion and material growth. The third stage, from 1781 to the incorporation of Baltimore in 1796, was a continuous struggle to adapt the resources of a straggling village to the needs of an expanding city.

For one hundred years, the original charter remained the basis of the city government of Baltimore. But although not displaced until 1898 by a second fundamental instrument, its practical significance had long before been reduced to a minimum by the mass of amendatory legislation enacted by successive General Assemblies. From the standpoint of financial as of economic and administrative development, the first century of Baltimore's corporate existence falls naturally into three periods: the first extending from 1797 to 1816; the second from 1817 to 1856; the third from 1857 to 1897.

From 1797 to 1816 administrative and fiscal organization, the details of which had in the main been left to local choice by the act of incorporation, underwent repeated and illogical change. Rapid municipal growth made necessary the extension and reorganization of local functions and this was undertaken tentatively and conservatively. Normal increase in expenditure was early checked by the marked inelasticity of the sources of municipal revenue, and the exigencies of the War of 1812 resulted in the accumulation of unpaid claims against the city—the nucleus of the funded municipal debt of the succeeding period.

The essential features of the present financial system of Baltimore were established in the period from 1817 to 1856. The introduction of new industrial methods succeeded the reactionary depression following the War of 1812. Beginning with the projection of the Baltimore and Ohio Railroad as a necessary measure for preventing the diversion of western trade, the municipality plunged recklessly into the policy of aiding works of internal improvement, from the construction of which an immediate local advantage was supposed to accrue. By direct municipal loans and the lavish extension of municipal credit, a relatively large funded and guaranteed debt was amassed, necessitating increasing resort to the corporate power of taxation, and limitation in municipal function and expenditure.

The forty years from 1857 to 1897 may be said to constitute the modern period of the corporate history of Baltimore. Economic interests suffered keenly from the events of the Civil War, but with the revival of the prostrate industrial life of the South, the city emerged into new economic importance and subsequent growth was substantial and continuous. The administrative organization of the city underwent spasmodic and unimportant change. The local supremacy of the Know-Nothing party was succeeded by the administrative laxity and waste of the War and Reconstruction periods, and these in turn by a long era of political stability. The financial characteristics of the period were rapid growth in municipal expenditure and in funded indebtedness, increasing inelasticity in the taxable basis and in sources of municipal revenue other than direct taxation, and a consequent uninterrupted rise in the tax rate.

In the following pages the financial history of Baltimore through these successive periods is traced in detail. The narrative proper is supplemented by a consideration of the present financial status of the city, including a cross-sectional view of municipal finances in a single typical year (1897), a description of the fiscal provisions of the new charter with which Baltimore is about to begin a second century of corporate existence, and a chapter of critical comments and constructive suggestions.

PART I

THE FINANCES OF BALTIMORE TOWN

1729-1796

CHAPTER I

THE BEGINNINGS OF THE TOWN, 1729-1744.

The proprietary government of Maryland emerged from an era of troublous times upon a period of active growth and development towards the close of the first quarter of the eighteenth century. Commerce expanded, population increased and settlements to the northward thickened. It was not long before the need of additional ports of entry near the head of Chesapeake Bay began to be felt. On July 14, 1729, a petition, signed by leading planters of Baltimore County, was presented to the General Assembly praying for the erection of a town on the north side of Patapsco River, upon a tract of land situated some fourteen miles from the waters of the Bay. Three weeks later a bill to this effect was passed, appointing seven well known residents of the County as "Commissioners," to purchase by agreement or by condemnation the site indicated in the petition, and "to lay out the same in the most convenient manner into sixty equal lots to be erected into a Town," with adequate provision for streets, lanes and public purposes. These lots were open for settlement, preferably to residents of Baltimore County, but after six months to any other person paying to the owner of the land a due proportion of its total valuation and agreeing to erect thereupon, within a period of eighteen months, a house covering at least four hundred square feet.[1]

Like the hundred or more earlier fiat towns of provincial Maryland, Baltimore Town was designed essentially as a market place and entrepôt, where local traffic could be carried on, imports be entered, exports be cleared and public dues and taxes be paid. It was endowed with no exceptional political or civil privileges, and had virtually no organic life of its own. The government of the Town, vested in the original Commissioners who held office for life and filled vacancies arising in their own number, consisted of little more than the disposition of vacant sites, and the adjustment of disputes between lot holders. The settlement itself was in the main a typical Maryland town of provincial times, " a collection of stores, warehouses, quays and government buildings " which tended to grow " not around the chapel or school, but around the custom house or court house."[2]

A local body thus constituted had manifestly little occasion and less opportunity for independent financial activity. In fiscal as in other matters, early Baltimore Town was simply a geographical unit within Baltimore County. Residents of the Town were assessed in ordinary manner by the county court, and paid the customary charges of the parish. Services were rendered, authorized levies were made and expended by county justices or parish vestry within the Town, precisely as in the county or parish proper.

A suggestion of local life in financial matters appears incidentally in the act erecting the Town. Many persons who originally took up lots in the statutory towns of Maryland, failed to fulfill the conditions of settlement and so forfeited title. For the purpose of preventing the continuance or growth of vacant tracts, the General Assembly early

[1] Bacon, " Laws of Maryland," 1729, ch. 12.

[2] Wilhelm, " Maryland Local Institutions," pp. 105, 111, in *Johns Hopkins University Studies in Historical and Political Science*, Third Series (1885), Nos. V-VI-VII.

provided for the re-entry of forfeited lots. The usual clause was inserted in the act erecting Baltimore to the effect that any person might take up a forfeited lot and acquire a valid title thereto by "paying the Commissioners or person by them thereunto appointed, the sum first set and assessed upon such lot, for the public use and benefit of the town."[1]

The water front of the new settlement was quickly taken up; but landwards Baltimore grew slowly, and forfeitures and re-entries of building sites were frequent. Yet the revenue trickling from this source was thin and uncertain. Persons taking up forfeited lots formally acknowledged themselves as "debtor to the said Town as ordered by Act of Assembly."[2] But immediate payment of the purchase money seems rarely to have been made. A title to the lot was recorded, ordinarily with the simple proviso that the taker up "promises and obliges himself and his heirs to satisfy the Commissioners of the said Town for the said lot."[3] For many years the familiar fate of the statutory Maryland town threatened Baltimore, and the Town Commissioners directed their efforts to an increase of population and the erection of buildings and took no steps to enforce early payment of the purchase money of lots. Not until the Town had struck healthy root, did the disposition of forfeited sites become an appreciable source of revenue.

Few occasions, however, arose in the early life of the Town for any expenditures of a distinctly local character. In 1752, twenty-three years after its erection, Baltimore was still a straggling settlement of some twenty-five houses and two hundred inhabitants.[4] Necessary offices of a general character were exercised by county and parish authorities. The Commissioners selected one of their own number as clerk, to keep a record of proceedings and to maintain a plat of the town, as provided by the act creating Baltimore;

[1] Bacon, "Laws of Maryland," 1729, ch. 12.
[2] "Records of the Commissioners of Baltimore Town" (MS), p. 3.
[3] *Ibid.*, p. 7.
[4] Griffiths, "Annals of Baltimore," p. 32; Scharf, "Chronicles of Baltimore," p. 48.

but his services were probably remunerated by fees for making entries and recording titles.[1]

The revenues accruing from the sale of forfeited lots, while small, were probably adequate for slight expenditures for local repair and construction. Now and then some larger local improvement became necessary and its cost was defrayed by voluntary subscriptions of residents of the Town. The authority of the Commissioners, absolute within narrow limits, did not of course involve raising money by local levy, or the exaction of local fees or dues. In default of specific legislation by the General Assembly, or extraordinary appropriation by county or parish authorities, additional local expenditure could only be defrayed in the voluntary manner indicated. Thus record is found of a bridge built across Jones' Falls in 1732 to facilitate communication with the adjacent newly erected Jonas or Jones' Town, the cost of which was met by "the inhabitants of the town."[2] Such expenditures were possibly assessed by the Commissioners upon residents of Baltimore. But returns could not be enforced by process of law, and it is more likely that the amount required was secured then, as somewhat later, by purely voluntary subscription.[3] The slow growth of local revenues in early Baltimore is suggested by the apparent inability of the Town even to maintain in repair the bridge thus constructed and the consequent provision in an act of the Assembly of 1745, that it "shall for the future be deemed a Public Bridge and repaired and kept at the charge of Baltimore County."[4]

[1] "Records of the Commissioners of Baltimore Town" (MS), pp. 1, 5, *et passim.*

[2] Bacon, "Laws of Maryland," 1745, ch. 9, sect. 4.

[3] There is nothing in the financial history of Baltimore Town corresponding to the action of the inhabitants of Charlestown, who, in 1744, "voluntarily advanced and paid into the hands of the Commissioners appointed for laying out the said Town, the sum of Twenty shillings upon every and respective lot by them taken up, over and above the price and purchase thereof,"—the aggregate sum of £200 thus realized "to be applied towards building a Public Wharf and Store-House in the said Town for the advancement of trade thereof." Bacon, "Laws of Maryland," 1744, ch. 22.

[4] Bacon, "Laws of Maryland," 1745, ch. 9.

CHAPTER II

EXPANSION AND GROWTH, 1745-1780.

The consolidation with Baltimore Town of an adjacent settlement, Jones' Town, authorized by the Assembly in 1745,[1] marks the beginning of a period of territorial expansion and material growth. Two years later, in 1747, a strip of land lying between the earlier settlements was absorbed. Successive acts of the Assembly in 1750 and in 1753 added territory almost as large as the tract out of which the original town was erected. Further additions were made in 1765, in 1773, and in 1781. The life of the settlement gradually developed from a mere struggle for existence to a race for supremacy in trade with older towns of the province. Baltimore with its fine harbor, numerous mill streams and rich iron deposits slowly forged ahead. The issue of the contest, not realized until after the close of the Revolutionary War, was anticipated in 1768, when the privileges and dignities of county town—a court house and a prison—were transferred from Joppa to Baltimore. The outbreak of the Revolutionary War cut off foreign supplies and stimulated local manufactures and shipping, making possible a period of remarkable commercial activity following the final suspension of hostilities.

The institutional development of Baltimore during this period was less marked than its material growth. The "consolidation act" of 1745 vested the administration of the larger Baltimore Town in a new board of seven Town Commissioners holding permanent tenure and filling their own vacancies, but in all other matters, like their predecessors, a mere standing committee of the General Assembly.

[1] Bacon, "Laws of Maryland," 1745, ch. 9.

Some recognition of local life in financial matters was, however, inseparably connected with territorial growth. The clerical duties of the Commissioners became more onerous and they were empowered by the act of 1745 "to levy, assess and take by way of distress if needful, from the inhabitants of the Town by even and equal proportion the sum of three pounds to be paid to their clerk."

Assessment by poll was virtually the only form of direct taxation known in Maryland prior to the Revolutionary War, and the phrase "by even and equal proportion" has been taken accordingly to mean that the Commissioners annually levied upon each actual resident of the Town his per capita share of the three pounds required.[1] In actual fact, although the selection of a clerk followed immediately upon the organization of the new board of Town Commissioners, no provision appears to have been made for his specific remuneration until 1750, when the Commissioners resolved "to levy a Tax of one Shilling Currency per Annum on Each Lott in the Town toward defraying the wages of the clerk and that the same be levied for the year past ending March 27, 1749."[2] A special tax on land—the germ of a general property tax—and not a poll tax is thus the first direct tax levied in Baltimore and probably one of the earliest forms of a property tax in Maryland.[3] Record is found of an apparently similar levy in 1752;[4] but thereafter the ordinary revenues of the Commissioners appear to have been adequate for the purpose, without necessary recourse to direct taxation.

The act of 1745 authorized a re-survey of the Town, and a clearer marking of the bounds of lots. The latter work extended over some years and involved a considerable cost —defrayed in part by the services of persons in debt for the

[1] "Report of Baltimore Tax Commission" (1885), p. 7.

[2] "Records of the Commissioners of Baltimore Town" (MS), p. 23.

[3] "Report of the Maryland Tax Commission" (1888), p. cxxiv.

[4] "Records of the Commissioners of Baltimore Town" (MS), p. 30.

purchase of forfeited lots, to whom a corresponding credit was allowed by the Commissioners.[1] An appreciable expenditure was however necessary, and when in 1750 the one shilling tax for clerical services was levied, the Commissioners, apparently by mere form of analogy, resolved to levy "also One Shilling currency per Annum on Each Lott for a Locust Post which is set up at the end of Each Lott."[2]

As an exercise of local power, this charge is anomalous. It was entirely without specific authority and ordinary processes of law could certainly not have been employed to enforce payment from delinquent lot owners. Both in regard to this and the preceding levy the Clerk was directed "to return a list of what he receives to the Commissioners at their next meeting." But such a report if made has not been preserved and we are left in doubt as to the results attending either levy. No other direct tax of any kind appears to have been levied in Baltimore until 1783.

As Baltimore Town developed, the administrative oversight exercised in theory by the county court inevitably involved the neglect of local needs. Thus the repair of the bridge made a county charge by specific enactment in 1745 became again in 1747 an object of local concern. The growth of local trade and commerce hastened the emergence of distinctly local demands clearly beyond the province of the county administration. A fence was erected about the town in 1746, either as tradition relates to serve as a wall of defense from a rumored Indian incursion, or more likely to keep stray swine and geese from trespassing. The earliest local functionary for other than clerical purposes,[3] was a person appointed in 1750 at "40 shillings per annum" to restrain residents from appropriating fence pickets for kindling wood. Need was early felt for public wharves, and the first of these was actually commenced in

[1] "Records of the Commissioners of Baltimore Town" (MS), pp. 22-23.

[2] *Ibid.*, p. 33.

[3] *Ibid.*, p. 23.

1750.[1] The erection of a market house, agitated as early as 1751, was finally consummated ten years later, and the appointment of a clerk of the market, by the Justices of Baltimore County Court, to receive "not more than 30 pounds per annum" from out the Town treasury, was authorized by the Assembly in 1765.[2]

The inception of improvements of this character proceeded ordinarily, as in the earliest days of the Town, from voluntary agencies. Thus in 1748 twenty-six residents of the Town subscribed "towards keeping, repairing, and making good the fence of the said town and supporting a person to keep it in order."[3] In 1751 an unsuccessful subscription was opened to erect a public market since "no provision hath yet been made by law or otherwise."[4] Three years later $450.00 were raised by a benefit lottery conducted by residents of the Town for building the public wharf,[5] and in 1764 a more liberal subscription, aided by a second lottery, secured enough to make possible the erection of the market house upon a site leased by the Town Commissioners. The maintenance and extension of local institutions, once provided, speedily devolved upon the Town and entailed a steadily increasing local expenditure.

The growing need of income was met, in part, by the larger revenue derived from the re-entry and sale of forfeited lots. The Act of 1745 transferring the administration of the Town to a new board of Town Commissioners, authorized them to recover "any money which shall be found due to the first commissioners from any takers-up of the lots by virtue of the original laws for laying out the same; which money they shall apply to the uses intended by the said original Act."[6] Having ascertained in 1747 that

[1] Griffiths, "Annals of Baltimore," p. 29.

[2] *Ibid.*, pp. 31-32; Scharf, "Chronicles of Baltimore," pp. 46-47; Bacon, "Laws of Maryland," 1765, ch. 35.

[3] Griffiths, "Annals of Baltimore," p. 30; Scharf, "Chronicles of Baltimore," p. 39.

[4] Griffiths, "Annals," pp. 31-32; Scharf, "Chronicles," pp. 46-47.

[5] Griffiths, "Annals," p. 34; Scharf, "Chronicles," p. 49.

[6] Bacon, "Laws of Maryland," 1745, ch. 9.

"there is 25 lotts which the proprietors have not paid for" in Baltimore Town, and twenty-four lots, in Jones' Town, the Commissioners promptly proceeded to enforce settlement.[1] In February 1748, it was further resolved that "when any person applies to the Clerk to take up any Lott either in Baltimore or in Jones's Town that they pay down the money to the Clerk, or the Clerk is not to enter it."[2] Payment of arrearages was gradually made and vacant sites remaining were taken up, sometimes at a considerable premium.[3]

The aggregate revenue derived from the sale of forfeited sites, even when supplemented by such occasional windfalls as the disposition of the town-fence remnants or the sale of deserted houses,[4] tended from its very nature to diminish as the Town became more thickly settled and the need for local revenues became more urgent. More productive sources of local revenues were (1) Fines and Forfeitures, and (2) Market Licenses and Rentals:

(Fines and Forfeitures.) No original power resided in the Town Commissioners to impose local fines, even in the exercise of specifically conferred authority. The town-fence was abstracted piece-meal, almost under the administrative nose of the Town, with confessedly no means of redress on the part of the Commissioners.[5] A general power conferred by the Assembly in 1747[6] to cause all nuisances to be abated was inadequate to effect the removal of any large inconvenience, and specific authority, enforcable by penalties, had to be sought from the Assembly when such an occasion arose.[7]

[1] "Records of the Commissioners of Baltimore Town" (MS), pp. 17-18.

[2] *Ibid.*, p. 21.

[3] *Ibid.*, p. 25.

[4] *Ibid.*, pp. 23, 30.

[5] *Ibid.*, p. 30.

[6] Bacon, "Laws of Maryland," 1747, ch. 21.

[7] *Ibid.*, 1766, ch. 22. As late as 1791, the Town Commissioners petitioned the legislature to impose penalties for enforcing authority vested in them several years earlier.

The earliest specific grant of authority for the imposition of local fines, is contained in an act of the Assembly of 1747, wherein the Town Commissioners were empowered broadly to make such rules and orders "as may tend to the Improvement and Regulation of said Town in general," and specifically to impose a fine of ten shillings upon every resident allowing his chimney to catch fire or failing to keep "a ladder high enough to extend to the Top of the Roof of such House."[1] Of more importance, financially considered, was the provision in the act of 1765, appropriating to the Town Commissioners "for the Use and Benefit of the Town," all fines and forfeitures accruing from neglect of the regulations prescribed for market sales.[2]

The development of local trade was followed by the institution of a system of local inspection of staple merchandise. In 1768 the General Assembly authorized the annual appointment by the Town Commissioners of an inspector of flour, three cullers or garblers of staves and shingles, three measurers of grain, and five weighers of hay and corders of wood; these officials were authorized to receive specified fees, but were required to transfer all fines and forfeitures accruing under the act to the Town Commissioners, "to be by them laid out and expended in mending the Public Wharfs and Streets in the said Town."[3]

Some few fines although locally imposed were not remitted to local use. Provision was made in 1774 for the annual appointment by the Town Commissioners of a gauger to measure liquids brought to Baltimore for sale. Fines and forfeitures therein accruing were however appropriated one-half to the informer and one-half toward defraying the county charge.[4]

(Licenses and Rentals.) The General Assembly in 1747 authorized the Town Commissioners to appoint two Fairs to be held annually in Baltimore, and to provide regulations

[1] Bacon, "Laws of Maryland," 1747, ch. 21.
[2] *Ibid.*, 1765, ch. 35.
[3] *Ibid.*, 1768, ch. 15.
[4] *Ibid.*, 1774, ch. 23.

therefor.[1] Aside from the fines and forfeitures accruing from violation of prescribed regulations, no regular revenue appears to have been derived from this source for several years. On February 6, 1751, the Town Commissioners ordered their clerk: "to put up advertisements, one Month before the Fairs kept in the Town to inform all persons that they are not to erect any Booth or Sell any Liquors at the said fairs before they obtain License from the Clerk and pay him for the same. The Clerk not to receive a Sum exceeding fifteen Shillings for any one Booth nor less than Two Shillings and Six Pence to be applied to the use of the Town."[2]

The collection of this earliest license tax probably came to an end with the completion of the Town market house. In 1765, the General Assembly authorized the Town Commissioners to appoint a clerk of the market, to rent the stalls and shambles, to designate two days in the week as market days, and to impose penalties for sales and purchases at any other time or place. Rentals, fines and forfeitures accrued to the Town Commissioners for "the public use and benefit of the Town."[3]

The disbursement of local funds was entrusted largely to the discretion of the Town Commissioners. Specific funds were sometimes appropriated to specific purposes, ordinarily to those representing local needs at the time most urgent. Thus fines imposed for chimney fires in 1747 were devoted "to some Building or Improvement in the said Town, such as the Repair of the Bridge or making and repairing a public wharf." Penalties and forfeitures accruing under the inspection act of 1768 were expended in "mending the public Wharfs and Streets." More commonly the Town Commissioners were directed simply to apply the sums accruing to "the public Use and Benefit of the Town." In any

[1] Bacon, "Laws of Maryland," 1747, ch. 21.

[2] "Records of the Commissioners of Baltimore Town" (MS), p. 29.

[3] "Laws of Maryland," 1765, ch. 35.

event a clause designating specific objects of expenditure must have had suggestive rather than mandatory force, and to have been subject in practice to the discretion of the Town Commissioners.

Provision was ordinarily made in every act appropriating funds for local use, that precise account of receipts and expenditures should be kept by the clerk of the Town Commissioners, or as he came gradually to be called, the Town Clerk; but nothing like a periodic fiscal statement seems to have been required or rendered during this period, and it is impossible to reconstruct any fiscal summary from the scanty records of the Town Commissioners.

CHAPTER III

THE GENESIS OF SELF-GOVERNMENT, 1781-1796.

At the close of the Revolutionary War, Baltimore Town had clearly outgrown its original administrative shell. A form of government devised for a port of entry and strained to satisfy the needs of a straggling village was manifestly inadequate for a town of some 8000 inhabitants. This was particularly evident in financial matters where the limited resources of a tentative commercial settlement, with little or no organic life of its own, were available for the expanding wants of an incipient city. A measure of local self-consciousness developed with the events of the War, and in 1782 the first of repeated unsuccessful attempts was made to secure the incorporation of the Town. Thereafter until actual incorporation in 1797, the administrative development of Baltimore was an unsatisfactory attempt to satisfy contingencies of material growth by an adaptation of old forms, and the duplication rather than the extension of administrative machinery. The Town Commissioners were vested with somewhat broader authority and remained nominally in control of the general administration of the city; but in the main, new functions of importance were entrusted to independent and practically co-ordinate boards or commissions, granted specific authority by the General Assembly and exercising independent financial powers. Thus the paving, repairing and cleaning of streets, with certain allied functions, were in 1782 entrusted to a special board of Street Commissioners. In 1783 the general care of the channel and harbor of Baltimore was vested in a board of Port Wardens, and in 1784 the functions of watching and lighting the town were conferred upon the then almost lifeless board of Town Commissioners. The financial history of Baltimore during this period resolves itself into an examination of the financial activity of these several bodies.

The Board of Special Commissioners.

The most urgent local improvement at the close of the War was the paving, cleaning and repair of streets. Arthur Young's familiar estimate of the Warrington turnpike, "most infamously bad" and "made with a view to immediate destruction" could have been applied in all propriety to Baltimore high-ways. Sidewalks and cart-roads had remained entirely unpaved since the erection of the Town, and the soft soil and heavy traffic combined to render many of them dangerous and all of them disreputable.[1] As early as 1768, an act of the Assembly authorized the Town Commissioners to expend fines and forfeitures therein accruing to "mending the public wharfs and streets." Larger recognition was accorded in an act of the Assembly of 1781, authorizing a local tax on auction receipts. A designated person was appointed Town Auctioneer, and penalties were imposed upon any one else conducting a public sale or employing a person for that purpose. The auctioneer was empowered to charge specified per centum fees upon the values of various classes of property sold, and was required to pay to the Town Commissioners, in quarterly amount, "one pound on every hundred pounds worth of property by him sold," to be expended in mending and repairing the streets of the Town.[2]

The Town Commissioners appear to have used their own discretion in the expenditure of the monies so accruing, without strict compliance with the letter of the law.[3]

[1] Griffiths, "Annals of Baltimore," p. 95.

[2] "Laws of Maryland," 1781, ch. 11.

[3] "Ordered that Vendue Master pay to Such Person as the Commissioners shall appoint, such sum as may be sufficient to pave and post the Market House and around it"; cf. "Records of the Commissioners of Baltimore Town" (MS), p. 36.

Whether as a result of this fact, or from dissatisfaction with the personnel of the board, or because of the inadequacy of the fund appropriated, or merely influenced by the practice of entrusting new functions to new commissions—a radical change was effected by the passage of an act in 1782 for "the speedy application of the monies appropriated for repairing the streets in Baltimore Town."

Functions. Seven designated persons were therein appointed a board of "Special Commissioners," to hold office for the term of five years during which the act was to continue in force, with power to fill vacancies arising in their number by reason of death, resignation or removal. They were authorized to "direct and superintend the leveling, pitching and repairing the streets, and the building and repairing the bridges within said town and to devise and do all and every thing necessary to promote this end, which they may judge for the benefit or advantage of the said town and its inhabitants."[1] Baltimore street was directed to be first paved, and thereafter those streets or parts of streets which were "most essential to the welfare and trade of the town," in a succession determined by the discretion of the Special Commissioners, until the completion of the whole.

To defray the expenditures thus incurred, the act empowered the Special Commissioners, (1) to collect either in person or by a treasurer by them appointed, the proceeds of the auction tax hitherto paid by the town auctioneer to the Town Commissioners; (2) to recover from the Town Commissioners "all monies paid to them or in their hands by virtue of their powers for repairing the streets of said Town," and (3) to receive the proceeds of fines and forfeitures theretofore or thereafter appropriated for the repair of streets, or for the general use and benefit of the Town. If these appropriations proved inadequate, the Special Commissioners were authorized to borrow from the

[1] "Laws of Maryland," 1782 (Nov. sess.), ch. 17.

inhabitants of the Town the amount of five thousand pounds to be applied as directed, for the ultimate payment of which the said appropriations were pledged.

Changed methods of expenditure rather than additional sources of revenue were provided by this act, and the Special Commissioners found the means available for general street paving entirely inadequate. A detailed measure for "the more effectual paving the streets of Baltimore-town" was accordingly passed by the General Assembly, in January 1783.[1] The Special Commissioners appointed in the previous measure were by this statute made a body corporate by the name of the "Special Commissioners for Baltimore-town." The incumbents were to stay in office, filling vacancies by co-optation until 1786. Thereafter a method of indirect election was to prevail. Residents of the Town qualified to vote for delegates to the Assembly or having real property therein above the value of thirty pounds were directed to elect by ballot in October 1786, and quinquennially thereafter, nine persons qualified to serve as delegates, to be "Electors of Special Commissioners." These Electors were directed to select by ballot out of their own number, having regard to integrity, industry, ability, and the equal representation of the several parts of the Town, seven Special Commissioners who must have been residents of Baltimore for three years next preceding election or own real and personal property therein above the value of five hundred pounds. Vacancies arising in the board in intervals between elections were filled by the choice of the survivors.

The general maintenance of the "road-way" of the town —streets, bridges, sewers—was thus vested in the Special Commissioners, and thereafter until 1796 when the authority had by the various local boards of the Town was transferred to the corporation of Baltimore City, this constituted their most important function. In 1789 conservative senti-

[1] "Laws of Maryland," 1782 (Nov. sess.), ch. 17.

ment succeeded in enacting a measure whereby the Special Commissioners were forbidden to proceed with the paving of any street or alley until their choice had been approved by the Town Commissioners.[1] Two years later, this statute was repealed, and the Special Commissioners were left in entire control of the care of the city highways.[2]

Certain additional powers were from time to time incidentally conferred upon the Special Commissioners. Such were the enforcement of certain regulations "for the more effectual remedy to extinguish fire," including authority to cause wells to be sunk and pumps to be erected in parts of the Town remote from water-supply, and the maintenance and repair of wells and pumps so provided;[3] the appointment of the assize of bread;[4] the extension of certain streets to the water front,[5] and the construction of sewers in the precincts of the Town.[6] Sometimes particular revenues were made available for such specific purposes, as in the sinking of wells and the erection of pumps. Otherwise the charge was directed to be paid out of the general funds in the possession of the Special Commissioners.[7]

Revenues. The inadequacy of the revenues appropriated in the original measure appointing Special Commissioners in 1782 has already been noted. The act of 1783 however authorized an important series of local exactions, which may perhaps be said to constitute virtually the earliest comprehensive recognition of local financial life in Baltimore. Subsequent fiscal legislation until 1797 was largely amendatory of or supplementary to this act, and can best be treated in connection with the detailed features of the meas-

[1] "Laws of Maryland," 1789 (Nov. sess.), ch. 45.
[2] *Ibid.*, 1791, ch. 59.
[3] *Ibid.*, 1787, ch. 4; 1792 (Nov. sess.), ch. 21.
[4] *Ibid.*, 1791, ch. 59, sect. 14.
[5] *Ibid.*, 1796, ch. 45.
[6] *Ibid.*, 1792 (Nov. sess.), ch. 21.
[7] Thus the provision directing the Special Commissioners to pay the assessors appointed to regulate the assize of bread out "of any of the funds, which, by the present laws of this state, have or may come to their hands." *Ibid.*, 1792 (April sess.), ch. 6.

ure. The revenues of the Special Commissioners may be distinguished as follows: (i) Fines and Forfeitures; (ii) Lotteries; (iii) Special Assessments; (iv) Taxes.

(Fines and Forfeitures.) By the act authorizing their appointment, the Special Commissioners were put in receipt of all fines and forfeitures theretofore accruing to the Town Commissioners, whether originally appropriated for the repair of the streets or for the common benefit of the Town. In 1782 an additional fine—"tax," it is termed in the statute—of thirty shillings was imposed upon chimney fires, and one of corresponding amount upon persons convicted in the county court of selling liquors without licenses. Ten years later, in 1792, the penalty upon chimney fires was curiously adjusted to the size of the structure—three pounds, if a house of three stories; twenty shillings, if one of two stories, and fifteen shillings, if one of one story.[1]

Occasionally penalties imposed to enforce authority not vested in the Special Commissioners accrued to this body. Thus fines imposed in 1791 upon unlicensed chimney sweeping were appropriated half to the informer, half "to the street commissioners for the paving and repair of the streets."[2] The same act provided that penalties and forfeitures arising from violation of regulations for gunpowder storage should be applied "towards the expense of paving and repairing the streets," doubtless at the discretion of the Special Commissioners. Similarly fines and forfeitures under an act of 1792 to regulate the exportation of potash accrued half to the prosecutor, and half to "the Street or Special Commissioners of Baltimore Town."[3]

(Lotteries.) From the early days of the Town, quasi-public lotteries had been employed to supplement private contributions as a means of effecting needed local improvements. Regular provision for a distinctly public and spe-

[1] Penalties in detail were also imposed by the act appointing the Special Commissioners, to enforce the various powers therein conferred.

[2] "Laws of Maryland," 1791, ch. 69, sect. 29.

[3] *Ibid.*, 1792, ch. 65.

cifically authorized lottery was first made in 1791,[1] probably to obviate the necessity, as will be noted hereafter, of a heavier direct tax. The Special Commissioners were therein authorized to raise annually by lottery a sum not exceeding £3500 per annum and to retain one-third of the proceeds, the remaining two-thirds being paid to the Wardens of the Port. The same act prohibited private lotteries in the Town, and in the following year this prohibition was extended to the State at large.[2]

The curious interweaving of various authorities in the administration of Baltimore Town at this period is illustrated by the measure prescribed for the regulation of the Baltimore Town lottery. The Special Commissioners were authorized to appoint, with the advice and consent of the Wardens of the Port, managers to conduct the lottery, whose bond must be approved by the Town Commissioners and recorded and lodged with the clerk of the Baltimore County Court.

(Special Assessments). The act of 1782 authorized the Special Commissioners to levy twelve shillings and six pence on every foot front of "improved and unimproved lots in those parts of the streets fixed on to be paved or that may have been paved," and six shillings and three pence on similar lots located in "lanes and alleys paved or to be paved." The charge was to be assessed and levied but once, and the selection of the particular localities to be paved was left to the direction of the Special Commissioners, "as appears to them essential to the growth and prosperity of the said town." The assessment could be laid upon tenants, who were authorized in such event to make a corresponding deduction from rental payment.

This charge was essentially a special assessment. It was "a payment made once and for all to defray the cost of a specific improvement to property undertaken in the public interest, and levied by the government in proportion to the

[1] "Laws of Maryland," 1791, ch. 59. [2] *Ibid.*, 1792, ch. 58.

particular benefit accruing to the property owners."[1] It was levied within a particular district; not however as a special tax according to the general ability to pay, of those residing within the district, but "according to the individual benefits accruing to the owners of real property." The "foot-front rule" was employed as an index to ascertain the amount of these individual benefits.[2]

In 1789 upon petition that "the price of materials and labour hath fallen very considerably," the General Assembly reduced the assessment charge one half, or, to six shillings and three pence per front foot of street lots, and to three shillings and two pence of lane or alley lots. The zeal of the Special Commissioners seems to have offended the conservative sentiment of the Town, and a clause was added, directing that streets selected for paving, hitherto at the mere discretion of the Special Commissioners, must thereafter receive the consent of the Town Commissioners.[3] The reduction came inopportunely. Legislative authority for the auction tax, imposed in 1781 and renewed in 1784, and for the property tax, imposed in 1783, expired in 1789, thus cutting off two important sources of revenue from the Special Commissioners. Funds accruing from other sources—specific taxes, fines, forfeitures—were required for maintenance and repair, leaving as the only fund available for further construction, the reduced assessment charge. This was promptly found to be "greatly inadequate" and "not more than sufficient to keep the streets already paved in repair." Experience having further shown that "the tax fixing the rate per foot at one price for streets and alleys of different widths, operates unequally and oppressively," a higher tariff of assessment charges, apportioned to the width of the respective streets or alleys was enacted in 1791 and remained in force until the incorporation of the Town.[4]

In 1787, an act of the General Assembly "for the more

[1] Seligman, "Essays on Taxation," p. 304; Rosewater, "Special Assessments," p. 9.

[2] *Ibid.*, pp. 63, 129-130.

[3] "Laws of Maryland," 1789, ch. 45.

[4] *Ibid.*, 1791, ch. 59.

effectual remedy to extinguish fire in Baltimore town" directed all householders assessed for £100 to provide, under penalty of fines, two leather buckets to hang near the front door for use in case of fire. In addition, the Special Commissioners were authorized to cause wells to be sunk and pumps erected in parts of the town remote from water supply, the expense thereof "to be raised and paid by the assessable property on the square that wants such wells or pumps, to be levied, collected and applied by the commissioners aforesaid for the purpose aforesaid." Provision was made that no steps should be taken until a majority of property owners on the square should have indicated by petition their desire therefor, and that fines and forfeitures accruing under the act should be used in part payment of this expenditure.[1]

(General Property Tax). The most significant provision of the act of 1782 was the authority conferred upon the Special Commissioners to levy a tax "not exceeding two shillings six pence on every hundred pounds of assessed property" within the Town. The assessment for the public levy was taken as the basis of the local tax. The Special Commissioners were authorized to appoint collectors of the tax who among other things should "call upon the county commissioners of the tax to know the yearly valuation of property within said town and to regulate the tax upon every £100 worth of property by said valuation." Appeal lay to the Special Commissioners who were empowered "to diminish and add to such person's rate or assessment as to them shall seem just and reasonable."

In 1785 was passed "an act to ascertain the value of the land in the several counties of this state, for the purpose of laying the public assessment." The bounds of Baltimore Town and "precincts"[2] were defined; local commissioners of the tax were appointed distinct from those of Baltimore County, and provision was made for a distinct

[1] "Laws of Maryland," 1787, ch. 4. [2] See above, p. 60, note 1.

local assessment. The commissioners of the tax for Baltimore Town were directed to appoint a proper person to ascertain and return "all rents, lots and parcels of ground of all kinds, and houses, buildings and improvements, in said town"—to be thereafter valued by them. As a rule for estimating the value of local ground-rents in Baltimore, as in other towns of the State, the local commissioners of the tax were directed to capitalize ground-rents at the rate of eight per cent. They assessed all improvements and increments in value upon lessees and demanded the sum rated of the lessees, who were authorized to make a corresponding deduction from rental payments. The value of rented houses was determined by capitalizing the annual rental at the rate of sixteen per cent. Where the property was leased for more than three years, the valuation was found by deducting the capitalized rental from the current valuation. Other forms of real property were to be "valued at their actual worth in ready current money." No specific mode was prescribed for the valuation of personal property. The governor of the State was directed to appoint in Baltimore Town as in each of the counties three persons, constituting a court of appeals, to review upon appeal the valuations of the commissioners of the tax.[1]

In 1792 a general reassessment of real and personal property in the state was again authorized. The number of commissioners of the tax for Baltimore Town was increased to five and therein appointed. They were directed to select as assessors, "one or more sensible and active persons," residents and property owners of the Town. In the valuation of real property, the provisions of the act of 1785 were to prevail. Slaves and silver plate were to be valued upon a fixed scale; but every other article of personal property, "at its actual worth in ready money made current by law," according to "the discretion and judgement of the several assessors." The board of appeals established by the act

[1] "Laws of Maryland," 1785, ch. 53.

of 1785 was abolished, and the commissioners of the tax were vested with power of final review.[1]

Legislative authority for the two shillings six penny property tax expired in 1790.[2] The growing burden of local and public charges discouraged its re-enactment and when in 1791 the necessity arose for additional revenues for street paving, recourse was had to an increased paving assessment, as described, to additional license taxes and to an annual public lottery, noted above.[3] Provision was however made that in the event of these several revenues proving inadequate, the Special Commissioners might levy a tax "not exceeding one shilling and three pence on every £100 of assessable property" within the Town. Prompt use was made of the authority conferred, and the tax was regularly imposed, at the maximum rate authorized, until the incorporation of the Town.

(Auction Receipts Tax). The origin of the tax on auction receipts has already been intimated. It was imposed in 1781, to remain in force for three years, for the purpose of providing the Town Commissioners with a special fund for the repair of streets. Exclusive auction privileges were conferred upon a designated person, the town auctioneer, who was authorized to charge specified fees, and directed to pay to the Town Commissioners in sworn quarterly account one per cent. upon the valuation of all property sold. By the statute of 1782 appointing Special Commissioners, the proceeds of the tax on auction receipts were transferred from the Town Commissioners to the Special Commissioners, but no change was made in the form of the tax. This transfer was confirmed by the measure of 1783, and additional fines were imposed upon "the vendue master" for refusal to render periodic settlement of receipts—the amount of the fine to be adjudged by "any two impartial persons," one of whom should be chosen by the Special

[1] "Laws of Maryland," 1792, ch. 71.
[2] *Ibid.*, 1782, ch. 17, sect. 2.
[3] *Ibid.*, 1791, ch. 59.

Commissioners, the other by the auctioneer, and to be recovered as in the case of small debts.[1]

The essential provisions of the statute of 1781 were reenacted in 1785.[2] Slight changes were made in the amount of the prescribed fees and the town auctioneer was authorized to receive over and above these "on all vessels at the rate of one quarter per cent., and on all other property, except as aforesaid, at the rate one half per cent.," to be paid to the Special Commissioners of Baltimore Town, as theretofore, in quarterly account and to be by them applied to "the mending and paving the streets thereof." This act was to remain in force for a single year; but at the following session of the General Assembly, it was continued for three years longer.[3] Authority for the tax thus expired at the end of the legislative session of 1789.[4] At the following session of the General Assembly the tax was re-imposed; but the occasion therefor as well as the further significance of the tax are associated with the activities of the Port Wardens rather than those of the Special Commissioners, and can most conveniently be considered in another connection.

(Specific Taxes). The revenue act of 1782 imposed annual specific taxes as follows: on four-wheeled riding carriages, 30 shillings; on chairs and sulkies, 15 shillings; on drays, 25 shillings; on wagons and cars, 25 shillings; on riding horses, 20 shillings; on billiard tables, 15 pounds. Tavern houses were subjected to an additional charge of £5 annually. A tax of £50 per annum was imposed upon the play house of the Town, and a license tax, to be fixed in amount by the Special Commissioners, upon all public exhibitions.

The Special Commissioners were empowered "to continue all or as many of the specific taxes above mentioned as may be judged least injurious to the welfare of the town, and towards a permanent fund to keep in repair the streets

[1] "Laws of Maryland," 1782 (Nov. sess.), ch. 17, sects. 3 and 24.
[2] *Ibid.*, 1784, ch. 61.
[3] *Ibid.*, 1785, ch. 77.
[4] *Ibid.*, 1791, ch. 59, preamble.

and for the purposes of this act." In actual fact these taxes were imposed until the incorporation of the Town, and indeed were continued thereafter.

(Collection and Recovery). The original act of 1782 appointing Special Commissioners merely directed the payment of all charges to "the said special commissioners, or to their treasurer, to be by them appointed." The act of the following session was more explicit. In addition to a clerk and a treasurer, the appointment was authorized of one or more collectors to assess the various charges upon the persons liable, to collect promptly, under penalty for neglect, the sums so assessed, and to make periodic returns thereof to the treasurer. Much difficulty was however experienced in the collection of taxes and fines. The annual balance-sheets of the Special Commissioners showed arrearages, at all times considerable in amount, and occasionally disproportionate.

Fines, penalties and forfeitures accruing to the Special Commissioners were recovered with costs of suit by and in the name of their treasurer before a justice of the peace or in the county court.[1] Civil procedure seems also to have been the only method at first available of enforcing the payment of local taxes. In 1792 the Special Commissioners were however vested with power to recover all taxes laid or to be laid, by distress and sale of the property of the persons chargeable—the procedure being as in cases of distresses for rent, and remedy lying in a writ of replevin sued out of the Baltimore County Court.[2]

(Gross Receipts). The special assessment for street paving—"the paving tax," as it was ordinarily called—and the tax on auction sales during the period of its imposition, formed the most important items in the receipts of the Special Commissioners. The yield of the special assessment declined from 1783 to 1789, recovering with the operation of the graduated scale enacted in 1791 to the close

[1] "Laws of Maryland," 1782 (April sess.), ch. 39, sect. 5; 1782 (November sess.), ch. 17, sect. 30.
[2] *Ibid.*, 1792 (November sess.), ch. 21, sect. 1.

of the period. The tax on auction sales showed an apparent decline from 1783 to 1788; but the parallel increase during this period of the amount of "taxes in arrears" suggests that this was in large measure due to the delinquency of the collector or auctioneer. The specific and license taxes were comparatively inelastic, the increase proceeding largely from the tax on liquor sales. The proceeds from fines and forfeitures remained relatively unimportant. Perhaps the most disappointing source of revenue was the general property tax. This was due in part to general evasion, in part to imperfect collection. The share of the Special Commissioners in the proceeds of the Town lottery was virtually constant.[1]

Rigidity and inelasticity were the manifest characteristics of the revenues of the Special Commissioners. Specific funds tending to slow increase, with the growth of the Town, rather than general sources of revenue, were available for purposes of expenditure. These funds proved inadequate not only for further construction and improvement, but even for necessary maintenance and repair.

Indebtedness. The earliest exercise of local borrowing power was authorized by the act of 1782 appointing the Special Commissioners, in the provision that should the several funds appropriated prove inadequate, the Special Commissioners might "borrow to the amount of £5000 current money, from the inhabitants of said town pledging for the discharge thereof the whole or any part of the above appropriations." Before any action was taken under this measure, the act of the following session was passed, enlarging the authority already conferred by empowering the Special Commissioners to anticipate by loan on the several taxes authorized "any sum not exceeding fifty thousand pounds and to mortgage the whole or any part of the said taxes for the payment of any part of the whole of such sum so borrowed."

No evidence appears of any formal exercise of the bor-

[1] See Appendix A.

rowing power thus conferred. The provision however gave undoubted credit to the warrants of the Special Commissioners, and was thus directly responsible for the accumulation of an appreciable floating indebtedness. Bills for work performed were paid by the Special Commissioners in the form of orders upon the treasurer. When the funds of the board were exhausted, as was ordinarily the case, the unpaid orders simply accumulated without appearing to have exercised any correspondingly unfavorable influence upon the credit of the board. Upon the incorporation of Baltimore in 1796, the unpaid orders then outstanding to the amount of some ten thousand dollars were assumed as a floating debt by the city government, and by the exercise of economy in expenditure together with the increase in municipal revenues were paid within a few years.

Audit. The act of 1782 appointing the Special Commissioners, required them to render an annual account of receipts and expenditures to the Town Commissioners and to publish a copy thereof in the first month of every year in the newspapers of Baltimore.[1] The revenue measure of the following session provided for more careful audit by authorizing the annual election by voters of the Town, of three Comptrollers of Accounts who should examine and certify to the correctness or error of the annual account of the Special Commissioners and should append this certificate to the published account.[2] The reports published were mere summarized balance sheets. The statement was occasionally appended that the particular items of expenditure were too numerous for insertion in the printed report, but might be examined in the books of the board. The certificate of the Comptrollers was usually printed with the report.

THE BOARD OF PORT WARDENS.

Functions. The rapid development of local commerce during and immediately after the Revolutionary War cen-

[1] "Laws of Maryland," 1782 (April sess.), ch. 39, sect. 8.
[2] *Ibid.*, 1782 (November sess.), ch. 17, sect. 28.

tered attention upon the condition of the wharves and harbor of Baltimore, and made apparent the necessity of more careful supervision of shipping than that theretofore nominally exercised by the Town Commissioners. In June, 1783, the General Assembly appointed nine residents of the Town as "Wardens of the Port" to hold office until October, 1786, and to be elected thereafter every five years by the Electors of the Special Commissioners. The Wardens were authorized to appoint a clerk and a treasurer, to survey and chart the harbor, to define the channel by buoys and water marks, and to clean and remove obstructions from the basin. The construction and extension of private wharves were made subject to the supervision of the Board, and general authority was conferred to make and enforce regulations for the protection of the harbor and the preservation of navigation, provided that such ordinances were given due publicity and were not repugnant to exisiting law.[1] These powers were enlarged somewhat in 1788 and confirmed in 1791.[2]

The total expenditures of the Port Wardens, for repairing wharves, surveying the channel and dredging and cleaning the harbor were inconsiderable up to 1791. Thereafter occurred a gradual increase to 1795. The administrative expenses of the board were throughout disproportionate to the work performed. The act of 1783 fixed the compensation of the chairman at *7s. 6d.* and that of other members of the board, at *5s.* per diem. In addition, the act of 1783 appropriated to the treasurer of the board a commission of two and a half per cent. on all monies received and authorized the naval officer of the port to deduct his usual commission from the proceeds of the tonnage tax.[3]

Revenues. The original measure of 1783 appointing Port Wardens, provided (sect. 16) that all expenditures incurred under the act, including the remuneration of the Wardens, should be defrayed from out the specific revenues therein

[1] "Laws of Maryland," 1783 (April sess.), ch. 24.
[2] *Ibid.*, 1788, ch. 20; 1791, ch. 60.
[3] See Appendix B.

appropriated. Subsequent legislation from time to time changed the precise nature of these revenues; but the entire independence of the financial operations of the Port Wardens was not thereby affected. The receipts of the board may be distinguished, for closer examination, as accruing from: (i) Fines and Penalties; (ii) Lotteries; (iii) Taxation.

(Fines and Penalties). The Port Wardens were authorized by the act of 1783 to impose fines not exceeding fifty pounds, for the violation of all rules and regulations by them established. Such fines were recoverable by civil suit before a magistrate, as in the case of small debts, the usual appeal lying to the Baltimore County Court.

(Lotteries). The circumstances leading to the institution of the Town lottery in 1791 have been described in another connection. The most important source of the Port Wardens' revenues had been cut off in 1789. The resultant deficit was doubtless responsible for the provision in the act of 1791, that two-thirds of the annual profits of the lottery should be paid to the Wardens "for the deepening and cleaning of the harbour and basin."[1] In practice, the lottery appears to have been conducted by a joint board, composed of five Port Wardens and three Special Commissioners, instead of by appointed managers as authorized. The gross value of the lottery was ordinarily $50,000, and the net amount to be raised, $8,510, something less than the sum actually authorized[2] (£3500).

(Tonnage Duty). The act of 1783 appointing the Port Wardens, empowered them to "impose on every vessel entering or clearing at said port one penny per ton." The naval officer of the port was directed to levy the tax and, after deducting his commission, to pay the proceeds in quarterly account, to the Wardens. This tax was to remain in

[1] "Laws of Maryland," 1791, ch. 59, sect. 7.

[2] See announcement of the lottery in *The Baltimore Daily Intelligencer*, April 16, 1794; and in *The Federal Intelligencer and Baltimore Daily Gazette*, March 30, 1795.

force "till a sufficient sum shall be raised for defraying the expense aforesaid." The proceeds of the charge proved entirely inadequate for necessary expenditures, and in 1788[1] the maximum levy was raised to "two pence current money per ton," and pilot boats and vessels not coming from sea and belonging to residents of Maryland were exempted from the charge. The adoption in 1789 of the federal constitution, which Maryland had ratified in the year preceding, annulled the power of the state to lay a local tonnage duty, and cut off the revenues of the Wardens accruing from this source.

In 1790 the then nugatory provision for the tonnage duty was repealed by the legislature, and a lower tax was imposed of two cents per ton upon every vessel entering the port—to go into effect upon confirmation of the act by legislation of the federal government.[2] No action was taken by Congress, and in 1791 the legislature again authorized the same duty, in identical terms and subject to the same condition.[3] It proved equally inoperative from lack of the requisite federal ratification. Not until May 12, 1796, a few months before the incorporation of Baltimore, was such confirmation obtained from the federal government.[4]

(Auction Receipts Tax). The expenditures of the Wardens from 1790 to 1797 were largely defrayed from another source. Authority for the auction tax, the proceeds of which at first accrued to the Town Commissioners and later to the Special Commissioners, expired in 1789. At the following session of the General Assembly the tax was reimposed, but with important changes. Two auctioneers' offices were established, with two incumbents in each office. Vacancies were filled and removals were made by the Governor and Council. The exclusive privilege of selling goods at auction was conferred as before upon the per-

[1] "Laws of Maryland," 1788, ch. 20.
[2] *Ibid.*, 1790, ch. 22.
[3] *Ibid.*, 1791, ch. 60.
[4] By an act of the first session of the Fourth Congress, ch. xxvi.

sons so appointed, and penalties imposed upon other persons doing so. The auctioneers were authorized to charge specified fees and were directed to pay to the Port Wardens in quarterly account at the rate of five shillings for every hundred pounds, or one fourth of one per cent., towards defraying "the expense of cleaning and deepening the basin." The act was to remain in force for a period of seven years.[1]

The passage of the act was received with marked dissatisfaction in Baltimore. This hostility was directed less against the burden or amount of the tax than against the form of its imposition. A meeting of the most influential citizens of the Town, held on January 4, 1791, issued a formal protest against the action of the General Assembly in "increasing and confirming a nuisance which it has been their anxious desire to remove." The grant of exclusive privileges to a handful of men, it was declared, not only tended to enrich the few at the expense of the many, but was the creation of a monopoly, in violation of the express declaration of the Maryland Bill of Rights. In conclusion the subscribers pledged themselves to make no purchases of goods sold at public auction, nor to patronize importers who acted otherwise.[2] Despite this vigorous protest, the statute remained unchanged and in force until its expiration in 1797—almost coincident with the incorporation of Baltimore.

(Gross Receipts). The revenues of the Port Wardens increased steadily after 1786. The tonnage duty and the tax on auction receipts were the important sources. Fines and wharfage receipts added much smaller but not insignificant amounts. The aggregate receipts of the Port Wardens were in regular excess of their disbursements and the net balance accumulated. An annual statement of the financial operations of the board was published in the newspapers of Baltimore. These statements as published, like

[1] "Laws of Maryland," 1790, ch. 12.
[2] *Maryland Journal and Baltimore Advertiser*, January 11, 1791.

the balance sheets of the Special Commissioners, were mere unitemized summaries.[1]

THE BOARD OF TOWN COMMISSIONERS.

The ordinary duties of the Town Commissioners were restricted, after the appointment of the boards of Special Commissioners and of Port Wardens, to the determination of lot boundaries, the regulation of the Town markets and the supervision of merchandise inspection. With these duties went in theory a general superintendence of the administrative affairs of the city, limited however in practice to a discretionary assent to powers otherwise exercised, such as the approval of streets selected for paving by the Special Commissioners,[2] or acceptance of the bond of the managers of the Town lottery.

The slight expenditures required for these several purposes appear to have been almost entirely defrayed by the receipts from market licenses and stall rentals. All other regular revenues theretofore accruing to the Town Commissioners—fines, penalties, forfeitures, the tax on auction sales—were transferred to the Special Commissioners by the act authorizing their appointment, while subsequent revenues were uniformly appropriated for specific purposes.

The Town Commissioners were from time to time vested with the discharge of particular duties. In such event the expenditures involved were defrayed by the appropriation of specific revenues. In 1784, two commissions of nine and six persons, respectively, were appointed to erect new market houses in the Town. The Town Commissioners were however authorized to provide the revenues therefor by the sale of the old market-house and site.[3] An act of the same session directed the Town Commissioners to cause a new survey of the Town to be made and to defray the

[1] See Appendix B.

[2] See above, p. 21; also "Records of the Town Commissioners" (MS), February 25, 1791.

[3] "Laws of Maryland," 1784, ch. 62.

expenditures incurred from out "the street tax" (*i. e.* the direct property tax) levied by the Special Commissioners.[1]

As Baltimore grew in area and population, the exercise of two functions inevitably associated with local growth became necessary, (1) widening and extending streets and (2) lighting and watching the town. The methods pursued by the legislature in providing for these local needs indicate the characteristic reluctance of that body to entrust new functions to the Town Commissioners or to other existing local authorities.

Street Reconstruction. In 1783 occurred the first of a long series of laborious, costly attempts to remedy the defects in the original arrangement of the Town as in that of successive additions. Upon the representation of a number of inhabitants of Baltimore that great inconvenience arose from the narrowness of Hanover-lane, the Town Commissioners were empowered to widen the lane to the width of the connecting street. The plan proposed by the petitioners to defray the expenditures involved was adopted in the statute—a special assessment upon property owners benefited, equivalent to the amount of damages awarded.

(Special Assessment). The Town Commissioners were directed to file with the clerk of the county court a plat showing the extent and limits of the proposed alteration. Then having given ten days' notice of their intention, they were directed to meet to ascertain the damages sustained by any persons by the alteration, and to determine the various proportions of this amount which should be paid by the several persons benefited in accordance with the particular advantage derived therefrom, both of which returns should likewise be lodged in the office of the clerk of the county court. The Town Commissioners were made a body politic to sue for the recovery of benefits assessed, for the use of the persons to whom the damages had been awarded.[2] A year later (upon representation that the Town

[1] "Laws of Maryland." 1784, ch. 39.

[2] *Ibid.*, 1783, ch. 22.

Commissioners had not, through misapprehension of the measure, assessed all persons benefited for the damages incurred), a supplementary act was passed directing the Town Commissioners to give twenty, instead of ten days notice, to assess all property benefited, regardless of its location, and in their discretion to summon a jury of twelve freeholders to award damages and to assess benefits in any or all cases.[1]

The local charge thus imposed is of particular interest as probably the earliest use in Baltimore of a special assessment with estimation of particular benefit in each case. The distinctive feature of the "paving tax," which the Special Commissioners had been authorized to impose in the year preceding, was the assessment of benefit by the imposition of a definite charge in proportion to frontage. In the present act as in a long succession of analogous measures there appear the essential features of the modern Baltimore special assessment as crystallized in subsequent legislation of the General Assembly of Maryland.[2]

There is no evidence as to the manner in which the Town Commissioners succeeded in the exercise of the power of eminent domain, and in the levy of the special assessment in 1783, other than the mere fact that Hanover-lane was actually widened. Whatever the results may have been, they were not enough to persuade the legislature again to vest this function in the Town Commissioners. In 1792 it

[1] "Laws of Maryland," 1784, ch. 46.

[2] It is possible that this is one of the earliest practical uses of a special assessment of this character in the United States. Dr. Rosewater has found the modern origin of the special assessment in an English statute of 1667, and Prof. Seligman has called attention to an earlier act of 1662, containing the same principle. The spirit and the letter of the English statute of 1667 were reproduced in a New York provincial law of 1691. Although this law remained upon the statute book, it appears that little or no actual use was made of the principle of betterment until the practical reenactment of the measure after the revolution of the new commonwealth government of April, 1787, four years after the passage of the present act. Cf. Rosewater, "Special Assessments," p. 23.

became desirable to construct an approach to the central market from the western part of the Town. It was impossible to effect the improvement save by the exercise of the right of eminent domain. Five designated persons were accordingly appointed commissioners with authority to lay out and open a series of streets for this purpose, and to award damages and assess benefits as in the act of 1783. Provision was made that in the event of the appointed commissioners neglecting to award and assess, the sheriff of Baltimore County should summon a jury of seven freeholders who should carry out the intention of the act. A clause was added to the effect that no street should be opened or extended until the damages awarded had actually been paid.[1] Similarly in 1795, the necessity having arisen for a road leading from the western and southwestern parts to the southern part of the Town, five designated commissioners were authorized to extend Pratt street westerly, and to award damages and to assess benefits for this purpose.[2]

Authority to lay out and open streets, subject however to an important limitation, was conferred upon the Town Commissioners by the act of 1784 authorizing a new survey of the town, as already noted. The Town Commissioners were therein vested with general power, "to survey, alter, amend and lay out anew, the streets, lanes and alleys, running through the same, with the consent of the proprietors thereof, or their guardians, first had and obtained, and at their own expense." They were further directed to open streets on land reclaimed along the water front, subject to the same conditions.[3] Thereafter until the incorporation of Baltimore, the activity of the Town Commissioners in opening and extending streets was confined within the narrow province here outlined.

[1] "Laws of Maryland," 1792, ch. 27. The contingency provided for actually occurred, and the award and assessments were made by the seven jurors. *Ibid.*, 1794, ch. 38.

[2] "Laws of Maryland," 1795, ch. 58.

[3] Repealed and re-enacted with changes by *ibid.*, 1794, ch. 62.

Watching and Lighting. The first general provision for policing and lighting Baltimore was made by the General Assembly in 1784 by the passage of an act "for the establishment and regulation of a night watch and the erection of lamps, in Baltimore-town."[1] The Town Commissioners were therein authorized to contract for the erection and maintenance of as many street lamps, and also for as many watchmen as might be deemed necessary. The Commissioners were constituted justices of the peace with authority to appoint constables, who in turn should superintend the watch and "use their best endeavors to prevent fires, murders, burglaries, robberies and other outrages and disorders."

To defray the expenditures involved in the exercise of these functions, certain revenues, ordinary and extraordinary, were appropriated. The heavy initial cost was met by the appropriation of the proceeds of the *2s. 6d.* general property tax levied by the Special Commissioners in 1785; and the proceeds of the tax on auction receipts accruing likewise to the Special Commissioners in 1785. The ordinary revenues provided were: (i) Fines and penalties; (ii) surplus revenues from the existing license tax on liquor sales in Baltimore; (iii) taxation. The Town Commissioners were authorized to appoint a treasurer subject to the same rules and regulations as the treasurer of the Special Commissioners, and to keep an exact account of receipts and expenditures, subject to the inspection of the Town Comptrollers.

(Fines and Penalties). Fines were imposed in detail for violations of provisions of the act. These were recoverable in the manner of small debts and were appropriated "towards defraying the charges of the said lamps and watches."

(License Tax). By an act of the same session (1784) erecting the University of Maryland, the proceeds of the existing state license tax on ordinary keepers and liquor re-

[1] "Laws of Maryland," 1784, ch. 69.

tailers, in so far as derived from the western shore of the state, were appropriated to the new foundation.[1] A provision of the Baltimore "watch act" was to the effect that should the aggregate funds appropriated to the University exceed the sum of £1750 current money, then the surplus of the monies collected from Baltimore for ordinary and retailers' licenses should be applied in part discharge of the expenses of the act.[2]

(General Property Tax). The most important fiscal provision of the measure was the authority conferred upon the Town Commissioners to assess and levy a tax not exceeding 1*s.* 6*d.* on every £100 of legally assessed property in the Town, to be collected in the same manner and subject to the same regulations as the public tax. To aid in providing immediate revenues, a levy for the current year, upon the valuation of property made in 1783, was authorized, and the county collector was authorized to make collections.[3] The entire act was to remain in force for three years. It was renewed in 1787 and in 1795 for seven and three years respectively and was made a perpetual law in the act incorporating Baltimore as a city.[4]

(House Tax). The ordinary revenues in aggregate appropriated by the act of 1784 soon proved inadequate. On March 15, 1787, the Town Commissioners resolved to discharge the watch "if the Funds which are appropriated for carrying them on are insufficient or cannot be collected."[5] Whatever result may have attended this declaration, certainly no relief was afforded until 1792 when authority was conferred for the imposition of an interesting house tax.[6]

[1] "Laws of Maryland," 1784, ch. 37.

[2] *Ibid.*, 1784, ch. 69, sect. 17.

[3] In actual fact the Town Commissioners at first received the proceeds of the tax from the sheriff and only subsequently from the county collector of Baltimore County. See "Records of Town Commissioners" (MS), p. 49.

[4] "Laws of Maryland," 1787, ch. 38; 1795, ch. 83; 1796, ch. 68.

[5] "Records of the Town Commissioners" (MS), p. 53.

[6] "Laws of Maryland," 1792, ch. 69.

The justices of the criminal court of Baltimore County, instead of the Town Commissioners, were therein authorized to appoint one or more persons to make an enumeration of all dwelling-houses, storehouses and warehouses in the Town, noting the names of the dwellers and occupiers thereof, and the number of stories of each building. On this return the justices were directed to levy taxes as follows:

"On every three story dwelling-house, store-house or warehouse, fifteen shillings current money; on every two story dwelling-house, storehouse or warehouse ten shillings current money; on every one story dwelling-house, storehouse or warehouse, five shillings current money; but, in case any three story house shall not be more than eighteen feet front on any street, lane or alley, then and in that case the said house shall be taxed at the rate of ten shillings current money; and in case any two story house shall be above thirty feet front on any street, lane or alley, that then and in that case the said house shall be taxed at the rate of fifteen shillings current money; which said tax shall be imposed, levied and collected, annually, one third thereof from the owner or owners, and two thirds from the occupiers or tenants of such dwelling house, storehouse or warehouse."

The tax thus imposed was to remain in force until October 30, 1793, or until the end of the legislative session happening thereafter. Distinct machinery for its collection was provided by authorizing the justices to appoint one or more bonded collectors who should be subject to the regulations imposed upon the county sheriff in the collection of the public tax, and who should complete all collections within twenty days after publication had been made of its imposition. The proceeds were to be paid to the treasurer of the Town Commissioners, appointed in the act of 1784, and were specifically appropriated as a fund for "the regulating a night-watch, and the erection of lamps, in the said town, and for no other purpose." The justices were directed to lay an account of all receipts and disbursements accruing from the act before the Town Comptrollers, who were to approve or disapprove and to publish the same.

It seems likely that the idea of a house tax was suggested by the use of this fiscal device in England. On the other hand, the curious adjustment of tax to height and frontage, and the division of burden between owner and occupier appear to be distinctive features of the Baltimore tax.

Transfer of Functions. The reluctance of the legislature to vest any further powers in the Town Commissioners evidenced in the recognition of Special Commissioners, Port Wardens, County Justices, has been repeatedly noticed. This distrust culminated in 1793, when the Town Commissioners were stripped of authority for watching and lighting the Town, conferred in 1784 and curtailed in 1793. Thereafter until the incorporation of Baltimore in 1796, the administrative importance and fiscal activity of the Town Commissioners were slight and virtually the same as in the period between 1782 and 1784.

The act of 1793 erected a Court of Oyer and Terminer and Gaol Delivery in Baltimore county, composed of a chief justice and four associate justices, to try all cases hitherto heard before the criminal court of the county. The several powers vested in the Town Commissioners by the act of 1784 were formally transferred to the justices so appointed, who were further authorized to levy the house tax until October, 1794, or until the end of the legislative session thereafter, in the manner provided by the act of 1792, and to impose a dog tax of *7s. 6d.*, the proceeds to form a further fund towards defraying the expenses of watching and lighting the Town.[1]

In 1794 the powers vested in the Court of Oyer and Terminer and Gaol Delivery, doubtless including the levy of the house tax, were transferred to the Baltimore County Court.[2] Finally, in a supplementary measure of 1795, the

[1] "Laws of Maryland," 1793, ch. 57.
[2] *Ibid.*, 1794, ch. 65.

house tax was specifically repealed and the justices of the county court were authorized to levy in lieu thereof a direct tax sufficient—in connection with the funds already provided by law—for the support of the town watch and the erection and maintenance of lamps.[1] No change was made in the machinery of collection, but the associate justices of the county court were directed to meet weekly in the Town to receive reports from the night watch, and to direct its movements. By the same act the justices of the county court were directed to levy on the assessed property of the Town and on "the wharfs adjoining thereto," the expenditures of a local committee of health during the current year, to be collected in the same manner as the county levy. A further anomalous provision directed that the expenses attending the act, and the cost of repairing the bridges of Baltimore Town to an amount not exceeding £100 should be paid by Baltimore County and collected with the county assessment. The entire act was to continue in force until January 30, 1798.

On December 31, 1796, Baltimore Town was incorporated. The functions of watching and lighting were vested in the corporation and the original measure of 1784 enacted into a perpetual law, subject however to future amendment and revision at will. The "watch tax" authorized in the act of 1795 could thus have been levied only once, if at all. No use was made of the authority conferred by the same act to assess the expenditures incurred by the health committee upon the Town, and it is possible that the watch tax was similarly allowed to go by default.

Revenues and expenditures. Neither details nor summaries of the financial activities of the Town Commissioners have been preserved. After 1789, the published balance sheets of the Baltimore County Court distinguish the receipts and expenditures of the Court in account with Baltimore Town.[2]

[1] "Laws of Maryland," 1794, ch. 29.

[2] See Appendix C.

Resumé.

A convenient resumé of the foregoing will be afforded by tracing the status of the individual resident and property-owner of Baltimore, with respect to local services and burdens, in the period surveyed.

In the first period, from 1729 to 1744, residence in Baltimore Town merely involved convenient location with respect to a port of entry. Public services were rendered and public charges were imposed by county justices or parish vestry within the Town, precisely as in the county or parish proper. Occasions for expenditures of a distinctly local character were exceptional and were met almost entirely by private subscriptions. The disposition of forfeited sites furnished a thin and inadequate revenue for maintenance and repair.

As Baltimore grew in area and population in the period from 1745 to 1780, the administrative oversight exercised in theory by the county court tended inevitably to the neglect of local needs. Local expenditures continued to be defrayed largely by voluntary contributions. The revenues accruing from the sale of forfeited sites, from fines and penalties for the violation of specifically authorized powers, and from market license taxes, were available for the extension and maintenance of local institutions once provided. The genesis of local taxation appeared in the levy of the amount of the clerk's salary upon the building lots of the Town.

The period from 1781 to the incorporation of Baltimore in 1796 was characterized by great complexity in the distribution of local functions and greater variety in the form of local charges. Construction and maintenance of the roadway of the Town and the provision of a public water supply were vested in the Special Commissioners. The opening, widening and extension of particular streets were entrusted variously to the Town Commissioners and to specifically appointed commissions. Supervision of local shipping was put in the hands of the board of Port Wardens. The functions of watching and lighting the Town were exercised first by the Town Commissioners, later by the justices of the Baltimore County Court. The Town Commissioners exercised in theory a general superintendence of the administrative affairs of the city, limited however in practice to a discretionary assent to powers otherwise vested. Each of these bodies enjoyed mutual independence in its financial operations.

The resident property owner was mulcted for the violation of local regulations, the proceeds ordinarily accruing to the body in which was vested the exercise of the particular function involved. His property was assessed for the special benefit derived from the paving or reconstruction of a particular street, the sinking of a well or the erection of a pump in the vicinity, either in the form of a definite charge per front foot, or a proportionate share as fixed by jury determination of the gross cost involved. He paid to the Special Commissioners a general property tax (2*s.* 6*d.* in £100 from 1782 to 1790, and of 1*s.* 3*d.*, from 1791 to 1796) to defray the cost of street repairs; to the Town Commissioners and later to the county justices, for watching and lighting the Town, a property tax (1*s.* 6*d.* in £100) from 1784 to 1796, a graduated house tax from 1793 to 1795, and an additional property tax thereafter. His property when sold at public auction was subject, in addition to specified auctioneer's fees, to a local tax varying from one-quarter to one-half per cent. of the gross receipts. The price he paid for goods coming by water to Baltimore was augmented by a tonnage duty of one and two pence. He paid specific taxes on his carriages, chairs, wagons, riding horses and billiard tables, and if the proprietor of a tavern, a play house or any place of public amusement, he was charged with a considerable license tax. Finally he might find consolation in the blank drawn in the Town lottery in the thought that to some extent he had contributed to the repair of streets and to the improvement of the harbor.

It is thus easy to see, why from the close of the Revolutionary War, agitation for the formal incorporation of Baltimore Town should have been continuous and persistent. Inhabitants of the Town had little voice in its administration; authority was scattered among irresponsible and independent commissions, and necessary functions were neglected or entirely omitted. Division of authority produced wasteful as well as inefficient administration. The property owner was subject to distinct assessment, the cost of collection was needlessly repeated, and methods of account were imperfect. After a series of unsuccessful attempts,[1] Baltimore City was incorporated by an Act of the General Assembly on the last day of December, 1796.

[1] For a brief summary of some of these, see T. P. Thomas, "The City Government of Baltimore," pp. 15-16, in *Johns Hopkins University Studies in Historical and Political Science*, Fourteenth Series, No. I.

PART II

THE FINANCES OF BALTIMORE CITY

FROM 1797 TO 1816

INTRODUCTION

Between the close of the Revolutionary War and the outbreak of the War of 1812 occurred a noteworthy expansion of local trade. Continental wars not only increased the demand for Maryland staples, but largely diverted the West India trade to this safer port. The rise and perfection of the "Baltimore Clipper" aided the opportunity, and during the whole period under consideration, Baltimore enjoyed a large part of European and West Indian commerce, together with no inconsiderable share of the world's carrying trade. This upward movement terminated with the outbreak of hostilities and the stirring events of the War of 1812. But even during these years, daring blockade running and indirect shipments enabled Baltimore merchants to retain possession of a considerable foreign trade, and the resulting depression was less acute than might have been expected.

The administrative history of the city during the same period reveals the gradual evolution of municipal organization. The act of incorporation established the general outline of municipal government, but left the details of administration to local choice. This determination proceeded tentatively and conservatively. At first the essential features of the town administration were incorporated into the municipal framework with the least change necessary. As at one point after another inadequacy and inefficiency in administration became evident, specific changes were introduced, without anything like a general reconstruction at any time occurring.

The influence of these two forces—rapid material growth and slow administrative development—is reflected in the financial history of the city from 1797 to 1816. The first fact rendered necessary an extension of local functions and the more regular performance of those already assumed. The second occasioned constant, illogical change in administrative and fiscal machinery.

CHAPTER I

MUNICIPAL ADMINISTRATION.

Corporate Powers.

By the act of 1796[1] Baltimore Town was erected into a city, and its inhabitants constituted a body politic and corporate by the name of the "Mayor and City Council of Baltimore." The authority before invested in the Town Commissioners, Special Commissioners and Port Wardens was transferred to the new corporation. Additional powers, corresponding in the main to those ordinarily possessed by a municipal corporation, were conferred by specific enumeration. In the following year the act of incorporation was made perpetual law, and certain supplementary powers were added.[2]

The powers conferred by the charter included authority to remove public nuisances, to provide for the safety and health of the city, to establish and reconstruct streets (with the consent of the owners of the ground), to improve the harbor, to erect bridges, to construct sewers, to regulate markets, to prevent and extinguish fires, to impose and appropriate fines, penalties and forfeitures, and to impose taxes not exceeding two dollars in the hundred pounds in any one year, and to enforce their collection, if necessary, by distress and sale.[3]

The supplementary statute of 1797 added authority to pave and repair streets, to license and regulate vehicles for hire, to make new assessment of real and personal property

[1] "Laws of Maryland," 1796, ch. 68. [2] *Ibid.*, 1797, ch. 54.

[3] A certain district of the city, Deptford Hundred, was exempted from any tax, direct or indirect, for the improvement of the docks and harbor.

as often as might be necessary, and to tax particular districts of the city for street paving, sinking wells or erecting lamps "which may appear for the benefit of such particular part or district."

Administrative Organization.

The government of the city was vested in a Mayor and a bicameral City Council. The lower house or First Branch was composed of two members elected annually by popular vote from each of the eight wards into which the city was divided. The upper house or Second Branch was composed of one member from each ward, elected by a miniature electoral college made up of one elector from each ward chosen by popular vote at the time of electing the members of the First Branch. The Mayor was elected at the same time and in the same manner as the members of the Second Branch of the Council. The Council was empowered to pass all ordinances necessary for the exercise of the power conferred upon the corporation, subject to a veto privilege on the part of the Mayor. In 1808 the high property qualifications of the Mayor and Councilmen were considerably reduced, and the method of choosing the Second Branch of the Council was changed to election by popular vote. The Mayor continued to be chosen indirectly, but the number of electors was increased from eight to sixteen.[1]

The Charter left the details of administrative machinery, as has been intimated, to local determination. Provision was, however, made that two candidates must be nominated for each municipal office by the Second Branch of the Council, one of whom should be appointed by the Mayor. After 1808 nominations were made jointly by the two Branches of the Council. The successive changes in the organization of municipal departments can be best noticed in connection with the particular functions with the exercise of which they were vested.

[1] "Laws of Maryland," 1807, ch. 152.

Financial Machinery.

The second ordinance passed by the newly organized City Council designated two persons to receive the records and the funds in the possession of the several town authorities.[1] This was speedily followed by the creation of the offices of Register and Treasurer.[2] The Register was directed to preserve all municipal records and accounts; to cause all ordinances to be published, and to affix the city. seal when required. The Treasurer was authorized to receive, deposit and draw, when directed by ordinance, the funds of the corporation, and to render account annually, or oftener if required, to the Mayor and to each Branch of the Council. A year later the office of Treasurer was abolished and the various duties and powers theretofore exercised by this officer were vested in the Register.[3]

Immediately after the organization of the Council, the appointment of a Collector was authorized, to enforce the payment of all municipal taxes and dues, and also to collect the proceeds of chimney fines. Subsequent local levies provided in each case for the appointment of a similar functionary, who was required to make returns within a specified period. Gradually the office came to be regarded as fixed, and its incumbent was vested with the collection of all local charges, save those specifically provided for.

The Budget.

Little evidence is available as to the extent and nature of budgetary procedure during this early period of municipal history. The problem was essentially simple. Local sources of revenue were utilized throughout to the maximum degree authorized, and the task was simply an adjustment of expenditure to relatively fixed and inelastic revenue. It is probable that the City Council simply followed the

[1] Ordinance of March 17, 1797.
[2] Ordinance of March 27, 1797.
[3] Ordinance of March 10, 1798.

practice of the state legislature, and that a general appropriation bill was prepared and reported by a joint Ways and Means Committee of the two Branches. This was the procedure a few years later, and it seems likely that the practice was at this time already in vogue. A detailed balance sheet of receipts and expenditures was published annually by the Register.[1]

[1] See Appendix D.

CHAPTER II

MUNICIPAL EXPENDITURE.

The disbursements of Baltimore City during the first twenty years of its corporate life differed in degree rather than in kind from those of the Town administration. Roads and highways, watching and lighting, administration, wharves and harbor, continued the primary objects of local expenditure, in much the order named. The development of local activity largely in these directions, made possible by formal incorporation, was reflected in a marked increase in aggregate disbursements until 1801. The succeeding decade revealed fairly uniform expenditures, followed in turn by a sharp increase after the War of 1812.

STREETS AND ROADWAYS.

Street Paving and Repair. By the charter of Baltimore City no authority was provided for the paving or repair of streets other than that implied in the transfer to the corporation of the several powers possessed by the authorities of Baltimore Town. The supplementary measure of the following year, however, specifically empowered the city to pass "all ordinances necessary for paving and keeping in repair the streets, lanes and alleys" and "to tax any particular part or district of the city for paving the streets, lanes or alleys therein." An ordinance passed at the first session of the City Council made provision for the continuous exercise of this power. A board of five City Commissioners was appointed and vested with "all the power over the said streets, lanes and alleys, lines and boundaries of lots, within the said city heretofore granted to the commissioners of Baltimore town."[1] The actual duties of the

[1] Ordinance of April 10, 1797.

Commissioners were the selection of the particular streets to be paved or repaired, and the contracting with proper persons for the performance of the work. The Commissioners were directed to give in the selection of streets "a preference to such as shall in their judgment be of most importance." This broad discretion was, however, limited by the provision that only such streets should be paved as "a majority of the proprietors and tenants inhabiting therein may require."

In 1806 the number of City Commissioners was reduced to three, of whom one must reside on the east side and two on the west side of Jones' Falls. The duties and powers of the board remained unchanged. This ordinance was to remain in force for a single year.[1] Upon expiration it was, however, re-enacted with a further statement of the powers of the City Commissioners in much the terms of the ordinance of 1797.[2] Two years later in the effort to introduce greater simplicity and economy into city administration, the distinct boards of City Commissioners and of Health Commissioners were abolished and a new joint board of four persons, styled "City Commissioners and Commissioners of Health," was created. The early principle of territorial representation was continued in the provision that two of the Commissioners must reside on the east side and two on the west side of Jones' Falls.[3] This was abandoned in 1814, when the number of Commissioners was reduced to three, independent of residence.[4]

The cost of paving public thoroughfares was defrayed, in large part, by a special assessment upon the property benefited, as noted below.[5] The proceeds of the assessment were ordinarily anticipated by draft upon the city treasury to which any surplus reverted. Deficits were met by special

[1] Ordinance of March 14, 1806. [2] Ordinance of March 19, 1807.
[3] Ordinance of March 22, 1809. [4] Ordinance of March 25, 1814.
[5] See below, page 80. For minor changes in the powers of the City Commissioners, cf. Ordinances of March 7, 1801; March 3, 1804; March 9, 1807.

appropriations.[1] Specific appropriations were sometimes also made in aid of special assessments levied upon a thinly-settled street;[2] or in the event of a depleted treasury, the Commissioners were occasionally authorized to borrow a specified amount upon the credit of the city, to be repaid within a definite period.[3] Less usual was the procedure in certain cases where the City Commissioners were directed to pave portions of certain streets, provided that the owners of abutting property satisfactorily paved the remainder.[4]

Side-walks were laid or repaired by the owners of abutting property. Tenants of not more than five years' possession were required to perform the work, with the privilege of making a corresponding deduction from rental payment. In the case of refusal or neglect upon the part of owners or occupiers, the City Commissioners made the improvement and levied the charge, together with a fine of one-eighth of a dollar per front foot upon the delinquent.

Sewers. Under the terms of the Charter, the corporation was empowered "to pave and keep in repair all necessary drains and sewers, and to pass all regulations necessary for the preservation of the same." This authority was vested in broad terms in the board of City Commissioners, appointed by the ordinance of April 10, 1797, as noted above. The City Commissioners were empowered to enter upon private property "through which the common sewers now or may hereafter run, or ought to run, to regulate, make or repair the same." The damages sustained by private property, if any, were to be assessed by two arbitrators (one of whom was chosen by the City Commissioners, the other by the owners concerned) with power to summon an umpire, whose award was final. The damages so ascertained were paid to the owners affected from out the city treasury. No essential change was made in this procedure in the ordi-

[1] Ordinance of April 29, 1797.
[2] Ordinances of June 18, 1797; February 20, 1799; March 15, 1800.
[3] Ordinances of February 26 and 27, 1799; April 7, 1800.
[4] Ordinances of August 2, 1809; March 10, 1810.

nance of March 9, 1807, revising the functions of the City Commissioners.

The construction and repair of sewers, however, formed but a small item of municipal expenditure. Within the period here considered, and indeed throughout the whole history of the city, dependence was had upon surface drainage, and anything approximating a system of municipal sewerage was unknown. Occasional appropriations were made for the construction of mere storm-water drains;[1] at other times recourse was had for nominal expenses of repair to the annual appropriations of the City Commissioners. In some cases the work was entrusted to specifically appointed commissioners. Of this character was an enabling act of the General Assembly in 1815, authorizing the construction of sewers in the western precincts of Baltimore.[2] Five persons were therein appointed commissioners to construct such sewers within the territory described "as in their opinion will conduce to the healthiness or beneficial improvement of the grounds lying adjacent thereto." The cost incurred was to be defrayed by a special assessment upon the proprietors of the lots benefited.

Bridges. With a site repeatedly cut by a water-course, the construction and repair of bridges in Baltimore City soon became necessary. As indicated above, this indeed formed one of the earliest and most urgent objects of public expenditure in the period before 1797.[3] Local resources were inadequate, and in 1796 the General Assembly incorporated a private company to construct a "Lower Bridge" across Jones' Falls, and appointed two boards of Commissioners to repair the "Upper Bridge" and the "Middle Bridge," respectively, and to levy for this purpose specified amounts upon the assessable property of Baltimore County.[4]

After the incorporation of Baltimore, and the grant of power "to erect and repair bridges," the burden appears

[1] Ordinance of February 27, 1799.
[2] "Laws of Maryland," 1815, ch. 82; cf. below, p. 60, note 1.
[3] *Ibid.*, 1796, ch. 56.
[4] *Ibid.*, 1796, ch. 55.

to have been assumed in large part by the municipality. During 1797 and 1798 the commissioners appointed by the Legislature in 1796 to repair the bridges across Jones' Falls were authorized by the City Council to borrow from local banks upon the credit of the city considerable amounts to be repaid within the two following years.[1] These larger works once completed, but small appropriations were made for construction or repair during the next decade.

In 1808 began a movement for the construction of more substantial and expensive bridges. These were built under the superintendence of the Mayor and City Commissioners, who were required to secure the consent of all property owners exposed to damage. It is likely that the several amounts appropriated were obtained wholly or in part by loans from the banks of the city and repaid out of accruing city revenues.[2]

Street Reconstruction.

By the original act incorporating Baltimore City, the Mayor and City Council were authorized to establish new and to alter old streets, with the consent of the owners of property affected. This last condition virtually limited the power to the extension into unbuilt territory of streets already established. The work was probably performed under the direction of the City Commissioners, and involved little, if any, unusual expenditure.

Where the consent of all property owners affected could not be obtained, specific legislative authority was sought for the exercise of the power of eminent domain. This authority was accorded in a series of special acts of the General Assembly of Maryland directing the extension or alteration of the particular streets in question.[3] The ordinary procedure therein authorized was for the City Com-

[1] Ordinances of April 24, 1797, and March 19, 1798.

[2] Griffiths, "Annals of Baltimore," pp. 196-197.

[3] "Laws of Maryland," 1797, ch. 64; 1798, ch. 19; 1799, ch. 31; 1800, ch. 56; 1801, ch. 81; 1803, ch. 68; 1810, ch. 153; 1811, ch. 24, 133; 1812, ch. 34, 40, 118, 171; 1813, ch. 97.

missioners to lay out or widen the particular street, to declare it a public highway and to return a plat thereof to the Register of the city. If the street extended into the "precincts" of the city,[1] or into Baltimore County, or occasionally in the case of a street within the city, the duties of the City Commissioners were performed by the "commissioners of the precincts" or by a specially appointed commission.[2]

Ordinarily the entire expenditure involved in widening or extending the street and in the award of benefits was defrayed by a special assessment upon the property benefited in the manner hereinafter described.[3] In some cases where the amount was unusually large the city was authorized to make an appropriation in aid.[4]

Street Cleaning.

The newly appointed City Commissioners were charged in an early ordinance with the cleaning of streets—a function consisting in the mere removal, bi-weekly, of dirt and refuse accumulated or deposited by householders in front of their respective lots.[5] A year later, the office of "Superintendent of Streets" was created, and the authority of the City Commissioners in this regard was transferred thereto. The Superintendent received a fixed salary and one-half of all fines collected upon his information; and was required to render weekly account of all funds received from fines and from sales of refuse.[6]

In 1801 two Superintendents of Streets were appointed, one for the district east, and one for that west of Jones' Falls. The incumbents were directed to execute all orders

[1] The "Precincts of the City" comprised certain parts of Baltimore County immediately without the corporate limits of Baltimore City. In 1817 these districts were defined and made part of the city ("Laws of Maryland," 1816, ch. 209, 218).

[2] "Laws of Maryland," 1807, ch. 31; 1812, ch. 120, 121; 1813, ch. 67; 1816, ch. 143, 218; 1817, ch. 71, 115, 117.

[3] See below, page 80.

[4] "Laws of Maryland," 1803, ch. 82; 1817, ch. 71, 115.

[5] Ordinance of April 11, 1797.

[6] Ordinance of March 19, 1798.

received from the Mayor and from the Commissioners of Health, and to render monthly instead of weekly account.[1] These powers were renewed in 1807,[2] and immediately thereafter the Superintendents of Streets were charged with the provision and care of the city's pumps and wells, under the new title "Superintendents of Streets and Pumps."[3] Their primary duties with respect to street-cleaning remained unchanged.

Watching and Lighting.

The charter of Baltimore vested the corporation with general authority "to establish night watches or patrols, and to erect lamps," and made the statute of 1784 perpetual, as already noted.[4] At the first session of the City Council, an ordinance was passed authorizing the appointment of three "Commissioners of the Watch and for Lighting the City." This board was empowered to employ watchmen and to contract for the erection and care of lamps.[5] Subsequent ordinances provided for the joint exercise of these powers by the Commissioners of the Watch and the Mayor.[6] This practice led to the gradual disuse of the Commissioners of the Watch. The offices seem never to have been formally abolished; but after 1804 no appropriations for salaries appear to have been made, and the duties of the board were doubtless assumed by the Mayor. In 1807, the City Commissioners were formally substituted for the Commissioners of the Watch to appoint and superintend the night watch, in conjunction with the Mayor.[7]

[1] Ordinance of March 10, 1801. [2] Ordinance of March 26, 1807.
[3] Ordinance of April 2, 1807; cf. p. 64, below.
[4] See above, page 44.
[5] Ordinance of April 3, 1797.
[6] Ordinances of November 28, 1797; March 2, 1799; March 15, 1800.
[7] Ordinance of March 9, 1807, sect. 20. During the entire period here under survey, periodic report of the proceedings of the night watch continued to be made to designated "Justices of the Peace" (cf. p. 44, above).

In 1816, the foundation of a general police system for Baltimore was laid by the passage of an ordinance providing for the appointment by the Mayor of a corps of thirty-four persons for the purposes of watching and lighting the city, receiving fixed remuneration and classified as watchmen, captains, and lieutenants of the watch.[1]

The police duties of the city watch consisted almost exclusively in the prevention and detection of crime. For the enforcement of city ordinances and the prevention of their neglect, dependence was largely put upon private information. As early as 1798, however, the appointment was authorized of a City Constable to ascertain all violations of municipal ordinances.[2] This limited provision was soon found inadequate, and in the following year the Mayor and City Council were directed to appoint one constable for each ward; but their aggregate compensation was fixed at five hundred dollars.[3] In 1807, the Mayor was directed to appoint "a suitable number of City Constables," and the same amount was appropriated annually.[4] Two such officials appeared in the list of municipal officers of 1812. In January, 1813, the Mayor was empowered to appoint at pleasure not less than twenty-five nor more than one hundred bailiffs, for the purpose of "aiding in the preservation of the peace, the maintenance of the laws and the advancement of the police and good government" of the city.[5]

Fire Protection.

The earliest suggestion of expenditure for fire protection in Baltimore is probably the proposal in 1763 for a lottery

[1] Ordinance of April 4, 1816. In the same year the Mayor was authorized to contract with the newly formed "Baltimore Gas Light Company" for one year, subject to renewal, for lighting the city with gas instead of oil-lamps, provided that no greater expenditure were entailed by the change; see Ordinance of June 17, 1816.

[2] Ordinance of March 19, 1798.

[3] Ordinance of February 26, 1799; continued by Ordinance of March 5, 1801.

[4] Ordinance of March 26, 1807.

[5] "Laws of Maryland, 1812 (November sesssion), ch. 194.

to raise £510, some part of which should be used for "Buying Two Fire Engines and a Parcel of Leather Bucketts for the Use of the said Town."[1] In 1769, the first of a long series of volunteer fire companies was organized and a fire engine purchased by means of popular subscription.[2] The statute of 1787, referred to above,[3] "for the more effectual remedy to extinguish fires," not only provided a means of water supply, but directed every householder to keep two leather buckets hung up near the door of his house.

Volunteer fire companies were so strongly intrenched in Baltimore upon the incorporation of the city in 1796, and their activity had grown so familiar that no provision was inserted in the charter for the municipal assumption of this function. For the next sixty-five years, the relation of the city to fire protection was free supply of water, extension of financial aid, and inadequate regulation of volunteer companies. The first direct grant was made in 1800.[4] Thereafter annual appropriations in general aid of the volunteer companies of the city, together with occasional specific grants for equipment, formed a feature of the municipal budget.

Water Supply.

Among the enumerated powers of the new corporation was included authority "to erect and regulate pumps in the streets, lanes, and alleys" of the city. At the first session of the Council, all pumps erected and to be erected under the provisions of the statute of 1787 were declared public, and their maintenance assumed by the city. In the same ordinance the City Commissioners were authorized to contract for the sinking of wells and the erection of pumps

[1] Scharf, "Chronicles of Baltimore," p. 56.

[2] *Ibid.*, p. 64.

[3] See above, page 25. In the same year (1787), the four volunteer fire companies then in existence in Baltimore agreed upon concerted action in case of fires.

[4] Ordinance of March 6, 1800; see also Ordinances of March 8, 1803, and March 2, 1804.

wherever such seemed necessary, and to provide for their maintenance and repair thereafter.[1]

In the following year this ordinance was repealed and more energetic measures were taken, by providing for the annual appointment in each ward of the city of a "Superintendent of Public Wells and Pumps," vested with the care and repair of old, and the provision of new pumps and wells. The cost of erecting new pumps was defrayed by a special assessment or "pump-tax"[2] upon the property benefited, levied by the Superintendent of the particular ward, acting together with the Superintendent of any adjoining ward. All Superintendents were required to render quarterly account to the Mayor.[3]

Five years later an ordinance was passed with the explicit preamble that the measure of 1798 "has been found insufficient and it is believed that if the superintendence of the pumps was concentrated in fewer hands that the complaints would be reduced." Instead of eight, two Superintendents were therein appointed—one for the district west, and one for that east of Jones' Falls. No change was made in the duties attached to the office, but penalties were added for the neglect of their performance.[4] In 1807 the duties of the "Superintendents of Wells and Pumps" were assumed by the Superintendents of Streets.[5]

But long before 1817 public pumps and wells had been found inadequate as the sole source of the growing city's water supply. In 1799 certain persons were authorized to raise by lottery a sum of money to be applied towards defraying the expenses of conveying and distributing "pure and wholesome water."[6] A second ordinance of the same day provided for carrying this project into execution, by authorizing the Mayor, with the advice and consent of

[1] Ordinance of April 24, 1797. For these several purposes the sum of one thousand dollars was appropriated!

[2] See below, page 82.

[3] Ordinance of March 10, 1798.

[4] Ordinance of March 25, 1803.

[5] See above, page 61.

[6] Ordinance of February 26, 1799.

a board of seven specially appointed commissioners, to contract for the conveyance into and distribution within the city of an adequate supply of water from one of the numerous adjacent sources. Any such contract to be valid must receive the approval of the Mayor and Council. The expenses involved were to be defrayed by a loan, made by the Mayor and the appointed commissioners, for the repayment of which all profits accruing from the supply of water, and the proceeds of all lotteries were pledged.[1] Beyond some preliminary work of examination, no practical result followed this measure, and in 1803, twelve new commissioners were appointed for the purpose of "introducing a copious and permanent supply of wholesome water into the City of Baltimore." They were authorized, in conjunction with the Mayor, to make detailed examination of the sources of supply and of the means of conducting it into the city, to invite proposals, and to make a contract subject to the approval of the Mayor and Council. A special session was authorized to consider the commission's report and to provide funds for defraying the expenses involved.[2]

This effort was likewise unsuccessful, and it was left for private enterprise to accomplish that at which public activity had stalled. Early in 1804, permission was granted certain owners of property along the water front to introduce, at their own expense with the aid of voluntary subscriptions, a supply of water into the city, and to erect a public reservoir for which the city appropriated the site.[3] A month later, the persons interested formed themselves into "The Baltimore Water Company" and received an act of incorporation in the following year.[4] In 1806 the powers conferred by the act of 1804 were virtually transferred to the Baltimore Water Company, which was thus given the free use of streets and public protection of property.[5]

[1] Ordinance of February 26, 1799.

[2] Ordinance of March 24, 1803. [3] Ordinance of March 8, 1804.

[4] Griffiths, "Annals of Baltimore," p. 171; Scharf, "Chronicles of Baltimore," pp. 296, 303.

[5] Ordinance of February 14, 1806.

The first step towards municipal control of the water supply was taken in 1809, when the City Commissioners were authorized, in conjunction with the Mayor, to contract with the Water Company for the transfer of all fire plugs erected by the Company, and further to erect as many more as might be necessary. An appropriation was made for this purpose, and the care of the fire plugs was vested in the City Commissioners.[1]

Health.

In addition to authorizing a special tax on the assessable property of the city to extinguish the debt incurred by the Committee of Health of Baltimore Town, the charter of Baltimore City vested the corporation with power to pass all laws and ordinances "necessary to preserve the health of the city; prevent and remove nuisances; to prevent the introduction of contagious diseases within the city and within three miles of the same." At the first session of the Council, an ordinance was passed authorizing the appointment of a new board of Commissioners of Health and vesting it, in conjunction with "the health officer for the time being," with the detailed execution and enforcement of these general powers. The appointment of a clerk was authorized, and all necessary expenses were assumed by the city; but the Commissioners themselves seem to have been unsalaried.[2]

In 1801, this body was succeeded by five Commissioners of Health, each of whom assumed sanitary control of an assigned district of the city. The powers of the board were enlarged, and the Superintendents of Streets and the City Constables were directed to execute the orders of any Com-

[1] Ordinance of March 11, 1809. The regulative power of the municipality was exercised in the following year by an ordinance imposing fines upon the Water Company for neglect to restore torn-up streets to their original condition, or to replace defective street paving (Ordinance of February 10, 1810).

[2] Ordinance of April 7, 1797.

missioner. The Commissioners were to receive fixed salaries, to draw on the Register for necessary expenditures, and to account quarterly with the Mayor and annually with the Council.[1] Two years later, a further reorganization took place. Four Commissioners of Health were then appointed, two of whom were chosen from the east side and two from the west side of Jones' Falls; their authority was extended to the sanitary care of docks.[2]

In 1807, recourse was again had to the district plan. The city was divided into four districts, sanitary control over each of which was assumed by a corresponding Commissioner. The appointment of a Health Officer and an assistant was also authorized, to carry into execution prescribed quarantine regulations.[3] Finally in 1809, the board of Commissioners of Health was merged with the board of City Commissioners in a new joint board, styled "City Commissioners and Commissioners of Health," as has been already described.[4] No further change in organization was made until the creation of a municipal Board of Health in 1820.[5]

Markets.

Prior to 1797, three markets had been successively established in Baltimore upon authority derived from the Legislature. The charter of the city vested general power in the corporation "to erect and regulate markets." An early ordinance of the City Council prescribed detailed rules for the conduct of such markets, and authorized the appointment of a clerk for each, who should enforce all market ordinances, collect stall rentals, and pay over the proceeds, together with all fines and forfeitures, to the City Treasurer.[6] A few years later, the erection of an additional market house was authorized, and special commissioners were appointed to borrow money for this purpose and to

[1] Ordinance of March 20, 1801.
[2] Ordinance of March 22, 1803.
[3] Ordinance of March 18, 1807.
[4] See above, p. 56.
[5] See below, p. 121.
[6] Ordinance of April 11, 1797.

superintend its expenditure. In 1804 the debt so incurred was discharged and a supplementary appropriation made.[1] In the following year, a general ordinance was passed for the regulation of the markets of the city, repealing all previous measures, and virtually constituting the general market code of Baltimore, throughout the period here considered.[2]

Wharves and Harbor.

The charter of Baltimore vested the power hitherto exercised by the Port Wardens in the corporation. Provision was immediately made for the detailed exercise of this authority by the appointment of a Harbor Master, empowered to select his own deputies subject to the approval of the Mayor.[3]

Further facilities for local commerce were afforded by the construction of public wharves in 1797, in 1803, and in 1806. In each case the work was entrusted to two or to three specially appointed commissioners, who were authorized to draw upon the City Register for the sum appropriated. Somewhat exceptional was the procedure in 1797, whereby the appointed commissioners were authorized to borrow the sum appropriated, to be repaid by the city within two years. Occasional appropriations for wharf repair were made to the City Commissioners.[4]

Specific provision was made for the expenditure of wharfage receipts by the passage of an ordinance in 1801, with the explanatory preamble: "it is but just and reasonable that the same (*i. e.* wharfage receipts) or as much thereof as may be necessary should be appropriated to the keeping the said wharves in repair, and in improving the streets and cleaning the docks thereof." The ordinance provided that

[1] Ordinance of March 2, 1804.

[2] Ordinance of March 25, 1805, supplemented by Ordinance of March 13, 1816.

[3] Ordinance of April 24, 1797.

[4] Ordinances of March 19, 1797; March 8, 1803; March 14, 1806. Compare also those of February 26, 1799, and March 15, 1800.

all wharfage charges should be specifically appropriated to the improvement of the particular wharf or dock from which they had been collected, and the Mayor was authorized to appoint one or more commissioners for each wharf to apply the money appropriated.[1] In 1809, the office of Harbor Master was duplicated by the appointment of one official for the east and one for the west side of Jones' Falls, each of whom was vested with exclusive jurisdiction within his respective field.[2] Finally in 1813 the board of Port Wardens was revived by the appointment of three persons, vested with the general care of wharves and docks, the inspection of local shipping and the preservation and improvement of the channel and harbor. The Harbor Masters were made subject to the directions of this board.[3]

Poor Relief.

Before 1818, there existed in Baltimore no distinct municipal agency for purposes of poor relief. As early as 1773, the erection of an alms-house in Baltimore County had been authorized, and trustees appointed to construct and maintain it.[4] In 1805 the conduct of the institution was transferred to the Levy Court of the County,[5] where it remained until vested by a statute of 1817 in a board of five trustees, appointed by the governor of the state.[6] It is probable that extreme cases of dependents and defectives encountered in the city were relieved by this agency. The expenses of the alms-house were defrayed by county taxation. As Baltimore grew in area and population the desirability of a distinctly local agency for poor-relief became more obvious; but not until 1818 was this afforded.[7]

Upon certain extraordinary occasions specially appointed agencies were vested with the administration of tempo-

[1] Ordinance of May 21, 1801. [2] Ordinance of March 22, 1809.
[3] Ordinance of March 24, 1813.
[4] "Laws of Maryland," 1773, ch. 30.
[5] *Ibid.*, 1805, ch. 94. [6] *Ibid.*, 1817, ch. 85.
[7] *Ibid.*, 1818, ch. 122; see below, p. 130.

rary aid. Thus in 1800 the subsequent organization of a permanent poor-relief board was anticipated by the appointment of persons in each ward to investigate the condition of the poor resident therein, and to issue recommendations to the Board of Health to any in real distress for relief at the public expense.[1]

Municipal provision for the pauper sick and insane was also late in emergence. The first general hospital in Baltimore appears to have been established by private benevolence in 1794, "as a temporary retreat for the Strangers and Sea-faring people."[2] During the ravages of yellow fever in 1798, the institution was purchased by the local Committee of Health and was maintained by state and city appropriation.[3] In 1808 the hospital was vested in private hands for a term of fifteen years. The city paid for the public patients at a fixed rate and exercised general control over the institution by a board of five visitors.[4] In 1814 this lease was extended under certain conditions for a further term of twenty-five years.[5]

Municipal Buildings.

Expenditure for the construction and maintenance of municipal buildings formed an insignificant item in the municipal budget prior to 1897. In 1801, five commissioners were authorized in conjunction with the Mayor to erect a city hall. Funds therefor were provided by the appropriation of one half of the proceeds of the fifteen shillings tax[6] for as long a period as might be requisite. In anticipation of this fund the commissioners were authorized to borrow money at six per cent., and in the interim to secure

[1] Ordinance of November 18, 1800, "to mitigate the distress occasioned by the late prevailing fever."

[2] Griffiths, "Annals of Baltimore," p. 145.

[3] Ordinances of February 20, 1798, and February 20, 1799.

[4] Ordinance of June 25, 1808. The number of visitors was increased to twelve by Ordinance of March 24, 1813.

[5] Ordinance of March 21, 1814.

[6] See below, page 75.

temporary quarters for the municipal government.[1] No action of importance appears to have been taken under this ordinance, and in 1806 it was specifically repealed.[2]

After 1807, occasional purchases of building sites and the erection of temporary structures for municipal purposes increased the ordinary annual outlay for maintenance and repair to an appreciable aggregate in certain years.

ADMINISTRATIVE EXPENSES.

The charter of 1796, as has been intimated, defined the mere framework of municipal government, and left the corporation to provide by ordinance for its own administrative machinery. At early sessions of the Council provision was made for the appointment of a Register, Treasurer, Collector, Commissioners of the Watch and for Lighting the City, Commissioners of Health, City Commissioners, Clerks of Markets, Harbor Master, Superintendents of Wells and Pumps, all of whose functions have been described above. At the end of 1798 the officers of the corporation included the Mayor, Register, Collector, twenty Councilmen and Council officers, twenty-eight commissioners constituting five boards, twenty-two inspection officers, and ten remaining functionaries performing more or less distinctly administrative duties. By 1812 the administration of the city had become appreciably reduced in complexity. The offices of Mayor, Councilmen, Register, and Collector were unchanged; those of Harbor Master, Superintendent of Streets and City Constable had been duplicated; the number of inspection officers had increased to twenty-four; but of the various boards of commissioners, the body of four City Commissioners was the only survival.

In the interval between 1812 and 1816, no marked reductions were made in the administrative force of the city; but on the whole, the salary list of the corporation was

[1] Ordinance of March 7, 1801.
[2] Ordinance of March 17, 1806.

much less than the formidable array of municipal officers would indicate. The entire body of inspection officers were paid by fees; the Collector was compensated by a commission on collections; and the same system reduced the salary of market officials to a nominal sum. The important salaried offices of the corporation in 1815 were: Mayor ($2500), Register ($1400), City Commissioners and clerk ($2400), Port Wardens ($1600), Health Officers ($600), Superintendent of Streets and Pumps ($960), Market Clerks ($972.50).

Interest on Debt.

The inherited Town debt was extinguished within a few years by payments from out the current revenues of the municipality. No appreciable expenditure for interest upon the incipient municipal debt became necessary before 1810, in which year a slight outlay was required. This increased gradually towards the close of the period.

CHAPTER III

MUNICIPAL REVENUE.

The characteristic feature of the municipal income of Baltimore in the years from 1797 to 1816 was its essential rigidity. The maximum tax levies authorized by the charter and by enabling acts of the legislature were imposed from the first. In the absence of any power to impose further local charges, receipts could only grow with the normal growth of the bases of revenue. An inadequate assessment machinery prevented the yield of the general property tax from keeping pace with the growth of the city in population and in wealth. Such was not the case with the license taxes and the tax on auction receipts, and these two items constituted the two most important items of compulsory revenue. The special assessment continued in the twenty years following the incorporation of Baltimore, as in the period immediately preceding, the ordinary fiscal device for effecting the opening and paving of streets, the construction of sewers, the sinking of wells and the erection of pumps. Wharfage receipts contributed appreciably to municipal revenue, and fines and forfeitures to a slight degree.

TAXATION.

General Property Tax. The charter of 1797 authorized the corporation "to lay and collect taxes not exceeding two dollars in the hundred pounds in any one year." A particular district of the city, Deptford Hundred, long pronounced in its opposition to the incorporation of Baltimore, was conciliated by specific exemption from any tax, direct or indirect, laid for the improvement of the harbor and wharves.[1]

(Assessment). The valuation of property made in 1792 and used thereafter as the basis of public levies constituted the basis of the first municipal levy in 1797.[2] In the same year an act for the general revaluation of real and personal property in the state was passed by the General Assembly.[3] General re-assessments were subsequently authorized in 1803 and in 1812.[4] These were designed primarily for state and county taxation, but were promptly utilized for the municipal charge as soon as available. In each of these acts as in the earlier statutes of 1785 and 1792,[5] a board of five Commissioners of the Tax was appointed for Baltimore City and for each county, and vested with general control of the revaluation of property. This board appointed a clerk with as many assessors as required, received the returns of the assessors upon the completion of the work, and acted as a board of review and appeal. In the counties, the boards of Commissioners of the Tax remained in activity in the intervals between general reassessments, assessing new property and allowing deductions for that destroyed or transferred.[6] In Baltimore City, the Commissioners of the Tax seem to have exercised no corresponding function after the completion of each reassessment.

Ample power for distinct local revaluation of property for purposes of local taxation was contained in the supplementary statute of 1797. The corporation was therein authorized "to make new assessment of all real and personal property as often as it may be necessary." But limited use was made of this broad authority. At an early session of the Council, the city was divided into three districts, for

[1] In 1806, "Rogers's Addition," then already a part of the city, was exempted from all corporate taxes and dues ("Laws of Maryland," 1805, ch. 42).

[2] See above, page 26.

[3] "Laws of Maryland," 1797, ch. 89.

[4] *Ibid.*, 1803, ch. 92; 1812, ch. 191.

[5] *Ibid.*, 1785, ch. 53; 1792, ch. 71.

[6] "Report of Maryland Tax Commission" (1888), p. cxxxiv.

each of which an assessor was appointed. These assessors were authorized to copy from the books of the Commissioners of the Tax for Baltimore Town the assessment of real and personal property made by them, and to add thereto the value of all alterations and improvements, and of all new and unassessed property. They could make no change in the valuation of property already assessed. Appeal from the valuation of any one assessor lay to the final judgment of his two associates. The Mayor was empowered to make transfers in assessed valuation and to allow for insolvencies, as theretofore done by the Commissioners of the Tax for Baltimore Town.[1] Similar provision for additions and transfers was made in the municipal levies of 1801, 1811, and 1816—the aggregate valuation of any one year serving as the basis for that of the following revision. In 1808 and thereafter, appeal from the valuation of an assessor lay to the Mayor instead of to the other assessors.[2]

The several reassessment measures provided for the valuation for purposes of taxation of all personal and real property. Slaves and silver plate were estimated at fixed rates, and churches, colleges, mechanics' tools and crops in the possession of the producer were ordinarily exempted from taxation.[3]

(Rate). The charter of Baltimore placed a statutory limitation, as noted above, upon the local tax rate. The maximum levy authorized, two dollars on every hundred pounds, was promptly imposed in 1797 in the equivalent form of fifteen shillings, and with the exception of 1800, when one half of the ordinary rate was levied, annually thereafter until the close of the period.[4]

[1] Ordinance of April 24, 1797.

[2] Ordinances of March 5, 1801; March 9, 1808; March 11, 1811; March 2, 1816.

[3] Thus see "Laws of Maryland," 1812, ch. 191. For details of the early state reassessments, *v.* "Report of Maryland Tax Commission (1888)," p. cxxx *et seq.*

[4] In 1812 the levy was first expressed in the national currency, *i. e.*, two dollars.

No other direct tax was levied in Baltimore prior to 1817. In 1815 renewed application was made to the General Assembly for authority to impose a special tax to discharge that part of the debt contracted in defense of the city in the War of 1812 and not assumed by the federal government; but the necessary power was not granted.[1]

(Collection). No permanent machinery at first existed for the collection of the tax. An early session of the City Council authorized the appointment of a collector to receive all Town taxes and local dues; but the activity of this functionary apparently ceased with the completion of this particular task.[2] In each municipal levy, provision was made for the appointment of an independent collector, bonded for the faithful performance of his duties. These consisted, in the main, of the delivery of a tax duplicate to every property owner, and in the completion of collection within a specified time. With this period expired the authority of the collector to enforce payment. If the collection was still unfinished, the securities of the collector became liable, and the passage of a special ordinance extending the time within which collection could be made was necessary.[3]

The annually recurring appointment of a collector tended to establish the office definitely, and by 1812 the "City Collector" may be said to have become a formal municipal officer.[4]

A characteristic of the direct tax was its high cost of collection. The collector was compensated by a commission varying from six to eight per cent. upon collections of the direct tax, and from five to eight per cent. of the collections of other local charges. The office soon became, as it throughout continued, one of the pleasant places in the municipal administration.

Specific Taxes. The specific taxes imposed in 1782 upon

[1] Resolutions of 1815, No. 1. [2] Ordinance of March 27, 1797.
[3] Ordinances of March 9, 1804; March 18, 1814; March 4, 1815.
[4] Thus see Ordinance of March 24, 1813.

four-wheeled vehicles, chairs or sulkies, drays, wagons or carts, and riding horses, as described above, remained in force in unchanged form after the incorporation of the city in 1796.

For some years such taxes, as all other municipal dues, were probably collected by the City Collector upon his own information. In 1812,[1] and in every subsequent levy of the direct property tax, provision was made for the appointment by the Mayor of a person to take account of all vehicles taxable, and to make return thereof. The authorized tax was then collected by the City Collector.

Auction Receipts Tax. The authority to impose a local tax upon auction receipts, renewed by the General Assembly to the Port Wardens of Baltimore Town in 1790 for a period of seven years and transferred to the Mayor and City Council in 1796, expired almost immediately after the incorporation of Baltimore.[2] The charter of the city authorized the corporation "to provide for licensing and regulating auctions and pawn-brokers within the city and precincts thereof." Apparently upon the strength of this general power, an early ordinance was passed by the Council, providing for the continuance of the tax in unchanged form. The auctioneers of the city were required to pay the City Treasurer one-fourth of one per cent. (five shillings on every hundred pounds) on all sales made by them. Quarterly account with the Treasurer was prescribed and the bondsmen of the auctioneers were made liable for any breach of the ordinance.[3]

In 1801 the tax was increased to one half of one per cent. (fifty cents on every hundred dollars). The Register instead of the Treasurer received quarterly returns, and auctioneers were required to keep exact account of all sales and upon demand to submit the same to the inspection of the Mayor.[4] In 1802 the tax was further increased to one

[1] Ordinance of March 6, 1812.
[2] See above, page 34.
[3] Ordinance of April 27, 1797.
[4] Ordinance of February 20, 1801.

per cent., at which amount it remained until the close of the period.

Lottery Tax. The General Assembly in 1791[1] prohibited any private lottery in Baltimore Town. After the incorporation of the city, special acts continued to be passed from time to time authorizing specific lotteries. In the confirmatory ordinances passed by the City Council, the provision was commonly inserted that six per cent. of the amount proposed to be raised should be paid to the Register of the city by the managers of the particular lottery.[2] This clause did not appear in every instance,[3] and no general statute was at any time passed. In 1817, lotteries were subjected to a five per cent. state tax on the value of the prizes, and thereafter yielded no revenue to the city treasury.[4]

License Taxes. Prior to the incorporation of the city, but slight fiscal use was made of the local license tax. After 1797, more frequent recourse was had thereto, and the revenues accruing from this source came ultimately to form an important item in the municipal budget. The important objects liable to such charges were, (i) Municipal Offices; (ii) Vehicles; (iii) Public Amusements.

(Municipal Offices). The administration of Baltimore Town was slow to add to its salaried officials. As from time to time necessary functionaries were appointed, fees and perquisites were ordinarily appropriated in lieu of salaries. This same tendency continued after the incorporation of Baltimore in 1796. As the city grew in population and wealth, the fees accruing became disproportionate to the service rendered, and the municipality endeavored to effect a proper adjustment, partly by substituting a fixed salary for remuneration by fees, more generally by imposing a license tax upon the official and his function.

[1] "Laws of Maryland," 1791, ch. 59.
[2] Ordinances of March 14, 1803; March 8, 1804; March 3, 1808; June 25, 1808; February 27, 1812.
[3] Thus see Ordinance of March 9, 1804.
[4] "Laws of Maryland," 1817, ch. 154.

In 1798 a general ordinance was passed directing all officers of the corporation to whom fees or perquisites were given in lieu of a salary, to obtain from the Mayor a license under the public seal of the city.[1] The same measure imposed license taxes upon inspectors of flour ($100), inspectors of salted provisions ($100), and upon gaugers of flour ($5). This was followed by a series of similar enactments, imposing license taxes of varying amount upon the inspection officers of the corporation.

Analogous to the license tax upon inspection officers was that imposed upon auctioneers, whose vocation was always regarded as quasi-public in character. In the same category may also be classed a license tax upon brokers imposed by an ordinance of 1798.[2]

(Vehicles). In addition to the specific taxes imposed by the act of 1782, all vehicles used for the transportation of goods were in 1798 subjected to an annual license tax and a slight registration fee.[3] In 1801, "to encourage the introduction and use of broad wheels," vehicles so provided were exempted from both the tax of 1782, and the license tax of 1798. Narrow wheel vehicles theretofore prohibited were permitted subject to special license taxes.[4]

(Public Amusements). In 1797 a general ordinance was passed requiring all theatrical and dramatic performances to be licensed by the Mayor and prescribing the charge ("tax or fine") to be imposed.[5] A supplementary ordinance of the following year imposed an annual license tax, in lieu of all other charges, upon public billiard tables.[6] License taxes were also imposed upon market traders and upon dogs.[7]

[1] Ordinance of March 19, 1798.

[2] Ordinance of February 28, 1798.

[3] Ordinance of March 10, 1798.

[4] Ordinance of March 21, 1801; re-enacted with a revised schedule of charges by Ordinance of March 8, 1807.

[5] Ordinance of March 28, 1797. [6] Ordinance of March 19, 1798.

[7] The license tax on dogs was collected first by the City Collector, then by the City Constables, and finally by the Superintendent of Chimney Sweeps!

Special Assessments.

The principal purposes for which special assessments were levied were the paving and reconstruction of streets, and the supply of public pumps and wells.

The proceeds of the special assessment imposed for street paving formed an important item of municipal revenue throughout the entire period from 1797 to 1816. The proceeds of the "pump tax" varied slightly during the first half of the period; after 1808 it became of little consequence, rallying somewhat just before 1816. The entire assessment levied in the course of street reconstruction was ordinarily awarded in the form of damages to property injured by the change, and consequently figured to but small amount in the municipal budget.

Street Paving. An early ordinance prescribed the machinery for levying the special assessment for paving purposes, or "paving tax," as it was commonly called. After determining the particular street to be paved, the City Commissioners were directed to make out a list of all persons liable to the assessment with the amount liable, and to present a revised copy thereof to the City Collector, who was required to make collections and to pay over to the City Treasurer the proceeds less his commission.[1] The City Commissioners were authorized to draw on the Treasurer for the aggregate amount of the assessment and to apply the same to the purpose designed. Any surplus remained in the Treasury for the use of the city, while deficits were met from out the funds appropriated for the use of the City Commissioners. The mode of estimating benefit continued, as provided by the statute of 1791, the foot-front rule, with the amount charged per foot varying according to the width of the particular street.[2] Experience soon showed that the "paving tax" thus assessed was insufficient in yield, and a few months later the City Commissioners were directed to increase the prescribed charges

[1] Ordinance of April 2, 1797.

[2] See above, page 24.

twenty-five per cent.[1] In 1800, upon the representation of the City Commissioners that "the present paving tax is unequal in its operation as the streets, lanes and alleys are of different width, and that an average tax on the square foot would be more just," an ordinance was passed fixing the assessment at nine cents per square foot upon the area to be paved.[2] The rule of apportionment still continued to be frontage as the assumed measure of benefit. The only change in the machinery of collection was that the City Commissioners issued their warrant to the Collector for the collection of assessments.

Occasionally the proceeds of the assessment were supplemented by a direct appropriation from out the City Treasury.[3] In paving Market Street in 1801, the chief thoroughfare of the city and a street of unusual width, the City Commissioners were directed to divide the street into three strips, two of which, thirty feet each in width, were to be paved by special assessment, while the Commissioners were to pave the middle strip at the expense of the corporation.[4] More curious was a case occurring in the same year, in which an appropriation having been made to a contractor for filling up a certain street, he was further authorized to receive from owners of abutting property, to defray the cost of paving the same street, sums of money identical in amount and mode of collection with a special assessment.[5]

Street Reconstruction. The charter empowered the corporation to establish new, and to alter old streets with the consent of property owners affected; but neither it nor the supplementary statute authorized a special assessment for this purpose. In consequence, a special act of the General Assembly was necessary whenever any important street reconstruction was contemplated. The procedure author-

[1] Ordinance of July 12, 1797. [2] Ordinance of March 6, 1800.

[3] Ordinances of February 20, 1799, and March 15, 1803.

[4] Ordinance of March 15, 1801.

[5] Ordinance of February 24, 1801. Procedure relating to the levy of the special assessment was re-enacted in Ordinance of March 9, 1807.

ized by such statutes, was ordinarily, as follows: The sheriff of Baltimore County, having given at least ten days' notice in one of the Baltimore newspapers, summoned a jury of twelve freeholders of the city, who, having been duly sworn, proceeded to make awards for damages and to assess a corresponding amount upon the property benefited. The sums assessed were filed in the Register's office and constituted a lien upon the property affected. Suit for the recovery of the damages awarded might be instituted within six months in the Baltimore County Court.[1] In the suburbs the Commissioners of the Precincts or specially appointed commissioners performed the duties ordinarily vested in the City Commissioners. Such bodies often acted also as a jury for the award of damages and the assessment of benefits.[2] Occasionally damages were awarded and benefits assessed by a board of five "disinterested assessors" appointed in each case by the Mayor, instead of by the jury summoned by the county sheriff.

The proceeds of the special assessment were designed to defray the entire expenditure involved. At times when the improvement was large and costly, the city, as has been said, made a direct appropriation in aid.[3]

Wells and Pumps. In the supplementary statute of 1797 wells and pumps were enumerated among the objects for which a special assessment might be levied. The procedure of assessment and collection was prescribed in detail in the following year.[4] When a new pump was to be erected, the Superintendent of Pumps in the ward wherein it was to be placed, acting with the superintendent of any other ward, levied on all assessable property liable to be benefited, wherever located, "such a sum on every hundred pounds of property as it may stand upon the books of the City Assessors as will be just and equal." The mode of

[1] See references in note 3, page 59, above.
[2] "Laws of Maryland," 1812, ch. 120; 1813, ch. 67; 1816, ch. 143; 1817, ch. 71, 115, 117.
[3] *Ibid.*, 1813, ch. 176, 182; 1816, ch. 62, 162, 171.
[4] Ordinance of March 10, 1798.

collection and expenditure of the "pump tax" was as in the case of the "paving tax."

In 1803 the objects for which the special assessment might be laid were extended to the sinking of new wells, and to any alteration or addition to any existing well or pump.[1] Authority was sometimes given for the construction of public wharves, the cost to be defrayed by special assessment. The procedure authorized was as in the case of street reconstruction—award of damages and assessment of benefits by a jury summoned by the county sheriff, later by a board of five assessors appointed by the Mayor.[2] More exceptional were the imposition of special assessments for the paving of gutters in 1807,[3] for the construction of sewers in the western precincts of the city in 1815,[4] and for the wharfing of the basin in 1805 and thereafter.[5]

FEES.

A fee has been defined as "a payment to defray the cost of each recurring service undertaken by the government primarily in the public interest, but conferring a measurable special advantage on the fee-payer."[6] So understood, local fees play an insignificant part in the early finances of Baltimore City. The exaction of such charges was authorized in the series of inspection ordinances, noted above; but the proceeds constituted the perquisites of the otherwise unpaid officials, and formed no part of the municipal budget. They indeed obviated the payment of salaries to a considerable number of municipal officials, and as such constituted an indirect form of municipal revenue. This connection is seen in the promptness with which the municipality intervened by means of license taxes when the fees aggregated

[1] Ordinance of March 25, 1803.
[2] "Laws of Maryland," 1805, ch. 84; 1810, ch. 103; 1815, ch. 34, 206.
[3] Ordinance of March 9, 1807.
[4] "Laws of Maryland," 1815, ch. 82.
[5] *Ibid.*, 1805, ch. 84; 1810, ch. 103; 1813, ch. 71; 1815, ch. 206.
[6] Seligman, "Essays in Taxation," p. 304.

more than a fair compensation, and in the rough adaptation thereafter of tax to proceeds.[1] On the whole however the method here pursued—neglect of both receipts and expenditures of this kind—appears the simpler device, and more in accord with actual experience.

A few instances occur in which an actual fee was exacted. Thus the City Commissioners were early directed to receive one dollar per day for the use of the city from persons requiring their services for determining lot boundaries or regulating party walls.[2] In 1798 the owners of wagons and carts were required to pay to the City Register a registration fee of fifty cents. In the same year the City Register was directed to charge $2 and $1, for every fixture of the city seal.

By an early ordinance of the City Council, the Mayor was directed to receive from the Maryland Fire Insurance Company a formal transfer of the right vested in that corporation of erecting a magazine for storing gunpowder. An appropriation was made for construction, and the Mayor was authorized to impose a reasonable "storage or rate" upon powder stored in the public magazine.[3] Income from this source was more in the nature of a quasi-private receipt than of a fee.

Fines and Forfeitures.

The charter of Baltimore vested the corporation with the expressed power "to impose and appropriate fines, penalties and forfeitures, for the breach of their by-laws or ordinances." Such charges when imposed by the ordinances of the city were recoverable before a single magistrate as in the case of small debts, if not exceeding twenty dollars; or in larger amount, by action of debt in Baltimore County Court.

All regulative ordinances of the corporation imposed spe-

[1] See below, page 78.

[2] Ordinance of May 6, 1797.

[3] Ordinance of April 10, 1797.

cific or maximum fines and penalties for non-compliance. A common provision was, that of the fines so recovered, one-half should be paid to the informer and the other half be appropriated for the use of the city. An early ordinance vested the Mayor with power to remit so much of the city's part of any fine, not exceeding twenty dollars, as seemed "just and reasonable."[1] The mode of recovery and collection varied. In some cases it was vested in the City Collector;[2] in others in the Mayor;[3] in still others, in the officials designed to enforce the provisions of the ordinances, as the clerks of the markets or the various inspection officers.

Quasi-Private Receipts.

Wharves. The ordinance of April 24, 1797, vesting in the corporation the powers before exercised by the Port Wardens definitely authorized the collection of wharfage charges by a Harbor Master therein appointed. In 1801, such receipts were appropriated to the improvement and repair of the particular wharves and docks from which they had been collected, and the Mayor was authorized to appoint one or more commissioners for each public wharf to superintend the expenditure of the funds so accruing.[4] This ordinance was to remain in force for a single year; but the practice appears to have continued, until again specifically authorized in 1807.[5] In 1813, the list of commodities liable to wharfage was enlarged so as to include every ordinary article of commerce. Rates varying from twenty cents to one-half cent per package were imposed, and a general clause added that all unenumerated articles should be charged proportionate to bulk. Owners of property front-

[1] Ordinance of June 26, 1797. [2] Ordinance of March 27, 1797.

[3] Ordinance of May 6, 1797.

[4] Ordinance of May 21, 1801. Municipal ownership of wharves originated in the extension of streets to the harbor and the reservation of the corresponding water front.

[5] Ordinance of April 8, 1807; see also ordinance of March 15, 1803.

ing upon any of the public wharves were exempted from the payment of wharfage charges upon goods received or delivered.[1]

Much dissatisfaction appears to have resulted from the operation of this measure, culminating in the passage of an act by the General Assembly of Maryland in January, 1814, prohibiting the Mayor and City Council from imposing any "tax, duty, toll, or wharfage upon any goods, wares or merchandise, or other articles for the passing of the same over any of the public wharves."[2] The power of the corporation to regulate by ordinance the time during which such goods might remain upon the wharves was reaffirmed. In accordance with this prohibition, ordinances were promptly passed repealing all specific wharfage charges, and substituting charges based upon tonnage. An attempt was made in the following year to return to the system of specific charges, but the illegality of this procedure in face of the specific prohibition of the Legislature soon became apparent and the ordinance was promptly repealed.[3]

Markets. Receipts from the rental of market stalls and shambles, which played so important a part in the economy of Baltimore Town, continued to figure to some extent in the corporate budget. The "market codes" of 1797 and 1805 alike provided for the appointment of a salaried clerk for each of the city markets, who was required to determine and collect the rental of all stalls, to keep fair and regular account of the proceeds, and to pay the funds so received into the city treasury.[4] Upon renting a stall the clerk issued a certificate, stating terms and tenure, to the applicant, which when approved by the Mayor was exchanged for a license recorded with the City Register, valid for one year and transferable with the approbation of the Mayor. All market traders were subject to an annual license tax.

[1] Ordinance of March 24, 1813.
[2] "Laws of Maryland," 1813, ch. 118.
[3] Ordinances of March 21, 1814; March 25 and July 27, 1815.
[4] Ordinances of April 11, 1797, and March 25, 1805.

Lotteries. An annual Town lottery was authorized by the General Assembly in 1791,[1] the proceeds of which were directed to be divided between the Port Wardens and the Special Commissioners, as described above.[2] This privilege was transferred to the municipality in 1796, but seems never to have been regularly exercised thereafter, if indeed the practice had not fallen into virtual disuse before the incorporation of Baltimore. In 1797, 1798 and 1808 special ordinances were passed authorizing public lotteries for the purpose of raising specific amounts ($9080; $9086 and $9333.33, respectively), in aid of municipal revenues. In the first two instances, three bonded commissioners were appointed to conduct the lottery and to defray all expenses, including their own remuneration from out a five per cent. commission upon gross receipts. In the third case, the Register of the city and six appointed persons were named commissioners to conduct the lottery.

Occasional use was made of the lottery for defraying specific municipal expenditures. Thus in 1799, commissioners were appointed to raise by lottery the sum of $4381, for providing an adequate water supply. In 1814 similar provision was made to raise the net sum of $100,000, to be expended by the Mayor and City Council in the erection of an arsenal,[3] and in 1816 a public lottery to raise the sum of $50,000—increased in 1817 to $1,000,000—was authorized, for walling in Jones' Falls and for improving Harford Street.[4]

GIFTS.

Voluntary contributions figured to small extent in local receipts after the incorporation of Baltimore City. In 1799 certain proprietors of ground are said to have "raised a considerable sum of money by subscription," for the purpose of erecting a bridge across Jones' Falls.[5] Simi-

[1] "Laws of Maryland," 1791, ch. 59.

[2] See above, page 22.

[3] "Laws of Maryland," 1813, ch. 125.

[4] *Ibid.*, 1815, ch. 209; 1816, ch. 138.

[5] Ordinance of February 27, 1799.

larly in 1808, the City Council, having appropriated the sum of ten thousand dollars for the erection of a stone bridge across Jones' Falls on Baltimore Street, authorized the Mayor "to accept for the use of the corporation any donation of land on each side of Jones' Falls, which may be useful to, or will improve the site for the aforesaid bridge."[1]

Under this head are perhaps also to be classed certain revenues appropriated by the state to the municipal treasury. Thus the city continued for a time after incorporation in receipt of the surplus proceeds of "ordinary and retailers" licenses issued by Baltimore County Court to taverns within the city, as provided in the statute of 1784.[2] In 1804, revenue from this source, then already amounting to some $5000 per annum,[3] was diverted by act of the legislature into the state treasury.[4]

[1] Ordinance of June 25, 1808.

[2] Ordinance of April 29, 1797; also see above, page 40.

[3] Griffiths, "Annals of Baltimore," p. 177.

[4] "Laws of Maryland," 1804, ch. 93. In 1815, the justices of the Orphans Court of Baltimore County were directed to pay the proceeds of intestate estates to the trustees or managers of the several free schools of Baltimore, in proportion to the number of children educated at each school; *ibid.*, 1814, ch. 131.

CHAPTER IV

MUNICIPAL INDEBTEDNESS.

An appreciable floating indebtedness—an heritage from the administration of Baltimore Town—devolved upon the municipality, with the assumption of corporate rights in 1796. A debt of $2200 had been incurred by the local "Committee of Health," and remained undischarged; while the unpaid accounts of the Special Commissioners of Baltimore Town aggregated $9981.15. A provision of the charter specifically authorized a levy upon the assessable property of the city for the discharge of the health debt; but no recourse seems to have been made thereto. Instead, the surplus revenues of the city were devoted to the discharge of the aggregate indebtedness. By 1798, upwards of six thousand dollars had been so paid, and by 1800 the entire debt had been extinguished.

In the decade following the incorporation of Baltimore, it became common to anticipate municipal income by informal loans, the proceeds of which were appropriated to specific purposes. In certain of these ordinances, the corporation formally guaranteed the repayment of the loans, indemnified the commissioners appointed to negotiate them, and pledged the revenue of the city for their ultimate repayment.[1] A more common clause was the provision that the indebtedness be discharged within the time specified

[1] Ordinances of April 24, 1797; March 19, 1798; April 23, 1798. In the ordinance of February 26, 1799, authorizing a loan to provide an adequate water supply, the profits arising from the undertaking and from all future lotteries were specifically appropriated for the repayment of the loan.

from out unappropriated revenues in the city treasury, or from funds accruing thereto.[1]

Prior to 1812, no serious difficulty was experienced in accomplishing this. Rigid economy in municipal administration, with strict limitation in expenditure, made it possible to defray from out the ordinary revenues of the city all current expenditures, to discharge the inherited Town obligations and to extinguish periodic floating indebtedness. The City Register's summaries from 1803 to 1815 disclosed appreciable balances in the municipal treasury at the close of each fiscal year. The balances of 1813 and 1814 were indeed more apparent than real. In 1813 a debt of $16,000 to the banks of the city remained undischarged and in 1814 this had increased to $20,000. But under normal conditions, little difficulty would doubtless have been experienced in extinguishing this obligation at the first favorable turn in the city's finances.

The stirring events of the War of 1812 however injected into the municipal budget a large and unforeseen item of expenditure, and contributed to reduce municipal revenue. Current indebtedness not only remained unpaid but steadily increased, and came eventually to form the nucleus of the funded municipal debt of the present day. Early in 1813 British vessels entered Chesapeake Bay, and established a blockade upon local commerce. The city at once prepared to supplement federal and state measures of defense by appointing a Committee of Supply, composed of the Mayor and seven citizens, and appropriating the sum of $20,000. This sum was found inadequate, and a municipal convention was called, made up of four delegates from each of the wards and precincts. This body recommended a municipal loan not exceeding $500,000, and advised that authority be sought from the General Assembly to levy a special tax in payment thereof. In May, 1813, the city petitioned the General Assembly "to assume the debts contracting for

[1] Ordinances of March 10, 1798; March 14, 1806; March 17, 1806.

public defense," and to authorize the levy of a special direct tax upon the city and precincts for their ultimate discharge. Both petitions were refused and the loan in the form proposed was abandoned. The city treasury having now become depleted and the local situation remaining serious, the corporation, without waiting for specific authority, authorized by ordinance of May 10, 1813, a loan of $80,000 from the banks of the city.[1]

Before the final suspension of hostilities occurred, the entire loan so authorized had been contracted. Renewed attempt to secure authority from the General Assembly to levy a special tax to extinguish it, was unattended with success.[2] The current obligations of the city were further increased by successive loans in 1815 and 1816 of $10,000 each in anticipation of municipal revenues,[3] making the aggregate indebtedness of the city at the close of the period considered about $100,000.

[1] Mayor's Communication of February 14, 1814; Griffiths, "Annals of Baltimore," pp. 204-205, 213.

[2] Resolutions of February Session, 1815, No. 1.

[3] Resolutions of February Session, 1815, No. 3; of 1816, No. 6.

PART III

THE FINANCES OF BALTIMORE CITY FROM 1817 TO 1856

INTRODUCTION

Relative stability in administrative organization and marked growth in municipal consciousness characterized the institutional development of Baltimore in the forty years from 1817 to 1856. The recovery of economic interests from the reactionary depression following the War of 1812 was succeeded by the introduction of new industrial methods and appliances. On July 4, 1828, Charles Carroll of Carrollton, the last surviving signer of the Declaration of Independence, laid the first rail of the Baltimore and Ohio Railroad, and thus "One man's life formed the connecting link between the political revolution of the last century and the industrial revolution of the present."[1]

Beginning with the projection of improved means of communication with the West as a necessary measure for preventing the threatened diversion of the trade of that region from local merchants, Baltimore plunged boldly into the policy of aiding works of internal improvement. The essential features of the modern financial system of the city were determined by 1856, and that determination was shaped largely by municipal activity in this direction. The city grew steadily in wealth and population and preserved

[1] Hadley, "Railroad Transportation," p. 1.

an industrial and commercial prominence, some part of which would perhaps otherwise have been lost. On the other hand by direct municipal loans and by extension of municipal credit to various railroads and canals, in the construction of which it was believed that Baltimore had a direct interest, a large and burdensome funded and guaranteed debt was incurred. This in turn necessitated larger resort to the corporate power of taxation, retrenchment in ordinary expenditure, and limitation of municipal activity to the functions already assumed. Normal development along these lines was interrupted by the emergence of a new municipal spirit, coincident with the completion of the Baltimore and Ohio Railroad in 1853, and expressed in the administration of Mayor Thomas Swann in 1856.

CHAPTER I

MUNICIPAL ADMINISTRATION.

Corporate Powers.

In 1818 the General Assembly passed an "Act relating to the City of Baltimore,"[1] which constituted an important supplement to the original charter. Powers before enjoyed by the commissioners of the several precincts were transferred to the corporation. The city was divided into twelve wards, instead of eight as theretofore, with provision for successive increase to fourteen, sixteen, eighteen and twenty, as population increased. The same act authorized the city to lay and collect direct taxes on the assessment of private property, "to such amount as shall be thought necessary for the public or city purposes"; to issue stock or borrow money to an amount not exceeding one million dollars "for the purpose of promoting or effecting any great or permanent improvements"; to exercise the right of eminent domain in effecting municipal improvements, and to levy special assessments for street reconstruction. In 1829, upon petition of the corporation, the Assembly authorized the Mayor and City Council to pass ordinances regulating the manner of appointing all municipal officers.[2] By the state constitution of 1851, Baltimore City was separated from Baltimore County, of which it had theretofore been a formal part.

Administrative Organization.

With the increase in the number of city wards in 1818, the number of City Councilmen and of Mayor's Electors un-

[1] "Laws of Maryland," 1817, ch. 148.

[2] Resolution of February 19, 1829, p. 155; "Laws of Maryland," 1828, ch. 114.

derwent corresponding change. Important modifications were made at the same time in the method of appointing municipal officers. Instead of merely selecting one of two candidates nominated for each office by the City Council,[1] the Mayor himself appointed all officers, subject to confirmation by the Council. The only exceptions to this were the City Register and the City Clerks who were elected by the two branches of the City Council in joint convention.

In 1833, influenced by the spirit of democracy then dominant in American political thought, the surviving remnant of the electoral system was swept away and the election of the Mayor was changed to direct popular choice.[2] The City Council was organized in its modern form in 1845. The city was divided by five commissioners, appointed by the governor of the state, into twenty wards "as nearly equal in population as may be, and the boundaries of which shall be as nearly as practicable in right lines."[3] The First Branch of the City Council consisted of twenty members, one from each ward; the Second Branch, of ten members, one from two contiguous wards.[4] Under this act the City Councilmen continued to be elected annually; but in the following year the term of members of the Second Branch was extended to two years.[5]

Detailed changes in administrative organization, such as the establishment of the Board of Commissioners of Public Schools in 1828 and the successive modification of the Board of City Commissioners, are noted below, in conjunction with the financial activity of the corresponding municipal department.

[1] See above, page 52.

[2] "Laws of Maryland," 1832, ch. 206; in response to resolution of Mayor and City Council of February 14, 1833, No. 16.

[3] It is curious to note that of these five commissioners, three were chosen from citizens of Baltimore residing west and two east of Jones' Falls.

[4] "Laws of Maryland," 1844, ch. 282.

[5] *Ibid.*, 1845, ch. 238.

Financial Machinery.

The financial mechanism of the municipality centered in the office of the City Register. After 1818 this official was elected annually by the two chambers of the City Council in joint session. He performed the functions both of treasurer and auditor, receiving and guarding all public moneys, examining all accounts presented for payment and making all proper disbursements. The appointment of a Deputy Register was authorized in 1836, for the performance of such duties as the Register might direct.[1]

The collection of municipal taxes, special assessments and other local charges, both current and in arrears, remained vested in the hands of the City Collector, save when otherwise provided. The Collector was charged by the Register with the maximum amounts collectible under the several levies and credited with the payments periodically made. Tax arrearages were carried forward from year to year in open account. In 1852-53 a City Auditor was appointed and vested with the audit of municipal tax and assessment collections, before performed by the Register.[2] A year later the function of the Auditor was changed to the collection of tax arrearages, of which duty the Collector was thereby relieved.[3] The audit and control of municipal accounts thus again devolved upon the City Register. In 1856, Mayor Samuel Hinks suggested the appointment of a City Comptroller to supervise the entire financial affairs of the corporation,[4] and the establishment of the office in 1857 may be regarded as one of the important features of the succeeding period of municipal history.

The negotiation of funded loans and the custody of the sinking fund were at first entrusted to the Mayor and the president of the two Branches of the City Council. In 1818

[1] Ordinance of January 30, 1836, No. 2.
[2] Ordinances of June 18, 1852; March 18, 1853.
[3] Ordinance of March 9, 1855.
[4] Mayor's Message of January, 1856.

a board of three Commissioners of Finance was vested with all duties relating to the issue of city stock, and a body of three Commissioners of the Sinking Fund, with the amortization of funded indebtedness.[1] In 1826 the Commissioners of the Sinking Fund were discharged, and their duties transferred to the Commissioners of Finance.[2]

The Budget.

The form of the municipal budget and the order of budgetary procedure may be said to have taken definite shape within the period here considered. Estimates of anticipated expenditures and revenues for the ensuing fiscal year were obtained by the joint Ways and Means Committee, at first directly from the several municipal offices, after 1840 through the instrumentality of the City Register.[3] Upon the basis of these estimates, a general appropriation bill was reported to the City Council and enacted, ordinarily without change, as any other municipal ordinance.

Municipal revenue was supplied in the main by the levy of a direct property tax, the maximum rate of which was changed in 1818 from one and a third per cent. to "such amount as shall be thought necessary for the public or city purposes," and the actual rate of which was determined by the Ways and Means Committee. With the growth of the city and the increase in municipal expenditure, larger recourse was necessarily had to direct taxation as a source of municipal revenue. Instead of utilizing for this purpose the original "Direct Levy" ("direct tax"), the fixture of the rate of which had been placed entirely within the power of the corporation by the act of 1818 above noted, specific authority was obtained from the General Assembly, ordinarily in connection with the act empowering the exercise of the particular function, for the annual levy of a special

[1] See below, pp. 196-197. [2] Ordinance of April 3, 1826, No. 3.
[3] Ordinance of March 12, 1840.

rate to an amount adequate to defray the total expenditure involved in each particular case. Between 1817 and 1856, five such special rates were annually imposed, in addition to the Direct Levy, and the Highway and Bridge Levy, employed in lieu of the Direct Levy for the taxation of the thinly settled outlying districts of the city. These special rates were: Court Levy, Poor Levy, School Levy, Levy for County Expenditures for City Purposes, and Internal Improvements Levy.

The explanation of this method of special levies, long a feature of the municipal budget, is probably to be found in two circumstances: (1) the influence of the "rate system" of the English municipal corporations, (2) the practical circumstance that the "Direct Tax" could be levied only within certain prescribed "limits of direct taxation," whereas the special levies authorized by distinct acts of the state legislature could be imposed upon the aggregate taxable basis.[1] It is probable that the special levies were originally precisely adjusted by the Ways and Means Committee of the City Council to the estimate of anticipated expenditures submitted by the respective municipal departments, and that the funds so provided were designed exclusively for the respective purposes for which they had been levied. In actual practice the rates although authorized by distinct ordinances were levied collectively and the proceeds covered into the municipal treasury in aggregate. Certain municipal departments, notably the Commissioners of Public Schools, repeatedly asserted their right to the entire proceeds of their respective rates and inclined to regard the annual appropriation of the City Council as a mere credit to this account. But this claim was never admitted, and before 1856 the use of special tax levies may be said to have become a mere budgetary form.

[1] See below, p. 146.

CHAPTER II

MUNICIPAL EXPENDITURE.

The growth of municipal expenditure in the period from 1817 to 1856 was continuous although irregular. The rapid increase in the years following the War of 1812 culminated in 1817, and was succeeded by a decade of normal development. The policy of municipal aid to works of internal improvement, inaugurated in the closing years of the third decade, was accompanied by increased expenditure in all branches of municipal service, continuing progressively until the dawn of the modern era of municipal activity.

From 1817 to 1835, street paving and repair, watching and lighting (the cost of which remained undifferentiated), harbor improvement, public schools, interest on the funded debt and administrative costs were the important occasions of local expenditure. After 1835, interest on the funded debt became the dominant item and formed from one-half to one-third of the ordinary net annual outlay. Expenditure for watching and lighting and for public schools increased rapidly, and the annual disbursement for judicial purposes, charities and corrections and administration, more gradually. The cost of harbor improvement, fire protection and sanitation underwent little change, while that of street paving and street cleaning declined relatively.[1]

Streets and Roadways.

The general improvement and maintenance of the city roadway, including the paving and repair of streets and the construction of bridges and sewers, remained until 1820 vested in the board of three "City Commissioners and

[1] See Appendix D.

Commissioners of Health," described above.[1] In 1820 occurred a natural differentiation and reassociation. The ordinance of 1809 appointing the joint board was repealed, the Commissioners of Health were continued in separate existence, and the City Commissioners were merged with the existent board of Port Wardens in a new board of three persons, styled "City Commissioners and Wardens of the Port of Baltimore." Warrants or other documents issuing from the new body bore the title, Wardens' Office, or City Commissioners' Office, as the case required.[2] The dual character of this board was clearly recognized in the general re-enactment of municipal ordinances, which took place in 1826 and in 1838.[3]

Not until 1850 was any change made in this anomalous exercise of distinct functions by a single board acting in dual capacity. In 1849 the board of City Commissioners was displaced by a single City Commissioner and two subordinate Assistant City Commissioners;[4] but these functionaries were at once constituted a board of Port Wardens, and vested with all the powers possessed by their predecessors.[5] Finally in 1850 the distinct office of Port Warden was created and the City Commissioner was relieved of duties relating to the care of the harbor and wharves of the city.[6]

Street Paving and Repair. The re-enacting ordinance of 1826 provided that all paving should be performed under

[1] Page 56.
[2] Ordinance of February 2, 1820.
[3] Ordinances of April 8, 1826; May 22, 1838, No. 47. In 1827 the board was required to submit to the City Council annually thereafter separate reports of its proceedings, as a board of City Commissioners and as a board of Port Wardens, with fiscal abstracts of each department separately signed (Ordinance of April 2, 1827). In 1838 provision was made that "the City Commissioners shall, *ex officio*, be Port Wardens" (Ordinance of May 22, 1838, No. 8).
[4] Ordinance of February 15, 1849, No. 3.
[5] Ordinance of April 25, 1849, No. 48.
[6] Ordinance of March 8, 1850. After 1851 instead of the two Assistant City Commissioners authorized, the subordinate force consisted of one Assistant City Commissioner and clerical aid.

the superintendence of the City Commissioners by contract, after public advertisement and award to the lowest bidder. This clause was incorporated in all subsequent municipal codes, and the contract system was essentially the method employed by the City Commissioners for new paving.[1] It was however neither the method now described by the term, contract system, nor what is understood as the modern day-labor system, *i. e.* where the municipality assumes direct control of the work and employs day labor. The actual practice was to invite bids and to make awards for detailed services—supply of materials, wages of laborers, and hire of carts and horses. Not until 1855 were contracts awarded for paving according to completed work, the unit being the square foot. A saving of at least one-third in the cost of the work was effected, it was stated, by this change.[2]

The cost of initial paving continued to be defrayed by the levy of a special assessment upon abutting property, as described above,[3] supplemented by occasional special appropriations. When municipal property abutted upon a street about to be paved, a corresponding assessment was levied upon and paid by the city. By an extension of the same principle, the entire cost of paving street intersections or "cross streets" continued a municipal charge.[4]

A characteristic feature of street maintenance during the period here considered was the increased cost of street repair, an outlay borne entirely by the city treasury. It was essentially a compulsory expenditure. Urban growth and local traffic played havoc with the crude paving of local streets, and the City Commissioners were throughout engaged in a constant and barely successful struggle to prevent the leading thoroughfares from becoming impassable.

[1] Ordinances of April 8, 1826, sect. 19; April 28, 1830.

[2] Report of City Commissioner, January 1, 1856.

[3] Page 80.

[4] Cf. Ordinance of February 16, 1832, No. 8; Resolution of March 27, 1845, No. 41.

Despite larger appropriations the necessity far outran the relief, and at best a policy of patch-work was pursued.

For a number of years the cost of repaving, as distinguished from repairing, paved streets continued to be defrayed, as in the case of initial paving, by a special assessment upon abutting owners. With rapid municipal development and the consequent need of street improvement, the municipal appropriations in aid of the sums so levied—from the first appreciable in amount—grew in frequency and in importance. This practice crystallized in April, 1833, in the adoption by the corporation of a resolution providing that upon the receipt of a petition from the proprietors of abutting property for the repaving of any particular street, the City Commissioners should ascertain the cost of such repaving, exclusive of cross-streets, and give public notice that the improvement would be undertaken under the supervision of the City Commissioners, as soon as the owners affected should deposit with the city a sum equal to two-thirds of the expenditure involved. The remaining third and the cost of repaving cross-streets were appropriated from out the city treasury.[1]

Although not specifically provided, this resolution was construed as requiring the application of *all* the property owners affected. This unanimous consent could rarely be obtained, and then only with much exertion and difficulty. In 1834 through the efforts of Mayor Jesse Hunt, the General Assembly authorized the corporation to repave and recurb any street whenever the owners of two-thirds of the abutting property had made application therefor. Leaseholders for ninety-nine years or more and mortgagees in possession were construed as owners.[2] This grant was immediately accepted by the corporation, and the Mayor was directed to refer all applications, made in proper form, to the City Commissioners, who thereupon levied two-thirds

[1] Resolution of April 24, 1833, No. 69.

[2] "Laws of Maryland," 1833, ch. 40; Mayor's Message of January 6, 1834.

of the aggregate expenditure upon the abutting property owners in the usual manner of a special assessment for street paving.[1] With a view to encouraging the further repaving of streets, the corporation in 1854 sought authority to reduce the requisite condition from the application of the owners of two-thirds of the abutting property to the owners of a major part, but without success.[2]

The aggregate expenditure for street paving and repair thus consisted, in addition to the administrative expenses of the City Commissioner's office, of the cost of paving cross-streets, of the repair of paved streets, of the city's contribution of one-third to the cost of repaving, and of occasional special appropriations. To these should be added minor items, such as the cost of paving and repaving in front of city property, the repair of unpaved streets, and the supply of flag and stepping stones. Estimates of the amounts required for each of these several purposes were annually submitted by the City Commissioner to the City Register, and by him incorporated in his general estimate of receipts and expenditures for the ensuing year. In the annual appropriation bill, specific appropriations were made for each of the purposes named, subject to the order of the City Commissioner for the amount actually expended; any balance of a particular appropriation over the corresponding expenditure remained in the city treasury.

In actual practice, however, estimates of the City Commissioner were materially cut down by the City Council, and the sums appropriated were considerably less than the several amounts required. In some cases in face of an inevitable expenditure, no appropriation whatever was made. An unauthorized deficit was thus created and carried forward in increasing amount from year to year despite the protests of successive Mayors and City Commissioners for larger appropriations and regular discharge of liabilities.

[1] Ordinance of April 19, 1834, No. 26; re-enacted in Ordinance of February 20, 1835, No. 7.

[2] Ordinance of March 4, 1854, No. 27.

The ordinary form of an appropriation for paving or repaving was, "including bills rendered, and orders unpaid." In some cases the standing indebtedness was actually more than the new appropriation. Thus the appropriation made by the City Council for the repair of paved streets in 1853 was some three thousand dollars less than the amount due by the city at the beginning of the year for that purpose.[1]

Compelled to choose between an utter neglect of streets, for the most part in deplorable condition, and an accumulation of a departmental floating debt, the City Commissioner, with the sanction of the Mayor, ordinarily pursued the latter policy. In consequence, at the close of the period here considered, an indebtedness of upwards of $60,000 had been created on account of street repair and cross-street repaving alone. Payment for contract work was thus subject to indefinite delay, and its cost was proportionately heightened.

Sewers. By successive re-enactment the City Commissioners remained vested with authority "for mending, making, or repairing of sewers within the city."[2] This power was manifestly unavailing in default of appropriations by the City Council. Dependence continued to be had entirely upon surface drainage, and no attempt was made to project anything approaching a general sewerage system.[3]

Appropriations of moderate amount were made from time to time for the construction and extension of underground drains or storm-water sewers. The trivial nature of such expenditures during the early part of the period is seen in a resolution of March, 1828, that the cost of constructing a sewer on Pratt Street, not to exceed one hundred and ninety-five dollars, should be taken out of the appropriation for the removal of nuisances! The entire cost

[1] Report of City Commissioner, January 2, 1854.

[2] Ordinance of April 8, 1826.

[3] "Sanitary Condition of Baltimore," by James Wynne, M. D.; extracted from the *First Report of the Committee on Public Hygiene of the American Medical Association*, and reprinted in "Municipal Reports" of Baltimore for 1849.

of such work was ordinarily defrayed from out the city treasury. Occasionally the special assessment was employed.[1] A small sum was also annually appropriated for the repair of sewers, subject to disbursement by the City Commissioners. As in the case of street paving, the sum available was rarely adequate for the needs of the Commissioners in this direction, and their accounts presented a chronic indebtedness, with a consequent mischievous delay in the discharge of incurred obligations.

Bridges. Specific appropriations of moderate amount were made from time to time to the City Commissioners for the construction and repair of bridges, ordinarily with the provision that power should be exercised subject to the approbation of the Mayor.

Appropriations thus authorized were commonly made from out current revenues. Somewhat exceptional was the procedure in March, 1832, when an appropriation was made for building a certain bridge, provided that designated individuals would lend the corporation a similar amount to be devoted to the same purpose;[2] and again in April of the same year, when the construction of a stone bridge was authorized and the Commissioners of Finance were directed to borrow funds for that purpose, to be repaid after 1845.[3] Extraordinary provision for bridge construction was at an early period supplemented by an annual appropriation of small amount for bridge repair, expended in the discretion of the City Commissioners.

The first measures of importance towards providing the city with adequate bridges were taken at the very close of the period here considered. In June, 1855, the City Commissioner was by resolution directed to submit different proposals for building iron bridges across Jones' Falls to three persons designated by the Mayor, and thereafter to contract for the construction of the bridges according to

[1] Ordinance of March 16, 1821.
[2] Ordinance of March 23, 1832, No. 20.
[3] Resolution of April 28, 1832, No. 1.

the plans selected. The cost of the work was to be defrayed from out the levy for 1856.[1] By the close of the year, three such bridges were in process of construction and a considerable obligation had been incurred.[2]

STREET RECONSTRUCTION.

General provision for the extension and reconstruction of streets was made in the important "Act relating to the City of Baltimore" passed at the legislative session of 1817. Nine commissioners were therein appointed to cause to be surveyed "all such streets, lanes and alleys, as they shall deem proper and convenient," and to return plats thereof to the City Register and to the Clerk of Baltimore County Court.[3] A majority of the commissioners were made competent to exercise all the powers of the board, and vacancies arising therein were filled by the Mayor and the presidents of the two Branches of the City Council. Any reconstruction included in the plan of the commissioners could be undertaken by the corporation upon the written application of the proprietors of not less than two-thirds of the property liable to damage. In 1835 the same action was authorized upon the application of the proprietors of a major part of the property to be taken.[4]

The street reconstructions recommended by the commission of 1818 were slowly introduced. This delay worked some hardship upon the owners of property lying in the path of proposed alterations. Improvements could be made and buildings erected only at the risk of having them destroyed without compensation to the owner, while on the other hand the property was subject to ordinary taxation. Relief was afforded in 1833 by a statute of the General As-

[1] Resolution of June 2, 1855, No. 135.

[2] Report of City Commissioner, January 1, 1856.

[3] "Laws of Maryland," 1817, ch. 148. The commissioners were further authorized to reserve parcels of ground for public purposes, to be purchased at the expense of the city, and to revise the names of streets.

[4] "Laws of Maryland," 1834, ch. 277.

sembly empowering the corporation to pass ordinances fixing a time limit for effecting alterations recommended by the commission; thereafter such improvements could only be made subject to full payment for all damages inflicted.[1]

The mode of procedure in the case of street reconstruction continued essentially that in vogue in the period before 1817. The City Commissioners, or more commonly, a board of specially appointed commissioners, five in number, and either designated or thereafter appointed by the Mayor, were directed to survey and lay out the street as specified, to cause a plat to be made and to be returned under their seal to the office of the City Register.[2] Despite the general power conferred by the statute of 1817, authority to open and extend particular streets continued to be sought and obtained in special acts of the legislature. Such special acts were often made conditional upon the assent of the Mayor and City Council and ordinarily authorized some modification of customary procedure.[3]

Some doubt having been expressed as to the power of the corporation to establish the grades of unpaved streets, specific authority was conferred by the General Assembly in 1836, and promptly embodied in a municipal ordinance.[4] It provided that whenever the owners of a major part of the ground on any thoroughfare laid out in the survey of 1817-18 should make written application for its regrading, the Mayor should appoint two disinterested persons who in conjunction with the City Commissioners should constitute a board of commissioners to perform the alteration in

[1] "Laws of Maryland," 1832, ch. 207. Frequent use was made of the privilege thus conferred; see Ordinances of March 23 and 25, 1835, Nos. 13, 14; April 23, 1839, No. 50.

[2] For typical illustrations: "Laws of Maryland," 1826, ch. 91; 1827, ch. 21; 1831, ch. 257, 292; 1832, ch. 214, 268; 1836, ch. 182; Ordinance of April 26, 1836, No. 39.

[3] "Laws of Maryland," 1817, ch. 168; 1820, ch. 56; 1821, ch. 45; 1823, ch. 136; 1827, ch. 58.

[4] "Laws of Maryland," 1835, ch. 390; Ordinance of June 16, 1836, No. 46.

the manner prescribed by existing ordinances. In 1839 the powers vested in the corporation relative to street reconstruction were again specifically reaffirmed by the General Assembly.[1]

Serious loss to both city treasury and to property owners resulted from the appointment, as commissioners or assessors for each reconstruction, of persons with no special qualification or experience for a work requiring expert skill. Attention was directed to this evil by Mayor Samuel Brady in his message of January 4, 1841, and a remedy proposed in the form of a permanent board of commissioners for opening streets. Two months later—doubtless as a direct result of this recommendation—an ordinance was passed establishing the essential features of the later system of street reconstruction in Baltimore.[2] Provision was made for the annual appointment in usual form of three "Commissioners for Opening Streets" with power to appoint necessary assistants and subordinates. Whenever directed by ordinance to proceed with any street reconstruction, these commissioners were required to effect the improvement and to assess benefits for all costs incurred and to award damages as hereinafter described.[3]

The gross expenditure, including both the amount of damages awarded and the actual cost involved in effecting the reconstruction, continued to be defrayed by a special assessment upon the property benefited. After 1837 specific provision was often made in ordinances authorizing any street reconstruction, "that in no event shall the Mayor and City Council of Baltimore be responsible for any expenses, costs, or charges relating to or connected with the opening of said street."[4]

[1] "Laws of Maryland," 1838, ch. 226.
[2] Ordinance of March 9, 1841, No. 10.
[3] See page 164, below.
[4] Ordinances of April 12, 1837, No. 40; March 6, 1843, No. 11; April 15, 1845, No. 20.

Street Cleaning.

With the exception of a brief and relatively unimportant interval, the function of street cleaning and scavenging remained under the nominal control of the Commissioners of Health. The detailed administration and organization of the service, on the other hand, varied repeatedly and was characterized by a weak and vacillating municipal policy.

The two Superintendents of Streets and Pumps appointed in 1807[1] were in 1817 increased to four—one for each of the corresponding districts into which the city was divided by the City Commissioners.[2] Like their predecessors, the new Superintendents were charged with the care of streets and with the repair of wells and pumps, exercising the latter function under the direction of the City Commissioners. A really important change occurred in 1827, when the Commissioners of Health were empowered to substitute, with the approbation of the Mayor, the day-labor for the contract system in street cleaning.[3] The change appears to have been promptly made and to have continued in force for a number of years.

A radically new policy was inaugurated in 1839 when the offices of Superintendents of Streets were abolished and the duties pertaining thereto were vested in a corresponding number of "city bailiffs and police officers."[4] This was supplemented in 1844 by the substitution in turn of the contract system for the day-labor system, and the virtual transfer of the control of the department from the Commissioners of Health to the City Commissioners.[5] At the same time the special police officers acting as Superintendents of Streets were discharged, and their duties were thereafter performed by the regular police force of the city, under the

[1] See above, page 61.

[2] Ordinance of March 14, 1817. The number of Superintendents was subsequently increased to five and later to six.

[3] Ordinance of April 29, 1827.

[4] Ordinance of March 9, 1839, No. 6.

[5] Ordinance of March 1, 1844, No. 5; Resolution of January 23, 1844, No. 1.

supervision of the Mayor and City Commissioners.[1] The innovation was short lived. In 1845 the Board of Health again assumed control of the work; the city was divided, as before, into districts, in each of which a Superintendent of Streets and Pumps exercised detailed supervision.[2] The contract system however continued in force practically until 1853, when the day-labor system under the direction of the district Superintendents of Streets and Pumps was again introduced.[3]

The results of this shifting, hap-hazard policy can be easily surmised. Despite considerable annual appropriations, together with the proceeds from the sale of street refuse, which in 1850 had become "the most valuable part of the remuneration," the condition of Baltimore streets during the greater part of the period here considered appears to have been a menace to both municipal health and public comfort.[4] The final adoption in 1853 of the day-

[1] Ordinance of March 1, 1844, No. 6; Resolution of April 13, 1844, No. 122.

[2] Ordinances of April 25, 1845, No. 35; May 2, 1846, No. 64; April 14, 1847, No. 27; 1848, No. 3; April 2, 1853, No. 26.

[3] Ordinance of April 2, 1853, No. 26.

[4] Evidence of this is contained in Dr. James Wynne's report on "the Sanitary Condition of Baltimore," to which reference has already been made: "There is no fixed time for cleaning the streets, and they receive attention in proportion to their tendency to accumulate filth, but never more than twice a week, more frequently once in two weeks. The narrow lanes, inhabited by the poor, although more liable to become filthy, receive less attention than the more public thoroughfares, and are always in a more dirty condition. It may be proper to remark that the refuse of the streets is not collected together by brooms, but is gathered into heaps by hoes and carted away. The most effectual scavenger is a copious shower, which, from the rapid descent of the streets, sweeps away with it an increditable amount of street washings. These showers are very frequent during the summer months, and are always hailed by me as a great blessing, on account of the manner in which they purify the streets. There are no regular depots for the street manure, but each contractor deposits the manure from his district on such vacant lots as he can obtain in the outskirts of the town, until disposed of to the surrounding country people, or carried away in boats" (Municipal Reports for 1850, p. 210).

labor system in place of the contract system—a substitution curiously described as "a novel experiment"—appears to have been attended with a measure of improvement. On the other hand it introduced, or at least emphasized, certain mischievous elements in municipal administration, the full evils of which were realized in a subsequent period of municipal history.[1]

WATCHING AND LIGHTING.

The tendency toward the differentiation of the functions of watching and lighting, perceptible before 1817, proceeded rapidly thereafter. This was hastened by the displacement of oil by gas as a public illuminant, and by reliance upon a private corporation for public lighting. Strangely enough, no change was made in the practice of a joint appropriation for the two services, and it is impossible to determine their respective costs, either from the annual appropriation bills or from the Registers' summaries.

Lighting. The contract made in 1817 with the Baltimore Gas Light Company for lighting the streets of the city was renewed in 1818.[2] The Mayor was therein authorized to contract for lighting "such squares, streets, lanes and alleys in the city as he may deem fit and advisable," at a price not exceeding $12.50 for each lamp per annum. This contract continued in force for a year, and was renewed with slight modifications annually thereafter. In efficiency the lighting of the city underwent but slight relative improvement. Municipal appropriations were inadequate as compared with the high charge for gas, and the policy of the Gas Company with respect to the extension of mains appears to have been narrow and short-sighted. In 1850 the lighting of the city was described as of "a most defective character," the prolific source of disorder and crime, and the occasion of great public inconvenience.[3] Some advance was made in

[1] "Report of the Board of Health," December 31, 1853.
[2] Ordinance of March 27, 1818. Cf. above, page 62.
[3] Mayor's Communications of November, 1850; January 19, 1852.

the form of a more favorable contract with the Gas Company in 1851,[1] but the situation in the following year was not inspiring: "the lamps, in a great majority of the streets, are so badly arranged, and at such a distance from each other, as to be little better than a mere apology for such light as the public wants and safety requires."[2]

The first of a series of identical errors in municipal policy with respect to gas supply was taken in 1851 in the grant of the use of streets to a new association (Thomas J. Clare & Co.), the head of which was "in possession of a patent right for the manufacture of water gas, which he believes to be superior in quality and cheaper in price than the gas now used in lighting the city."[3] More fortunate than in many subsequent experiences the city seems to have escaped the normal results of its reckless grant, by the apparent failure of the project at an initial stage; but the episode is of interest as an early local instance of mistaken policy with respect to industries of service.

In 1852 Mayor John H. T. Jerome strongly urged an increased appropriation for public lighting, and recommended the enactment of legislation compelling the Gas Company to supply gas wherever required by the city. Should this effort fail, or the gas corporation prove recalcitrant, the municipal ownership and operation of the gas supply were recommended. This forcible suggestion of an efficient executive is worthy of citation in full: "If nothing can be accomplished by legislation or negotiation with the present Gas Company, to have the city brilliantly and economically lighted, why, then I say, at once establish a City Gas Works under your own control and direction; but, perhaps the great objection to such an undertaking will be the heavy expense necessarily incurred. To this I answer, will not the profits to the corporation be as great as to an inde-

[1] Resolution of May 9, 1851.
[2] Mayor's Communication of January 19, 1852.
[3] Ordinance of May 29, 1851, No. 55.

pendent company? Most assuredly it will. Therefore it is reasonable to infer, that instead of an expense, it will in the course of a few years, be a source of great revenue to the corporation, whilst the benefits to the citizens of having the city properly lighted will be beyond estimation."[1]

Police. The police force of the city continued a composite of two practically independent bodies, (1) the night watch acting as a night patrol, and (2) the city bailiffs as a day constabulary force. Despite urban expansion, the former body increased slowly and inadequately in numbers. Similarly the inefficiency of the force of bailiffs as a day police grew more and more pronounced; until at the very close of the period was foreshadowed that reconstruction and unification of the system which distinguished the succeeding period of municipal development.

(Night Watch). The formal organization of the night watch remained much as established in 1816. The city was divided into districts, and captains, lieutenants and watchmen were appointed for each district. Three justices of the peace were annually selected, as before, to receive the report of the watch.[2] In 1835 the system was officially described as "efficient and well organized"; but the employment of additional watchmen was recommended as necessitated by the extension of the city.[3] The increased appropriations

[1] This recommendation was probably suggested by Philadelphia's experience in municipal ownership of gas supply. In the "Sanitary Report on Baltimore" of 1850, to which reference has already been made, Dr. Wynne stated that the price of gas in Philadelphia was "believed to be the lowest price demanded in any town in the United States," and that the use of gas in private dwellings was much more common there than in other places. With reference to conditions in Baltimore, he added: "It becomes a question of importance to the companies themselves, as well as to the consumers, whether large profits might not be derived from a reduction in price and a consequent extension in its use. If a city can supply gas and water at a less rate than the incorporated companies constituted for that purpose, its obligations in assuming these important functions become obvious and imperious.

[2] Cf. Ordinances of February 20, 1821; March 9, 1826.

[3] Mayor's Communication of January 5, 1835.

required for this purpose were not forthcoming and in 1844 the Mayor was requested "to reorganize the night watch of the city in such a manner as he may deem best for the protection of the persons and property of the citizens, and that he be authorized for that purpose to employ such additional watchmen as he may deem necessary."[1] No action appears to have been taken under the terms of this resolution, and in 1850 the existing system was extended rather than reconstructed.[2]

(Day Police). Increase in the number of city bailiffs brought little improvement in efficiency. In 1835 the service was described by Mayor Jesse Hunt as "lamentably defective," and the propriety of the term will be appreciated when it is understood that the aggregate compensation of the force was $750 per annum, and that this amount was distributed exclusively among those bailiffs in attendance upon the city markets, leaving the remainder of the force entirely unpaid, save by the receipt of fees for judicial services and one-half of fines and penalties collected upon their information.[3]

In 1838 the number of bailiffs was increased to thirty-six, and the body formally organized as a "city police," with the high constable acting as chief of police. One-third of the force received fixed salaries; the remainder, termed "extra city bailiffs," were compensated by the Mayor from out the proceeds of fines accruing from the violation of city ordinances.[4] The appointment of additional bailiffs was again authorized in 1839, 1841, 1848, and 1850. These moderate additions proved however utterly unavailing in face of the growing turbulence of the city,[5] and a radical reorganization of the system became imperative. In 1853 the necessary authority for the reconstruction of the police

[1] Resolution of March 24, 1844, No. 70.
[2] Ordinance of April 5, 1850.
[3] Mayor's Communication of January 5, 1835.
[4] Ordinance of May 23, 1838, No. 45.
[5] Cf. Mayor's Communication of January, 1856, p. 18.

department was obtained from the General Assembly of Maryland,[1] and in 1856 detailed recommendations were made to this end by Mayor Samuel Hinks.[2] The nature of these measures can be best described in conjunction with the actual reorganization of the department.[3]

Fire Protection.

Fire protection in Baltimore continued to be afforded by volunteer companies, receiving annual appropriations from out the city treasury for the maintenance and repair of equipment, and after 1834 formally associated in an incorporated body. The unnecessary multiplication of companies early threatened the efficiency of service and unduly increased its cost. In 1823 the City Council declared by resolution that the organization of additional companies was extravagant and inexpedient.[4]

Some measure of united action had been adopted by the various volunteer fire companies as early as 1787; but not until 1831 was a regular association evolved in the form of the "Baltimore Association of Firemen." This body was reorganized three years later and incorporated by the General Assembly as the "Baltimore United Fire Department." Each company was represented by seven delegates in the Department, and by one member in a standing committee or board of select delegates. The Department was authorized to provide for the better regulation of companies in service, for the settlement of disputes and for the creation of a relief fund for injured firemen or their families.[5]

The rivalry and jealousy of the several companies, which for many years had made of each fire alarm the occasion of disturbance and sometimes of riot, was not appreciably reduced by this formal act of association. In 1838 the legis-

[1] "Laws of Maryland," 1853, ch. 46.
[2] Mayor's Communication of January, 1856, p. 18.
[3] See below, page 223.
[4] Resolution of February 8, 1823.
[5] Scharf, "History of Baltimore City and County," pp. 240-241.

lature of Maryland attempted to correct the growing evil by imposing heavy penalties upon persons convicted of destroying or injuring fire apparatus, or assaulting firemen while engaged in the performance of duty. The standing committee of the Department and the presidents of the several companies were further vested with the power of justices of the peace while in active service.[1] In the same year the Mayor was empowered to withhold authorized appropriations from any company, of which the members had engaged in riot or disorder in connection with any fire.[2]

In 1842 the city was divided into three fire districts, in each of which a Chief Marshal was appointed by the delegates of the United Fire Department, to have entire control of the companies present at any fire within the district. In 1848 the Mayor was empowered at his discretion to suspend or entirely withhold annual or special appropriations from any particular company. The city was divided anew into four districts, and the proper ward of each company was made the district in which its engine house was situated, unless otherwise prescribed by the Mayor.[3]

The characteristic features attending the operations of the fire department of Baltimore continued to be disorder and turbulence. In Mayor Samuel Hink's annual communication of January, 1856—by all odds the best document pre-

[1] "Laws of Maryland," 1837, ch. 190.

[2] Resolution of April 10, 1838; similarly, of February 13, 1840, No. 14. This clause ordinarily appeared in subsequent appropriation bills.

[3] Ordinance of March 23, 1848, No. 28. The discretionary power of the Mayor was further enlarged in the following year; see Ordinance of April 13, 1849, No. 33.

At about the same time the interesting suggestion was made that the municipality should undertake to insure private property within the corporate limits against loss by fire. It was asserted that the revenues so accruing would be "amply sufficient, after discharging the ordinary losses by fire, to defray the whole expense of the internal government of the city, and pay a considerable part of the annual interest growing out of the improvident legislation of the state, and ultimately relieve the citizens from the payment of tax." Resolution of March 27, 1846, No. 89.

pared by a Baltimore executive up to that time—important recommendations were made relative to the reorganization of the department. These proposals are directly associated with the changes introduced in 1858, and can be most intelligently considered in connection therewith.[1]

In addition to the annual appropriations for maintenance, extraordinary grants were made from time to time, either from out the city treasury or by the issue of city stock, to specific companies for the purchase of apparatus and the erection of engine houses. The property in possession of the companies appears to have been held in outright ownership even when purchased by special municipal appropriation. In some cases at least, explicit provision was made that property so obtained should be deeded to the corporation, and that any rents accruing therefrom should be paid annually into the city treasury.

WATER SUPPLY.

The water supply of the city was derived to an increasing extent from the service of the Baltimore Water Company. This corporation enjoyed a practically unqualified franchise, having full power to convey water under any of the streets of the city, and to open the street-bed as often as might be necessary for that purpose. In return therefor the Company was required merely to restore torn-up streets to their original condition, to replace defective piping, and to maintain fire-plugs in good condition—the last service at the expense of the city.[2]

The inherent defects of water supply by private agency gradually became pronounced. The cost of service was high; the source of supply unsuited for an expanding city, and, most serious of all, a short-sighted policy of extending service only into immediately remunerative districts seems

[1] See below, page 228.

[2] Ordinances of January 28, 1826; cf. ordinance of April 3, 1843, No. 25.

to have been pursued throughout. Thus in 1850, mains were laid in but one half of the populated portion of the city, and not more than five thousand houses in all were supplied.[1] Efforts in the direction of municipalization were made in 1830, in 1833, and in 1835;[2] but no agreement as to the proper valuation of the existing plant could be reached. For the next fifteen years public sentiment in Baltimore may be said to have steadily crystallized in favor of municipal ownership and operation of water supply, if necessary at the expense of entirely independent construction.

The first of the series of steps ultimately resulting in municipal ownership was the appointment by the City Council in 1852 of a special committee "to enquire into the propriety of supplying the city with water."[3] In 1853 a formal effort was made by the city to secure specific enabling legislation from the General Assembly.[4] This led to the passage of an act authorizing the corporate purchase or condemnation of any lands and water rights, including the property and plant of the Water Company, and the issue for this purpose of municipal stock to an amount not exceeding $2,000,000.[5] Although not required by statutory provision, the City Council determined to submit to a popular referendum the expediency of exercising the power thus conferred.[6] An overwhelming majority in favor of municipal purchase resulted.[7] The Commissioners of Finance had already been instructed to negotiate with the Water Company for the purchase of the existing plant,[8] and in the summer of 1854 the transaction was completed. In return

[1] Cf. "Sanitary Report of Baltimore," p. 214.
[2] For details of these, see Scharf, "History of Baltimore City and County," pp. 216-217; also Resolution of April 13, 1835.
[3] Resolution of May 11, 1852, No. 97.
[4] Resolution of April 12, 1852, No. 101.
[5] "Laws of Maryland," 1852, ch. 376.
[6] Resolution of October 5, 1853, No. 252.
[7] 9727 votes were cast in favor of the undertaking and 304 votes against it; see Scharf, "History of Baltimore City and County," p. 218.
[8] Resolution of October 5, 1853, No. 254.

for an absolute conveyance of all property and privileges, the city issued to the Water Company six per cent. stock, redeemable on or after January 1, 1875, to the amount of $1,350,000. The annual revenues accruing from the municipal operation of the water works were specifically pledged for the payment of interest on the stock so issued.[1]

A municipal water department was organized early in 1855 by the creation of a Water Board, composed of a president, a first assistant commissioner, and a second assistant commissioner, appointed for a term of three years, but with tenures so arranged as to permit the retirement of one member each year. The Water Board was vested with practically absolute control of the department, including the administration, extension, and maintenance of the supply. Expenditures were met by requisitions upon the City Register to the amount of the appropriations made by the City Council, and funds received were deposited with the Register to the credit of the department.[2]

In sections of the city not penetrated by the mains of the Water Company, dependence was necessarily had as before upon wells and public springs. New pumps were erected upon the petition of any eight property owners in the particular locality, and the expenditure was defrayed by a special assessment upon property presumably benefited.[3] Once erected, such pumps might be transferred to the city and maintained in repair at the public expense.[4] Public springs were located in various sections of the city, often surrounded by a grass plot or small parked area, and maintained from out the city treasury.

Health.

Upon the dissolution of the joint board of City Commissioners and Commissioners of Health in 1820, as described

[1] Ordinance of July 29, 1854, No. 80.

[2] Ordinance of December 29, 1854, No. 1.

[3] "Sanitary Report of Baltimore" in Municipal Reports for 1850, p. 207.

[4] Resolutions of March 21, 1832, No. 53; January 24, 1839, No. 4.

above,[1] the sanitary control of the city was vested in a Board of Health, composed of three Commissioners and a Consulting Physician, appointed, as all other municipal officers, by the Mayor and confirmed by the Council. The Mayor was directed to divide the city into three districts, assigning a Commissioner to each district. The functions of the Board consisted in the general sanitary care of the city, including the superintendence of street-cleaning and the enforcement of sanitary ordinances;[2] while all quarantine regulations remained vested in a Health Officer, a practising physician, annually appointed by the Mayor and acting only in informal association with the Board of Health.[3]

In 1839 the office of Consulting Physician was abolished, and provision made that one of the three Commissioners of Health should be a physician of experience, should perform all the duties of the Consulting Physician as president of the board *ex-officio*, and should receive a slight extra compensation therefor.[4] With the change came inefficiency in service, and in 1841 Mayor Samuel Brady voiced the complaint that "The present organization of the Health Department, from all the information furnished me, has failed to answer the expectations of those who were friendly to the change." Accordingly a return to the earlier organization of the department was recommended, and at once made.[5] In 1844 one of the waves of mistaken economy that periodically swept over the city government of Baltimore again entirely abolished the Board of Health and transferred its functions to the City Commissioners, vesting the duties of the Consulting Physician in the Health Officer of the city.[6] It was impossible for this concentration to endure for any length of time. The City Commissioners were then already, in addition to their own specific functions, exercis-

[1] Page 101.
[2] Ordinances of February 10 and 29, 1820.
[3] Ordinance of May 25, 1838, No. 12.
[4] Ordinance of February 15, 1839, No. 3.
[5] Ordinance of February 10, 1841, No. 3.
[6] Ordinance of March 1, 1844, No. 6.

ing the duties of Port Wardens. To these were now added a series of more or less independent functions, and the anomalous spectacle was presented of a single board acting in a triple capacity, and presenting a distinct report for each class of activities.[1]

Accordingly in 1845 the appointment of an independent Commissioner of Health and a City Physician was again authorized, and these two officials together with the Health Officer were reconstituted a Board of Health, of which the City Physician was president *ex-officio.*[2] An Assistant to the Commissioner of Health was appointed in 1846, and soon became practically, although apparently without specific authority, a member of the Board of Health.[3]

In 1846 the Commissioners of Finance were empowered to sell the structure theretofore used for the reception of small-pox patients, and an appropriation was made for the erection of a new building.[4] Upon the completion of this "Small Pox Hospital" in 1847, its control was vested in the Board of Health under the direct charge of a Resident Physician.[5] In the following year the name of the institution was changed to the "Marine Hospital," and its management entrusted to a Marine Hospital Physician. in whom were merged the duties of both the Health Officer and of the Resident Physician.[6] Thereafter the Physcian to the Marine Hospital figured as practically a fourth member of the Board of Health.

Unwholesome sanitary conditions and location on the seaboard combined to render Baltimore constantly exposed and periodically subject to epidemic small-pox. Successive visitations, threatened and actual, led to the development of a supplementary sanitary force, designed primarily

[1] See Municipal Reports for 1844.
[2] Ordinance of May 2, 1845, No. 39.
[3] See Report of Board of Health, December 31, 1847.
[4] Resolution of May 25, 1846, No. 155.
[5] Ordinance of May 27, 1847, No. 48.
[6] Ordinance of May 20, 1849, No. 8; Report of Board of Health, January 1, 1850.

as vaccine physicians, but exercising other functions. A permanent vaccine corps was created in 1846 by empowering the Mayor and Council to appoint annually one vaccine physician for each ward, who should also act as "Health Warden" within his respective district.[1] The duties of this additional obligation were defined in 1853 as the detailed inspection of sanitary conditions within respective wards, and the report of existing cases of nuisance and contagious disease to the Board of Health.[2]

Markets.

All ordinances relating to local markets were codified in 1826 in a detailed measure "to regulate the several markets in the City of Baltimore." The limits of the five city markets were defined and the annual appointment of a clerk for each market and a chief clerk for each of the two more important was authorized.[3] In 1834 a sixth market was established and authority obtained from the legislature to levy a direct tax to defray the cost of acquiring the necessary site by condemnation.[4] Provision was made for two smaller markets in 1835 and in 1846 respectively.[5]

The only regular expenditure of importance connected with the maintenance of the municipal markets was the salary list of the clerks. Outlays for repair were necessary from time to time but were inconsiderable in amount. The periodic extension of market places and the reconstruction of market houses entailed somewhat larger expenditures.

Wharves and Harbor.

The board of Port Wardens continued in independent existence until 1820, in which year it was merged, as has been noted, with the City Commissioners in a new joint

[1] Ordinance of February 17, 1846, No. 3.
[2] Ordinance of March 11, 1853, No. 16.
[3] Ordinance of April 7, 1826.
[4] "Laws of Maryland," 1833, ch. 35.
[5] Resolutions of April 16, 1835, No. 64; February 17, 1846, No. 30.

board of three persons, styled City Commissioners and Wardens of the Port of Baltimore and vested with all the powers of both bodies. The organization and functions of the board remained in general unchanged, and in 1826 and again in 1838, all provisions relating to local wharves and harbor were codified in detailed ordinances. These provided for the annual appointment of three Port Wardens, who should be the same persons as were appointed City Commissioners, and of two Harbor Masters, each of whom should exercise exclusive authority on one side of Jones' Falls. The Port Wardens were directed to deepen a channel within designated limits, to cause all public wharves to be rebuilt or repaired when necessary, to erect substantial wharves or abutments at the end of all streets leading to the water front, and to compel the maintenance in repair of all private wharves; in short, to exercise general superintendence over local shipping. The Harbor Masters exercised subordinate powers in reference to the care of city wharves, the mooring of vessels, the collection of fines and wharfage dues.[1] Wharfage receipts were appropriated as before to the improvement of the particular wharves and docks where collected, and were expended under the direction of the Port Wardens with the approbation of the Mayor. The City Commissioners continued to act as Port Wardens until 1850 when a single distinct Port Warden was appointed, and the general charge of the harbor and wharves of the city was vested in him.[2]

The annual expenditures for the repair of public wharves were relatively small and fixed in amount. Specific appropriations were made from time to time for the construction of additional wharves, either by the Port Wardens independently or subject to the approbation of the Mayor.[3] A

[1] Ordinances of February 27 and April 3, 1826; May 22, 1838, No. 8.

[2] Ordinance of March 8, 1850.

[3] Resolutions of June 12, 1818; March 27, 1828; April 2, 1835, No. 46; Ordinance of February 26, 1822. Ordinance of May 20, 1853, No. 42.

larger expenditure was entailed by the necessity for straightening and walling in Jones' Falls, the city water course.

Annual appropriations for deepening and preserving the harbor continued to be made from out the proceeds of tonnage and auctioneers' dues. In 1828 the proceeds of the local tax on auction receipts was diverted from the city to the state treasury, as hereinafter described; but $20,000 of the revenues accruing therefrom was annually appropriated by the General Assembly for the improvement of the harbor of Baltimore.[1] This appropriation was ordinarily anticipated by the Port Wardens drawing upon the City Register.[2] Occasional appropriations were also made by the federal government.[3]

Despite these efforts, serious loss and inconvenience were suffered by the commercial interests of the city from the inability of vessels of heavy draught to reach its wharves. Intelligent agitation for the construction of a ship channel in the Patapsco River resulted in the passage by the General Assembly in 1852 of an act empowering the city to issue stock to the amount of $50,000 "for removing the obstruction in the bed of the Patapsco River beyond the limits of direct taxation," and authorizing the levy of an additional tax to defray interest and to provide principal therefor.[4] A special board of commissioners, composed of the Mayor, the Port Warden and seven designated persons, was promptly appointed for exercising the authority thus conferred.[5]

Courts.

A distinct criminal court for Baltimore City was erected in 1817 under the name of the Baltimore City Court. All salaries and expenditures were to be ascertained by the Court, and levied by the Levy Court of Baltimore County

[1] "Laws of Maryland," 1827, ch. 111; see below, p. 156.
[2] Ordinance of April 6, 1829; Resolution of March 15, 1832, No. 44.
[3] Mayor's Communication of January 1, 1838.
[4] "Laws of Maryland," 1852, ch. 296.
[5] Ordinance of June 18, 1852, No. 59.

upon the assessable property of the city and precincts of Baltimore.[1] A year later the levy of this "court tax" was transferred to the Mayor and City Council of Baltimore.[2]

Jurisdiction over civil cases in Baltimore City continued to be exercised by the Baltimore County Court, the maintenance of which remained a joint charge upon the city and the county. At first the city's share seems to have been levied directly by the Levy Court of Baltimore County. After the administration of the county was vested in the County Commissioners in 1828, the County Court ascertained and certified to the Mayor and City Council the share of the city, "having regard to the quantity of business transacted therein for the said county and city," respectively. This amount, together with certain other semi-judicial charges—coroners' fees, removal of criminal trials, maintenance of court-house—was then levied as a direct tax ("certain expenses levy") upon the city.[3]

Two justices for each ward of the city were appointed in 1819 by the governor and council of the state. They received specified fees and were styled "Justices of the Peace of the State of Maryland in and for the City of Baltimore."[4] In 1822 the total number of justices authorized was increased to thirty-six,[5] but it is doubtful whether the entire number was actually appointed. In 1847 it was proposed to reduce the number of justices to sixteen, to be appointed as before but to receive fixed salaries from out the municipal treasury, into which in turn were paid all fees. The city protested vigorously against the change as devolving upon "local authorities the maintenance of judicial functions, when they are to have no voice in the appointment of judicial officers."[6] Despite this protest the plan was adopted

[1] "Laws of Maryland," 1816, ch. 193, 227; 1817, ch. 190.
[2] *Ibid.*, 1817, ch. 195.
[3] See below, page 148. "Laws of Maryland," 1827, ch. 80, 167; Ordinances of March 25, 1829, March 9, 1830, April 25, 1831, No. 32.
[4] *Ibid.*, 1818, ch. 209.
[5] *Ibid.*, 1821, ch. 249; supplemented by 1824, ch. 189.
[6] Resolution of February 23, 1848, No. 18.

by the General Assembly,[1] and in the same year the appointment of four additional justices was authorized.[2]

The Maryland Constitution of 1851 definitely incorporated the courts of Baltimore with the judiciary of the state, and reduced the city, for judicial purposes, to a mere district of Maryland. The new courts located in Baltimore were a Court of Common Pleas, a Superior Court, a Criminal Court—each with a judge and clerk elected by popular vote but paid by the state. An Orphan's Court was established, with three judges elected by popular vote receiving per diem compensation from the city. The legislature was further authorized to erect at its pleasure an additional city court, which power was exercised in 1853 by the establishment of a Circuit Court.[3] Local justices of the peace and constables were appointed by the governor, and a sheriff was elected by the voters of the city.[4] The expenses of the courts, exclusive of the salaries of the judges and the clerks, were defrayed by the city. Nominally provided by the municipal levies for "court" and "certain expenses," the aggregate sum was really paid, as an ordinary municipal expenditure, by an annual appropriation from out the city treasury.

Schools.

As early as 1723, public provision was made in Maryland for the support of county and parish schools.[5] Not however until 1812 was a considerable fund made available for the establishment of free schools throughout the state. This was done by requiring the banks of Maryland to make an aggregate payment of $20,000 per annum—to be apportioned according to their respective capitals—in return for

[1] "Laws of Maryland," 1847, ch. 77. The salary of a justice of the peace was fixed at $1000 per annum; in the event, however, of the aggregate fees paid into the municipal treasury not amounting to $16,000, an equal distribution of the actual receipts was made.

[2] *Ibid.*, 1847, ch. 316. [3] *Ibid.*, 1853, ch. 122.

[4] Constitution of 1851, Article IV.

[5] Scharf, "History of Baltimore City and County," p. 223.

an extension of their charters to 1835. The revenues thus received were to be divided equally among the several counties of the state, and to be utilized exclusively as a public school fund.[1]

In 1813 an annual tax of twenty cents on every hundred dollars of capital stock, payable to the treasurer of the Western Shore of Maryland, was substituted for the fixed charge upon the banks.[2] This tax was to go into effect on January 1, 1815; but not until February, 1817, were nine Commissioners of the School Fund appointed for each county and authorized to receive and expend the respective sums allotted.[3] In 1821 Commissioners of the School Fund for Baltimore City were appointed distinct from those of Baltimore County. The share of the fund allotted to the county appears to have been thereafter divided equally between city and county.

In 1826 provision was made by the General Assembly for the establishment of a distinct system of public schools in Baltimore, by empowering the corporation to levy additional local taxes to an amount necessary for their establishment and support.[4] A year later the statute received the requisite assent of the corporation,[5] but not until March, 1828, were steps taken to put the system into operation. The two branches of the City Council elected annually in joint convention six Commissioners of Public Schools, constituting a School Board of which the Mayor was president *ex-officio*. This Board was directed to divide the city into certain districts, in each of which a school was to be established, and to make all necessary provision for the establishment, government and maintenance of the schools.[6]

[1] The provision was inserted in the act incorporating the Cumberland Turnpike Road Company: "Laws of Maryland," 1812, ch. 79.

[2] "Laws of Maryland," 1813, ch. 122.

[3] *Ibid.*, 1816, ch. 246.

[4] *Ibid.*, 1825, ch. 130.

[5] Ordinance of January 17, 1827.

[6] The number of school commissioners was increased to nine in 1834, to thirteen in 1837, to fourteen in 1842, and to twenty in 1846—one from each ward of the city, elected by the two Branches of the City Council in joint convention.

The School Board appointed its own secretary and treasurer, but enjoyed little fiscal independence. With the annual report to the City Council, an account of the expenditures of the Board in the past year and an estimate of the funds required for the ensuing year were submitted. This estimate influenced, to a greater or less degree, the City Council in fixing the rate of the direct "school levy," authorized in 1826 and imposed annually for the support of the schools. The proceeds of this rate when paid into the city treasury were nominally treated as a "public school fund," subject to disbursement by the Register upon the draft of the president of the School Board, countersigned by the Mayor. It was common for the Board to anticipate the proceeds of the school tax by temporary loans, and in some cases specific provision was made that the expenditures of the Board should not exceed the fund in the possession of the Register for the use of schools.[1] Undrawn amounts, however, appear to have been covered into the general municipal balance at the close of each fiscal year.

The public schools were practically free to the children of residents of Baltimore. A nominal fee of one dollar per quarter was charged, but any child could be exempted from payment by the Board of School Commissioners.[2] Municipal taxation formed the most important item in the maintenance of the system. After 1827 the city received the distributive share of the school fund hitherto appropriated to the Commissioners of the School Fund for the City of Baltimore.[3] This sum was deposited at first with the Commissioners of Finance; but afterwards was drawn directly by the City Register, and placed to the credit of the public school fund. Of less importance as sources of revenue were the proceeds of intestacies in the city of Balti-

[1] Ordinance of February 21, 1843, No. 6.
[2] Ordinance of March 8, 1828.
[3] Ordinance of June 29, 1828.

more, appropriated in 1845 to the support of local schools,[1] and occasional special appropriations.[2]

CHARITIES AND CORRECTIONS.

A local poor relief board was first appointed in 1818, when the Mayor and City Council were directed to select annually from each ward of the city one "sensible and discreet inhabitant" as Manager of the Poor, with power to commit indigent sick and defectives to the county almshouse. The trustees of the almshouse were instructed to prepare annually a separate estimate of the expenses incurred in the maintenance of city inmates, and this amount was levied on the property of the city in the same manner as the charges of the City Court,[3] and the proceeds paid to the trustees of the almshouse.[4] In 1822 the maintenance of the almshouse was transferred to a corporate body styled "The Trustees for the Poor of Baltimore City and County," consisting of seven persons, of whom four were residents of the city and were annually appointed by the Mayor and Council, and three were residents of the county and

[1] "Laws of Maryland," 1845, ch. 129.

[2] The interest of Maryland's share of the surplus revenue of the United States was appropriated for distribution among the counties and Baltimore City, in the same proportion as the school fund was then distributed ("Laws of Maryland," 1836, ch. 220). In 1838 this mode of distribution was changed. One-half of the interest fund was divided among the counties and Baltimore in proportion to the white population of each as determined by the federal census; the other half was divided among the counties and the city in equal parts. Distributions were made annually at the same time as the division of the free school fund ("Laws of Maryland," 1837, ch. 285). In 1840 the whole residue of the surplus revenue and of the interest received thereon, less the appropriation to the school fund for the current year, was applied to the payment of the interest upon the state debt. Instead thereof, the sum of $33,069.36 was annually appropriated to the school fund from out the revenues to accrue after June 30, 1840, from the Baltimore and Washington Railroad, to be distributed as the previous fund ("Laws of Maryland," 1839, ch. 33).

[3] See above, page 125.

[4] "Laws of Maryland," 1818, ch. 122.

were similarly selected by the Governor.[1] The mode of commitment remained unchanged until 1854, when the judge of the Criminal Court of Baltimore or any justice of the peace was authorized to commit vagrants and paupers.[2] During the last decade of the period here considered, the almshouse appears to have suffered at least relative deterioration in condition and management. Joint ownership with the county discouraged that expansion of the institution which urban growth made necessary. The energies of the Trustees of the Poor seem to have been absorbed in the struggle to maintain the institution even in its actual condition with the tardy and insufficient revenues available. A dissolution of joint ownership and the erection of a larger municipal building was urged repeatedly.

The lease of the city hospital to private hands, as described above, was confirmed in 1821.[3] In 1827, the Mayor was authorized to cede to the State of Maryland, through an incorporated board ("the President and Board of Visitors of the Maryland Hospital"), the city's right in and title to the hospital, provided that the state guaranteed the repayment to the city of the several amounts already expended in the purchase and construction of buildings, such repayments to be utilized in making provision for a hospital for contagious diseases.[4]

Persons convicted of criminal offenses were committed as before to the jail of Baltimore County. In 1817 the judges of the newly created Baltimore County Court were directed to examine the jail accounts, and to ascertain what portion thereof, as determined by the relative number of prisoners from Baltimore, should be paid by the city.[5] In the following year, this function was transferred to the Levy

[1] "Laws of Maryland," 1822, ch. 167.

[2] *Ibid.*, 1854, ch. 116.

[3] Ordinance of March 16, 1821.

[4] "Laws of Maryland," 1816, ch. 156; 1826, ch. 259. Ordinance of April 2, 1827. Resolutions of February 23, 1827, and February 4, 1828.

[5] "Laws of Maryland," 1817, ch. 142.

Court of Baltimore County.[1] The cost of all repairs was paid in equal proportions by the city and the county, respectively.[2] In 1832 the management of the jail was transferred to a board of seven persons, annually appointed and commissioned by the Governor of the state, of whom four were required to be residents of Baltimore City and three of Baltimore County. The board was constituted a body corporate by the name of "The Visitors of the Jail of Baltimore City and County." As before, one-half of all expenditures for repairs and improvements and a proportionate share of the cost of maintenance, determined by the relative number of prisoners from the city, were paid from out the municipal treasury. The Visitors submitted an annual statement of receipts and expenditures to the Mayor and City Council, together with estimates for the ensuing year.[3] In 1839 the appointment of the city members of the Board of Visitors was transferred to the Mayor and City Council, and of the county members to the County Commissioners. No change was effected in the powers and duties of the board.[4]

The necessity for more ample accommodations for local delinquents revived the project of separating the city's and the county's joint interest in the institution.[5] This separation was finally consummated in November, 1853, and thereafter the Baltimore jail was a distinctly municipal institution, at which county prisoners were received subject to specific charges for maintenance.[6] A committee of the City Council had already reported in favor of building a city jail upon the site of the old structure, and in 1851 an appropriation was made for this purpose.[7] Difference of opinion arose as to the precise form and location of the

[1] "Laws of Maryland," 1818, ch. 141.

[2] *Ibid.*, 1827, ch. 167.

[3] *Ibid.*, 1831, ch. 58.

[4] *Ibid.*, 1838, ch. 75; see, for an earlier attempt to secure this method of appointment, Resolution of March 19, 1829.

[5] Resolution of April 18, 1849, No. 103.

[6] Cf. Report of the Visitors of the Jail, 1853.

[7] Ordinance of May 23, 1851, No. 42.

building, and not until 1856 was its actual construction undertaken.[1]

In 1831 the General Assembly authorized the establishment in Baltimore of a "house of refuge" for juvenile delinquents, to be managed by an incorporated board of twenty-four managers, of whom eight were appointed by the Governor and Council of Maryland, eight by the Mayor and City Council of Baltimore, and the remaining by private subscribers. Certain state funds were appropriated to the use of the institution, but it was to receive no direct municipal aid.[2] Probably because of this latter reason, the plan proved unsuccessful. The project was again revived in 1845 and remained under discussion until 1849, when a number of philanthropic citizens reorganized under the act of incorporation of 1831. Place was given upon the directorate to representatives of the city and state, from both of which aid was expected. The city at once appropriated a definite amount together with the proceeds accruing from the sale of certain municipal property.[3] A site was purchased and the erection of a building commenced. The legislature however refused all pecuniary aid and in 1853 entirely severed the state's connection with the institution. Municipal spirit intervened at this critical juncture; two additional appropriations were made, and in 1855 the first inmate was admitted.[4]

Parks and Squares.

The early municipal history of Baltimore reveals the characteristic neglect of the American city to make adequate provision for unbuilt areas in residential quarters and for extensive pleasure grounds in suburban districts. In

[1] "Laws of Maryland," 1852, ch. 200; Resolution of July 16, 1853, No. 214. Also Scharf, "History of Baltimore City and County," p. 201.

[2] "Laws of Maryland," 1830, ch. 64.

[3] Resolution of April 12, 1849, No. 88.

[4] Scharf, "History of Baltimore City and County," p. 826.

1827 a prominent citizen, William Patterson, agreed to present to the city two adjoining squares of ground, containing five or six acres, in the eastern section of the city to be used as a public walk or park. The tract was accepted by the city and provision made for its enclosure and improvement. This gift formed the nucleus of the present Patterson Park.[1]

A further nucleus of a system of public squares in Baltimore was provided in 1839 by the corporate acquisition of a small area in the northwestern section of the city (Franklin Square). The tract was purchased from the owners of adjacent property, subject to the condition that the purchase price should be credited by the city to the account of the special assessment levied thereon for street paving.[2] This arrangement was never carried out, and in 1844 provision was made for the payment of the specified amount in four equal installments, whenever a designated number of buildings should be erected abutting upon or adjacent to the square.[3] Other public areas were acquired in 1846 (Union Square) and in 1853 (Eutaw Square), by gift; in 1852 (Federal Hill) and in 1853 (Madison Square) by condemnation and purchase.[4] Payment for Madison Square was made in six annual installments from out the current revenues of the city. The cost of laying out and condemning a public square on Federal Hill was defrayed in part by the levy of a special assessment upon property owners to the amount benefited. Expenditures for improving and maintaining areas thus acquired were irregular in time and for the most part inconsiderable in amount. After 1853 the desirability of a system of public parks became generally recognized and public sentiment was ripe a few years later for prompt adoption of the sagacious policy proposed by Mayor Thomas Swann.

[1] See below, page 246. [2] Ordinance of April 23, 1839, No. 47.
[3] Ordinance of April 13, 1844, No. 32.
[4] Ordinances of May 15, 1846, No. 69; March 19, 1853, No. 18; July 22, 1852, No. 71; April, 1853, No. 27.

Municipal Buildings.

The legislative and administrative departments of the municipal government continued to be housed in quarters leased of private individuals. In 1821 the City Commissioners were instructed to present to the Council plans for the erection of a general municipal building.[1] No definite results followed, and additional quarters were leased as the increase of administrative needs required. In 1830 a joint committee of the City Council reported the quarters then occupied by the corporation as inadequate, and recommended the purchase of a separate building. The structure was promptly acquired and remained the seat of municipal government for some twenty years. The necessity of erecting a permanent city hall became generally recognized in 1844, and for the next ten years the determination of plan and site was under discussion. In 1854 the Legislature authorized the corporation to purchase a site, to erect a building and to issue $400,000 in city stock in payment thereof. No immediate steps were taken and in 1857 it again became necessary to provide temporary quarters for city officials.[2]

The court house of Baltimore County was badly injured by fire in 1834 and a special commission of six designated persons, three of whom were residents of the city and three of the county, was appointed to reconstruct the building. To defray the expenditures involved, the Mayor and City Council were authorized to issue stock to an amount not exceeding $80,000, bearing interest at five per cent. and irredeemable for twenty years. Interest and sinking fund were provided by an annual levy in equal parts upon the taxable property of Baltimore City and County, respectively. The commissioners were required to account to the corporation for all moneys disbursed, and in the event of future separation between Baltimore City and County, provision was

[1] Resolution of November 20, 1821.

[2] Scharf, "History of Baltimore City and County," p. 175. Resolutions of April 16, 1844; May 2, 1845; May 28, 1853, No. 167.

made that the whole estate of the court house should be vested in the city upon the payment to the county of one-half of the value thereof.[1]

Special appropriations continued to be made from time to time for the construction of minor municipal buildings, as in 1819 for the erection of a new powder magazine;[2] in 1821 for the purchase of site and erection of an engine house.[3]

Administrative Expenses.

Municipal expenditure for administrative purposes, including the diary of the City Council and the salaries of strictly administrative officers, rose sharply during the early years of the period here considered. This was due to a marked increase in the amount of municipal salaries rather than to any multiplication of municipal offices or to an increase in minor disbursements.[4] In the decade beginning with 1820 retrenchment and consolidation kept the total administrative expenditures of the city fairly constant, at a figure somewhat less than the aggregate for 1819. After 1830 municipal outlay for this purpose increased gradually but continuously, with the accompanying growth of the administrative force throughout the remainder of the period. There was little or no qualitative change in the character of expenditure.

[1] "Laws of Maryland," 1834, ch. 151. In 1838 a further issue of $25,000 was authorized subject to the same conditions.

[2] Ordinance of March 18, 1819.

[3] Resolution of February 27, 1821.

[4] A comparison of the important salaries paid by the city in three successive periods is interesting in this connection:

	1815	1819	1823
Mayor	$2500	$3600	$2000
Register	1400	1810	1289
City Commissioners	2400	4598 74	2750
Port Wardens	1600	1875	——
Health Officer	600	1000	600
Supts. of Streets and Pumps	960	2500	2250
Clerks of Markets	972 50	1500	1699 99
Diary of City Council	1039 50	2765	2971

Interest on Debt.

Interest charges upon the funded debt of Baltimore first figured to any considerable amount in the municipal budgets of 1818 and 1819. The inappreciable growth of funded indebtedness in the succeeding decade was reflected in a practically fixed charge from 1820 to 1830. During the next twenty-five years the normal course of debt accumulation was radically changed by the large participation of Baltimore in the policy of internal improvements, the details of which are presented in another connection. Municipal subscriptions, loans and guarantees in aid of various railroad and canal projects contributed to swell the funded liabilities of the city to an amount utterly disproportionate to its financial resources, and to convert the annual interest payment into a heavy and oppressive charge. In 1830 the funded debt of the city was little more than $500,000 with an annual interest burden of some $25,000. Fifteen years later (1844) the debt had increased to $5,493,773.03 with an annual interest charge of $313,408.88. The policy of internal improvements was responsible for practically the entire addition. No appreciable increase in indebtedness took place between 1844 and 1850; but in the next six years occurred an increase absolutely greater than that characterizing the period from 1828 to 1844. This increment was however made up of direct and guaranteed loans upon which there occurred no default in interest payment by the recipients, and of stock issued for the purchase of the water plant, interest upon which was paid from out of water rentals. In consequence the direct interest charge of the city underwent little change from 1844 to 1856.

Of those who clamored for the successive extension of municipal aid to works of internal improvements, few, if any, anticipated that a continuous municipal burden would be thereby entailed. In addition to the advantage derived by the general economic interests of the city, it was confidently expected that large direct returns would be received by the city for its loans and subscriptions. In the case of municipal subscriptions to the Baltimore and Ohio Railroad, this was partly realized in the form of small and irregular dividends;[1] from the city's important interests in other improvement projects, practically no direct return was received.

[1] See below, p. 172.

CHAPTER III

MUNICIPAL REVENUE.

The relative importance of the several forms of municipal revenue underwent radical change in the period from 1817 to 1856. During the first two decades of the corporate existence of Baltimore, the general property tax was, comparatively speaking, a minor source of income. It was ordinarily surpassed in yield by the auction receipts tax and by the license tax, and, not uncommonly, by the special assessment for street paving. After 1817 this gradation was completely reversed. The proceeds of the auction receipts tax remained almost stationary until diverted into the state treasury in 1827. The paving assessment declined absolutely and became an uncertain source of municipal income. License taxes and wharfage dues increased absolutely in amount, but suffered marked relative decline. The growing demands of the municipal budget were thus borne almost entirely by the direct taxation of general property.

TAXATION.

General Property Tax.[1] Within the period here examined were developed the characteristic features of the modern[2] general property tax of Baltimore: the employment of a common basis for state and municipal taxation, the absence of any periodic local reassessment, the levy of nominally distinct rates, and the allowance of discounts for prompt payment.

(Assessment). The results of the general reassessments authorized from time to time for state and county taxation

[1] See Appendix D.
[2] That is to say, the system in vogue until 1896.

were promptly utilized for local purposes. In addition special acts of the legislature vested the city at irregular intervals with authority for local revaluation, without conferring power, however, for continuous or periodic reassessment.

Thus local reassessments of real and personal property were made in 1817 and 1822 by the Commissioners of the Tax for Baltimore City in the manner prescribed by the general reassessment act of 1812.[1] These revaluations were designed primarily for the public levy, but provision was made in each case for the employment of the new basis for municipal purposes.[2] The act of 1812 authorized the Commissioners of the Tax to provide for the annual addition to the assessment books of unassessed property; but beyond the initial review of the assessors' returns, the Commissioners could not revise valuations once made. In March, 1827, the administration of Baltimore County was transferred from the justices of the Levy Court to an elected board of three commissioners. All powers of the Levy Court relating to Baltimore City, including the assessment of property and the levy of municipal taxes, were vested in the Mayor and City Council, instead of in the new county administration.[3] It accordingly became necessary for the city to make independent provision for the limited revision of property valuation, hitherto performed by county authorities. This was first done in 1829. Three assessors were appointed, in the same manner as other municipal officers, and charged with the addition of all unassessed property to the general tax lists. The Mayor and the City Collector

[1] "Laws of Maryland," 1817, ch. 142; 1822, ch. 130. Also cf. above, page 74.

[2] Ordinance of February 22, 1819. Resolutions of May 5, 1823; April 15, 1826; February 3, 1827; January 24, 1828.

[3] "Laws of Maryland," 1826, ch. 217. This general transfer was confirmed by a supplementary statute of the following year, wherein the board of Commissioners of the Tax for Baltimore City was formally abolished, and its power and property vested in the corporation (*ibid.*, 1827, ch. 80).

were constituted a Board of Appeals, with power of final review.[1] In 1830 provision was made for similar appointments and additions each year thereafter until a new general reassessment should be made.[2]

Specific authority was conferred upon the corporation in 1832 to provide by ordinance for the revaluation of all property, real and personal, within the city.[3] The total assessed valuation of Baltimore was then $3,564,904, while the municipal levy had reached $4.92½ upon every $100. Despite the urgent need of revision, indicated by these figures, no immediate use was made of the power so conferred. Problems of sanitation, presented by the periodic recurrence of plague and fever, were engaging the corporate administration to the neglect of problems of finance.[4] In the following year the power of the city to make a new assessment of property "whenever they may deem it expedient" was renewed by the General Assembly in even broader terms, and under this second grant, provision for the first distinctly local reassessment of property in Baltimore was made.[5] Five Commissioners of Tax were elected by the two branches of the City Council in joint convention, and two Assessors were appointed for each ward in the usual manner of corporate officers. The Assessors were required to ascertain and assess the value of "all lands and lots of ground, all houses and other buildings, and improvements of every description, and all furniture, plate and slaves." Every taxable person was obliged to return an itemized account of the value of his personal estate—neglecting to do which, such estimate was to be prepared by the Assessors to the best of their ability. The Commissioners of Tax formed a final board of review, with power to add to or deduct from the valuations returned "so as to conform the

[1] Ordinance of March 19, 1829.
[2] Ordinance of February 16, 1830.
[3] "Laws of Maryland," 1831, ch. 214.
[4] "Report of the Tax Commission of Baltimore," 1885, pp. 10-11.
[5] "Laws of Maryland," 1833, ch. 143.

same to the acts of Assembly, and usage in the counties of this State."[1]

Great difficulty was experienced in organizing the machinery contemplated by the ordinance. The Assessors were entirely without experience, and the interval of twenty-one years that had elapsed since the last general revaluation of property in Baltimore rendered the entire procedure unpopular.[2] After six months delay, a supplementary measure was passed, enumerating in greater detail the taxable forms of personal wealth and authorizing the Assessors to make aggregate instead of itemized return therefor.[3] New boards of Commissioners of Tax and Assessors were then appointed, and a complete reassessment of property in Baltimore was made. The results of the revaluation were more favorable than the most sanguine had anticipated. The taxable basis was increased from $3,787,762 to $42,931,960, permitting a reduction of the tax rate within the limits of direct taxation, from $4.77⅚ in 1835, to $ .66⅝ in 1836.

The extraordinary results of the reassessment of 1834-35 made evident the desirability of periodic revaluation. Machinery for this purpose was provided in 1836 by the appointment in the usual manner of three Assessors exercising all the powers vested by the ordinances of 1834 in both the Assessors and in the Commissioners of Tax. The new Assessors were given final power of review and were required to return to the City Register assessed valuations of real and personal property in the several wards, distinguishing property "within" from that "without" the limits of direct taxation.[4] In the following year the City Collector was authorized to make transfers on the assessment books, to allow for insolvencies and removals from the city and to made abatements and releases required by error.[5] Finally

[1] Ordinance of May 12, 1834, No. 32.

[2] See Ordinance of June 10, 1834, providing for temporary appointments by the Mayor.

[3] Ordinance of February 23, 1835, No. 9.

[4] Ordinance of April 22, 1836, No. 31.

[5] These powers were exercised subject to the approbation of the Mayor.

in 1839 provision was made for the annual appointment of two Assessors of Tax, constituting together with the City Collector a final board of review for the revision of all valuations.[1]

The logical development of a system of local assessment along the lines projected by municipal legislation in 1836-39 was interrupted by the revival of direct taxation for state purposes in 1841. The reckless participation of Maryland in various schemes of internal improvement in the decade from 1830 to 1840 resulted in the accumulation of a large and oppressive state debt. Direct taxation, hitherto distinctly an emergency resource in Maryland, became in 1841 the only means of averting repudiation. The imposition of a general property tax was opposed, resisted, delayed, and finally effected by the passage on April 1, 1841, of "an act for the general valuation and assessment of property in this state, and to provide a tax to pay the debts of the state." It authorized the first general reassessment of property in Maryland since 1812, and imposed a direct property tax for state purposes of one-fifth of one per cent.[2]

The act of 1841 introduced the essential features of the modern property assessment system of Baltimore. Specific provision was made therein that the resulting valuation, although designed primarily for the levy of the state tax, should be utilized after 1841 for municipal taxation. The twelve wards of the city were divided into six assessment districts, in each of which three designated Assessors were appointed. These Assessors were directed to ascertain and value, by oath or affirmation if necessary, all property liable to assessment, and to make return thereof with values annexed under specific categories: (1) Land, (2) Slaves, (3) Stock in trade, (4) Public securities, (5) Bank and other stocks, (6) Private securities, (7) Live stock, (8) Household furniture, (9) Plate, (10) Gold and silver watches, (11) Property of any other description. Private corporations were

[1] Ordinance of March 25, 1839.
[2] "Laws of Maryland," 1841, ch. 23.

required to return account of all stock held by non-residents. The tax levied upon such stock was collected from the corporation and charged to the account of the particular stockholders. The collector of the state tax was directed to assess any property liable to taxation which might have been omitted in the regular course of assessment. The Mayor and City Council were required to appoint annually a board of three persons, to be styled the Appeal Tax Court of Baltimore City, to receive and record the reports of the Assessors and to act as a board of review. A final right of appeal from the decisions of the Appeal Tax Court lay to the Court of Appeals of the Western Shore of Maryland.

The Appeal Tax Court was at once organized by the appointment of the two acting Assessors and the City Collector, as Judges.[1] The Court was merely empowered to review the valuations of assessors made under the statute of 1841, to allow for transfers of property, to make abatements in case of loss or destruction of property, to assess the stock of corporations annually returned for valuation, and to increase the assessment of persons applying for abatement, should it appear that any new property had been acquired. Aside from these limited powers, the Court, as originally constituted, seems to have possessed no authority whatever to revise or correct valuations once made.

The taxable basis of Baltimore remained practically constant from 1841 to 1846, when the General Assembly authorized a local revaluation of all property subject to taxation under the terms of the statute of 1841. The corporation was given absolute authority to arrange the machinery of assessment, "for ascertaining and determining, by a fair and just valuation, the actual wealth of the citizens of Baltimore, which shall be chargeable according to such valuation, with the public assessment." State as well as municipal taxes were to be levied upon the resulting basis.[2] Steps were at once taken for local reassessment. The city

[1] Ordinance of May 8, 1841, No. 1.
[2] "Laws of Maryland," 1845, ch. 336.

was divided into five districts, in each of which three Assessors were appointed by the Mayor and charged with the revaluation of all taxable property. A Board of Control and Review composed of five persons, one from each district and likewise appointed by the Mayor, was created—to remain in existence until February, 1847, when its functions were to be assumed by the Appeal Tax Court.[1] Thereafter the Appeal Tax Court continued charged with the correction of assessments arising from the transfer or loss of old and the acquisition of new property, but without power to revise and correct ordinary valuations.[2]

The second general revaluation of property for purposes of state taxation was made in 1852 in much the form prescribed by the reassessment act of 1841. Baltimore was divided into ten districts, in each of which three designated persons acted as assessors. The Appeal Tax Court, temporarily enlarged by the addition of two designated persons to two assessors annually appointed by the corporation, served as a board of control and review. When completed, this revaluation was likewise utilized for municipal taxation.[3]

(Exemption). In 1822 the Mayor was authorized to make abatements upon assessed valuations of other than real property, when such appeared "just and reasonable," in the same manner as done by the Commissioners of Tax under the provision of the general assessment act of 1812.[4] In cases where an abatement had already been made on real property for state and county taxation, similar action with respect to the municipal levy was authorized. Specific power to make abatements and releases of taxes on real property, subject to the approbation of the Mayor, was conferred upon the City Collector in 1828.[5]

[1] Ordinance of May 14, 1846, No. 71.
[2] Ordinance of May 14, 1846, No. 71.
[3] "Laws of Maryland," 1852, ch. 337.
[4] Ordinance of January 28, 1822.
[5] Ordinance of April 8, 1828.

The local reassessment of 1834 exempted from taxation estates in personal property not exceeding $500 in value, together with all "property belonging to the United States, the State of Maryland, the city or county of Baltimore, houses for public worship, burying grounds, college buildings, the working tools of mechanics and manufacturers, ships, boats and other vessels, and all such property as is exempted from taxation by special acts of the legislature."[1]

In 1839 the City Council resolved "that it would not be proper, where the stock of corporations is assessed to individuals owning it, to tax also property held by corporations themselves."[2] This was followed by the specific exemption in the reassessment of 1841 of all "judgments, bonds, mortgages, promissory notes or other securities belonging to any bank or other incorporated institution, the capital stock whereof is made subject to taxation by the provisions of this act."[3] In the same measure the maximum value of exempted estates was reduced to $200, apparently including both real and personal property.[4]

(Rate). In 1818 the charter limitation of the local tax to a maximum levy of 15 shillings on £100 (.75 on $100), was displaced by a provision authorizing the corporation to levy direct taxes to "such amount as shall be thought necessary for the public or city purposes."[5] Prompt use was made of the extensive power thus conferred. In 1818 the rate of the direct tax, the proceeds of which were available for general municipal purposes, was raised from .75 to $1.50 upon each $100 of assessed valuation. In 1819 occurred a further increase to $2.00, at which amount it remained fixed until 1824, when it was raised to $2.50. Five years later, in 1830, it was again increased to $3.00.

Long before this, the imposition of the direct tax upon

[1] Ordinance of May 12, 1834, No. 32.
[2] Resolution of June 25, 1839, No. 17.
[3] "Laws of Maryland," 1841, ch. 23.
[4] This amount was further reduced to $50 (*Ibid.*, 1841, ch. 116).
[5] "Laws of Maryland," 1817, ch. 148, sect. 4.

the outlying, thinly settled sections of the city created dissatisfaction, as entailing a burden with no corresponding benefit. Accordingly, the General Assembly in the act of 1817 authorized the Governor of Maryland to appoint three non-residents of Baltimore "to ascertain and mark out the limits within said city, so far as the same is in their judgement thickly settled, built up, or improved; and in which the usual regulations for watching and lighting, or clearing the streets are or ought to be applied." Beyond the limit thus established the city was prohibited from imposing the direct property tax for municipal purposes, and the dividing line was designated as "the limit of direct taxation."[1] In 1831, provision was made for the extension of the boundary, so as to include such portions of the area excluded by the survey of 1817 as stood in need of the primary municipal services of watching, lighting and street paving.[2] In 1842 the corporation was authorized to extend the limits of direct taxation within the city boundaries at discretion, subject only to the limitation that no block should be included upon which less than six houses had been erected.[3] Such extensions were made in 1842, 1850 and 1853.

Increased municipal expenditure for specific purposes was defrayed, as noted above,[4] not by increasing the "Direct Levy," but by the levy of special rates as required for meeting the expenditures entailed by the several new functions. Such special levies were imposed upon the taxable basis of the entire city, without regard to the limit of direct taxation, and the proceeds were probably at first designed as distinct funds for specific municipal purposes, instead of, as they later became, mere contributions to the general municipal treasury. During the greater part of the period from 1817 to 1856, five such rates were annually

[1] "Laws of Maryland," 1817, ch. 148, sect. 19.
[2] "Laws of Maryland," 1830, ch. 139; Ordinance of April 6, 1831, No. 21.
[3] "Laws of Maryland," 1842, ch. 218; Resolution of February 21, 1843, No. 23.
[4] Page 98.

imposed in addition to the Direct Levy, *viz.*, Court Levy, Poor Levy, School Levy, Levy for County Expenditures for City Purposes, and Internal Improvements Levy. The area of the city lying without the limits of direct taxation was subject to a special Highway and Bridge Levy. The development of the municipal tax rate is essentially a history of the emergence of these successive levies.

Court Levy. Upon the erection of Baltimore City Court in 1817, the Levy Court of Baltimore County was authorized to assess annually upon the taxable property of the city the salaries of the judges and all other incidental expenditures as ascertained by the City Court itself.[1] A year later, the levy of this aggregate outlay was transferred to the Mayor and City Council.[2]

Poor Levy. In 1819 the trustees of the almshouse of Baltimore County were instructed to prepare an annual statement of the expenses incurred in the maintenance of city inmates, and this amount was levied upon the city in the same manner as the court tax.[3] After the transference of the care of the institution to the Trustees of the Poor for Baltimore City and County in 1822, the annual statement was prepared by that body.[4]

School Levy. Authority for the establishment of a distinctly local system of public schools was conferred by the General Assembly of Maryland in 1826.[5] The Mayor and City Council of Baltimore were therein empowered to levy and collect in addition to existing taxes and with due regard to the actual wealth of tax-payers "such further and other taxes, rates or assessments, as may be necessary for the support of such public schools." The first actual levy for school purposes was made in 1830, and the charge was imposed annually thereafter.

Levy for County Expenditures for City Purposes.[6] After

[1] See above, page 125.
[2] "Laws of Maryland," 1817, ch. 195.
[3] *Ibid.*, 1818, ch. 122.
[4] *Ibid.*, 1822, ch. 167.
[5] *Ibid.*, 1825, ch. 130.
[6] Designated also as "Certain Expenses Levy."

the transfer of the powers of the Levy Court of Baltimore County to a board of County Commissioners in 1828, the Mayor and City Council were authorized to levy upon the city its proportion, for the year elapsed, of the judicial expenses of Baltimore County and of certain allied charges theretofore assessed upon the city by the Levy Court of the county.[1] This function was re-imposed in successive years, and in 1831 a general ordinance was passed authorizing an annual levy for the payment of expenses "formerly required to be paid by the late Levy Court of Baltimore County."[2] These included the city's proportion of the expenses of the courts, the court-house and the jail of Baltimore County, the removals of criminal trials, the payment of coroners, federal and state elections, collection of the levy and of certain miscellaneous services.

Internal Improvement Levy. Prior to 1839 the interest charge upon that part of the municipal debt contracted in aid of works of internal improvement was defrayed from out of the general fund of the municipal treasury. In 1839 the burden had become oppressive and authority was obtained from the General Assembly to levy on all assessed property of the city, both on that within and on that without the limits of direct taxation, "any sum or sums which may be necessary to pay and discharge the principal and interest of any loan or loans which may have heretofore been obtained or which may hereafter be obtained by the said Mayor and City Council of Baltimore, for the purpose of prosecuting and completing the works of internal improvement now authorized by law."[3] A week later a tax of ten and one-half cents was levied, the proceeds to be applied by the Commissioners of Finance for the payment of interest upon one million dollars of the city's subscription to the Baltimore and Ohio Railroad Company.[4] Thereafter

[1] "Laws of Maryland," 1827, ch. 80 and 167.
[2] Ordinance of April 25, 1831, No. 32.
[3] "Laws of Maryland," 1838, ch. 168.
[4] Ordinance of March 14, 1839, No. 14.

the levy was annually made in aid of the interest charge upon the internal improvement debt.

Highway and Bridge Levy. The area of the city lying without the limit of direct taxation, although exempt from any direct municipal tax, was nevertheless the occasion of considerable municipal expenditure, notably for the repair of highways and the construction of bridges. To remedy this inequality, the General Assembly in 1824 authorized the corporation to levy upon this district a special direct tax of thirty-five cents upon every hundred dollars, the proceeds to be so expended.[1] In February, 1828, the maximum rate of the tax was increased by act of the General Assembly from thirty-five to fifty cents.[2] In actual practice the tax was levied at the rate of thirty-five cents from 1824 to 1832, and of fifty cents from 1832 to 1836, in which latter year the results of the general assessment of property became available. Nominally the tax was levied only on real property ("houses and lands"). State and local assessments, however, failed to make separate return of realty and personalty and in practise the charge seems to have been imposed upon the aggregate assessment.[3]

(Statutory Limitation). The statutory limitation fixed by the original charter of Baltimore upon the rate of municipal taxation was annulled in 1818 and unqualified authority vested in the corporation to impose direct taxes to the amount required for municipal purposes.[4] Not until 1831 was this broad power restricted by the provision that the municipality should not in any one year raise by direct taxation a sum exceeding $120,000, nor by all forms of taxation a sum exceeding $220,000.[5] The municipal treasury suffered serious embarrassment from this limitation. To comply therewith, it became necessary to cut down the rate of the direct tax from the figure before levied and still

[1] "Laws of Maryland," 1823, ch. 185; continued by *ibid.*, 1827, ch. 87 and made perpetual by *ibid.*, 1836, ch. 120.

[2] *Ibid.*, 1827, ch. 87.

[3] See below, p. 267.

[4] Cf. above, p. 95.

[5] "Laws of Maryland," 1830, ch. 139, sect. 3.

required by ordinary municipal expenses. Moreover the limitation practically prevented the extension of municipal aid to the works of internal improvement then projected.[1]

In March, 1832, the city representatives in the state legislature were requested by resolution of the City Council to secure amendatory legislation whereby the restriction of tax proceeds to $120,000 should apply only to the original "direct tax," thereby excluding "city poor, city court, school, county tax for city purposes, paving tax, pump tax, specific tax, road and bridge tax, and the interest on the railroad stock, exclusive of any dividends thereon."[2] The desired relief was promptly afforded by the repeal of all limitation upon the taxing power of the corporation.[3] When in 1834 such a limitation was again imposed, the maximum amount was fixed at $200,000 and specific provision was made that this applied only to taxes "for the purpose of defraying the corporation expenses, exclusive of all others," *i. e.* to the proceeds of the "direct tax."[4] Five years later the municipality found itself again hampered by the rigid statutory limit and made application for a further increase.[5] This too was successful, and the maximum sum to be raised by direct taxation for defraying "the expenses of the corporation" was fixed by the General Assembly at $350,000 per annum. From this amount were expressly excluded the proceeds of all municipal taxes, for the imposition of which specific authority had been or should be conferred upon the corporation.[6] In 1853 upon petition of the corporation, the General Assembly increased the maximum yield of the "direct tax" to $500,000.[7]

(Collection). Before 1817 the collection of local dues and charges had become a formal municipal office. Exist-

[1] Cf. Mayor's Message of January 2, 1832.
[2] Resolution of March 1, 1832, No. 24.
[3] "Laws of Maryland," 1831, ch. 214.
[4] *Ibid.*, 1833, ch. 143.
[5] Resolution of February 28, 1839, No. 35.
[6] "Laws of Maryland," 1838, ch. 208.
[7] *Ibid.*, 1852, ch. 233; Resolution of May 10, 1853, No. 131.

ing provisions were collated in a single ordinance in 1826.[1] The annual appointment was therein authorized of a City Collector, who was required to enter into heavy bond with the corporation and to account monthly with the Register for funds received. The provision for the annual appointment of a Collector practically resulted in the successive reappointment of the actual incumbent. Largely in consequence, the earlier practice of requiring the completion of collections within a definite period, unless extended by special ordinance, continued for several years but appears thereafter to have fallen into disuse.[2] The personal liability of the Collector for the return of all taxes levied remained unchanged. He was charged each year with the aggregate amount levied, and credited with the sums returned and with remissions made in cases of insolvency and removal. Arrears were carried forward from year to year until extinguished by outright sale to the Collector. This was ordinarily done by special resolution of the corporation. Thus in 1829 the Collector was discharged from liability for the taxes of 1821, 1822 and 1823 upon the payment of $225, and in 1830 from liability for the taxes of 1824, 1825 and 1826 upon payment of $542.47.[3] The machinery thus provided was extremely defective as a means of securing prompt collection of the annual municipal levy. In 1836 of the aggregate property tax levied, $153,230 was paid into the city treasury, while the sum of $142,014.24 remained in arrears. In 1837 "as much money was collected for street opening as for city taxes, without the twentieth

[1] Ordinance of April 7, 1826.

[2] Ordinances of March 24, 1819; February 11, 1820; March 29, 1821.

[3] Resolutions of April 6, 1829; April 8, 1830; February 16, 1832; February 26, 1833; April 3, 1838, No. 35. The continued liability of the Collector led to somewhat anomalous results when the actual incumbent was not reappointed. Thus in 1837 two City Collectors were in office—the new one charged with the collection of the levy for 1836, the old one with the completion of the levies of 1833, 1834 and 1835.

part of the complaints."[1] The acute industrial depression following the crisis of 1837 accented the evil. Tax collections diminished alarmingly and the credit of the city was threatened.

In August, 1840, a resolution of the Mayor and City Council declared all taxes to be payable within the year for which they were assessed. An emphatic note of warning was sounded in Mayor Samuel Brady's Message of January 4, 1841: "It is very evident that some more summary process must be adopted in the collection of taxes than that heretofore pursued or else the city will be compelled to dishonor its obligations, from the inability to meet the demands upon the Treasury." This state of affairs, it was stated, was largely due to the fact that the Collector could only proceed against delinquent tax-payers as in ordinary cases of indebtedness. The remedy proposed was that taxes upon property should be made liens, and that property itself should be applied to their payment by immediate sale instead of by execution upon judgment. Application to this effect was made to the General Assembly,[2] and in February, 1841, the necessary authority was conferred.[3] The City Collector was directed to enforce the prompt collection of taxes and of special assessments for street paving, levied upon city lots, by public sale after due notice. Property thus sold might be redeemed by the delinquent tax-payer within two years of the time of sale, upon payment of all advances with interest together with a penalty of eighteen per cent.[4] No change was made in existing procedure with respect to houses and personal property.

To simplify the book-keeping of the City Collector's department, provision was made in 1845 for a general account to be kept by the Register with the Collector for all taxes levied by the corporation. To this end, the Appeal Tax

[1] Mayor's Message of January 4, 1841.
[2] Resolutions of 1841, No. 13.
[3] "Laws of Maryland," 1840, ch. 63.
[4] Ordinance of March 9, 1841, No. 13.

Court was required to transmit annually to the Register written statements of the whole assessable basis, of additional assessments and of abatements made in the preceding year. The Register was directed to charge the Collector in a general account with the net amount of taxes so levied, and to credit him with the sum of all funds collected, as well as with all discounts allowed for prompt payment. At the close of each fiscal year the old account was closed, and arrearages carried forward as a charge against the Collector in the new account. Similar procedure was prescribed for the special assessments levied for paving and repaving and for wells and pumps.[1] In 1852 a new official, designated the City Auditor, was appointed for the purpose of keeping the accounts between the city and the City Collector;[2] but the old system was probably again introduced in 1855, when the duties of the Auditor were changed to the collection of taxes in arrears.[3]

With the view of encouraging the prompter payment of municipal taxes, the City Collector in 1835 proposed the introduction in Baltimore of the practice prevailing in other cities, where "inducements are held out for the prompt and punctual discharge of the public dues, by allowing to those who pay before certain periods, a discount graduated agreeably to the times of payment, and by charging interest on all sums remaining unpaid after a certain day."[4] The suggestion was adopted in the following year, when provision was made for the allowance of a discount for prompt payment of the local taxes of the current year and for the charge of interest upon taxes in arrears.[5] Essentially similar action was taken in 1837,[6] and in 1841 the use of dis-

[1] Ordinance of March 10, 1845, No. 10. The state tax on property within the city was collected by the City Collector ("Laws of Maryland," 1841, ch. 325 and 328; Ordinance of April 8, 1842, No. 34).

[2] Ordinance of June 18, 1852, No. 58.

[3] Ordinance of March 9, 1855, No. 10.

[4] City Collector's Report of January 5, 1835.

[5] Ordinance of April 14, 1836, No. 62.

[6] Resolution of March 22, 1837, No. 46.

counts for prompt payment of taxes and of interest penalties for arrearages, which has since remained a feature of the Baltimore tax system was permanently introduced. In succeeding years the rates of discount and interest were varied, often in accord with the fiscal exigencies of the corporation, but the practice remained essentially unchanged.

Notwithstanding these devices, the aggregate arrearages increased more than proportionately with the increase in the amount of municipal taxes levied. This was due partly to the failure to enlarge the force of the Collector's office, partly to the limited power possessed by that official to enforce collections. Various remedies were proposed, such as an advance in the beginning of the fiscal year, an increase in the rate of discount allowed for prompt payment and the appointment of a special collector of taxes in arrears.[1] This last suggestion was practically adopted in 1855 by the change in the duties of the City Auditor already noted.[2] The remuneration of the Collector continued for some years to be a definite percentage upon his collections, ordinarily specified in the ordinance authorizing the levy. As the aggregate yield of municipal charges increased, the rate of the commission was successively reduced from eight and six per cent. prevailing before 1817, to four, three and a half and three per cent. In 1841 a fixed annual salary was substituted for the fees and commissions before received.[3]

Specific Taxes. Specific taxes continued to be imposed upon four-wheeled riding carriages, sulkies, riding horses, wagons, as prescribed in the enactments of 1782 and 1801.[4] Distinct provision for the assessment of the tax was made in each annual levy until 1818, when a general ordinance was passed for the annual appointment of one or more Assessors of Specific Taxes. These Assessors were required

[1] Mayor's Messages of January, 1855, and January, 1856.
[2] See above, p. 97.
[3] Ordinance of March 3, 1841, No. 7, sect. 15.
[4] See above, pp. 28, 76.

to make sworn return to the City Collector of every vehicle taxable, with the name and residence of the owner. Failing to locate the owner the tax was imposed upon the person in whose possession the object was found.[1] In 1840 the duties of the Assessors of Specific Taxes were vested in the Board of Assessors appointed by the ordinance of March 25, 1839,[2] and in 1843 the specific taxes were abolished and a general tariff of license taxes on vehicles was adopted in lieu thereof.[3]

Auction Receipts Tax. The tax on auction sales remained fixed at one per cent. of gross receipts. Certain forms of property were occasionally exempted and slight modifications were introduced in the authorized auctioneers' fees; but in 1826 the tax was continued in practically unchanged form.[4] For some years before this, the large yield of the tax had been regarded with jealous eye by the state legislature at Annapolis. Formal attempt was made at the legislative session of 1820 to divert the proceeds of the tax from the municipal into the state treasury, but without success.[5] Seven years later this was however accomplished. The Governor and his Council were then authorized to appoint auctioneers, not exceeding twenty in number, for the city of Baltimore, upon whom the exclusive right of conducting public sales was conferred. The rate of the tax remained unchanged at one per cent.; but the proceeds thereof, as well as of the license taxes on auctioneers, were paid into the state treasury. In place of this revenue, the sum of twenty thousand dollars from out of the proceeds of the tax on auction sales was annually appropriated to the city of Baltimore to be expended exclusively in deepening and improving the harbor. If the proceeds of the tax did not aggregate the sum appropriated, the appropriation was

[1] Ordinance of March 20, 1818.
[2] Ordinance of February 27, 1840, No. 6.
[3] Ordinance of April 11, 1843, No. 33. Cf. below, p. 158.
[4] Ordinance of March 16, 1826.
[5] Resolution of January 13, 1821.

reduced to the amount realized.[1] This appropriation was made annually thereafter and served in some measure to allay local feeling against the assumption by the state of what had long been regarded as a source of distinctly municipal revenue.

In 1836 the General Assembly appointed three persons as commissioners to assess the damages suffered by certain citizens of Baltimore in the bank riots of August 8-10, 1835, and to make return thereof to one of the state treasurers, who was in turn directed to issue to the parties affected interest-bearing stock of the State of Maryland to the amount of the award. Upon the ground that the violence was the result of the neglect of the municipal authorities, the payment of the indemnity was imposed upon the city. Provision was made that the annual appropriation of $20,000 from out the proceeds of the auction tax should be withheld from the city and should be utilized for the redemption of state stock thus issued, unless the corporation should provide for its prior payment by a levy upon the assessable property of the city or by a corporate loan. Should this be done within two years, the annual state appropriation was to be renewed, subject as before to the future control and disposition of the legislature.[2] The awards of the commissioners were made a year later and fixed the aggregate damages suffered at the sum of $102,552.82.[3]

The action of the General Assembly excited much bitterness and hostility in Baltimore. With the avowed purpose of testing the legality of the diversion, an ordinance was passed in 1836 declaring the action of the legislature unconstitutional and restoring the proceeds of the auction tax to the city treasury. The preamble of this ordinance indicated the attitude of the city: "It is the opinion of this corporation that the act of Assembly . . . is in its operation

[1] "Laws of Maryland," 1827, ch. 111.
[2] *Ibid.*, 1835, ch. 184; also cf. *ibid.*, 1835, ch. 226.
[3] Scharf, "Chronicles of Baltimore," p. 489.

unequal, oppressive and unjust; and in so much as it imposes pecuniary burdens upon the citizens of Baltimore, for the use of the state, from which all other citizens of the state are free and exempt, is in violation of the bill of rights and constitution of Maryland."[1] The protest of the municipality was unavailing. Indemnity stock was issued by the state and the customary appropriation from out the proceeds of the auction tax was withheld from the corporation.

In 1844 the City Council represented to the legislature that principal and interest of the indemnity loan had long since been redeemed from out the proceeds of the auction tax, and, the citizens of Baltimore being "grievously burthened with the weight of taxation imposed on them for the improvement of the state," besought the restoration of the auction duties to the municipal treasury.[2] A similar petition for the annual appropriation of twenty thousand dollars from out the proceeds of the auction tax receipts to be applied as before to deepening and improving the harbor was made in 1852.[3] Finally in 1853 the annual state appropriation for this purpose was resumed.[4]

License Taxes. Changes in detail rather than in essence were made in the license taxes imposed upon municipal officials, upon vehicles and upon public amusements. A rough adaptation of tax to income continued to characterize the license charge upon city officials. With the gradual substitution of fixed salaries for fees and perquisites, this source of municipal revenue became insignificant. The tariff of license taxes upon vehicles was modified from time to time until in 1843 the specific tax was repealed, and provision was made for the annual registration in the City Register's office of all vehicles and for the fixture thereupon of a corresponding numbered tin plate. A

[1] Ordinance of June 24, 1836, No. 52, sect. 14.
[2] Resolution of January 23, 1844, No. 2.
[3] Resolution of April 21, 1852, No. 69.
[4] Ordinance of June 16, 1853, No. 66.

schedule of license taxes was prescribed, renewable annually and subject to a slight fee for transfer.[1] License taxes upon public amusements underwent repeated and spasmodic change in amount. In general they remained imposed upon all theatrical and musical entertainments, museums, circuses, bowling alleys, public billiard tables and shuffle boards.

To discourage the further influx of pauper immigrants and to provide for the support of those in Baltimore, the General Assembly in 1833 authorized the corporation to require every master of a vessel landing alien passengers at Baltimore, to pay a tax of $1.50 for each such person or to enter into indemnity bond to the sum of $150 for each immigrant for public charges that might be incurred within a period of two years. The proceeds of the tax, as well as penalties and forfeitures accruing under the act, were appropriated to the Trustees for the Poor of Baltimore City and County, and to the German Society of Maryland and the Hibernian Society of Baltimore in such proportions as the Mayor and City Council of Baltimore might determine.[2] In 1834 two-fifths of the revenues accruing under the act were appropriated to the two benevolent societies,[3] and in 1842 the remaining three-fifths were specifically appropriated to the Trustees of the Poor for Baltimore City and County—two-fifths to be credited to the account of the city and one-fifth to that of the county.[4] The tax had been made compulsory some years before by the repeal of the alternative right of ship-owners to enter into indemnity bond,[5] and the city's share of the proceeds became considerable after 1843.[6] This source of revenue was threatened by the decisions of the U. S. Supreme Court declaring

[1] Ordinance of April 11, 1843, No. 33.
[2] "Laws of Maryland," 1832, ch. 303.
[3] *Ibid.*, 1833, ch. 117.
[4] *Ibid.*, 1841, ch. 174.
[5] *Ibid.*, 1834, ch. 84; 1849, ch. 46.
[6] "Report of the Trustees for the Poor of Baltimore City and County," for 1849.

similar acts of the states of New York and Massachusetts, levying taxes on foreign passengers, to be in conflict with the 8th section of Article I. of the U. S. Constitution.[1] The New York legislature promptly enacted a modified law, presumably meeting the decisions of the Supreme Court. Such action, although recommended, was apparently not taken in Maryland; yet the imposition of the charge seems to have continued uninterruptedly.[2]

Market-houses had been erected in the city, primarily for the sale of food supplies. From time to time special permits were issued by the municipal authorities for the sale of general merchandise, until inconvenience and loss were suffered by the original occupants. In 1824 a tariff of license taxes was imposed upon such transactions, and the sale of imported goods in the markets was entirely prohibited.[3] This tariff was reenacted in almost unchanged form in 1826,[4] but in the following year the whole schedule was repealed and the retail sale of merchandise in any of the markets of the city was entirely prohibited after March, 1827.[5] An annual license tax upon all hucksters was imposed in 1823. This was repealed in 1832 and a per diem charge was substituted therefor.[6] Representation being made to the General Assembly that this charge was "unequal, unjust and oppressive," the city was forbidden in 1835 to impose any local market license tax or charge upon non-residents of Baltimore offering for sale either in person or by agent articles of their own production.[7]

A special license tax ($4 per annum), in addition to the regular state tax ($12 per annum), was imposed in 1829

[1] *Passenger Cases* (Smith *vs.* Turner, Health Commissioner of the port of New York, and Norris *vs.* The City of Boston), 7 How. 283.

[2] See "Register's Summary," January 22, 1856. In the succeeding period of municipal history, the charge, although apparently never repealed, was allowed to lapse.

[3] Ordinance of March 9, 1824.

[4] Ordinance of April 7, 1826.

[5] Ordinances of February 12 and March 2, 1827.

[6] Ordinance of March 31, 1832, No. 31.

[7] "Laws of Maryland," 1835, ch. 297.

upon all retail liquor dealers in Baltimore, and the proceeds appropriated to defraying the city's share of the expenses of the jail.[1] Application was made to the legislature of 1839 for the appropriation of all the receipts from liquor licenses in Baltimore City and County to the Trustees for the Poor, but without favorable results.[2] License taxes were also imposed on dogs, on the vending of charcoal and foreign fruits, on pawnbrokers, on the excavation of vaults and areas, and on the sale of firewood at public wharves.

SPECIAL ASSESSMENTS.

Street Paving. In form and mode of imposition, the special assessment for street paving, or "paving tax," underwent little change from 1817 until the close of the period here considered. The General Assembly in 1818 restrained the Mayor and City Council from causing any unpaved street or alley to be paved until there had been secured, not as theretofore, the consent of a majority of the owners of the abutting property, but "the assent in writing of the proprietors of a majority of the ground fronting and binding" on the particular part paved.[3] Subject to this condition, the special assessment was to be levied in the case of all paving and repaving embracing fifty square yards.[4]

Changes of slight importance in the established procedure were also made in 1823. Before proceeding with the paving of any unpaved street, lane or alley, the City Commissioners were required to obtain not only the consent of the owners of a major part of abutting ground, but the approbation of the Mayor testified in writing on the list of proprietors' names, and finally to give seven days' notice in one or more of the newspapers of the city of the fact of such application, as also of the time and place of their meeting for the purpose of taking action thereupon.[5]

[1] "Laws of Maryland," 1827, ch. 117, sect. 2.
[2] Resolution of February 22, 1839, No. 29.
[3] "Laws of Maryland," 1817, ch. 148.
[4] Ordinance of June 5, 1818.
[5] Ordinance of March 14, 1823.

The City Collector was instructed to collect special assessments within sixty days from the issue of the warrant of assessment and to enforce payment of arrears by distress or otherwise upon not less than sixty days' notice. Failing to do so, he became personally responsible for the payment of the assessment.

The aggregate cost of repaving streets was at first assessed upon benefiting property owners. After 1834 the repaving of any street was undertaken upon the application of the owners of two-thirds of the abutting property. One-third of the total expenditure was paid by the city and the remaining two-thirds assessed by the City Commissioner upon abutting property in proportion to frontage.

Street Reconstruction. Supplementary to the creation by the General Assembly in 1817 of the board of nine commissioners to lay off and extend streets, provision was made in each specific case of opening, closing, widening or grading a municipal thoroughfare, for the appointment by the Mayor and City Council of five assessors to ascertain the damages sustained by property owners by reason of the reconstruction, and to return a report thereof to the City Register. The damages awarded were to be paid out of the city treasury to the persons thereto entitled before any actual work was undertaken, and appeal lay to the Baltimore County Court. Although no specific mention was made, the act doubtless contemplated the levy of a special assessment upon property benefited by the improvement to the amount of the entire expenditure involved; but no instrumentality for the continuous performance of this function was designated.[1]

In actual practice, the city does not appear to have taken any direct part in the assessment of benefits for street improvements in the manner provided by the act. Upon the receipt of a written application from the proprietors of not less than two-thirds of the property damaged, five assessors were ordinarily appointed to ascertain the actual damages

[1] "Laws of Maryland," 1817, ch. 148.

sustained. Not until the petitioners had paid to the City Register this aggregate amount, together with the estimated expenses to be incurred in effecting the improvement, were the City Commissioners at liberty to proceed with the work. There is apparently no evidence of the municipality undertaking to allot the shares of the assessment to be borne by the several property owners benefited, nor is it entirely clear whether the assessment was distributed among all such or only among the petitioners.

Specific provision was made by the General Assembly in 1835 that in all applications for street reconstruction made by virtue of the act of 1817 and signed by the proprietors of a major part of the property liable to condemnation, the corporation should appoint three or more commissioners to award damages and assess benefits in the manner prescribed in specific statutes.[1] The more important street extensions and reconstructions were however made not under authority derived from the general statute of 1817, but from specific enabling acts passed by the General Assembly as noted above.[2] The particular agency selected for effecting the improvement in such cases was vested with the levy of the corresponding special assessment. It was ordinarily a board composed of three or more designated commissioners or of five assessors appointed by the Mayor. Exceptional cases were presented by boards consisting of seven assessors appointed by the Baltimore County Court,[3] of the City Commissioners and two or four persons named by the Baltimore City Court,[4] of the City Commissioners and two designated persons,[5] of seven commissioners appointed by a board of seven designated electors.[6]

The procedure was much the same in all cases. The as-

[1] "Laws of Maryland," 1834, ch. 277. The statutes referred to were *ibid.*, 1826, ch. 91; 1827, ch. 21.

[2] Page 108.

[3] "Laws of Maryland," 1818, ch. 198.

[4] *Ibid.*, 1817, ch. 12; 1824, ch. 152.

[5] *Ibid.*, 1827, ch. 58.

[6] *Ibid.*, 1827, ch. 71.

sessing board, after giving due notice in the local newspapers, proceeded to examine upon oath the persons affected by the improvement, with a view to determining the damages sustained. To this amount was added all actual expenditures incurred, and the aggregate was assessed by the board upon all persons benefited by the improvement "having regard to all circumstances." The assessment list was filed with the Register of the city and the specific amounts levied were collected by the City Collector, paid into the city treasury and then disbursed to the proper recipients.[1] Ordinarily the action of the assessing board was final. In some cases appeal was authorized, either to the judge of the Baltimore City or County Court or to a jury empanelled by the Court. The aggregate cost involved was usually defrayed by the proceeds of the special assessment. In certain more important improvements, municipal appropriations in aid were made. Thus in opening Pratt, South and Lombard streets, authorized by the General Assembly in 1817, one-third of the total cost involved was borne by the city. In other cases appropriations of specific amount were made.

The act of 1841 appointing the board of Commissioners for Opening Streets effected slight modification in the levy of the special assessment for street reconstruction. Whenever authorized by ordinance to proceed with any specific work, the Commissioners were required to give at least sixty days' notice in two local newspapers of a time and place of meeting for the assessment of benefits and the award of damages. Damages were awarded to the amount "of any right or interest claimed in any ground or improvements—over and above the amount in value of benefit which will thereby accrue to such owner, for which, taking into

[1] "Laws of Maryland," 1823, ch. 72; 1826, ch. 202; 1834, ch. 43. In 1837 the City Collector was authorized to receive from persons to whom damages had been awarded and upon whom benefits had been assessed, an assignment of benefits in part discharge of the amount assessed, instead of requiring payment to and disbursement by the City Register in full (Ordinance of March 3, 1837).

consideration all advantages and disadvantages, such owner ought to be compensated." The amount assessed included the aggregate damages and the estimated expenses of reconstruction, levied "on all the ground and improvements —the owners of which, as such, the said commissioner shall decide and deem to be benefited—in just proportion according to the value of the benefit, which in the estimation of the said commissioners will accrue to each owner." The prosecution of the work was contingent upon the preliminary payment to the persons entitled thereto of the amount of damages awarded, or the written consent of such persons to proceed in lieu thereof. Upon the completion of the valuation and assessment, the Commissioners made return to the Register, and having given due notice, sat for ten days thereafter to hear appeals and to make reviews. A final right of appeal lay to the judges of the Baltimore City Court, who were authorized to hear such cases fully and to summon a jury, in their discretion. The sums assessed upon the property benefited, if paid within thirty days after public notice had been given by the Register, were subject to a three per cent. discount. Sums then unpaid were collected by the City Collector, and paid over to the persons entitled to receive them. In 1843 an assessment so levied was made a prior lien upon property, to be collected if necessary by distress and sale as any other public tax.[1]

Wells and Pumps. Minor changes were introduced after 1817 in the special assessment levied for the supply and repair of public wells and pumps. In February, 1819, the maximum expenditure for this purpose, which might be defrayed by municipal appropriation instead of by the levy of a special assessment, was limited to fifty dollars.[2] Subsequent ordinances provided that the cost of all repairs "within" the limits of direct taxation should be defrayed from out the city treasury, and of all "without," by a special

[1] Ordinance of March 28, 1843, No. 24.
[2] Ordinance of February 25, 1819.

assessment.[1] Further restrictions were imposed by requiring the written application of eight or more of the property owners affected and the approval of the City Commissioners, for every new well or pump for which the levy of a special assessment was necessary. The contractor was, moreover, required to signify his willingness to receive the proceeds of the assessment in discharge of the work performed.[2]

Miscellaneous Purposes. A special assessment was occasionally levied to defray the cost of some particular improvement, as in 1817, for the acquisition by the City Commissioners of a piece of public ground for the improvement of the harbor;[3] in 1823 by the Port Wardens for the improvement of the water front;[4] in 1832 by a board of five commissioners appointed by the General Assembly for the condemnation of a site for a public market;[5] in 1833 for the repair of certain wharves;[6] and in 1852 for the acquisition of a public square.[7]

Interesting light upon the broad use to which the special assessment as a fiscal device might be put, as well as upon the early attitude of Baltimore to the street railway problem, is thrown by the action of the corporation in 1832. On April 1, 1832, the line of the Baltimore and Ohio Railroad was completed and in operation from Baltimore to Point of Rocks, a distance of seventy miles. In Baltimore tracks had been laid, under authority given by the City Council, parallel with the water front.[8] It was believed that greater facilities for travel and traffic would be afforded residents of Baltimore by the construction of "branch railways" within

[1] Ordinances of February 10, 1820, and February 11, 1822; Resolution of September 2, 1828.

[2] Ordinance of March 10, 1819.

[3] "Laws of Maryland," 1817, ch. 85.

[4] Ordinance of March 11, 1823.

[5] "Laws of Maryland," 1831, ch. 327; Ordinance of March 30, 1832, No. 28.

[6] "Laws of Maryland," 1832, ch. 57.

[7] Ordinance of July 22, 1852, No. 71.

[8] Ordinance of April 4, 1831.

the city. The president of the Baltimore and Ohio Railroad Company expressed his willingness to connect such branch lines, when constructed, with the main stem. In April, 1832, upon authority derived from the General Assembly, the City Commissioners were directed, upon receipt of the written application of the owners of a major part of the ground fronting on certain streets, to contract for laying such tracks. The aggregate cost involved was to be defrayed by a special assessment upon the owners of property abutting on the particular streets, levied in proportion to frontage and collected in the manner of city taxes.[1] Tracks were laid in 1832 on Howard, Patterson and Paca streets in accordance with these provisions, and the total expenditure was assessed upon the property benefited.[2]

FEES.

From the sources already described[3]—determination of lot boundaries, fixture of the city seal and storage of gunpowder—small amounts, which may fairly be described as fees, continued to trickle into the city treasury. These were supplemented by an appreciable revenue from the municipal operation of hay scales, fish-houses, dredging machine,[4] and from quarantine, court and inspection fees.

In 1818 an appropriation was made for the erection of a municipal hay scales, and the remuneration of the weigher was changed from the perquisites of office to a definite salary.[5] Municipal operation of the scales proved unsatisfactory and in 1824 the Mayor was authorized to rent them

[1] "Laws of Maryland," 1831, ch. 252; Ordinances of April 6, 1832, No. 41 and April 3, 1833, No. 26.

[2] Report of the City Collector in "Municipal Reports" for 1833, p. 98.

[3] See above, p. 84.

[4] The essentially compulsory character of such revenues constitute them fees rather than quasi-private receipts. The distinction is however only of theoretic interest in this connection.

[5] Ordinances of April 3 and September 21, 1818; supplementary to original ordinance of March 13, 1807.

from year to year upon the best terms procurable.[1] Administrative control of the scales was however retained by the city until 1838, when the function was definitely assumed by the state.[2] Provision was made in 1822-23 for the erection of municipal fish-houses, and for the compulsory inspection and storage of fish brought in any large amount to Baltimore. Keepers were appointed and authorized to receive certain fees, and monthly account with the City Register was required.[3] The fees received by the City Commissioners and Port Wardens for the hire of the municipal dredging machine were in 1839 added to the annual appropriation for deepening and improving the harbor.[4]

A schedule of quarantine fees to be collected from incoming vessels by the Harbor Master and paid over to the City Register was adopted in 1823 and reenacted in the general health ordinance of 1826.[5] Fees and charges for judicial services were fixed by the General Assembly, and constituted the remuneration of local court officials; after 1823, when in excess of $1500 per annum, twenty-five per cent. of the surplus was appropriated by the State.[6] In 1839 provision was made for the remuneration of the clerk and crier of Baltimore City Court by the payment of definite salaries and for the payment into the city treasury, in sworn quarterly account, of all fees and perquisities hitherto accruing to these officials.[7] After the incorporation of the local courts with the state judiciary in 1851 all judicial fees reverted to the state treasury.

A nominal text-book and tuition fee—$1 per quarter, with entire exemption, if expedient—was exacted of the

[1] Ordinance of January 30, 1824.

[2] "Laws of Maryland," 1836, ch. 238; 1837, ch. 319.

[3] Ordinances of 1821, No. 67, and February 4, 1823.

[4] Ordinances of May 10, 1839, No. 54; April 23, 1849, No. 46.

[5] Ordinances of March 11, 1823, and March 24, 1826, sect. 40; also January 8, 1855, No. 6.

[6] "Laws of Maryland," 1823, ch. 146.

[7] Ordinance of April 23, 1839, No. 42; but see "Laws of Maryland," 1838, ch. 314; 1841 (extra session), ch. 40; Ordinance of March 4, 1852, No. 18.

children of residents of Baltimore for attendance upon the public schools. Higher charges were imposed upon non-resident pupils. The revenue accruing from this source appears sometimes to have been paid direct to the School Commissioners, instead of being covered into the municipal treasury and then credited to the account of the "public school fund."[1]

Fines.

The place of fines and penalties in the municipal economy underwent no change beyond that incident to the multiplication of municipal ordinances and the growth of the city.

In 1818 all informers, other than municipal officers, were restricted from using the name of the Mayor and City Council in suits brought for the recovery of fines and forfeitures, and the city declined all liability for costs thus incurred. Measures were also taken to enforce payment by delinquent Justices of the Peace or other municipal officers of the city's share of fines and forfeitures.[2] The mode of collection was changed somewhat in 1824 by the provision that all information of the breach of municipal ordinances should be made before one of the Justices of the Peace appointed to receive the report of the night watch, or one of three Justices selected by the Mayor, and that a monthly return of all warrants issued by the Justices to the city bailiffs on such information, should be made to the City Register.[3] In 1838, the High Constable and his deputies were constituted *ex-officio* informers against all breaches of municipal ordinances, and no part of municipal fines was allowed for service thus rendered.[4]

Quasi-Private Receipts.

Wharves. A graduated tariff of wharfage charges was established in 1819, somewhat lower than the schedule then

[1] See, for example, "Report of the Commissioners of Public Schools" of December 31, 1853, p. 232.
[2] Ordinance of June 1, 1818.
[3] Ordinance of February 28, 1824.
[4] Ordinance of May 23, 1838, No. 45.

in force. Charges were collected daily by the Harbor Master, and monthly return was made to the City Register.[1] This tariff was re-enacted without change in the codification of municipal ordinances in 1826 and in 1838. In 1827 the corporation was again specifically authorized to levy upon all vessels landing, receiving or transporting other than Maryland products at city wharves, local tonnage charges of "reasonable amount," and statutes in conflict were repealed.[2] This power was supplemented in the following year by authority to recover in the name of the corporation charges so imposed.[3] A local tonnage duty of two cents per ton upon all vessels of sixty or more tons arriving at the port of Baltimore—originally authorized in 1791 and ratified by successive acts of the U. S. Congress—was reimposed by the city in April, 1830. The Collector of the Port (the federal customs officer) was authorized to collect the tonnage charge from all vessels entering at the Custom House, and to retain ten per cent. of the proceeds as a commission. Upon all other vessels, the duty was levied by the Harbor Masters; in the case of vessels arriving more frequently, it was levied but once a month.

In 1838 and 1839 new schedules of wharfage charges were adopted by the corporation, appreciably higher than those before in force. The result was marked dissatisfaction throughout the state, and in March, 1842, in "an act to prevent the collection of excessive wharfage in the city of Baltimore," both ordinances were declared inoperative, and the municipality was prohibited from imposing higher charges than those existing before 1839.[4]

Wharfage dues were collected after 1839 by three annually appointed Harbor Masters, to each of whom a designated territory was assigned.[5] Their compensation was fixed at ten per cent. of the tonnage charge and twenty per

[1] Ordinances of March 30, 1819, and February 27, 1822.

[2] "Laws of Maryland," 1827, ch. 162.

[3] *Ibid.*, 1828, ch. 162.

[4] *Ibid.*, 1841, ch. 311.

[5] Ordinance of April 19, 1839. In 1840 the number of Harbor Masters was increased to four; in 1846-47 the power of the Mayor to regulate wharfage dues was reaffirmed.

cent. of all other duties collected; but the aggregate commissions were divided equally among the several incumbents.[1]

Markets. The procedure in vogue with respect to the rental of market stalls and shambles was extended to the additional market-houses erected. In 1822 the clerks of the markets were directed to present annual reports to the Mayor of the number of stalls rented, the amount of rentals and kindred information.[2] In the market code of 1826, as already noted, detailed schedules of stall rentals were prescribed and the clerks were required to account monthly with the City Register for all funds received.[3]

The rental of stalls in the usual manner in Belair Market being represented in 1823 as an obstacle to their speedy occupation, the Mayor was authorized to offer at public sale two and three year leases thereof.[4] In more or less modified form, this method was frequently employed thereafter, even to the point of leasing stalls in perpetuity or for ninety-nine years, subject to the payment of specific annual rentals and charges.

Municipal Property. The city was in irregular receipt of a small revenue from the lease and sale of municipal property not utilized for public purposes and originally acquired by purchase, by the extension of the water front, or by the dispossession of delinquent tax-payers. Originally the disposition of each piece of municipal property was prescribed by a specific ordinance, and the proceeds were ordinarily covered into the city treasury for general municipal purposes. Gradually this function was relegated to the Commissioners of Finance and the accruing revenue was utilized in aid of the annual interest upon the funded debt of the city, and in the accumulation of a sinking fund.[5]

Viewed as immediately productive investments, the muni-

[1] Ordinance of February 27, 1840, No. 5.
[2] Resolution of March 21, 1822.
[3] Ordinance of April 7, 1826.
[4] Resolution of March 17, 1823.
[5] Ordinance of April 25, 1850.

cipal loans and subscriptions of Baltimore to the internal improvement projects were practical failures. The only important dividends realized were from the Baltimore and Ohio Railroad,[1] and even there the aggregate receipts were far less than the corresponding municipal interest payments. By 1857 all hope of securing any income from the city's subscriptions to the Baltimore and Susquehanna Railroad Company and from the Susquehanna Canal Company had been apparently abandoned.[2]

Lotteries. No municipal or quasi-municipal lottery was authorized after 1815. The drawings of the state lottery and of many private lotteries took place in Baltimore, but did not contribute directly to the municipal treasury. In 1839 the General Assembly appointed six designated persons as Commissioners of Lotteries to raise the sum of $150,000 for the purpose of constructing an armory and town-hall in Baltimore and for rebuilding and improving the Hanover Market-house. The Commissioners so appointed were vested with power to effect these improvements, provided the assent of the Mayor and City Council should be given to the act.[3] The measure was promptly confirmed by the corporation with the express conditions that the board of Commissioners satisfy the Mayor of the adequacy of their resources, and that the city assume no liability for expenditures incurred in the course of the work.[4]

[1] The dividends paid by the Baltimore and Ohio Railroad from 1827 to 1853 were as follows: 1831, 3/8 per cent.; 1832, January, 5/8 per cent.; 1832, July, 3/4 per cent.; 1833, 3/4 per cent.; 1835, 1 1/8 per cent.; 1840, 2 per cent.; 1841, 2 per cent.; 1843, 2 per cent.; 1844, 2 1/2 per cent.; 1846, 3 per cent. (of which 2/3 in scrip); 1847, 3 per cent. (scrip); 1848, 3 1/2 per cent. (scrip); 1849, 5 per cent. (scrip); 1850, 7 per cent. (scrip); 1851, 7 per cent. (scrip); 1852, 7 per cent. (scrip); 1853, 3 per cent. (scrip). See Reizenstein, "The Economic History of the Baltimore and Ohio Railroad, 1827-1853," in *Johns Hopkins University Studies in Historical and Political Science*, Fifteenth Series, VII-VIII.

[2] Cf. Register's Statement, January 30, 1857; cf. below, p. 198.

[3] "Laws of Maryland," 1838, ch. 323.

[4] Ordinance of April 20, 1839, No. 39. In 1840 the net sum to be raised was increased to $225,000 ("Laws of Maryland," 1839, ch. 52).

Water Supply. The municipal assumption of the function of water supply was consummated in the summer of 1854.[1] The tariff of charges exacted by the private corporation was retained by the city until June, 1855, when a new and lower schedule was introduced.[2] In January, 1856, Mayor Samuel Hinks recommended upon the score both of economy and equity, the adoption of a general water rate to be levied upon all houses within the water belt, instead of the system of graduated rentals then in force.[3] The proposal was apparently neglected, only to be revived at periodic intervals during the next forty years. The operations of the Water Board for the first fourteen months of its existence, ending January 1, 1856, showed an appreciable net balance in favor of the department.

Gifts and Subsidies. Voluntary or gratuitous revenues were occasionally received by the municipal treasury. Under this category should be grouped the gift of sites of public markets and buildings,[4] the bequest in 1839 of certain annuities for the relief of the poor of the twelfth ward of the city,[5] and the transfer to the public school fund of the property of intestates dying in the city of Baltimore.[6]

Of greater practical importance in the municipal budget was the regular appropriation of certain state revenues in aid of specific municipal funds. Thus, the proceeds of the local tax on auction receipts were diverted by the General Assembly in 1827 to the state treasury. But of these proceeds the sum of $20,000 was annually appropriated to the corporation, to be expended exclusively in deepening and

[1] See above, p. 119.

[2] Resolutions of June 16, 1855, No. 159, and April 3, 1856, No. 101.

[3] Mayor's Message of January, 1856, p. 12.

[4] Ordinances of April 10, 1818, and February 25, 1819. Resolutions of March 20, 1828; April 16, 1835, No. 67; March 11 and 21, April 13, 1844, Nos. 54, 64, 125.

[5] Ordinance of April 23, 1839, No. 48.

[6] The first provision of this kind seems to have been made in 1815. In 1839 such revenues were diverted to the public school fund of Baltimore County, but were again restored in 1846 ("Laws of Maryland," 1814, ch. 131; 1838, ch. 407; 1845, ch. 1203).

widening the harbor.[1] Similarly, after 1827, certain extraordinary revenues accruing to the school fund of the state were apportioned among the counties and Baltimore City, and the share of the city was credited to the municipal school fund.

In 1850 John McDonogh, a wealthy merchant resident in New Orleans but born and educated in Baltimore, died, leaving the bulk of a large fortune to be devoted by the cities of New Orleans and Baltimore to the education of the poor. The control of the estate (valued in 1855 at $2,272,406.05) was entrusted, in accordance with the terms of the bequest, to six commissioners, of whom three were appointed by Baltimore and three by New Orleans. The cumbersome plan of administration prescribed by Mr. McDonogh's will was soon found impracticable, and in 1857 a partition of the estate between the two cities was decreed. Owing to the overestimate of the original appraisement and the persistent litigation connected with the trust, the share realized by Baltimore was in 1860 only $579,715.53. The public school system of the city being then in successful operation, the entire fund was set apart for the establishment of a farm school for poor boys.[2]

[1] Laws of Maryland, 1827, ch. 111; Resolution of March 6, 1834, No. 34; cf. above, p. 156.

[2] William Allen, "Life and Work of John McDonogh," pp. 75-92.

CHAPTER IV

MUNICIPAL INDEBTEDNESS.

The most striking feature of the financial development of Baltimore from 1817 to 1856 was the growth of municipal indebtedness. The genesis of the funded debt occurred in the decade from 1817 to 1826 in the form of small loans for various municipal purposes. The fever for internal improvements ran full course in the period from 1827 to 1843, and left the city burdened with a modern funded debt. The years from 1843 to 1850 witnessed no considerable increase, but thereafter, by the issue of direct municipal loans and the extension of municipal credit in further aid of works of internal improvement, the funded debt was practically doubled and a large " guaranteed debt " was incurred. The issue of corporate stock for the purchase of a water plant in 1854 foreshadowed the extensive use of municipal borrowing for public improvements in the succeeding period of municipal history.

The history of municipal indebtedness within the forty years is essentially a narrative of successive funded and " guaranteed " issues. The loans were few in number, of large amount, and often issued to the beneficiary, who in turn negotiated them. In the absence of any important provision for amortization, the problem of debt administration was accordingly simple. Floating indebtedness played no considerable part in municipal finances during the period considered.

Growth of Indebtedness.

Origin of Funded Debt. The genesis of the funded debt of Baltimore is found in an ordinance of June 10, 1817, " for the creation of a six per cent. stock of the City of Baltimore." The ordinance authorized the issue, primarily for the purpose of acquiring a municipal dumping ground, of six per cent. stock in certificates of one hundred dollars each with interest payable quarterly. The certificates were redeemable at the pleasure of the corporation and were transferable at the Mayor's office in person or by attorney. The faith of the corporation and all corporate property were pledged for the payment of interest and principal. Some $40,000 appeared to have been issued under the provisions of the ordinance.[1] On August 15, 1817, a supplementary ordinance authorized a loan from the banks or from individuals of the city of a sum not exceeding $30,000, to be expended in repairing damages caused by late heavy rains. The Mayor and the presidents of the two Branches of the City Council were authorized to issue stock in prescribed form, or—at the option of the persons making the loan—to give the Mayor's note for a corresponding amount. Finally, on October 5 of the same year, the Mayor and the two Council presidents were authorized to issue stock in payment, wholly or in part, of the amount due the banks of the city. Provision was made that should the banks decline to receive the stock at or above par, it should be sold to individuals without discount and the proceeds devoted to the payment of the bank indebtedness. Six per cent. stock to the amount of some $30,000 was issued under this ordinance, swelling the total funded indebtedness of the city at the close of 1817 to nearly $100,000.

It is noteworthy that this entire indebtedness was incurred without any specific authorization to issue municipal stock, either in the city charter or in a subsequent enabling act of the legislature. The municipality seems simply to have assumed the power from the provision of the charter

[1] See the tabular statement of the successive issues of city stock, prepared by the Register for the City Council in 1850 and included in the Municipal Reports of that year. Statistics relating to the early growth of the funded debt of Baltimore must unfortunately be derived in great part from this not entirely trustworthy table.

permitting the corporation to purchase and hold real, personal and mixed property, and to dispose of the same for the benefit of the city.[1] Specific authority to issue negotiable securities or to borrow money was first conferred by the General Assembly in the important "Act relating to the City of Baltimore," passed in February, 1818. Section vii of this measure empowered the Mayor and City Council to borrow money upon the credit of the corporation or to issue stock to any amount not exceeding one million dollars in certificates of not less than one hundred dollars, "for the purpose of effecting any great or permanent improvement." Maryland banks were authorized to lend money to the corporation, and to purchase, hold or dispose of its stock. But an appreciable funded debt had already been contracted, as has been seen, prior to the passage of this act. Further, the funding of floating indebtedness, concerning which nothing was said, and the issue of stock for municipal improvements, neither "great nor permanent," continued periodically. In short, the early growth as well as the actual inception of the funded indebtedness of Baltimore involved the exercise of the implied or incidental, rather than the expressed power of a municipal corporation to borrow money and to issue negotiable securities.[2]

The grant of specific power to the corporation to incur a funded debt resulted in neither alarming nor continued use of municipal credit. In 1818, successive issues of stock were authorized in aid of city revenue, for the opening of Pratt and South streets, for funding the military debt and for minor purposes. The sum of $242,300.10, considerably less than the maximum amount authorized, appears to have been actually issued.[3] Between 1819 and 1827, the increase of the funded debt was inconsiderable, the only issue of importance being $80,000 in 1824, in payment of current

[1] See preamble to Ordinance of June 10, 1817.
[2] Cf. Dillon, "Municipal Corporations," §117 *et seq.*
[3] See tabular statement in "City Register's Report" for 1850.

M

municipal obligations. Ordinances were passed from time to time authorizing stock issues of slight amount for varied purposes—probably in face of a depleted treasury; but recourse was not often had to the power so conferred. In 1821 the issue of $340,000 of five per cent. stock was authorized for refunding the older six per cent. loans.[1] In 1827 the aggregate indebtedness of the city was less than $500,000, and of this more than three-fourths was in five per cent. stock.

Era of Internal Improvements. The mad fever for internal improvements that swept over the United States in the second quarter of the century ran its full course in Maryland. The results of the reckless use of public credit were, in the state's finances, the accumulation of a large funded debt, resort to direct taxation, and perilous approach to repudiation. In the finances of Baltimore the most characteristic effect was the creation of a modern municipal debt with its burdens and problems. In 1842 the City Register noted that, "a few years since . . . our entire issue of stock was less than a million, and the other engagements of the city were very limited, . . . but we now have fourteen different issues of stock, amounting to upwards of five millions." This transformation was essentially the result of bold extension of municipal credit in aiding the construction of the Baltimore and Ohio Railroad, and to a less degree, that of the Baltimore and Susquehanna Railroad and the Susquehanna Canal.

(Baltimore and Ohio Railroad). Baltimore formed a natural market for the agricultural products of the West. Active communication had long been maintained with that region—in early days by pack horses, later by long wagon trains that traversed the northern turnpikes as far as the Ohio River. The introduction of steamboats upon the navigable waters of the West displaced this means of transportation. Trade was diverted to other centres, and the commercial importance of Baltimore was threatened. Pub-

[1] Ordinance of November 9, 1821, No. 59.

lic-spirited citizens immediately began an agitaton for improved means of communication with the West. A plan for the organization of the Baltimore and Ohio Railroad Company was drawn up, and an act of incorporation was secured from the General Assembly of Maryland on February 28, 1827, nine days after the detailed project had first been made public.[1]

The capital stock of the new corporation was fixed at three million dollars, of which one million was reserved by the state of Maryland and five hundred thousand by the city of Baltimore. Payment for stock was to be made at the rate of one per cent. at the time of subscription; thereafter in installments as required by the directorate, provided that not more than one-third of the total amount subscribed could be called for in any one year. Baltimore was to be represented by two, and Maryland by four directors in addition to the twelve chosen by the stockholders.[2] The city promptly subscribed the maximum amount authorized, and made provision by appropriation and loan for the payment of the early installments.[3] In further aid of the railroad, the city agreed in 1830 to make anticipatory payments to the full amount of its subscription, upon evidence that thirty per cent. of the par value of all shares subscribed had been paid by other stockholders. To this end the Commissioners of Finance were empowered to issue five per cent. city stock in such amounts as might be demanded, not exceeding $70,000 in any one month. Interest was to be received by the city upon the amount advanced in excess of the quota called for from other stockholders.[4] The Company availed itself of the privilege conferred by the ordi-

[1] For further details see Reizenstein, "The Economic History of the Baltimore and Ohio Railroad, 1827-1853," in *Johns Hopkins University Studies in Historical and Political Science*, Fifteenth Series, Nos. VII-VIII.

[2] "Laws of Maryland," 1826, ch. 123.

[3] Resolution of March 20, 1827; Ordinances of June 26, 1828, No. 3; March 2, 1829, No. 15.

[4] Ordinance of June 25, 1830.

nance, and in 1833 the Commissioners of Finance advertised the necessary loans.[1]

In December, 1834, the Baltimore and Ohio Railroad was completed to Harper's Ferry and preparation was made for its further extension westward, to Cumberland, Wheeling and Pittsburg. The Company had at this time completely exhausted its own financial resources. Accordingly, in 1835, aid was sought from both state and city. The response of the city was cordial in the extreme. In 1836 the municipality was authorized to make an additional subscription to the stock of the Baltimore and Ohio Railroad Company, to an amount not exceeding three million dollars, to borrow money and to impose taxes for this purpose, and to appoint an additional representative upon the directorate of the Company for every five thousand shares ($100 par value per share) of stock thus subscribed.[2] In availing itself of this authority, the municipality simply added the provision that the subscription should be made in installments of not more than one million of dollars in any one year. The city stock was to bear interest at six per cent., and to be redeemable before July 1, 1890.[3] Any premium accruing from its sale was appropriated to the sinking fund, less a commission of three-tenths of one per cent. of the sum negotiated, which was allowed as compensation to the Commissioners of Finance.[4]

The acute depression of financial interests throughout the country subsequent upon the crisis of 1837 made difficult the sale of any considerable part of the stock thus authorized. The city met the early calls for installments upon its subscription by loans from local banks, aggregating $500,000 and secured by deposits of stock. After the bank crash of 1839 and the general suspension of specie payments by the banks south of New York in the autumn of that year,

[1] Mayor's Message of January 6, 1834.
[2] "Laws of Maryland," 1835, ch. 127.
[3] Resolution of March 17, 1836, No. 40; Ordinance of April 26, 1836, No. 37.
[4] Ordinances of April 12, 1837, No. 37, and May 19, 1838, No. 21.

it became practically impossible to obtain further loans upon any terms or to dispose of corporate stock, save at ruinous sacrifice. The fiscal exigencies of the Company growing more pronounced, recourse was had to a novel and interesting device—proposed by the Company and acquiesced in without formal action by the city—for making the municipal subscription immediately available.

The Baltimore and Ohio Railroad Company received city stock at par in payment of future installments upon the $3,000,000 subscription. In so far as possible, this stock was used in direct discharge of obligations incurred in construction. For smaller amounts and for current expenditures, "stock orders" were issued in denominations of $100, $5, $3, $2, and $1, fundable in stock at par in amounts of not less than $100, but designed as a local medium of exchange. For their ultimate security, stock to the full amount of the orders issued was deposited with two commissioners in trust for the holders, and to add to their acceptability the Company received them in discharge of all debts.[1] The profit arising from the circulation of these

[1] The economic character of the "stock orders" is described, in favorable light, in the Fourteenth Annual Report of the President and Board of Directors to the Stockholders of the Baltimore and Ohio Railroad Company (1840): "The orders do not promise to pay money, nor, indeed, are they, in any respect, promissory in their character. They confer an absolute authority for the transfer of City Stock, and finally cancel the obligation for which they are received in satisfaction. From the nature of the case, they cannot exceed in amount the City subscription and the stock actually transferred to the Commissioners in trust for the holders. They, in fact, represent City certificates, though in smaller denominations; and, in the requisite sums, may be funded and converted into coin or bank paper, at the pleasure of the holder. They are, therefore, not liable to the risk, or any other objection to which irresponsible paper issues, professing to pay money, are exposed; and every citizen, liable to the payment of a city tax, has an immediate interest in maintaining their value. Nor need the purpose or utility of these orders cease after the resumption of specie payments. On the contrary, they would, in that event, if they should be employed for such purpose, prove valuable auxiliaries in aiding the operations of the banks; they would, in no respect, impair the soundness of the regular currency, but might be advantageously maintained in general credit."

"stock orders" accrued to the city. In March, 1840, the Company agreed that city stock held in trust for the redemption of the orders should bear interest from the date of funding and not from the date of issue. A year later, the Register of the city was authorized by resolution of the Mayor and City Council to receive them in payment of all city dues and taxes and to pay them out again in discharge of the various demands upon the city treasury.[1] The saving of interest by the absorption of orders into local circulation was for several years important. A proportion of city stock was utilized by the Company in direct payment of its obligations, and another part was employed in funding orders presented for redemption. By far the largest amount of the outstanding stock, however, was held as a non-interest bearing collateral against the orders in circulation.

For a brief period the scheme worked successfully. The suspension of specie payments by the banks and the withdrawal of city scrip, described below,[2] gave a place for a local currency of small denominations. The orders were received by contractors in payment for materials and services, were distributed among laborers and tradesmen, and continued to circulate freely in the channels of retail trade. In October, 1840, stock orders to the amount of $515,000 had been issued and distributed, as follows: 100 of $100 each; 6,800 of $5 each; 13,000 of $3 each; 39,000 of $2 each; and 354,000 of $1 each. Of this entire amount, only the $10,000 in $100 denominations had been funded, and the credit of the orders in circulation was good.[3] Encouraged by these results, the Company proceeded during the next twelve months to issue stock orders in large amounts to defray the heavy expenditures entailed by the extension of the road to Cumberland. In October, 1841, the aggregate

[1] Resolution of February 9, 1841, No. 9; also Report of Commissioners of Finance, January, 1841.

[2] Page 189.

[3] Fourteenth Annual Report of the President and Directors to the Stockholders of the Baltimore and Ohio Railroad (October, 1840).

amount of outstanding orders was $1,449,051. As a medium of exchange, the orders had now suffered marked depreciation, and were becoming an instrument of oppression to the wage-earner and an element of disturbance in local trade. The Company continued to justify the issue of the orders, but their uninterrupted depreciation was an irresistible argument *contra*.[1] Early in 1842, the orders, then outstanding to the amount of $1,500,000, "had reached a depreciation which effectually excluded them from the operations of trade."[2] The ordinance permitting them to be used in payment of municipal taxes and dues was repealed, and the orders, by funding into stock and by outright purchase, soon disappeared from circulation.[3]

The history of the stock orders repeats the familiar experience of an inconvertible currency issued to the point of redundancy. At first emitted in moderate amount upon a market suffering from monetary stringency, the orders circulated easily. The action of the city in making them receivable for local dues opened a new outlet and maintained their credit for a period. Increasing issue, in no degree adjusted to the currency needs of the community, brought depreciation, until with the withdrawal of a quasi-tender quality, the notes lost all acceptability and soon disappeared from circulation. It is difficult, if not impossible, to determine the influence of the issue of stock orders upon the finances of Baltimore. Leaving aside the injury done the economic interests of the city by a mass of inconvertible depreciating currency of small denominations, it can hardly be doubted that the credit of Baltimore suffered from the presence of discredited paper fundable in its own obligations. On the other hand, any attempt to realize funds by direct sale of municipal securities must have meant, with prevailing finan-

[1] Fifteenth Annual Report of the President and Directors to the Stockholders of the Baltimore and Ohio Railroad Company (October, 1841).

[2] Mayor's Message of January 16, 1843.

[3] Resolution of March 17, 1842, No. 52.

cial conditions, a heavy loss to the city treasury and a no less serious blow to municipal credit. A conservative statement is, perhaps, that by the issue of stock orders the finances of the city escaped from greater loss, at the expense of the general economic interests of the city.

The final installments of the city's $3,000,000 subscription to the Baltimore and Ohio Railroad Company were paid by temporary loans, by transfer of city stock at par, by the sale of scrip dividends of the Company, and by outright appropriations from out the municipal treasury. In January, 1842, only $440,000 remained yet undischarged,[1] and during 1843 the last installment was paid.[2]

(Baltimore and Susquehanna Railroad.) Just as the Baltimore and Ohio Railroad was expected to link Baltimore commercially with the undeveloped country of the interior and the west, so the Baltimore and Susquehanna Railroad, the nucleus of the present Northern Central Railway, was designed to render the rich country lying to the north of the city, tributary to local trade and manufacture. It was projected with feverish enthusiasm in 1827, and an act of incorporation was secured from the General Assembly of Maryland in February, 1828. The capital stock of the Company was fixed at $1,000,000, of which the city of Baltimore subscribed $100,000. The railroad, as planned, was to extend from Baltimore to York Haven on the Susquehanna River, where connection was to be made with the Pennsylvania Canal. It was to be constructed at moderate cost and to be open for traffic within a few years.[3]

The unexpected opposition of the Pennsylvania legislature to granting the charter necessary for operation within that state, and the incorrectness of original estimates as to the expense of construction, prevented the attainment of either of these results. In 1837 nearly one-third of the road from Baltimore to York remained unfinished, and the

[1] Mayor's Message of January 17, 1842.
[2] Mayor's Message of January 15, 1844.
[3] "Laws of Maryland," 1827, ch. 72.

financial resources of the Company were completely exhausted. At this juncture recourse was had to the public treasury. Local enthusiasm for internal improvements was still keen. The state had passed the "Eight Million Loan Bill," extending large aid to most of the works then under construction, and the city had made a lavish subscription to the Baltimore and Ohio Railroad. In March, 1837, the General Assembly authorized the municipal loan of a sum not exceeding $600,000 for the completion of the Baltimore and Susquehanna Railroad. The property and income of the Company were pledged to the repayment of interest and principal, subject to the claim of the state for prior repayment of its own advances.[1] The Commissioners of Finance were promptly authorized to issue certificates of stock to the maximum amount, bearing interest at six per cent. and redeemable after 1870.[2]

A year later, with the projected terminus of the railroad almost within sight, the Company again found itself "reluctantly compelled to apply to the state and to the city for further aid to enable them to complete the enterprise in which they are engaged."[3] The city responded in February, 1838, by authorizing the Commissioners of Finance to issue city stock, bearing interest at five per cent. and redeemable in 1870, to the amount of $150,000, with a further sum of $100,000 available upon the completion of the line to York. These loans were made subject to the conditions: (1) that the Maryland legislature should agree to a similar loan, (2) that city and state should be vested with a preferred lien upon the profits of the road for the prompt payment of interest and principal upon the stock so advanced, (3) that the Company should obtain a supplement to its charter, reorganizing the directorate and giving to the city of Baltimore three additional directors to represent the

[1] "Laws of Maryland," 1836, ch. 236.

[2] Ordinance of April 10, 1837, No. 42.

[3] Report of the President and Directors of the Baltimore and Susquehanna Railroad, December 20, 1837.

new municipal subscription. As an inducement to grant the loan of $250,000 the city relinquished to the state any preference enjoyed as to the security of the loan of $600,000.[1] These several conditions were satisfied by the General Assembly in March, 1838, and a state loan of $500,000 to the Company was authorized.[2] In November, 1838, the terms of the loan of the preceding year whereby the sum of $100,000 became available only upon the completion of the line to York, were modified so as to make the whole payable in installments proceeding with the progress of the work.[3] Finally, in 1839, the city consented to the postponement of the liens and incumbrances on the property and revenues of the Company secured by the acts of 1836 and 1837,[4] in favor of similar rights in favor of the state to secure a loan of $750,000. In addition to these formal loans, the city upon several occasions extended temporary credit to the Company, as in 1838 in anticipation of a municipal loan, and in 1838 as an advance upon the state subscription made in that year.[5]

(Susquehanna Canal.). As early as 1783, the Maryland legislature had granted a charter to a corporation organized to construct a canal along the Susquehanna River from the state line to tide-water. A portion of the work was actually completed, but proved of little practical value. Repeated efforts to revive interest in the project were without success until June, 1835, when the Susquehanna Canal Company was organized under a charter obtained from the legislature of Pennsylvania. In the following year the powers

[1] Ordinance of February 24, 1838, No. 3.

[2] "Laws of Maryland," 1837, ch. 302; Ordinance of April 11, 1838, No. 13.

[3] Ordinance of November 5, 1838, No. 1.

[4] "Laws of Maryland," 1838, ch. 395; Ordinance of 1839, No. 40. The ordinance was neither approved nor vetoed by the Mayor and consequently became valid five days after its presentation.

[5] Resolutions of February 27 (No. 20) and March 10 (No. 26), 1838; Ordinances of August 28, 1839 (No. 2), and April 28, 1840 (No. 3).

of the corporation were enlarged, and in 1837 requisite authority for operation in Maryland was obtained by the incorporation of the Tide Water Canal Company. Under this legislation the property of the old Maryland Susquehanna Canal Company was acquired, and preparations were made for the construction of a canal along the west shore of the river, from Columbia to tide-water.[1]

The direct economic interest of Baltimore in the construction of such a canal had long been recognized. Most of the capital expended in the construction of the old Maryland canal had been contributed by its citizens, and a commission appointed by the Maryland legislature in 1822 to lay out and survey a route for a canal from Conewago Falls to Baltimore had recommended that it be constructed by the Mayor and City Council in their corporate capacity.[2] In 1837, with the successful revival of the project and with the public mind then predisposed in favor of any work of internal improvement, little difficulty was experienced in obtaining municipal aid. In April, 1837, the Mayor was authorized to subscribe for 7600 shares of the Susquehanna Canal Company of a par value of $50 each,[3] and the Commissioners of Finance were directed to issue city stock, bearing interest at six per cent, and redeemable after July 1, 1870, to the amount of $380,000, in payment thereof. Any premium accruing from the sale of the stock was appropriated to the creation of a sinking fund for its redemption.[4] In January, 1838, the city had paid upon its subscription the sum of $228,000, of which $152,000 was really a temporary interest-bearing loan to the Company in advance of the installments then actually called for.[5]

[1] Report of the President and Directors of the Susquehanna Canal Company, December 14, 1837. Scharf, "History of Baltimore City and County," p. 343.

[2] *Ibid.*, p. 343.

[3] Resolution of April 10, 1837, No. 84.

[4] Ordinance of April 12, 1837, No. 39.

[5] Mayor's Message of January 1, 1838.

(Minor Issues.) By 1843 the local craze for aiding works of internal improvement had passed its most acute form. Municipal credit in large amount was indeed extended to such works thereafter, but it was largely in consequence of interests assumed and obligations contracted during this period. The effect of the city's participation upon municipal finances was marked. In 1827, the funded debt of Baltimore was less than $500,000, with an annual interest charge of about $25,000; in 1844 the debt of the city had increased to $5,493,773.03, with an annual interest charge of $313,408.88.[1] Of this entire amount, $4,967,215.30 was issued in aid of works of internal improvement.[2] The remaining $526,557.73 represented unredeemed parts (1) of the debt contracted prior to 1827, (2) of the $105,000 Court House Loan authorized in 1835 and 1838 (one-half of the interest upon which was paid by Baltimore County),[3] (3) of stock issued in small amounts for various municipal improvements, and (4) of $332,000 authorized in 1838 and 1839 for the redemption of municipal scrip.[4] Of these several items, only the last requires any additional comment.

In May, 1837, for the purpose of meeting "the present wants of the community for sums of a small amount," six designated persons were appointed commissioners to prepare certificates receivable in payment of taxes and debts due to the corporation, in denominations of five, ten, twenty-five, fifty cents, one and two dollars respectively, to an aggre-

[1] Exclusive of interest upon Court House Loan. Mayor's Message of January 15, 1844.

[2] The important items were: Baltimore and Ohio Railroad Company, $3,500,000; Susquehanna Railroad Company, $950,000; Susquehanna and Tide Water Canal Company, $380,000.

[3] See above, p. 135.

[4] Issues of stock aggregating $60,000 were authorized in aid of the Baltimore and Chesapeake Steam Towing Company, as security for which a lien was taken upon the property of the Company (Ordinance of April 19, 1839, No. 37, and April 21, 1843, No. 35; Resolution of March 13, 1840, No. 55). In 1838 an issue of stock to the amount of $50,000 was authorized for the improvement of Jones' Falls (Ordinance of May 28, 1838, No. 23).

gate amount of $100,000.[1] The certificates were to be issued by the Register and the proceeds applied under the direction of the Commissioners of Finance towards the redemption of any of the loans authorized by the city. Six weeks later upon representation that "the wants of the citizens of Baltimore require a further issue of certificates for small sums of money," the total amount authorized was increased to $350,000, of which the Commissioners of Finance were empowered to loan to the Mayor and City Council of Baltimore a sum not exceeding $100,000, "to pay all expenses accruing from the consequences of the late freshet."[2] With the recovery of economic interests from the panic of 1837, the scrip flowed back into the municipal treasury. In 1838 the issue of city stock to an amount not exceeding $309,000, bearing interest at 6 per cent. and redeemable at will—increased in the following year by $23,000 redeemable in 1860[3]—was authorized for the redemption of the municipal currency as it accumulated in the hands of the Register. The further increase or reissue of the scrip in any denomination less than one dollar was prohibited. Provision was also made that within twenty days after the resumption of specie payments by the banks of the city, the Commissioners of Finance should issue $100,000 of city stock, the proceeds to be applied by the Register to the general redemption of the scrip.[4] Finally, in June, 1839, the Commissioners of Finance were authorized to substitute for the stock issued in the preceding year, sterling bonds to the same amount, payable in London and bearing interest not exceeding six per cent.

Guaranteed Debt. The funded debt of Baltimore re-

[1] Ordinances of May 16 and 20, 1837. The prescribed form of the certificate was as follows: "This certificate will be received by the Mayor and City Council of Baltimore, in payment of taxes or debts due to the corporation, for the sum of ———, pursuant to the ordinance in such case made and provided."

[2] Ordinance of June 30, 1837.

[3] Ordinance of March 22, 1839, No. 18.

[4] Ordinance of May 28, 1838, No. 23.

mained practically stationary from 1844 to 1850. Whatever slight issues may have been made for miscellaneous purposes were counterbalanced by cancellations from out the sinking fund. A detailed statement of the City Register in February, 1850, showed the aggregate existent funded debt to be $5,454,389.17.

Between 1850 and 1856 occurred a second increase of municipal indebtedness absolutely, although not relatively, greater than that occurring between 1828 and 1844. By January 30, 1857, the funded debt of the city had increased to $11,996,675 and a "guaranteed debt" of $2,000,000 had been contracted. This marked expansion resulted from two causes: (1) further extension of municipal credit in aid of works of internal improvement, (2) municipal purchase and improvement of water works.

Three railroads were projected in 1851-53, in the construction of each of which Baltimore was supposed to possess a direct economic interest: The Northwestern Railroad Company, incorporated by the Virginia legislature in 1851, proposed to construct a tributary to the Baltimore and Ohio Railroad, extending from Three Forks on the main line of that road, to Parkersburg; the Susquehanna Railroad Company, incorporated by the Pennsylvania legislature in 1851, undertook to connect the terminus of the York and Cumberland Railroad at Bridgeport with Williamsport; the Pittsburg and Connellsville Railroad Company, incorporated by the Pennsylvania legislature, offered a direct connection between Pittsburg and Cumberland, or some adjacent point on the line of the Baltimore and Ohio Railroad.[1]

Each of these projects was launched with a capitalization inadequate for the construction of the work, probably with the intention of securing additional funds by the issue of mortgage bonds. The credit of all railroad securities continued at low ebb, however, and such a method of finan-

[1] For details of Baltimore's interest in the construction of these roads, see Mayor's Message of January 19, 1852.

ciering became impossible. Recourse was accordingly had to Baltimore City for municipal aid, as the only means of preventing abandonment of the proposed works. Despite general recognition of the public utility of the railroads, the experience of Baltimore with works of internal improvement had proven so unsatisfactory, and the immediate result, in the form of an augmented tax levy to provide interest upon the city stock issued in aid thereof, had proven so disastrous, that no serious attempt was made to secure direct municipal grants or subscriptions. Instead, a method of municipal endorsement of corporate securities was proposed, whereby the city guaranteed the payment of interest and principal of definite issues of railroad securities and was secured by liens upon the property and revenue of the respective corporations. This plan of extending municipal credit without assuming any direct municipal burden was recommended by Mayor J. H. T. Jerome in 1852, and the necessary enabling legislation having been obtained from the General Assembly of Maryland,[1] the municipality undertook the guarantee of the bonds of the Northwestern Railroad Company, of the York and Cumberland Railroad Company (controlling the Susquehanna Railroad Company), and the Pittsburg and Connellsville Railroad Company, to the maximum amounts of $1,500,000, $500,000 and $1,000,000, respectively. The city reserved the right to take capital stock to the amount of bonds guaranteed, and was protected in the interval by the conveyance of a deed from each corporation, pledging its property for the payment of interest and principal of the bonds guaranteed.[2]

Practically the same period witnessed a critical turn in the affairs of the public work to which Baltimore had given largest aid and in the success of which she conceived her largest interest—the Baltimore and Ohio Railroad. Com-

[1] "Laws of Maryland," 1851, chs. 141, 146; 1852, ch. 269.

[2] Ordinances of June 14 (No. 40), June 17 (No. 44), July 22 (No. 76), 1852; June 24, 1853, No. 74; June 10, 1856, No. 29.

pleted to Wheeling on January 1, 1853, the railroad was now open for traffic over its full line from the Chesapeake to the Ohio. But this result had been attained only by straining every resource and the Company was now confronted by a financial *impasse*. A large amount of floating indebtedness had been incurred which required early discharge or funding; much remained to be done to complete permanently the road to Wheeling, and there was great need of a second track to accommodate the growing traffic of the road. In the face of urgent pressure from these several directions for large and immediately available funds, the Company found itself practically unable, with prevailing financial conditions, to negotiate its own securities.

On December 14, 1853, the municipality agreed to guarantee the payment of interest and principal of an issue of Baltimore and Ohio six per cent. bonds to the maximum amount of $5,000,000, in manner and subject to conditions closely resembling the guaranteed issues already described.[1] At the last moment, doubt seems to have been experienced as to the ability of the Company to realize upon such securities, for a fortnight later the ordinance authorizing the municipal guarantee was repealed and a direct loan of $5,000,000 to the Company was substituted therefor. The Commissioners of Finance were therein instructed to issue and sell municipal stock—in 5 per cent. sterling securities payable in London or 6 per cent. currency securities in their discretion—to the amount of $5,000,000, redeemable on January 1, 1890. The proceeds as received were to be paid to the Company, less a reservation of 10 per cent. which with its accumulations was to be invested by the Commissioners of Finance as a sinking fund and to be ultimately credited to the Company in aid of the redemption of the debt. The Company executed a full mortgage to the city of all property and revenues for the discharge of interest and principal. In order to meet the immediate exigencies of the railroad, an issue of city scrip to the amount of $1,000,000 was author-

[1] Ordinance of December 14, 1853, No. 2.

ized, fundable in the later bond issue. The entire ordinance was made conditional upon the assent of the succeeding General Assembly of Maryland.[1] This confirmation was not secured until March, 1854, and then only subject to the provision that no mortgage conveyed to the city should lessen or impair any of the liens or securities held by the state for loans theretofore made or for interest then due.[2]

The difficulty of negotiating any large amount of municipal securities, even though strengthened by municipal guarantee, which the Baltimore and Ohio Railroad had anticipated, was actually experienced by the Pittsburg and Connellsville Railroad. In June, 1856, the guaranteed bonds, before authorized, were replaced by a direct municipal loan of the same amount and secured as before.[3]

Purchase of Water Plant. The General Assembly of Maryland in 1853 authorized the municipality to issue stock to the maximum amount of $2,000,000 for the purchase of the plant of the Baltimore Water Company.[4] The transaction was completed in the summer of 1854, and $1,350,000 in six per cent. stock, redeemable in January, 1875, was given to the Baltimore Water Company in return for an absolute conveyance of property and rights.[5] During 1855 and 1856 specific ordinances authorized the issue of the remaining $650,000 for the extension and improvement of the plant.[6] By January 30, 1857, of the total amount authorized, $1,540,786.73 had been issued.[7]

The stock issued for the purchase and improvement of the water works stood on a different basis from ordinary

[1] Ordinance of December 27, 1853, No. 5; cf. Resolution of January 19, 1854, No. 1.

[2] "Laws of Maryland," 1853, ch. 34.

[3] Ordinance of June 10, 1856, No. 29.

[4] "Laws of Maryland," 1853, ch. 376.

[5] Ordinances of July 29, 1854, No. 80.

[6] Ordinances of October 19, 1855, No. 68; May 13 (No. 20), June 25 (No. 32) and July 17 (No. 40), 1856.

[7] Register's Report of January 30, 1857, p. 83.

municipal stock, being practically independent and self-sustaining. In the enabling ordinance of 1854 specific provision was made that the annual interest of the stock so issued should be defrayed from out "the net annual rents and revenues of the property." In 1856 the clause was added that all the surplus from water rentals in excess of the interest upon water stock and of the expenses of operation should be paid over to the Commissioners of Finance, who were directed to invest the proceeds as a separate fund in trust for the Water Department. The city pledged its faith to preserve this fund inviolate as a sinking fund for the redemption of water stock, and authorized a special annual levy of one-half per cent., for twenty years or less if necessary, in aid of the sinking fund so provided.[1]

Administration and Limitation.

The negotiation of loans, the issue of stock and the custody of the sinking funds was originally vested in the Mayor and the presidents of the two Branches of the City Council.[2] In June, 1818, a board of Commissioners of Finance, composed of two members of the First Branch and one member of the Second Branch of the City Council, designated by the Mayor, was constituted and charged in conjunction with the Mayor with the negotiation of certain loans.[3] A month later this board was substituted for the Mayor and the Council presidents in one of the earlier ordinances.[4] In 1833 the Board of Commissioners of Finance was definitely reorganized by substituting for the Council presidents, two persons annually elected by a joint convention of the City Council. The Mayor continued to form a third member of the board and was authorized to fill all temporary vacancies.[5]

The original statute authorizing the creation of a funded

[1] Ordinance of May 13, 1856, No. 20.
[2] Ordinances of August 15 and October 5, 1817; March 28, 1818.
[3] Ordinance of June 11, 1818.
[4] Ordinance of July 22, 1818.
[5] Ordinance of March 13, 1883, No. 16.

debt "for the purpose of promoting or effecting any great or permanent improvements" limited the maximum issue of corporate stock to one million dollars.[1] This power was further reduced in 1830 by the enactment of the provision that "the debts which the mayor and city council of Baltimore may contract on behalf of said city, shall not, in the aggregate, at any time, exceed the sum of one million of dollars, including as a part of said sum whatsoever amount the city may now owe."[2] Two years later this limitation was repealed and a somewhat vaguer provision adopted, whereby the corporation was authorized to borrow "such sum or sums of money, and to such amounts, not exceeding one million of dollars, for the use and improvement of the city of Baltimore, and of the property of the corporation, and to aid in the construction of any useful public work, authorized by any law of the state, or ordinance of the said mayor and city council, and on such terms as they, from time to time, shall deem proper and necessary."[3] This limitation remained in force, practically without change, until 1861.[4]

The statutory limitation upon the corporate borrowing power was greatly reduced by the facility with which the General Assembly authorized, by the passage of special acts, municipal loans or the use of municipal credit for specific purposes. The statutory limitations doubtless served to prevent an even more reckless issue of funded securities and in so far performed an important negative service. In practice, however, almost every important issue of city stock was based upon special legislative authority, and the actual effect of the one million authorized for general purposes was to restrict minor uses of municipal credit, as the issue of the "water stock"[5] and the negotiation of temporary loans.

[1] "Laws of Maryland," 1817, ch. 148, sect. 7.
[2] *Ibid.*, 1830, ch. 139.
[3] *Ibid.*, 1831, ch. 214.
[4] *Ibid.*, 1861, ch. 75.
[5] See below, p. 306.

Sinking Fund.

No provision for the amortization of funded indebtedness was contained either in the loan ordinances of 1817 or in the statute of 1818, formally authorizing the issue of city stock. In April, 1818, a sinking fund "for the reimbursement and redemption of the debts of the city of Baltimore" was created by the annual appropriation of $6,000 to be paid in quarterly installment from out the city treasury. The fund was vested in the care of three unsalaried "Commissioners of the Sinking Fund of the City of Baltimore," consisting, respectively, of the cashiers of the Bank of Baltimore, of the Union Bank of Maryland and of the Franklin Bank of Baltimore. Investments were limited to Baltimore City stock, United States six per cent. stock, and stock of the Bank of the United States and of any of the city banks. Preference in purchase was to be given to city stock when obtainable at or below par, but at no time could such stock be purchased above par. Purchases were to be made and transferred to the Commissioners of the Sinking Fund in trust for the corporation, and annual report as to the condition and progress of the fund was required.[1]

In practice the investments of the sinking fund appear to have been confined from the first to city stock. It became increasingly difficult, with the improvement of municipal credit and in consequence of the limitation to purchase at par or less, thus to invest increments of the funds and the proceeds of the annual appropriation. In January, 1821, the discontinuance of the appropriation and application of the fund, then containing city stock to the amount of $32,-487.17, to the direct cancellation of city indebtedness were recommended. In lieu of a sinking fund, it was suggested that unexpended annual balances should be devoted to the extinguishment of the debt. This recommendation was renewed from year to year, but was never actually adopted. The annual appropriation of $6000 continued to be made,

[1] Ordinance of April 1, 1818, No. 23.

but with irregularity both in payment and in investment.[1] As a result of this experience and influenced to a considerable degree by the amortization policy of the federal government, an important change in the maintenance of the sinking fund was made in 1826. The Commissioners of the Sinking Fund were discharged and the custody of the fund was transferred to the Commissioners of Finance. An annual appropriation of $27,000, together with the rents and proceeds of the sales of property belonging to the corporation, was made to the fund. The annual interest charge upon the total funded debt and the principal of maturing loans was paid from out this fund, and any resulting surplus was employed in the purchase of city stock. Such purchases were not, however, permitted to accumulate as a redemption fund but were promptly cancelled by an auditing committee of the City Council.[2] This was manifestly a sinking fund only in name. Certain funds were annually appropriated to the Commissioners of Finance for the payment of the annual interest charge upon the funded debt of the city, and any resulting surplus was devoted to the reduction of the principal of that debt.

The history of the sinking fund for the next twenty-five years is neither interesting nor instructive. The fund continued to receive the net income from municipal property; but as a result of the accepted policy of disposing of real estate as soon as an opportunity presented, the annual revenue from this source rarely exceeded four or five thousand dollars. With the issue of the large internal improvement loans, the practice of direct appropriations to the sinking fund was omitted. In 1850 the provision "that the

[1] Mayor's Message of January 1, 1821. On January 2, 1826, Mayor John Montgomery complained: "Up to November, 1825, that is, during a period of seven years, only the sum of $42,132.79 was paid over in cash to this fund, being the mere amount of the annual appropriation of $6,000, and that, too, without even simple interest, when the active principal of the Ordinance was founded upon compound interest."

[2] Ordinance of April 3, 1826, No. 3.

sum of six thousand dollars be annually appropriated in aid of the sinking fund" was specifically renewed, but not until the eve of the succeeding period of municipal history was it practically enforced. Despite the provisions of the ordinance of 1826 the revenues of the sinking fund were at first permitted to accumulate by re-investment. Somewhat later the policy of purchase and immediate cancellation of municipal securities was again adopted. After 1845, the annual revenues of the sinking fund were carried forward from year to year as an uninvested balance. Finally in 1855 the Commissioners of Finance were directed to invest in city stock all funds in their possession or to their credit, and the nucleus of the modern sinking fund was formed by the purchase of municipal securities to the amount of $143,279.11.[1]

The only special sinking fund created in Baltimore before 1857 was that for the amortization of the Five Million Baltimore and Ohio Loan of 1853-54. The ordinance authorizing the loan required a reservation of ten per cent. of the proceeds, to be invested by the Commissioners of Finance as a sinking fund and to be ultimately credited to the railroad in the repayment of the loan. Faithful compliance was had with this provision, and on January 1, 1857, the "Five Million Sinking Fund" aggregated $456,845.54.

Some explanation of the inadequate provision made by the city for the amortization of municipal indebtedness within the period here examined is to be found in the roseate view taken of the objects for which that indebtedness was in great part incurred. The various subscriptions, loans and guarantees made by the city in aid of works of internal improvement, were at first regarded as highly profitable investments, which instead of entailing any burden upon the municipality would at no distant date permit a reduction of those already borne. The early failure of the enterprises to realize the profits anticipated was ordinarily explained as

[1] Mayor's Message of January, 1856.

due to unexpected difficulties of construction, and the municipality delayed to provide for the amortization of the indebtedness incurred. When the final awakening came, bringing with it the certainty that the indebtedness contracted in aid of works of internal improvement would remain for many years an annual charge upon the tax-payer, public sentiment was in no mood to add to the burden of interest payment by making adequate provision for sinking funds.

Municipal Credit.

A characteristic feature of the deficit financiering of Baltimore has always been the use of par rather than discount bonds. This practice was fully established in the period from 1817 to 1856. In every loan ordinance provision was made that the stock therein authorized should be negotiated at a designated rate of interest and at not less than par. A considerable part of the funded indebtedness, contracted prior to 1857, however involved the direct issue of municipal securities to the ultimate beneficiary at par valuation and without public negotiation and sale. This was true of the more important municipal subscriptions to internal improvement projects and of the stock issued for the purchase of the water plant. The condition of municipal credit was thus represented with more or less exactness by the interest rate of the successive loans issued. In some cases difficulty was experienced in negotiating municipal securities at the designated rate of interest and limited to sale at par; in other instances a slight premium was realized and appropriated to the sinking fund. Similarly municipal securities were bought and sold by investors in the open market at terms varying widely from par valuation; but such fluctuations ordinarily corresponded to movements in general financial and industrial conditions rather than to changes in municipal credit, and exerted no considerable influence upon municipal finances.

The earliest issues of corporate stock in 1817-19 bore

interest at six per cent. These seem to have been taken easily at par, and in 1821 a refunding ordinance at five per cent. was passed. In 1827 more than three-fourths of the funded indebtedness, then aggregating about $500,000, was in the form of five per cent. stock. The original subscriptions to the Baltimore and Ohio and the Baltimore and Susquehanna Railroads were met by the issue of five per cent. stock, and no difficulty appears to have been experienced in gradually negotiating these at par. In 1831 five per cent. refunding stock, redeemable in 1845, was negotiated at an appreciable premium.[1]

The second important issue of municipal securities in aid of internal improvement projects occurred immediately before and during the crisis of 1837. It was found impracticable, in the complete prostration of financial interests, to negotiate at par a six per cent. bond. Rather than suffer the risk of amendatory legislation or the loss of delayed sale, the beneficiaries accepted the city stock in payment of subscriptions and loans, and then proceeded to realize thereupon by direct sale at discount or by indirect devices such as the issue of "stock orders." The effect upon municipal finances was as of the direct issue at par of a corresponding amount of six per cent. stock. In 1850 the total funded debt of the city was $5,454,389.17, of which $4,456,713.12 bore interest at six per cent. From 1850 to 1856 municipal credit was expressed in ability to borrow large funds at a rate slightly better than six per cent. The $5,000,000 loan to the Baltimore and Ohio Railroad was successfully negotiated, in so far as issued, in the form of six per cent. currency bonds, and the bonds accepted at par valuation by the Baltimore Water Company in payment of the water works were of the same character.[2]

[1] The price realized seems to have been 104; cf. Register's Statement of December 31, 1832.

[2] Municipal bonds were exempt from local taxation, and the state tax imposed thereon was paid by the city.

PART IV

THE FINANCES OF BALTIMORE CITY FROM 1857 TO 1897

INTRODUCTION

The modern era of the municipal history of Baltimore, regarded both in its financial and in its administrative aspects, is represented by the period from 1857 to 1897. Local trade and commerce suffered keenly from the events of the Civil War. Communication with the South was completely cut off, and western trade diverted to other channels. But the causes of prosperity were suspended, not destroyed, and as the prostrate industrial life of the territory naturally tributary to Baltimore revived, the city emerged into new importance as an industrial centre. Thenceforth economic development proceeded uninterruptedly. Population increased from 212,418 in 1860, to 267,354 in 1870, to 332,313 in 1880, to 434,439 in 1890. The residential section of the city expanded and in 1888 a large area or "belt" of suburban territory was annexed to the corporate limits. The diversification of manufactures, the growth of commerce, the extension of trade, the increase of population, the influx of foreign elements, the rise of economic standards, the development of social consciousness were the essential elements in the later economic history of Baltimore.

The year 1856 marked the complete ascendency of the Know-Nothing party in local politics. This domination was retained until the passage of the "Reform Bills" in

1860 and the correction of grave abuses in police administration and in election methods. It is an extraordinary circumstance that these years, although characterized by the use of fraud and intimidation in municipal elections to a degree almost unique in American political history, were, upon the whole, progressive in municipal policy. War and Reconstruction brought looseness and irregularity into municipal affairs. There was perhaps no actual misappropriation of corporate funds, but waste and laxity were the dominant notes. The modern phase of the political history of the city began with the success of the democratic party at the municipal election of 1867. The political complexion of the city remained unchanged from that time until 1895, when a wave of municipal reform swept the full republican ticket into office.

The administrative history of Baltimore since the Civil War confirms the experience of the ordinary American city. The affairs of the municipality were conducted as no man of ordinary sagacity would manage his own private business. There was no great municipal scandal nor palpable maladministration in detail; but the actual results attained—the burdens imposed, the benefits conferred, the obligations accumulated—were very different from those which an enlightened municipal policy would have secured. In reaching this end, political creed played no part whatever. It so happened that one party was in office during practically the entire period considered; but it may safely be asserted that no more favorable results would have followed had the opposing party been in continuous power. Neither corruption of parties nor incompetency of individual officials, but the mischief of prevailing methods and the indifference of popular sentiment were responsible for the feebleness and inefficiency of municipal government during the period considered.

CHAPTER I

MUNICIPAL ADMINISTRATION.

Corporate Powers.

The original charter of 1796, as modified by the mass of amendatory legislation enacted at successive sessions of the General Assembly, remained the basis of the municipal government of Baltimore in the period from 1857 to 1897. Certain important features of the existing administrative framework were incorporated in the Maryland Constitution of 1867, but the right of subsequent legislative control was expressly reserved to the General Assembly. From time to time; the accumulation of supplementary laws became intolerable and relief was afforded by the codification and incorporation into the statute law of Maryland of all legislation relating to Baltimore. The latest of such codifications (Article 4, "City of Baltimore," of the Public Local Laws of Maryland, 1888) together with a very considerable number of supplementary statutes thereafter enacted constituted the actual "charter" of Baltimore at the close of the period under consideration. It was described by a distinguished jurist of the city as "an incongruous medley of constitutional provisions and statutes enacted at various times and often for merely temporary purposes." To this might have been added the equally conservative statement that no city in the United States labored for so long a period under a more antiquated, cumbrous, and inadequate instrument of government.

Administrative Organization.

The actual form of the city administration underwent partial and spasmodic change by special acts of the legislature, and, within authorized limits, by ordinances of the City Council. Few, if any, of these modifications touched the essential features of the municipal government. Under the vigorous administration of Mayor Thomas Swann, the Board of Fire Commissioners was organized in 1858, and the Park Board in 1860. The political excesses of the Know-Nothing rule in Baltimore resulted in the transfer of control of the local police force from the city to a state Board of Police Commissioners in 1860. The Harbor Board was established in 1876, and the Mayor was made a member, *ex-officio*, of all important municipal boards in 1888. Other administrative charges are noted in succeeding pages in connection with the fiscal activity of the particular branch of municipal service affected.

Financial Machinery.

In 1857 the office of Comptroller was established for the examination, audit and settlement of all accounts in which the corporation was concerned either as debtor or creditor, a duty before performed by the Register. The new official was appointed biennially by the Mayor, subject to the confirmation of the City Council. In 1877 vouchers for all departmental expenditures were audited, adjusted and filed in the Comptroller's department, and paid by the City Register upon the order of the Comptroller. The money received by each department was not, as theretofore, retained and disbursed in the payment of bills incurred, but was regularly reported in amount, as required, to the Comptroller, who issued his warrant to the City Register to receive the specific sums.[1]

By the terms of the ordinance of 1857 creating the office of Comptroller, the office of Auditor was abolished and the actual incumbent retained only until March 1, 1858, for

[1] Resolution of February 14, 1877, No. 32; Report of City Comptroller of January 1, 1878.

completing the collection of tax arrears.[1] The office however continued in formal existence for several years longer, but its duties were actually performed by the Comptroller and the Collector. After 1862 taxes in arrears as well as those for the current year were collected by the Collector.

In 1872 the title of Board of Commissioners of Finance was changed to that of Department of Finance, and the income from all real estate and corporate securities belonging to the city, and the proceeds of all taxes levied for sinking fund purposes were specifically appropriated to the Department for the amortization of the funded debt.[2] Despite the repeated recommendations of the Comptroller, the auditing power of that official was never extended so as to include the fiscal operations of the Department of Finance.[3] The fiscal year of the corporation corresponded with the secular year, save for a brief period from 1873 to 1877, during which municipal accounting was made to terminate on October 31 of each year.

The Budget.

The essential form of the municipal budget and the general course of budgetary procedure had been definitely established in Baltimore before 1856 and underwent no important modification thereafter. To recapitulate what has been already stated elsewhere:[4] at the close of each fiscal year, detailed estimates of expenditures for the ensuing twelvemonth were sent by the heads of the several municipal departments to the City Register, who summarized them and added thereto the existing unpaid claims against the city ("floating debt"). This aggregate represented merely the direct charges upon the municipal treasury, and did not

[1] See below, p. 270.
[2] Ordinance of March 27, 1872, No. 26.
[3] Reports of City Comptroller of November 1, 1871; November 1, 1872; November 1, 1875.
[4] See above, p. 98.

include such indirect costs as that involved in the operation of water-supply, and in the maintenance of the parks, for which purposes specific sources of revenue were appropriated. The City Register also prepared a memorandum of estimated receipts from sources other than current taxation. These two summaries were submitted to the City Council and referred to the joint Ways and Means Committee, as were also the Appeal Tax Court's estimate of the taxable basis for the ensuing year and the City Collector's estimate of the proportion of taxes collectible within the year. With these data as a basis, the municipal budget was determined.

The budget, as presented to the City Council, consisted of a general appropriation bill and a series of specific tax levies aggregating the total municipal tax rate. The mode of submission and enactment was that of an ordinary municipal ordinance; but in actual practice the bills presented by the Ways and Means Committee were commonly adopted by the City Council without change. The general appropriation bill was however often supplemented in the interval between the adoption of the budget and the close of the fiscal year by the passage of special appropriation bills to be met from out of unappropriated funds in the city treasury or in some other extraordinary manner. This vicious practice was largely responsible for the periodic accumulation of floating indebtedness and for other defects in local finances.[1] The survival of the practice of levying distinct rates, nominally for the different items of municipal expenditure, instead of one aggregate rate to provide the total amount required by direct taxation, formed a curious archaism in the budgetary procedure of Baltimore. The proceeds of the several rates were paid into the municipal treasury, subject to ordinary appropriation, and were never segregated as distinct funds. Whatever practical significance the practice may have originally possessed was early

[1] See below, p. 330.

lost, and its later effect was simply to bewilder the tax-payer and to complicate the bookkeeping of the Collector's department.[1]

[1] The system of separate levy ordinance was finally abandoned in 1899, and a single ordinance imposed the aggregate tax rate. But provision was made that receipts should be "apportioned" as though imposed in the form of separate levies of designated amount.

An interesting suggestion has been made to me by a distinguished lawyer of Baltimore, to the effect that the city might perhaps have been prevented by legal process from devoting the proceeds of a special tax levy to any purpose other than that prescribed in the levy ordinance. The point, which might also be raised in connection with the "apportionment" of the 1899 levy, has never, I believe, been submitted to judicial determination.

CHAPTER II

MUNICIPAL EXPENDITURE.

The advent of the modern era in the administrative and financial history of Baltimore was signalized by a sharp increase in municipal expenditure. A metropolitan police force, a paid fire department, a municipal water service, a series of public parks, and a growing public school system introduced new elements of importance into the municipal budget and entailed a progressive increase in municipal expenditure. The net disbursements of the city in 1860 were more than three times as great as in 1850 and nearly twice as great in 1870 as in 1860. This rapid rate of increase terminated in 1870, and in the succeeding decade municipal expenditures remained practically uniform. After 1880 the growth in expenditure was continuous and large in absolute amount; but the rate of increase was less than in the period before 1870.

The explanation of this relatively slower growth in the ordinary expenses of the city government after 1870 is to be found in the increasing rigidity of municipal revenue. The need and the desire for progressively increasing expenditure were present throughout the subsequent twenty-five years—repeatedly to the point of administrative embarrassment. But with the slow increase in the taxable basis and the inappreciable growth in revenues from sources other than direct taxation, the only method of defraying larger municipal disbursements was by raising the rate of the general property tax. This soon attained burdensome proportions and further additions meant to imperil the success of the party in power at the ensuing municipal election. The periodic accumulation and funding of floating indebtedness afforded some margin for increased expenditure, but the practise was early discredited. In consequence the ordinary rule of public finance was reversed, and revenues limited expenditures instead of expenditures determining revenue.

After 1886 the occasion for largely increased expenditure for street paving, school houses, water sewers and bridges became imperative and resort was had to funded loans.[1] Increased requirements in other branches of municipal service were met by a steady rise in the rate of property taxation to the oppressive figure levied at the close of the period.

Streets and Roadways.

The care of the city's roadways, including the paving and repaving of streets, the erection and repair of bridges and the construction of sewers, remained vested in the hands of the City Commissioner. Similarly, the functions of street cleaning and street reconstruction continued entrusted to distinct and independent municipal officials. In 1856 the "City Commissioner's Office" consisted of a City Commissioner, an Assistant City Commissioner and a varied subordinate force. This organization was replaced in 1861 upon the recommendation of Mayor George William Brown by the revival of the old composite board of three City Commissioners and Port Wardens.[2] The change was found to work neither efficiently nor economically, and in 1863 the offices of City Commissioner and Assistant City Commissioner were revived.[3] The number of Assistant City Commissioners was increased to three in 1875, and the tenure of both City Commissioners and Assistant City Commissioner was changed, with that of other city officers, from one to two years in 1887.[4]

[1] See below, p. 320.

[2] Message of January 7, 1861, p. 5; Ordinance of February 28, 1861, No. 3.

[3] Mayor's Message of January 8, 1863, p. 8; Ordinance of February 14, 1863, No. 6.

[4] Ordinances of June 10, 1875, No. 112; February 25, 1887, No. 4.

The radical reorganization of the City Commissioner's department was repeatedly urged by Mayor F. C. Latrobe[1] between 1880 and 1892, but without effect. The plan most frequently recommended was the displacement of the City Commissioner by an unsalaried board of from three to six commissioners, acting essentially as a Board of Public Works. The detailed operations of the department were to be in charge of a skilled engineer, appointed by the board and subject to its control and direction. In 1895 the biennial appointment of a City Commissioner and three Assistant City Commissioners was confirmed. Specific provision was made that the Assistant Commissioners should be under the direction of the head of the department, and that the participation of an official in any business or pursuit other than that appertaining to his formal duties should be deemed sufficient cause for removal by the Mayor.[2] This ordinance resulted in a change of the personnel of the department and in an increase of salaries, but left its organization otherwise unaffected.

Street Paving and Repair. The paving and repair of streets, which formed the most important activity of the City Commissioner after 1856, included at least three functions closely related in character but more or less distinct in fiscal treatment: (1) paving and grading of unpaved streets; (2) partial repair of paved streets; (3) repaving of streets already paved.

(1) Unpaved streets were graded and paved by the City Commissioner upon the application of the owners of a major part of the ground binding thereon, or upon the passage of a specific enabling ordinance. The total expenditure—including the cost of collection but not that of paving cross streets, which was paid by the city—was levied as a special assessment upon abutting property in proportion to frontage. The requirement that pavements or footways must

[1] Thus see Mayor's Messages of January 1, 1881, and January 1, 1892.

[2] Ordinance of May 17, 1895, No. 71.

be laid and kept in repair by the owners of fronting property underwent no important change. The contract system, already in vogue for the repaving and repair of streets, was in 1859 extended to the grading and paving of unpaved streets.[1] As population increased and residential areas were extended to the corporate limits, the number of unpaved streets was rapidly reduced and municipal expenditure for initial paving was largely limited to that made necessary by street reconstruction. Streets were often opened, graded and paved, and then deeded to the city by owners of large suburban areas, in the hope of hastening the development of the surrounding district.[2]

(2) The statute of 1833 authorized the repaving of any street of the city upon the application of the owners of two-thirds of the abutting property. Two-thirds of the expenditure involved was defrayed by special assessment—the remainder by municipal appropriation.[3] This procedure continued until 1874, when the requisite condition was reduced to the application of the owners of one-half, instead of two-thirds of the abutting property.[4] In the absence of such application the improvement might be effected by the passage of a specific enabling ordinance. In 1874 the city began slowly to repave its principal thoroughfares with Belgian blocks, distributing the cost as above.

But even after the introduction of Belgian block paving and recognition of its superiority, the larger part of local repaving continued to be done in cobblestones. Between 1874 and 1881, 5,405,394 square feet of cobblestones were laid and only 87,628 square yards of Belgian blocks.[5] The general character of the work done was graphically described by Mayor F. C. Latrobe in 1881, as "the very poorest of its kind." The fixity of real estate values and

[1] Ordinance of March 23, 1859, No. 34.

[2] The careless acceptance of such gifts by the city has appreciably contributed to the irregularity of its suburban thoroughfares.

[3] See above, p. 103.

[4] Ordinance of June 4, 1874, No. 44.

[5] Report of City Commissioner, January 1, 1878.

the burden of direct taxation discouraged any general employment of the special assessment for the costly replacement of cobblestones by modern pavements. The use of short term funded loans of moderate amount for this purpose was recommended by the city executives in 1876 and in 1879. This dangerous procedure was first employed in 1880 in the form of a "paving loan" of $500,000, and thereafter formed the characteristic feature of modern repaving. In 1888 the issue of $1,000,000 city stock, redeemable in 1928, and in 1892 the issue of $1,600,000, redeemable in 1940, were authorized for this purpose. The cost of repaving important streets with asphalt blocks after 1888 was paid from out the proceeds of these loans.

(3) Street repair, like street paving and repaving, was originally done by contract through the agency and under the supervision of the City Commissioner. The actual expenditure of the city for this purpose continued in excess of the amount annually appropriated, yet the condition of the streets remained materially unimproved. In 1858 the City Commissioner himself described them as "in worse condition than they have been for many years; in many places almost, if not entirely, impassable."[1] In 1865 the repair of streets by the direct employment of day labor, instead of by contract was strongly recommended.[2] The change was actually made several years later, and the day labor system continued thereafter in force.

No form of municipal expenditure was so sharply criticised by reform sentiment in Baltimore as that involved in the paving and repair of streets. There were occasional charges of outright corruption and criminal waste, and a disposition was widespread to regard municipal expenditure for this purpose as throughout unfavorably disproportionate to the improvement effected. The organization of the City Commissioner's department and the conditions of labor employment there prevailing were in largest part re-

[1] Report of City Commissioner, January 1, 1858, p. 140.
[2] Report of City Commissioner, January 1, 1865, p. 164.

sponsible for this result.[1] There was never a pretense at conducting the affairs of the department upon any other than a political basis of the cheapest sort. The inevitable effect of these influences was however intensified by the repeated tearing up of streets and their wretched replacement by corporations and individuals—the former engaged in laying gas-mains, the latter in placing drain-pipes. Within a limited period, Baltimore was afflicted with five successive gas companies, each of which tore up the most important thoroughfares of the city and replaced them in a manner requiring early repair by the city. Similarly a mere application to the City Commissioner secured a license to lay drain-pipes from private premises to a city water sewer.[2]

Sewers. At the beginning of the period here considered, Baltimore was entirely dependent upon surface drainage for the disposition of its sewerage. A few miles of underground drains had been laid to overcome grades in the surface, but these were built in the crudest manner and utterly without system.[3] The Board of Health, endeavoring in 1856 to learn something of the disposition of the city's sewage, found that "there is not now, and apparently there never has been, a plat of the sewers prepared or recorded in this office. No one can now tell the forms, sizes, grades of descent, connections nor directions of the sewers."[4]

Attention appears to have been directed to the inadequacy of the existing system, less because of its effect upon the health and sanitary condition of the city than because of the loss and inconvenience suffered from the periodic flooding

[1] All laborers employed by the city were required to be registered voters and to receive a minimum wage of $1.66⅔ for an eight-hour working day.

[2] In many cases a special resolution of the City Council permitted private drains to be laid even without the payment of the nominal fee otherwise charged.

[3] See above, page 105.

[4] Report of Board of Health, January 1, 1857. It is said that even at the present time the city is without accurate knowledge relating to certain of its important storm-water sewers.

of houses and cellars through the inability of gutters and drains to carry off the volume of storm water. In 1859 at the instance of Mayor Thomas Swann a commission of three persons was appointed "to report upon a full, comprehensive and adequate system of underground drainage, as well as how our present sewers, tunnels and culverts can be altered and adapted to that end; what new works are requisite, as well as the cost thereof."[1] Certain cities were visited, expert opinion was secured and in 1862 a report was presented recommending the construction of additional drains for the reception of house drainage and surface water. The additional sewers recommended aggregated 5⅞ miles and involved an estimated expenditure of $91,491.[2] The report of the commission was approved by a joint committee of the City Council, who recommended the levy of a special assessment on property to the amount of the benefit accruing from the construction of the sewers and the appropriation of any necessary balance from out the city treasury.[3]

The stirring events of the Civil War diverted attention from the recommendations of the commission and left the situation essentially unchanged until several years after the actual cessation of hostilities. Preparation was made in 1868, in accordance with a special enabling act of the legislature,[4] for an improvement of the sewage methods of the city in much the manner recommended by the commission of 1859. The Commissioners for Opening Streets and the City Commissioner were constituted a board of "commissioners for the construction of sewers," and were authorized, whenever directed by ordinance of the City Council, to construct, open, enlarge or straighten any sewer, to effect the improvement, to award damages and to levy a special

[1] Resolution of September 26, 1859, No. 248.

[2] See Report of Sewerage Commission in "Municipal Reports," 1862, pp. 615-631.

[3] "Municipal Reports," 1862, pp. 633-635.

[4] "Laws of Maryland," 1868, ch. 1.

assessment upon the property benefited. Any resulting deficit was to be met by direct municipal appropriation.[1]

In the decade from 1869 to 1879 a limited number of sewers or storm-water drains were constructed in the manner provided by this ordinance. The work remained, nominally, vested in the composite board of commissioners for the construction of sewers; but practically, construction as well as repair were put in the charge of the City Commissioner.[2] After 1879 successive Boards of Health and city executives called attention in forcible terms to the evil effects of cesspools and surface drainage upon public health and municipal development. Under Mayor Ferdinand C. Latrobe in 1881 a civil engineer was appointed by a joint resolution of the City Council to examine and report upon the question of establishing a general system of sewerage in the city. A report was made to the same Council, but, although endorsed by the committee to which it was referred, it resulted in no practical action.

The introduction of the Gunpowder water-supply in 1881, by stimulating the use of house fixtures, resulted in an enormous increase in the domestic consumption of water and a consequent strain upon the primitive methods in vogue for the disposition of surface water and general sewage. This recurring emergency, accented by "the growth of the city, the extension of its paved streets, and the covering of its vacant lots with continuous rows of houses" was met, to the minimum degree necessary, by three devices: (1) the construction and extension of additional so-called sewers—in reality mere storm-water drains; (2) connection of private cesspools with the public storm-drains for the purpose of getting rid of the overflow—a privilege "at first refused absolutely, then granted conditionally, and later accorded freely, then again resolutely refused, and at present once more permitted under circumstances and conditions appealing to the favorable judgment of the authori-

[1] Ordinance of May 7, 1868, No. 52.
[2] Cf. Report of City Commissioner, November 1, 1875.

ties"; (3) construction of private drains by corporations and persons of wealth from their premises to the nearest water course, where storm-water drains have not been available.

The construction and extension of water-drains after 1879 together with the maintenance and repair of those already in existence entailed a large municipal expenditure. In 1897 the aggregate length of the storm-drains was estimated at some 33 miles, constructed at a cost of not far from $4,000,000.[1] This money was provided generally by the issue of funded loans. For the construction of the important Harford Run Sewer, loans of $250,000 in 1879 and $350,000 in 1884 were authorized. The "Five Million Loan" of 1888 included $1,750,000 for the construction of storm sewers and the "Six Million Loan" of 1892 provided for an expenditure of $1,000,000 for the same purpose.[2] By January 1, 1897 practically the entire amount authorized by these loans had been expended.

While costly provision was thus being made for mere surface drainage, attention was from time to time directed to the inevitable inadequacy of such expenditures and to the urgent necessity for some general sewerage system.[3] This agitation culminated in 1893, when an unsalaried commission of three persons was appointed "to examine into the necessity for a more perfect system of sewerage for the city of Baltimore."[4] After an exhaustive investigation extending over a period of more than four years, the commission under the chairmanship of Mr. Mendes Cohen, a representative citizen and a distinguished engineer of Baltimore, presented a notable report upon which the future sewerage system of Baltimore will doubtless be based. It recommended the separate collection and separate disposition of storm-water and domestic sewage. Storm-water

[1] "Report of Sewerage Commission," 1897, p. 10.

[2] See below, pp. 320-321.

[3] Mayor's Messages of January 1, 1884, p. 61; January 31, 1887, p. 57; January, 1891, p. 59.

[4] Resolution of May 25, 1893, No. 189.

should pass by way of the existing drains and natural watercourses to the river and harbor as now. Domestic sewage should be collected by a system of high level and low level intercepting sewers and disposed of by a continuous discharge into Chesapeake Bay. An alternative method of disposal was offered in the form of filtration upon lands in Anne Arundel County. The dilution method was recommended by the commission as serving practically the same purposes, while its final cost of completion was estimated as less than one-half and its annual cost of working about one-third as much as the other.[1]

Bridges. With the growth of the city's traffic and the spread of population to the west and northwest, the more or less temporary bridges before in use became inadequate and in absolute need of continual repair, necessitating an annual appropriation to the City Commissioner for mere maintenance.

Special provision was made from time to time for the construction of new bridges. The important improvement of Jones' Falls, projected in 1870 and noticed elsewhere,[2] involved the construction of permanent structures across certain of the most important thoroughfares of the city.[3] The large expenditures therein entailed were defrayed from out the proceeds of the Jones' Falls improvement loans, and the work was performed under the direction of the special Jones' Falls Commission. The "Five Million Loan" of 1888 and the "Six Million Loan" of 1892 authorized extraordinary expenditures for bridge construction of $250,000 and $600,000, respectively.

[1] The approximate cost for the first installation of the filtration project (to which public opinion seems to incline) is about $3,250,000. For the completion of the system so as to serve the needs of a population of one million, the estimated cost is about $6,700,000 additional. These figures do not include the cost of the reticulation system which it is proposed to defray by the levy of a special assessment upon property benefited.

[2] See below, p. 319.

[3] Mayors' Messages of January 1, 1880, p. 22; January 1, 1881, p. 42.

STREET RECONSTRUCTION.

For several years after 1856, the important function of street reconstruction remained under the control of the Board of Commissioners for Opening Streets, without important change in existing procedure.[1] In 1861, Mayor George William Brown recommended the abolition of the board and the transfer of its duties to the Appeal Tax Court, which was deemed "peculiarly fitted to discharge them by reason of the intimate acquaintance of the judges of that court with the value of property in the city."[2] This recommendation was promptly adopted and during the next five years the powers before vested in the commissioners were exercised by the Appeal Tax Court. A per diem compensation, which had been one of the objectionable features of the old system, continued to be assessed as part of the expenses of the particular improvement; but the proceeds were paid into the city treasury and the members of the Appeal Tax Court received definite salaries.[3]

In 1866 upon the representation of the judges of the Appeal Tax Court that the combined functions of street reconstruction and tax assessment were more than could be properly performed by a single agency, the former board of three Commissioners for Opening Streets was revived and again entrusted with the extension and reconstruction of the city's streets.[4] A more important change effected by the same ordinance was in regard to the method of defraying the cost of the reconstruction. The entire cost involved in any improvement, including all damages awarded, had theretofore been levied as a special assessment upon the property-owners benefited. Latterly with the growth in the city's density and the increase in the value of its real estate,

[1] Thus see Ordinance of April 14, 1857, No. 30.

[2] Message of January 7, 1861, p. 5.

[3] Ordinance of February 28, 1861, No. 4.

[4] Ordinance of April 3, 1866, No. 26. The tenure of office of the Commissioners was increased from one to three years in 1876 (Ordinance of May 31, 1876, No. 100) and reduced to two years in 1887 (Ordinance of February 25, 1887, No. 4).

this procedure had entailed an increasing burden upon property-owners, and had stimulated the practise of securing street reconstructions for speculative purposes. The ordinance of 1866 provided that the special assessment should be levied only to the amount of the estimated benefit, and that any deficit resulting from the greater cost of the improvement should be paid by direct municipal appropriation.[1] No essential change was made in the mode of effecting the extension or reconstruction. Whenever directed by specific municipal ordinance, the Commissioners proceeded after due public notice to effect the improvement, and to award damages and to assess benefits in the manner hereinafter described.[2]

As long as the benefiting property-owners were assessed to the gross cost of the improvement, street reconstruction involved no considerable direct municipal outlay. This state of affairs underwent radical change in 1866 with the adoption of the principle of levying the special assessment only to the amount of estimated benefit and of supplying the remainder by municipal appropriation. In 1869 a levy to defray the cost of street reconstruction appeared for the first time in the tax rate, and thereafter annual appropriations of considerable amount were made for this purpose. In 1871 it was proposed to limit the liability of the city to one-third of the expenditures incurred in street reconstruction,[3] and in 1880 the revival of the earlier form of special assessment was recommended;[4] but neither plan was adopted. A more successful suggestion was made in 1884, to the effect that the cost of important reconstructions be defrayed from out the proceeds of funded loans instead of out of current revenues.[5] The "Five Million Loan" of 1882 and the "Six Million Loan" of 1892 authorized expenditures of $1,200,-

[1] That is to say, "should be assessed upon the city."
[2] See below, p. 287.
[3] Report of City Comptroller, January 1, 1871, p. 131.
[4] Mayor's Message of January 1, 1880, p. 33.
[5] Mayor's Message of January 1, 1884, p. 66.

000 and $300,000, respectively, for this purpose. Certain of the most expensive street reconstructions in succeeding years were made possible by the funds thus provided.

Street Cleaning.

Despite urban growth, the functions of street-cleaning and scavenging remained under the nominal control of the Board of Health. The work was actually directed by five Superintendents of Streets, appointed by the Mayor, and charged with the care of designated sections of the city. The day labor system was employed, and each Superintendent appointed his own force. There was neither unification nor responsibility in the system.

In 1872, with a view to securing some general superintendence of the work, the Assistant Commissioner of Health was put in control of the department of street-cleaning "in all matters that relate to the operations and efficiency of the same, its economy in the employment of labor and the disbursement of money for such service." He was required not only to inspect and direct the work of the Superintendents, but to examine their weekly reports and to audit their pay-rolls.[1] In 1882 Mayor F. C. Latrobe urged that the functions of street-cleaning and scavenging be entirely withdrawn from the Board of Health and be vested in a special department in charge of a "commissioner of street-cleaning."[2] The letter rather than the spirit of this recommendation was incorporated in an ordinance of 1882. Provision was therein made for the annual appointment by the Mayor of a Commissioner of Street-cleaning who was vested with "exclusive charge of the cleaning of the public streets, lanes and alleys, and of the collection and removal of ashes, garbage, street and household refuse, in the city of Baltimore." Specifically, the powers before exercised by the Health Officers with respect to the operations and

[1] Ordinance of February 28, 1872, No. 20.
[2] Message of January 23, 1882, p. 16.

conduct of the Superintendents of Streets were transferred to the Commissioner for Cleaning Streets. The new official was also authorized to change the dividing lines of the six street-cleaning districts of the city, subject to the approval of the Mayor.[1] The reorganization resulting from this ordinance was nominal rather than real. An independent department was created, but the only real change involved was that the general superintendence before exercised by the Assistant Commissioner of Health was thereafter vested in the Commissioner of Street-cleaning. There was no centralization of responsibility in the relation of the Commissioner to the district Superintendents of Streets. These subordinate officials were appointed by the Mayor and in turn appointed their laboring force, entirely independent of the Commissioner. In other words the administrative head of the department, nominally responsible for its efficiency, was utterly without any direct influence in the selection and regulation of its personnel.

Between 1882 and 1896 no single feature of the city administration was so confessedly a failure and in such urgent need of reorganization as the street-cleaning department. That a branch of municipal service, requiring an expenditure of a quarter of a million dollars annually, should have been organized and continued in operation virtually without an executive head, was properly described as "simply incomprehensible to the minds of unsophisticated citizens."[2] In 1887 Mayor James Hodges declared that "the people are inexpressibly aggravated at this condition of things in that department and demand reorganization without delay."[3] Five years later, Mayor F. C. Latrobe repeated "The public will never be satisfied until this change is made. It is common sense that the man who is

[1] Ordinance of February 21, 1882, No. 6. The additional district had been created and a corresponding Superintendent appointed in 1881 (Ordinance of March 1, 1881, No. 19).

[2] Mayor's Message of January 31, 1887, pp. 32-33.

[3] *Ibid.*, p. 33.

responsible should have full power over every man in his department."[1] Practically every Mayor's message prepared during this period contained a more or less forcible recommendation for the reorganization of the department. Yet despite this apparent unanimity in intelligent sentiment, not the slightest essential change was made. The street-cleaning department continued in its primitive and inefficient organization until the advent of the new city charter.[2]

Inefficiency in organization resulted in costliness of maintenance. During the greater part of the period here considered, the street-cleaning department was relatively one of the most expensive branches of municipal service. The topography and natural environment of Baltimore were potent allies; yet at no time were the results attained commensurate with the money expended. The tenacity with which this notoriously inefficient organization was retained is explicable in the peculiar facilities it afforded for the dispensation of municipal patronage to the politically deserving.[3] Striking evidence of this was afforded in 1890 when a proposition was submitted to the city by an association of responsible citizens to engage to clean the streets of the city for a period of five years for the sum of $175,000 per annum, or about $110,000 less than was expended by the city for this purpose in 1890. Mayor F. C. Latrobe strongly advised that consideration be given this proposition, or least the adoption of the contract system; but both the proposition and the recommendation were ignored by the City Council.[4]

[1] Mayor's Message of January 1, 1892, pp. 61-62.

[2] Not until 1892 were sweeping machines and sprinklers employed, and then only for purposes of experiment; see Mayor's Message of January 1, 1893, p. 47.

[3] Not only in the employment of laborers, but as a result of the sub-contract system whereby one person undertook to supply any number of carts and drivers at the rate of $18 per week, as fixed by municipal ordinance, and made his own terms with his sub-employees.

[4] Mayor's Message of January 26, 1891, pp. 47-48.

POLICE.

The reorganization of the local police force, authorized by the legislature in 1853, actually took place under Mayor Thomas Swann's administration in 1857.[1] The existing night watch and day constabulary were then consolidated in a general police force under the control of a marshal annually appointed, as were all other members of the department, by the Mayor. The city was divided into four police districts, and provision was made for a patrol force of three hundred and fifty men. This reorganization was practically coincident with the rise and growth of the American or Know-Nothing party in Baltimore. The new police force, at first an important influence in repressing riot and disorder, was rapidly recruited from the Know-Nothing clubs, and ultimately became the ally and abettor of political violence and outrage.[2]

The reform party gained dominance in Maryland in 1860, and one of their early acts was to transfer the control of the police department of Baltimore City from the municipal authorities to the state legislature. To this end provision was made for the election by the General Assembly of a Board of Police Commissioners, composed of four citizens of Baltimore, serving a term of four years. One Commissioner retired every second year, and the Mayor of the city constituted a fifth member *ex-officio*. The new Board was authorized to organize and equip a metropolitan police force and to assume full control thereof. The Commissioners were directed to submit annually to the corporation an estimate of the sum of money necessary for the discharge of the duties imposed upon them, and the Mayor

[1] Ordinance of January 1, 1857, No. 4; authorized by "Laws of Maryland," 1853, ch. 46.

[2] The nature and results of this vicious alliance are described in detail in an excellent monograph upon "The History of the Know-Nothing Party in Maryland," by Mr. L. F. Schmeckebier, in the *Johns Hopkins University Studies in Historical and Political Science*, Seventeenth Series, Nos. III-IV.

and City Council were required to levy this amount upon the assessable property of the city. In default of such action, the Police Commissioners were authorized to issue municipal scrip bearing interest at six per cent. and payable at not more than twelve months after date.[1] The Board was required to make periodic reports of its proceedings and disbursements to the General Assembly. The first Police Commissioners were named in the statute, and the legality of the reorganization having been upheld by the courts, the new system went into effect on May 1, 1861. During 1861-62 the police force of the city was under the control of the federal authorities, and when the state again assumed control in 1862, it was under a new police law passed in that year by a legislature in full sympathy with the federal government. The Board of Police was reduced to two commissioners, with the Mayor *ex-officio*, and an oath of allegiance to the federal government was prescribed as a preliminary qualification.[2] After the cessation of direct federal interference with the affairs of the state in 1867, the Board of Police Commissioners was reconstituted so as to consist of three persons, elected by the General Assembly for a term of four years. The Commissioners were required to be residents of Baltimore for three years, and of Maryland for five years preceding the day of their election. The financial powers of the Board were practically as provided in the reorganization of 1860.[3] In 1874 the term of office of the Police Commissioners was increased to six years, so arranged that one member retired biennially.[4]

In 1867 the surviving remnant of local control over the police force vanished with the omission of the provision making the Mayor *ex-officio* a member of the Board of Police Commissioners. In the succeeding period the entire independence of the police force from municipal control formed a local grievance and complaint. The propriety of

[1] "Laws of Maryland," 1860, ch. 7.
[2] *Ibid.*, 1861-62, ch. 131.
[3] *Ibid.*, 1867, ch. 367.
[4] *Ibid.*, 1874, ch. 2.

the demand that "the City, which pays all the bills, should have a representative in the Board which spends the money"[1] was represented by successive city executives, and repeated petitions and drafts of bills were vainly submitted to the legislature to remedy this condition of affairs.[2] State control of the municipal police force was aggravated by the periodic interference of the state legislature in the internal affairs of the department, as by the enactment of mandatory legislation for an increase of salaries or an addition to the number of patrolmen.[3] It was often contended, with probable correctness, that the reluctance of the legislature to relinquish control of the city police force was due less to any uneasiness as to the possible recurrence of the conditions prevailing in the Know-Nothing period, than to the loss of the degree of patronage which state control ensured to the county members.

LIGHTING.

For some years before 1856, illuminating gas had been generally introduced in Baltimore for public lighting, and the municipality had become practically dependent upon private enterprise for this service. The project of municipal gas works was renewed from time to time thereafter, but rather as an expression of personal sentiment or for the purpose of influencing the policy of the private corporation than with a view to any practical outcome.[4]

[1] Moreover, "All revenue received by the department from fines, etc., instead of being paid into the City Treasury, as is that from every other department, goes into what is called the reserve fund of the Board, and is used as the Board thinks proper in building station-houses, etc. It purchases its own stationery, instead of obtaining it, as do all other City departments, through the City Librarian" (Mayor's Message of January 1, 1892, p. 84).

[2] Mayors' Messages of January 10, 1876, p. 75; January 21, 1878, p. 7; January 23, 1882, p. 43; January 31, 1887, p. 84; January 1, 1892, pp. 84-86; Resolution of January 31, 1882, No. 19.

[3] Thus see Resolution of March 15, 1872, No. 96; Message of January 27, 1890, p. 47.

[4] Thus see Message of Mayor Robert T. Banks, January 21, 1868, p. 18, and Resolution of May 21, 1877, No. 58.

But even this policy of dependence upon private activity was not consistently pursued. The city should have recognized the monopolistic character of gas-supply as an industry of service, and sought to make the best of the situation by allowing the original company the exclusive right of supply in return for important concessions in price and in franchise payment. Instead of this, rival company after company was encouraged and given unlimited use of streets and free right of operation. The persistent effort of the municipality was to secure a competitive price for public and private consumers in an industry which both practical experience and theoretical analysis had shown to be essentially non-competitive and monopolistic. The course of events was in every case the same: the projection of a "competing" gas company, a rate war in which the city ordinarily failed, because of an existing contract, to secure even temporary gain, and finally, consolidation with its incidents of increased capitalization and abandonment of the duplicated plant.[1] Within the period here examined, occurred no less than five such successive attempts at competition, of which several were mere speculative raids and of which none remained for more than a brief period in independent existence.

The effect of this short-sighted policy upon the municipal treasury was direct and important. Independent of the failure to secure any return for the use of the city's streets and of the positive loss entailed by the tearing up of the paved thoroughfares—the city was throughout forced to pay more for its gas than would otherwise have been the case, because of the apparent necessity the gas company was under to provide interest and dividends for a capitalization

[1] The attitude of the municipality towards these successive combinations is indicated in a resolution of March 10, 1880 (No. 30), wherein the General Assembly was "respectfully and most earnestly petitioned to investigate the said combination or conspiracy of said gas companies, and to use its power to prevent the oppression of the people of Baltimore that would result therefrom."

hopelessly swollen and represented in great part by duplicate, rusting plants. It is however improbable that the price actually paid by the city for its lighting during this period represented a minimum charge even under existing conditions. Originally the city paid a specific sum for each public light, independent of the amount of gas consumed. In 1871 a contract for five years was made at the rate of $2.50 per thousand feet.[1] This price was reduced, probably in 1879, to $2.25, and in 1880, to $1.85. In the latter year a five years' contract was made at the rate of $1.85, with the result that during a considerable part of this period the city actually paid a higher rate than private consumers.[2] After a brief rate war between rival companies, the maximum price of gas was fixed by legislative statute in 1888 at $1.25,[3] after which time no further contracts were made and the relation of the city to the gas company was precisely that of a private consumer.

The service rendered by the gas company was confined to the extension of plant and the supply of gas. Street lamps were erected at public expense and the whole cost of lamplighting devolved upon the municipality. This latter function was vested in 1857 in a body of Superintendents of Lamps and a large number of lamplighters, all of whom were appointed by the Mayor.[4] In 1878 general superintendence of street lighting was entrusted to a General Superintendent of Lamps and Inspector and Sealer of Gas Meters.[5] By a characteristic anomaly this official, although nominally responsible for the efficiency of the department, possessed no power of selecting either the district superin-

[1] Ordinance of May 10, 1871, No. 76.

[2] Mayor's Message of January 1, 1884, p. 42.

[3] Mayor's Message of January 1, 1888, p. 71; "Laws of Maryland," 1888, ch. 322.

[4] Ordinance of January 1, 1857, No. 4, sect. 13.

[5] Ordinance of October 23, 1878, No. 100. As suggested by the composite title, the duties of the Inspector and Sealer of Gas Meters (Ordinance of May 28, 1861, No. 53) were incorporated in this new office.

tendents nor the general body of lamplighters, both of whom continued to be appointed by the Mayor. In consequence the lamplighting department early became one of the defective branches of the city administration, of which the cost was largely in excess of the benefit derived, and of which the largest usefulness was the patronage it offered to ward workers.

The experience of the city with electrical illumination, introduced for public purposes in 1881-82, was in many respects the same as with gas lighting. Dependence was throughout put upon private enterprise, and successive companies were given the use of the city's streets in the hope of securing competitive prices. The actual results were either outright consolidation, or an amicable division of territory and the fixture of an arbitrary non-competitive price. Despite improvements in methods of electrical lighting and the rapid extension of its use for municipal purposes, the contract cost of lighting underwent slow reduction—from 70 cents per arc light at the time of its introduction, to 50 cents in 1887, to 40 cents in 1889. In 1890 a contract for five years was made at 35 cents per arc light and in 1894 this was extended for five years. The project of a municipal electric lighting plant was suggested from time to time but never seriously agitated. It was strongly recommended in 1891 by Mayor Robert C. Davidson, who estimated that a well-equipped plant, available for the public illumination of the city would entail a capital expenditure of $2,000,000 and an annual outlay of $170,000—thus effecting a saving of about $90,000 annually.[1]

A slow and short-sighted extension of service into thinly settled districts characterized the policy of the private lighting agencies of Baltimore. This was in part counteracted by contract provisions for the annual expenditure by the gas company of specified amounts in the extension of piping and for the erection of lamps at such points within cer-

[1] Mayor's Message of January 26, 1891, p. 66.

tain limits as might be designated by municipal ordinance.[1] Outlying sections continued to be lighted by oil lamps, for the maintenance of which annual contracts were made by the city with private individuals.

Fire Protection.

The unsatisfactory condition of the local fire department had become generally recognized in 1856. Suggestions were made from time to time for a modification of the existing system,[2] but the drift of opinion was toward the entire displacement of volunteer service by a paid department. Under Mayor Thomas Swann's administration a joint commission of nine persons, representing the city and the Baltimore United Fire Department, was appointed to present a plan for "the thorough organization of the Fire Department of Baltimore."[3]

A paid fire department was established at the close of 1858 and placed under the control of an unsalaried Board of Fire Commissioners, consisting of five persons appointed by the Mayor for a term of five years, so arranged that one member retired annually. The number and the remuneration of the force were fixed by municipal ordinance, but the actual appointments were made by the Fire Commissioners.[4] The volunteer companies remained in activity until the thorough organization of the new department, and then having sold the best part of their equipment to the city, gradually disbanded. The reorganization was completed

[1] Thus see Ordinances of November 2, 1876, No. 165; March 3, 1880, No. 15; March 22, 1882, No. 30.

[2] Thus see Mayor's Message of January, 1856, pp. 20-21.

[3] Resolution of May 31, 1858, No. 82.

[4] Ordinance of December 10, 1858, No. 5. Forty thousand dollars were appropriated for the equipment of the department, but the actual payments were made in the form of long time city notes. An interesting survival of the volunteer system was contained in the provision that the Fire Commissioners might allow persons to become "honorary members" of the department upon the payment of an annual sum of five dollars.

by the introduction of a police and fire alarm telegraph, and the results of the new system were promptly seen in an extraordinary reduction in the number of fires and alarms of fire from 428 in 1858 to 267 in 1859.[1]

The size and equipment of the fire department increased steadily with the growth of the city in the thirty years succeeding the substitution of the volunteer for the paid system. Certain changes were also made in the administration of the department. In 1868 the term of office of the Fire Commissioners was reduced to four years,[2] and in 1877 they were given full control of the police and fire alarm telegraph.[3] In 1878 an additional member was added to the Board, making six in all,[4] and in 1881 the term of office was changed back again to six years.[5] In 1883, in the hope of removing the department from the influence of local politics, the existing Board of Fire Commissioners was replaced by a Fire Marshal, biennially appointed by the Mayor.[6] None of the results sought for were attained,[7] and in 1884 the office of Fire Marshal was in turn abolished, and upon the recommendation of Mayor Ferdinand C. Latrobe the Boston system of a paid board of three Fire Commissioners, holding office for three years and retiring in succession, was substituted therefor.[8] The appointment and control of all employees of the department were entrusted to this board, and provision was made that all supplies must be purchased after advertisement and award to the lowest bidder. In 1888 the Mayor was made a fourth member of the board, *ex-officio*,[9] and in 1892 the term of office was reduced to two

[1] Mayor's Message of January 16, 1860, pp. 12-13; Resolutions of July 6, 1858, No. 123, and December 7, 1858, No. 11; Ordinance of June 24, 1859, No. 94.
[2] Ordinance of February 21, 1868, No. 7.
[3] Ordinance of March 29, 1877, No. 18.
[4] Ordinance of October 4, 1878, No. 87.
[5] Ordinance of February 24, 1881, No. 16.
[6] Ordinance of February 19, 1883, No. 1.
[7] Mayor's Message of January 1, 1884, p. 65.
[8] Ordinance of March 24, 1884, No. 21.
[9] Ordinance of April 14, 1888, No. 28.

years.[1] In 1893 the last vestige of the volunteer system was swept away by the replacement of "call men" by full paid employees.[2]

WATER SUPPLY.

After the municipal purchase of the existing water-works in 1854, early steps were taken to extend the plant and to furnish all sections of the city with an abundant supply of wholesome water.. The work of extension and the general administration of the department were vested in 1857 in a reorganized Water Board, composed of six members, appointed biennially by the Mayor who was also *ex-officio* a member of the new Board.[3] Under the direction of this body, the introduction of water from Jones' Falls was accomplished between 1858 and 1862. The aggregate cost of constructing the new water-works was defrayed from out the proceeds of special funded loans hereinafter described.[4] The Jones' Falls supply was completed by the construction of two additional reservoirs—Druid Lake in 1863-65 and the High Service Reservoir in 1871-74. Like the works proper, these additions were built from out the proceeds of special funded loans.

After several years of agitation during which the inadequacy of the existing water-supply for the wants of the growing city became increasingly apparent, the construction of a metropolitan system by the introduction of water from the Gunpowder River was definitely undertaken by the municipality in 1874 through the agency of the Water Board. A municipal loan of $4,000,000 was authorized for this purpose, and after seven years of practically continuous labor the new system was completed in October, 1881. It was further extended by the construction of a storage reservoir (Lake Clifton) from out the proceeds of additional

[1] Baltimore City Code, Art. XX, sect. 1; apparently upon the authority of the codifier.

[2] Ordinance of February 4, 1893, No. 8.

[3] Ordinance of April 14, 1857, No. 28.

[4] See below, p. 306.

loans to the amount of $1,500,000, authorized in 1883-86. Finally the extension of service into the recently annexed portions of the city was proposed in 1894, and the "Four Million Loan" authorized an expenditure of $2,000,000 for that purpose.[1] It will thus be seen that the cost of constructing and extending the local water-works was defrayed from out the proceeds of funded loans, and aggregated more than $12,500,000. Of this amount more than $4,500,000 was authorized prior to 1868; more than $5,000,000 between 1868 and 1888, and the remaining $3,000,000 after 1888.

Independent of the original cost of construction and extension, municipal ownership and operation of the water-works entailed an annual expenditure for the payment of interest upon the funded water debt, and for actual maintenance and operation, including the extension of mains within the city. From the very purchase of the original water-works these recurring expenditures were defrayed wholly or in part from out the rental receipts of the plant, and the Water Board was vested with virtual independence in fiscal matters.[2]

Health.

The Board of Health was reorganized in 1861 by consolidating the offices of Commissioner of Health and of City Physician.[3] The Assistant Commissioner of Health and the Physician to the Marine Hospital formed the additional members of the Board—the latter official by usage rather than by formal authorization. In 1886 the title of the Commissioner of Health was changed to "Commissioner of Health and Register of Vital Statistics,"[4] and in 1888 the Mayor was made a third member of the Board, *ex-officio*.[5]

[1] See below, p. 321.

[2] Occasional special appropriations were made by the City Council; but for a discussion of the financial policy of the Water Department, see below, p. 290.

[3] Ordinance of February 28, 1861, No. 5.

[4] Ordinance of June 4, 1886, No. 83.

[5] Ordinance of April 14, 1888, No. 29.

The activities of the department underwent little change. The functions of street-cleaning and garbage removal remained under the special charge of the Assistant Commissioner of Health, until vested in 1882 in an independent department.[1] The Marine Hospital became in 1881 the "Quarantine Hospital," and continued to serve both as a quarantine station and as an emergency hospital for the reception of infectious diseases. In 1890 a City Morgue was established and placed under the control of the Board of Health.[2]

Under the stress of recurring fever and epidemic, actual or threatened, the powers and resources of the Board of Health were greatly enlarged.[3] In the main, however, the functions of the health department in Baltimore as in the ordinary American city were restricted to merely remedial measures—the abatement of nuisances, the isolation of contagious disease, the enforcement of quarantine. The department was never vested with adequate power for the general sanitary control and improvement of the city. Successive health boards called attention in urgent terms to sanitary reforms made necessary by the growth of the city, such as the erection of a suitable hospital for infectious diseases or the establishment of a municipal abattoir, but the municipality was slow to extend the activities of the department by placing large resources at its disposal.[4] It is evidence of remarkable natural conditions rather than of efficient sanitation, that—with the existing facts of surface drainage, exposed water-supply, inadequate provision for infectious disease—the health of the city should have remained as favorable as was actually the case.

Markets.

At the outset of the period here considered, permanent market houses had been erected on all the designated

[1] See above, p. 220. [2] Ordinance of July 9, 1890, No. 156.

[3] Resolution of January 27, 1873, No. 68; Mayor's Message of January 23, 1883.

[4] Thus see Report of Board of Health, October 31, 1875; few of the evils therein pointed out have since been remedied.

market places of the city. The cost of maintenance, including expenditures for repairs and the salaries of the market clerks, was defrayed by annual appropriations from out the municipal treasury, into which were paid all market dues and rentals.[1] These ordinary expenditures remained practically constant in amount. From time to time it became necessary to replace or extend existing market houses, and special appropriations were made for this purpose from out current income and expended under the direction of the Inspector of Buildings.[2]

Wharves and Harbor.

General charge of the wharves and harbor of the city remained for some years vested in the Port Warden. In 1861 the office of Port Warden was consolidated with that of City Commissioner, as already noted,[3] but two years later it was again differentiated.[4] In the succeeding decade the Port Warden's department or "City Yard" was an offensive plague spot in the municipal administration. At its best, it was an extravagant and wasteful branch of municipal service; under ordinary circumstances, it was a haven of refuge for worn-out political hacks and ward-heelers. In 1876, largely through efforts of Mayor F. C. Latrobe, the office of Port Warden was entirely abolished and its duties transferred to an unpaid Harbor Board composed of the Mayor and six commissioners appointed by the Mayor for terms of four years, arranged so that half of the body re-

[1] See below, p. 296.

[2] The fixed character and insignificant amount of market expenditures are indicated in the following table:

Year.	Salaries.	Repair and Construction.
1856	$5,614.94	$ 8,406.13
1866	5,928.67	——
1876	4,670.81	3,297.16
1886	5,238.51	16,478.96
1896	4,725.07	——

[3] See above, p. 209.

[4] Ordinance of February 17, 1863, No. 8.

tired biennially.[1] In 1887 the tenure of the members of the Harbor Board was reduced with that of other city officers to two years.[2]

The functions of the Harbor Board, from the time of its creation, were threefold in character: (1) supervision and improvement of the harbor, (2) operation and maintenance of ice-boats, (3) repair of docks and wharves.[3] Specific appropriations were made annually by the City Council for each of these purposes, and unused balances remained in the city treasury.

(1) The most important activity of the Harbor Board was the maintenance by systematic dredging of specified depths of water in the various sections of the harbor, constantly threatened by tidewater deposits and drainage sediment. The work was done by specific contracts awarded to the lowest competent bidder.[4] Immediate superintendence was vested in a skilled engineer, whose continuous tenure was in considerable measure responsible for the excellent results accomplished.

The widening and deepening of the ship-channel of the city, undertaken by the commission of 1852,[5] languished with the abolition of the distinct office of Port Warden in 1861 and the expenditure of the original appropriation. In 1862 provision was made for the biennial appointment of six commissioners, serving without pay and, with the Mayor, constituting a board of commissioners "for deepening and improving the channel of Chesapeake Bay and the Patapsco River, below Fort McHenry." This body was

[1] Ordinance of March 24, 1876, No. 28.

[2] Ordinance of February 25, 1887, No. 4.

[3] An important additional service of the Harbor Board, aided by the federal government, was the establishment of the Port Wardens Line.

[4] "The average cost of dredging, including department expenses, under the old system was from 37 to 38 cents per cubic yard. Under the present system of a Harbor Board, the average cost, including departmental expenses, is from 11½ to 12 cents per cubic yard" (Mayor's Message of January 8, 1877, p. 84).

[5] See above, p. 125.

authorized to receive and disburse the twenty thousand dollars annually appropriated by the state from out the proceeds of auction duties, but no distinct municipal funds were made available.[1] During the next decade the work of improvement was prosecuted spasmodically as federal appropriations supplemented this inadequate fund. With a view to greater activity the powers of the commission were in 1872 transferred to the "Patapsco River Improvement Board," composed of three designated citizens, serving without pay, and the sum of $200,000 to be raised by temporary loans was appropriated for this purpose.[2] A second appropriation of the same amount was made in 1873,[3] and larger funds were at the same time made available by the federal government. In 1876 the newly created Harbor Board absorbed the duties of the Patapsco River Improvement Board. Thereafter the maintenance and improvement of the ship-channel were carried on under federal direction and, in the main, by means of federal appropriations; while the Harbor Board concentrated its efforts upon providing equal facilities within the harbor proper.

(2) The preservation of a navigable approach to the city during the winter season was vested in 1867 by act of the General Assembly in a "Harbor and River Relief Board" composed of the President of the Board of Trade, the President of the Corn and Flour Exchange and a member chosen by the presidents of the several marine insurance companies of the city.[4] Provision was made for an outright appropriation of $150,000 to be paid in equal parts by the city and the state for the construction of an ice-boat, and for an annual appropriation of $10,000 by the city thereafter for its maintenance. Similar provision for the joint construction and operation of a new ice-boat was made in 1888, and the

[1] Ordinance of August 9, 1862, No. 53.
[2] Ordinance of May 30, 1872, No. 66.
[3] Ordinance of March 25, 1873, No. 13.
[4] "Laws of Maryland," 1867, ch. 248; Ordinance of June 10, 1867, No. 40.

Mayor was substituted for the representative of the insurance companies in the Harbor and Relief Board.[1] In 1877 the newly organized Harbor Board was authorized to construct and operate an independent ice-boat for the protection of local commerce.[2] The exercise of the same function by two practically distinct bodies resulted in inefficient service and unnecessary friction. Some improvement was effected by the appointment of the Mayor as a member of the Harbor and River Relief Board in 1888; but the evil was not entirely corrected until 1894 when the ice-boat operated by the Harbor and River Relief Board was put under the control of the municipal Harbor Board.[3]

(3) The early practice of devoting the revenues collected from each wharf to its specific improvement fell into disuse and an annual appropriation of small amount was made from out the municipal treasury for the repair and cleaning of wharves.

Courts.

The incorporation of the city courts with the judicial system of the state, effected by the Maryland constitution of 1851, established the essential features of the local judiciary. The constitution of 1864 defined Baltimore, for judicial purposes, as the thirteenth judicial circuit of Maryland, with four courts, styled the Superior Court of Baltimore City, the Court of Common Pleas, the Circuit Court and the Criminal Court.[4] The term of the judges was fixed at fifteen years and that of the clerks at six years; the organization of the probate court was unchanged. Provision was made for the appointment of local constables by the corporation instead of by the state, and for the election by popular vote of a state's attorney for Baltimore City, with

[1] "Laws of Maryland," 1888, ch. 259.

[2] Ordinance of May 3, 1877, No. 33.

[3] See "Report of Harbor Board," January, 1895.

[4] The legislature was empowered to establish another court if it saw fit.

power to appoint a deputy attorney, both of whom were paid by fees.[1]

The modern organization of the local judiciary was determined by the state constitution of 1867. Baltimore was therein denominated the eighth judicial district of Maryland, with six courts (the Supreme Bench, the Superior Court, the Court of Common Pleas, the Baltimore City Court, the Circuit Court and the Criminal Court), presided over by one chief judge and four associate judges, together constituting the Supreme Bench of Baltimore City. The judges were elected by popular vote for a term of fifteen years and received an annual salary of $3500 from the state, with an additional allowance of $500 at the option and expense of the city. A clerk was elected for each court at an annual salary of $3500 for a term of six years, paid in so far as possible from out the fees of his office. Three judges of the Orphan's Court were elected every fourth year and received per diem compensation. Justices of the peace were appointed biennially by the governor, and constables by the corporation. A city sheriff was elected by popular vote every second year, and a state's attorney in Baltimore, every fourth year—the latter appointing a deputy attorney as before. The Supreme Bench appointed the necessary judicial officers (criers and bailiffs), whose compensation was fixed by the General Assembly.[2] In 1888 a second civil court, designated as Circuit Court No. 2, was established, and provision was made for the election of an additional judge and clerk in the same manner and receiving the same compensation as other members of the city bench.[3]

The entire cost of the local judiciary, with the exception of the salaries of judges and clerks, was imposed upon the city and defrayed by annual appropriations from out the city treasury. On the other hand, all judicial receipts and

[1] Constitution of 1864, Art. IV.
[2] Constitution of 1867, Art. IV.
[3] "Laws of Maryland," 1888, ch. 194.

excess of fees, reverted to the state treasury, despite repeated protest as to the injustice of such procedure.[1]

SCHOOLS.

The administration of the public school system remained vested in the Board of Commissioners of Public Schools, consisting of one person from each of the twenty wards of the city. In 1876 the term of office of the Commissioners was extended from one to four years, so arranged that one-fourth of the board retired annually.[2] With the addition of two suburban wards by the incorporation of the "Annex" in 1888, the number of Commissioners was increased to twenty-two. The members of the school board were nominally elected by the two branches of the city council in joint convention. At an early period, however, councilmanic courtesy permitted the practical appointment of Commissioners by the representatives of the ward within which the vacancy occurred. The actual supervision of instruction was in the hands of a Superintendent of Public Instruction, aided after 1872 by an Assistant Superintendent who, together with all teachers and persons employed in connection with the schools of the city, were appointed by the school board.

The public school system developed in scope and in proportions with the extension of the city and the growth of population.[3] Separate instruction was provided for males and females in primary, grammar and high schools. Provision was made for separate schools for colored children in

[1] Thus see Comptroller's Report of January 1, 1889; also Resolution of October 16, 1875, No. 486.

[2] Ordinance of October 30, 1876, No. 164.

[3] This is shown in the following tabular statement:

Year.	Schools.	Teachers.	Pupils.
1856	77	253	11,936
1866	88	411	17,967
1876	119	731	31,404
1886	136	969	41,256
1896	173	1,673	76,192

1867 and for the application to such schools of the proceeds of school taxes levied upon colored persons. It was however found impracticable to distinguish this revenue and the colored schools were thereafter supported as an integral part of the educational system of the city.[1]

In 1884 the fee of one dollar per quarter for the use of school books, from the payment of which the children of parents in moderate circumstances had already been exempt, was abolished and school attendance was made absolutely free to residents of Baltimore.[2]

Whatever fiscal independence the school board may have enjoyed prior to 1856 was gradually lost. During the greater part of the period here considered, the proceeds of municipal taxation for school purposes, the city's distributive share of the state school tax, tuition fees and miscellaneous receipts were paid to the city register and constituted a municipal "school fund." But this fund was neither segregated nor placed under the control of the school board, and the items constituting it are most conveniently regarded as ordinary municipal revenues and discussed in their proper connection. Estimates of anticipated expenditure were submitted annually by the school board, and embodied with more or less change in the municipal budget. Specific appropriations were made by the City Council, and the drafts of the school board were honored by the City Register only within these limits. This procedure was apparently modified in 1883 in the case of funds from intestacies, which, although nominally appropriated for the sole benefit of the public schools, had theretofore been paid into the city treasury and treated as a mere addition to the illusory "school fund." Such revenues were thereafter constituted a separate and distinct fund, held subject to the order of the school board.

[1] Ordinances of July 10, 1867, No. 45; May 5, 1868, No. 36; Report of Board of School Commissioners, January 1, 1869.

[2] Ordinance No. 141 of 1884; passed over the Mayor's veto. Tuition fees were retained for the children of non-residents.

The maintenance of the public school system, including the erection and equipment of school buildings, was throughout one of the largest items of municipal expenditure. Subject to the indirect credit of the other sources contributing to the "school fund," the entire cost of the schools was an immediate charge upon the municipal treasury. With increasing expenditure in other departments of municipal service and an uninterrupted rise in the rate of direct taxation, it was found impossible to provide the necessary number of additional school buildings from out of ordinary municipal revenues. Each of the composite loans of 1888 and of 1892 contained an appropriation of $400,000 for the provision of additional school-houses. But even these large sums were entirely inadequate, and one of the most urgent occasions for large municipal expenditure in the closing years of the period here considered was that entailed by the insufficient number and defective character of the public school buildings.[1]

CHARITIES AND CORRECTIONS.

Municipal expenditure for the support of dependent and delinquent classes developed along the lines indicated before 1856. The joint interest of city and county in the almshouse and the jail was dissolved and each institution passed under municipal control. No other charitable or corrective institution was established and maintained by the city; but increasing use was made of private agencies, to which annual municipal appropriations were made.

The dissolution of the joint interest of the city and county in the almshouse, although authorized several years before, was not consummated until 1858, when the property was offered at public sale and purchased by the county.

[1] For painful but graphic evidence of this, see "Report on the Sanitary Condition of the Primary Schools of Baltimore" (1898), made by Professor S. Homer Woodbridge of the Massachusetts Institute of Technology of Boston, by request of the Arundell Good Government Club.

Pending the erection of a new building the city leased the old structure, but continued to share the cost of maintenance with the county. In 1861 the city assumed direct control, agreeing to maintain paupers belonging to the county at a per capita charge.[1] The new almshouse or Bay View Asylum was erected in 1862-66 by a special commission ("The Building Committee of the Baltimore City Almshouse") of four persons appointed by the Mayor, who served as president, *ex officio*. Funds were provided by the sale of the city's share in the old almshouse property and by three successive issues of municipal stock.[2] The building was subsequently enlarged as required, and in 1880 provision was made for the erection of an additional structure.[3] From 1858 until 1862, the management of the almshouse appears to have remained in the hands of the city members of the joint board. In the latter year control was vested in an incorporated board of five Trustees of the Poor of Baltimore City, annually appointed in the manner of other city officers.[4] Six years later the full title of the almshouse was transferred to the Mayor and City Council without any change however in the administrative duties of the Trustees.[5] In 1886 the number of Trustees was increased from five to seven, and in 1892 the term of appointment was extended to two years.[6] Sick and indigent persons were admitted to the almshouse by the Trustees of the Poor, or their representatives, and by "managers of the poor," one of whom was annually appointed by the Mayor in each ward of the city. Vagrants and tramps were committed to the institution by police magistrates and by the Criminal Court.

A new city jail was constructed in 1856-60 by a specially

[1] "Baltimore City Code," 1879, p. 74, note; cf. "Report of the Trustees for the Poor," December 31, 1861.

[2] See below, p. 309.

[3] Ordinance of May 5, 1880, No. 91.

[4] "Laws of Maryland," 1861, ch. 279.

[5] *Ibid.*, 1868, ch. 1.

[6] Baltimore City Code, 1892, Art. II, sect. 2.

appointed building committee. Funds were provided by direct appropriations and by funded loans.[1] After the severance of the county's interest in 1853, the affairs of the institution appear to have been directed by the four city members of the joint board established in 1832. In 1861 provision was made for the annual appointment of a board of five persons, designated "The Visitors of the Jail of Baltimore City" and this body remained thereafter in control of the institution, with full power of appointing its officers.[2] In 1881 the number of Visitors was increased to six, together with the Mayor who served *ex officio;* the term of office was increased to six years, with two members retiring biennially.[3] Two years later the tenure was reduced to three years with one member retiring annually.[4]

The cost of maintaining the almshouse and the jail was defrayed by annual appropriations from out the city treasury. Nominally the proceeds of the "poor levy" and of a portion of the "certain expenses levy" of the general property tax were designed for this purpose. But the claim of the Trustees of the Poor to the aggregate yield of the "poor levy," although asserted at the beginning of the period, was at no time recognized. The rate of the levy was ordinarily adjusted to the expenditure anticipated; but the actual proceeds were never segregated, and if they exceeded the appropriation made by the City Council, the surplus remained in the general treasury instead of being credited to any special account.

The characteristic feature of local expenditure for charities and corrections was the system of municipal subsidies to private institutions. Prior to the Civil War small and irregular appropriations had been made to private institutions, for the most part to medical dispensaries. In 1864, probably as a result of the greater drain upon their ordi-

[1] See below, p. 309.
[2] Ordinance of May 16, 1861, No. 45.
[3] Ordinance of February 8, 1881, No. 4.
[4] Ordinance of March 5, 1883, No. 10.

nary resources resulting from prolonged military operations, a number of private relief agencies made successful application for municipal aid. This action was promptly accepted as a precedent, and within a decade indirect contributions to the support of dependent and defective classes had become the established municipal policy.[1]

The experience of Baltimore in granting public subsidies to private charities confirms in almost every detail the results attained in other American cities. The cost to the city was probably less than municipal institutions would have involved, but the benefits derived were certainly less satisfactory. Municipal subsidies stimulated the organization of unnecessary agencies and resulted in the wasteful duplication of institutions. The development of the system was, moreover, entirely unaccompanied by any of the checks upon which its successful working depends. No provision was made for the thorough inspection of subsidized institutions or for the systematic auditing of their accounts. The municipality had no voice in controlling the affairs of the institutions, including the terms of admission and discharge. Finally, municipal appropriations were ordinarily made in bulk and not on "the principle of specific payment for specific work."[2]

[1] The growth in the number of institutions aided and the increase in the aggregate municipal appropriation are indicated by the following statement derived from the Registers' estimates of probable expenditures for the ensuing years:

Year.	Number of Institutions.	Estimated Appropriations.
1870	7	$22,000
1880	15	100,000
1890	32	183,990
1896	51	277,275

[2] Warner, "American Charities," ch. XVII. Professor Warner was for several years secretary of the Charity Organization Society of Baltimore, and it is no hazardous conjecture to suppose that his admirable review of the system of public subsidies to private charities stands in some definite relation to conditions in Baltimore. Certainly the concluding sentence of Professor Warner's chapter may be cited as the practical lesson to be drawn from the experience of this city: "As a transition policy for growing communities,

PARKS AND SQUARES.[1]

A series of small unimproved public squares constituted the "lungs" of Baltimore in 1856. The present system of municipal parks originated in a proposition to establish a boulevard around the city, first entertained by the Mayor and City Council in 1851. A commission of representative citizens was appointed in that year to inquire into the feasibility of the plan and its probable cost. After careful surveys the commission reported that the plan was entirely practicable, but estimated its cost at $641,300, exclusive of right of way; subsequent modifications of route reduced this estimate nearly fifty per cent. The boulevard, as planned, extended in part beyond the city limits, and would have required an act of the legislature for the annexation of the section of Baltimore County included. This extension of the city confines was strongly opposed by residents of the county, and there appeared to be little likelihood of securing the requisite legislation from the General Assembly. The finances of the city were, moreover, in no condition to warrant the large expenditure required, and after some further discussion the entire boulevard project was dropped.

In 1856 the far-sighted sagacity of Mayor Thomas Swann proposed a practicable method for securing the desired improvement. To representatives of the Baltimore City Passenger Railway Company, then seeking an original franchise from the city, Mayor Swann announced his intention of approving such a grant only in the event that it

or for new and developing varieties of benevolent work, it may possibly have its place; but it should never be entered on inadvertently, for while all its advantages and economies are greatest at the beginning, the disadvantages and dangers of it increase as time goes on."

In this connection mention should also be made of the excellent report of the municipal commission appointed in Baltimore in 1897, under the chairmanship of Dr. Jeffrey R. Brackett, to propose improvements in the care of certain city poor.

[1] For details of the acquisition of the parks of Baltimore, see "Report of Public Park Commission," January 1, 1860; reprinted, with additions by Hon. F. C. Latrobe, in "Report," December 31, 1895.

provided for the payment to the city of one-fifth of the gross receipts of the railway, to be applied exclusively to the construction of the boulevard or to the purchase and maintenance of parks. With a veto power that could be overridden only by a three-fourths vote of the City Council, and with a public sentiment strongly in sympathy with his proposal, Mayor Swann was in a position to dictate terms. The franchise finally granted, as well as subsequent concessions to local street railways, provided for a "park tax" of twenty per cent. of gross receipts.

The proceeds of the franchise tax were allowed to accumulate until 1860, when—the plan of the boulevard being practically abandoned—an unsalaried commission consisting of the Mayor and four citizens was appointed for the selection and purchase of the sites of the proposed parks. After public advertisement and careful deliberation, the present site of Druid Hill Park, a highly developed country seat of nearly five hundred acres, was selected. This was soon after supplemented by the purchase of ground adjacent to the tract which William Patterson had given the city nearly thirty years before, now known as Patterson Park. The City Register was immediately authorized to issue city stock, redeemable at the end of thirty years and designated as "Public Park Stock," to defray the obligations incurred by the commission in the purchase of park sites. The certificates of stock were to be issued direct to the vendors upon the conveyance of the property purchased.[1] The proceeds of the franchise tax were pledged and set apart primarily for the payment of interest upon stock so issued. Of the amount remaining after the payment of interest, one-fifth was to be invested by the Register as a sinking fund for the ultimate redemption of the stock

[1] The entire arrangement was threatened by the unwillingness of the owner of the site to receive city stock in full payment. Delay and litigation were averted by the action of a number of public-spirited citizens, each of whom purchased $10,000 of city stock at par, and thus provided funds for the payment of one-fourth of the purchase money in cash.

and the remaining four-fifths devoted to the maintenance and improvement of the parks.[1] By the same ordinance a formal Public Park Commission was constituted by the addition of a sixth member to the original commission. The commissioners served without salary or emolument of any kind and held permanent tenure, provision being made that any vacancy from death, resignation or failure to serve should "be filled by the said commission itself and be by them reported to the Council for and subject to its approval, at the first session thereafter."

Subsequent to the acquisition of the first parks in 1860-61, important additions were made by purchase, condemnation and gift to the public areas of the city.[2] For the more important of these, special issues of city stock were authorized; minor purchases were made from current revenues. The procedure adopted with respect to the maintenance and administration of parks and squares was anomalous. The larger areas were put under the care of the Park Commission; but most of the smaller squares were placed in the control of separate commissioners appointed by the Mayor ordinarily from among the residents of the locality. A distinct appropriation was made for each such area, and expended independently by the corresponding body of commissioners. The system was wasteful and inefficient in the extreme and would probably soon have yielded to centralized control[3] but for the modicum of local patronage and petty authority which it afforded ward politicians.

To defray the heavy cost of initial improvements in Druid Hill and Patterson Parks, additional "Park Stock" to the amount of $150,000 was issued, and the proceeds put at the disposal of the Park Commission. From time to time special appropriations were also made from the general

[1] During 1860-61 the sum of $511,323.75 was issued for the acquisition of Druid Hill Park and $42,642.50 for the purchase of additions to Patterson Park. Cf. below, p. 310.

[2] Scharf, "History of Baltimore City and County," pp. 279-281.

[3] This was introduced in the new charter.

municipal treasury. But in the main the parks were maintained from out the proceeds of the street railway franchise tax. Despite successive reductions in the rate of the tax, receipts increased with the growth of local transportation and the amortization of the original park indebtedness. The Commission was charged by later ordinances with the improvement and maintenance of certain areas, for which special appropriations had theretofore been made. Finally, after 1891, all parks and squares, whether under the control of the Park Commission or of special commissioners, were improved and maintained from out the "park fund."[1]

In the absence of legislative interference, the Park Commission enjoyed practically absolute control over the disposition of the "park fund."[2] The franchise tax was paid by the several street railways to the city treasury and credited to the account of the Park Commission. Specific appropriations were then made by this body for the several parks and squares and for interest and sinking fund charges upon park indebtedness. Undrawn balances reverted back to the fund instead of to the general city treasury.

The organization of the Park Commission underwent but slight modification from its original form. In 1888 the number of commissioners was increased to six, exclusive of the Mayor, who served *ex officio*. The members were appointed by the Mayor, subject to the confirmation of the Council, and held office during good behavior.[3] In the codification of municipal ordinances in 1892 this last provision was coolly omitted by the codifier, without any authority whatever, and a clause providing for biennial appointment inserted.[4] This substitution was more or less responsible for an unfortunate change in the administration

[1] Ordinance of March 24, 1891, No. 14.

[2] In addition to the proceeds of the franchise tax on gross receipts of street railways, the Park Commission received small amounts from the sale of materials, privileges, etc., in the parks.

[3] Ordinance of November 5, 1888, No. 119.

[4] Baltimore City Code, 1892, Art. 37, sect. 1.

of the parks. From its organization the Park Commission was one of the few branches of municipal service removed from direct political influence. The incumbents were representative citizens whose tenure was practically permanent. The necessity for biennial appointment brought the Commission under political influence with corresponding loss in economy and efficiency.

MUNICIPAL BUILDINGS.

The construction and repair of all municipal buildings was vested in the City Commissioner in 1868.[1] The duties of that official were already multifarious, and in 1871 the new office of Inspector of Public Buildings was created. The incumbent was required to be an experienced builder or mechanic, and was appointed annually as other city officers. In addition to acting as a general building inspector and issuing permits for special building privileges, he was authorized to make all contracts, with the approbation of the Mayor, for the construction and repair of city buildings and to superintend the work when in progress.[2]

Ordinary municipal structures—school-houses, fire engine-houses, market-houses—were erected and kept in repair under the superintendence of the Inspector of Public Buildings, as thus provided. The municipal budget contained appropriations for each specific purpose and unexpended balances remained in the general treasury. Special funds for the purchase of sites and the erection of school-houses were provided by items of $400,000 in the composite loans of 1888 and 1892 respectively.[3]

[1] Ordinance of February 29, 1868. The Water Board and the Port Warden were specifically exempted from the operations of the ordinance. The construction of police station-houses was entirely within the control of the Board of Police Commissioners.

[2] Ordinances of June 10, 1871, No. 87; February 28, 1883, No. 9. The term of office of the Inspector seems to have been changed to two years in the codification of 1892.

[3] The $4,500,000 loan ordinance, defeated by popular vote on November 8, 1898, contained an item of $1,000,000 for school-houses.

For the construction of the four important municipal buildings erected within the period here considered—Almshouse, Jail, City Hall and Court House—special building commissions were created and special construction loans were authorized. The procedure with respect to the Almshouse and the Jail has already been described.[1] The City Hall was erected in 1867-75 under the direction of a building committee, composed at first of four, later of six members appointed by the Mayor, who served as chairman *ex officio*. The composition of the committee was afterwards changed to five members elected by the two branches of the City Council in joint convention. The cost of construction was defrayed by a series of funded loans aggregating $2,500,000. The amount actually expended, including cost of furnishing, was $2,375,400.41, or $124,599.59 less than the amount made available. An unsalaried board, consisting of seven members, with the Mayor *ex officio*, styled "the Building Committee of the New Court House," was appointed by ordinance in 1893 for the construction of that building. Funds were provided from out the composite loans of 1892 and 1894, to the aggregate amount of $2,750,000. In most of the special building commissions thus appointed, care was taken to select representative citizens of known integrity and capacity, and the results were on the whole far in advance of the architectural mediocrity and commonly defective character of the structures erected under the superintendence of the Inspector of Public Buildings.

An important item of municipal expenditure in conjunction with the maintenance of public buildings arose from the reprehensible practice of acquiring a mere leasehold interest instead of a freehold estate in the sites of certain schools, engine-houses and market-places. The system was mischievous in that it encouraged false estimates as to the cost of proposed improvements; it was expensive in

[1] See above, pp. 242-243.

that the city could borrow at a lower rate than that at which the ground-rent was capitalized.

Administrative Expenses.

The assumption of new municipal functions and the greater magnitude of ordinary municipal activities resulted in an appreciable and continuous increase in the administrative expenses of the city after 1856. The rise was most pronounced in the first fifteen years of the period examined. Aggregate expenditures for purposes that can fairly be described as administrative were in 1870 nearly five times as great as in 1855. Some part of this extraordinary increase was due to the laxity and waste of the War and Reconstruction periods; but the largest part was the accompaniment of marked expansion in the administrative and fiscal life of the city. After 1870 expenditures of this class developed normally with the increase of the general municipal budget, until in 1895 an increase of somewhat more than fifty per cent. for the twenty-five years was revealed. The multiplication of strictly administrative offices, the increase in the number of positions not directly connected with any existent department of municipal service and the gradual increase in the level of municipal salaries were responsible in the main for the growth of administrative expenses in this later period. More distinctive in character was the increasing cost of local elections and registrations of voters.[1]

[1] In 1876 the conduct of local elections, before entrusted to the police department, was vested in a bi-partisan Board of Supervisors of Elections, composed of three voters of the city, appointed biennially by the Governor of the State ("Laws of Maryland," 1876, ch. 223). The salaries of the Supervisors and all attendant expenses of elections and registrations were paid by the city. The introduction of the Australian ballot system in 1890 and of annual registration of voters in 1896 largely increased municipal expenditures for these purposes.

Similarly the city was charged with all salaries and expenses of the bi-partisan Board of Liquor License Commissioners, constituted in 1890 (*ibid.*, 1890, ch. 393) for the administration of the high-license system in Baltimore and composed of three persons biennially appointed by the Governor.

Interest on Debt.

The annual interest charge upon the funded debt constituted by far the largest single item in municipal expenditure during the entire modern period of the city government. In the first twenty years (1856-1875) the aggregate outlay for this purpose increased rapidly, corresponding to an uninterrupted accumulation of funded indebtedness and an unchanged interest rate. In the succeeding twenty years the slower growth of the funded debt was supplemented by the continuous decline in the rate of interest upon municipal securities, and there occurred no further increase in the annual interest payment. Charges upon that part of the funded debt issued for the purchase and extension of the water works were defrayed—at first in part, later in entirety—by the Water Board from out the revenues of the department. Similar provision was made by the Park Commission for the interest upon the park indebtedness. The remaining charges were paid by the Commissioners of Finance by means of direct appropriations from out the general municipal treasury. The chronic practice of making temporary loans in anticipation of current loans entailed an appreciable interest charge. This became of greater importance in the recurring intervals between the accumulation of floating indebtedness and the funding of permanent deficits. The provision made for the amortization of funded indebtedness is described in another connection.[1]

[1] See below, p. 333.

CHAPTER III

MUNICIPAL REVENUE.

The dominance of the general property tax among the various sources of municipal revenue, clearly established before 1856, became in the succeeding period of municipal history the characteristic feature of the local budget. Revenue from other sources was either small and inelastic, as receipts from markets and wharves; or temporary and uncertain, as dividends upon the city's holding of Baltimore and Ohio Railroad Company stock; or appropriated to special purposes, as the franchise tax upon street railways, devoted to the maintenance of parks and squares, and water rentals, to the maintenance of water-supply. Revenue from license taxes declined in relative importance until after the adoption of high license taxes on liquor sales in 1890. The special assessment no longer defrayed the entire cost of street reconstruction and street repaving; although authorized, it was not actually employed in connection with the construction of sewers.

Progressive expenditure was thus met almost exclusively by direct taxation. After the taxable basis had become practically inelastic, and the tax rate had reached oppressive proportions, an effective check was put upon municipal spending. Some further latitude was afforded by the issue of funded loans for purposes theretofore the object of current expenditure. But the financial status of the city at the close of the period disclosed the urgent necessity of new sources of local revenue.

TAXATION.

General Property Tax.[1] The development of the general property tax from 1856 to 1896 presented no novel feat-

[1] See Appendix F.

ures. The city remained without power of local assessment and the revaluations for state purposes were made at long and irregular intervals. With the assessment of realty at its full value and the failure to reach intangible wealth, the aggregate basis soon became practically rigid and the tax rate rose steadily thereafter. In 1896 an important reassessment act was passed and provision was made for the biennial revision of local valuations.

(Assessment). At the outset of the period here considered, the basis of local taxation was the periodic revaluation made primarily for the levy of the state tax, but promptly utilized for municipal purposes. Three persons, annually appointed by the Mayor and styled "Judges of the Appeal Tax Court," were charged with the correction of local assessments made necessary by the transfer or loss of old, and the acquisition of new property since the last general revaluation. No agencies existed for the revision and correction of valuations in the intervals between the general reassessments. The last general revaluation of property in Baltimore had thus been made in 1852.

The need of local revaluation became apparent in 1857,[1] and in the following year the city secured from the state legislature authority for a local reassessment, upon the condition that state as well as municipal taxes should be levied upon the new basis.[2] The machinery of assessment, the determination of which was left to the city, was very similar to that employed in 1852. The city was divided into ten districts of two wards each, and three residents of each district were appointed a board of assessors for the valuation of property therein. The revision of assessments was made by a board of control and review, composed of five persons similarly appointed by the Mayor. All real and personal property was returned by the taxpayer, presumably at its full cash value. Upon the completion of

[1] Mayor's Message of January 19, 1857; Report of Appeal Tax Court, January, 1857.

[2] "Laws of Maryland," 1858, ch. 241.

the revaluation, the Appeal Tax Court resumed exercise of the limited powers of correction before possessed without apparently any new powers of revision.[1]

In 1859 the Appeal Tax Court was nominally constituted a permanent board of assessment and review. All persons liable to local taxation were required to submit annually a revised list of real and personal assessments, or in default thereof the valuation was made by the Appeal Tax Court. The Court then sat as a board of review with final power to add to or deduct from the valuations submitted. This extensive power was rendered virtually nugatory by the absence of any adequate provision for its exercise. The appointment of only two assessors was authorized, one of whom was by virtue of his appointment clerk of the Court, and each of whom received for services as assessor the ridiculous sum of $250 per annum.[2] In consequence of the inadequate assessment machinery provided by the ordinance of 1859, the revaluation of 1858 remained for some years the basis of local levies with only slight changes. In 1862 the city petitioned the legislature for a general reassessment of property throughout the state—less however for the purpose of increasing the local basis than of removing existing inequalities in valuation between city and county, in anticipation of the imposition of a direct federal war tax.

In 1866 occurred another general reassessment of property throughout the state. Baltimore City was divided into five assessment districts of four wards each. In each district, a board of three assessors and a board of control and review consisting of the same number of persons was appointed by the governor of the state. The method of valuation was essentially that prescribed by the local act of 1858.[3] The work of the assessors in Baltimore appears to have been characterized by negligence and incapacity. Com-

[1] Ordinance of May 26, 1858, No. 25.
[2] Ordinance of February 21, 1859, No. 22.
[3] "Laws of Maryland," 1866, ch. 157.

plaint was so bitter that upon the completion of the assessment in 1868, the General Assembly authorized the reopening of the assessment books and imposed upon the Appeal Tax Court the task of adjusting as far as possible the grievances and inequalities complained of.[1] The number of written appeals from the decision of the boards of review which were filed with the Appeal Tax Court was 3063, and the total abatements made by order of the Court were $42,536,337, out of an aggregate assessment of $238,545,866. By far the largest proportion of this was caused by the carelessness of the assessors: "Millions of stocks exempt from taxation by the charters of the companies, and by acts of the legislature, were returned by the assessors, and of course had to be abated. Churches, literary and charitable institutions, being also exempt by law, had to be stricken out. Personal property was, in numerous instances, assessed twice, and not infrequently three times, and necessarily caused abatements to be made in order to do justice to the parties."[2] Upon the completion of this extraordinary revision, the Appeal Tax Court resumed exercise of its customary power.

A general reassessment of property in Maryland was authorized by the legislature in 1874,[3] but the measure was subsequently declared invalid by the Court of Appeals. Of no greater practical importance was the power conferred upon the corporation at the same session of the legislature to reassess all property in the city "whenever they think the public interest may require it."[4] The propriety of action under this enabling act was urged by all branches of the city administration; but no practical measures were taken, doubtless in anticipation of an early reassessment of property in Maryland.

In 1876 the General Assembly authorized the anticipated

[1] "Laws of Maryland," 1868, ch. 126.
[2] Report of the Appeal Tax Court, January 1, 1869.
[3] "Laws of Maryland," 1874, ch. 514.
[4] *Ibid.*, 1874, ch. 357.

reassessment of all property in the state.[1] In Baltimore a board of three assessors for each ward and a similar board of control and review for every five wards was appointed by the governor, and general superintendence of the work was vested in the Appeal Tax Court. In details of organization and in methods of assessment, the act was essentially the same as the preceding measures of 1858 and 1866. The results attained in Baltimore by the reassessment of 1876 remained practically the basis of local taxation for the next twenty years, during which time occurred no general revision of valuations. The activities of the Appeal Tax Court during this entire interval were limited to the revising powers already noted. In 1878 the Court was authorized to correct annually the assessment upon all property that had undergone change in value since last assessed; but the measure remained without important consequence.[2] The legislature passed a radical reassessment act in 1892, but it was vetoed by the governor. In 1896 the long deferred reassessment was authorized. For municipal purposes the results of this revaluation were not available until 1897, but the measure can properly be described in this connection.[3]

The characteristic features of the assessment act of 1896 were (1) the listing on oath of all real and personal property; (2) the local taxation of securities other than the shares of stock of all Maryland corporations at a fixed rate; (3) the taxation of the income from mortgages at a fixed rate and the apportionment of the proceeds between state and city; (4) provision for the biennial revision of assessments of real property and the biennial listing of personal property.

Each of the twenty existing wards of the city was constituted an assessment district, and an assessor was ap-

[1] "Laws of Maryland," 1876, ch. 260.
[2] *Ibid.*, 1878, ch. 178.
[3] *Ibid.*, ch. 120, 140-143.

pointed by the governor for each precinct.[1] These one hundred and ninety-eight precinct assessors were organized by the Appeal Tax Court into groups of three, and assigned at the discretion of the Court. The governor also appointed six Boards of Control and Review for Baltimore City, each composed of three persons, one of whom belonged to the minor political party. Schedules and interrogatories were prepared for the local assessors by the State Tax Commissioner—in whom was vested a general supervision of the assessment—and by them delivered to all persons taxable. Sworn listed return was required of all real and personal property, and persons convicted of false or fraudulent return were deemed guilty of willful perjury and were liable to a fine not exceeding five hundred dollars or imprisonment not exceeding two years, and to perpetual disqualification from being a witness in any matter or controversy.[2] The corrected assessments of property were returned by the Boards of Control and Review to the Appeal Tax Court and constituted a final valuation, save that persons claiming exemption or denying ownership of property assessed to them might appeal to the Baltimore City Court. Stocks of foreign corporations and bonds of all corporations were assessed at their marked valuation, and were subject to a local tax of three-tenths of one per cent., in lieu of the municipal levy upon other forms of property. Unreleased mortgages in Baltimore City were subject to a tax of eight per cent. upon the annual interest charge, one-fourth of the proceeds of which was paid to the state. Provision was made for the biennial revision of the valuation of real and for the relisting of personal property, and the

[1] The nominal qualifications were that the assessor must be a property-owner and taxpayer; a resident of Baltimore for two years prior to his appointment; and in possession of adequate knowledge of the value of property in the assessment district for which he was appointed.

[2] Additional heavy penalties of fine and imprisonment were imposed for failure to comply with any provisions of the measure.

Mayor and City Council were authorized to appoint the assessors and clerical force required for this purpose.[1]

Corporate securities were at first treated as all other forms of personal wealth. The local reassessment act of 1858 required all domestic corporations to furnish lists of individual stockholders. Resident stockholders were taxed directly; in the case of non-residents, the tax was paid by the corporation. The corporation might however, if it so elected, pay the entire tax and charge the amount expended to the account of the several stockholders. The actual value of corporate securities was fixed by the boards of control and review, and revised by the Appeal Tax Court annually thereafter.[2] The extension of the principle of "stoppage at the source," that is to say, the obligatory payment of taxes in one amount by the corporation, instead of by the several shareholders, was repeatedly recommended by municipal officials after 1866, but no immediate change was made.[3] Renewed attention was directed to the matter by the extraordinary decline in the assessments of the stock of incorporated companies in the years following 1875. The aggregate valuation of such securities fell from $30,510,260 in 1875 to $27,636,677 in 1876, to $25,597,870 in 1877, to $21,280,438 in 1878.[4]

Prior to 1874 corporations appear to have been taxed both upon their capital stock and upon their property. In that year deduction was allowed in the taxation of domestic corporations for any funded debt of the state or tax-paying stock of other domestic corporation, held as part of the investment of their capital or assets. Other forms of per-

[1] For an instructive discussion of the operation of the assessment act of 1896, as well as of other phases of property taxation in Baltimore, see the excellent essay by Mr. T. S. Adams on "Taxation in Maryland" in the volume of "Studies in State Taxation," now in course of publication as an Extra Volume of the *Johns Hopkins University Studies in Historical and Political Science.*

[2] Ordinance of May 26, 1858, No. 25.

[3] Report of City Collector, January 1, 1867; Report of Appeal Tax Court, January 1, 1871.

[4] Report of Appeal Tax Court, January 1, 1878.

sonal property and all real property owned by corporations continued to be taxed in addition to their capital stock until 1877, when the Court of Appeals pronounced this practise double taxation and unconstitutional.[1] In 1878 the modern method of assessing the stock of domestic corporations was adopted.[2] The office of "Tax Commissioner of the State of Maryland" was created and vested with the duty of assessing for purposes of state taxation the stock of all Maryland corporations.[3] The mode of procedure was for the Tax Commissioner to deduct from the aggregate market value of the shares of capital stock of each corporation the amount of credits allowed for tax-paying or tax-exempt investments of part of its capital. The net result, divided by the number of shares of capital stock, constituted the assessed taxable value of the respective shares of stock. The Tax Commissioner was required to certify to the Appeal Tax Court the assessed value of the stock of corporations of which any shareholders resided in Baltimore City, and upon this valuation the full municipal tax rate was imposed and "stopped at the source." The stock of foreign corporations, to which this procedure could of course not be applied, was valued by the local assessors in the hands of the owners as other forms of personal property. Bonds and certificates of debt were treated precisely as shares of stock.[4]

The reassessment act of 1896 imposed, as stated above, a maximum tax of three-tenths of one per cent., in lieu of all other municipal charges, upon the actual market value of the bonds and certificates of indebtedness of all corporations and upon the actual market value of shares of stock of foreign corporations, owned by residents of Baltimore. National bank stock and the stock of domestic corporations

[1] County Commissioners of Frederick County *vs.* Farmers and Mechanics Bank of Frederick, 48 Md. 188.

[2] "Laws of Maryland," 1878, ch. 178; amended by *ibid.*, 1880, ch. 20.

[3] The stock of national banks was similarly treated.

[4] For further details, see "Report of Maryland Tax Commission," 1888, pp. clxvii *et seq.*

were taxed at the full local rate.[1] The tax on domestic securities was paid by the corporation; but listed return of such securities was also required of the individual holders. All securities were assessed by the Appeal Tax Court at the valuation made by the State Tax Commissioner.

The experience of Baltimore in the attempt to assess general property for direct taxation in the forty years examined exemplifies in almost every particular the familiar operation of the general property tax in an industrial community possessing large amounts of intangible wealth. The great bulk of stocks, bonds and other securities, not taxed at the source, escaped assessment, and this fact was of necessity acquiesced in by the assessing agencies. The valuations of all forms of personal property were aggregated in the reports of the Appeal Tax Court until 1897, and there is no statistical evidence as to the extent to which intangible wealth figured on the assessment books. The repeated testimony of municipal officials on this score, however, leaves little doubt but that a small proportion was reached.[2] The adoption of the principle of taxing the capital stock of domestic corporations at the source effectively prevented the escape of such securities from assessment. The practise of deducting the tax-paying and tax-exempt property from the assessed value of the capital stock was attended with less satisfactory results, and the discrepancy between the taxable basis and the actual tax-paying capacity of certain classes of corporations became notorious.[3]

A further source of loss arose from the removal to Baltimore County, for residential purposes, of wealthy persons

[1] The courts have been called upon to determine whether national bank stock should be taxed at the full local rate or at the prescribed maximum of three-tenths of one per cent.

[2] Report of Appeal Tax Court, January, 1857; Mayor's Message of January 23, 1871, p. 6; Mayor's Message of January 1, 1881; "Report of Baltimore Tax Commission of 1885," p. 22; "Report of Maryland Tax Commission of 1888," p. 78 *et seq.*

[3] For the relation of this principle of deducting corporate property to the municipal credit of Baltimore, see below, p. 349.

engaged in business in Baltimore City. The General Assembly in 1862 and in 1865[1] undertook to subject to municipal taxation all property located in the city, even though the owners resided elsewhere. The Constitution of 1867 (Art. 3, sect. 51) prohibited this by providing that "the personal property of residents of this state shall be subject to taxation in the county or city where the resident *bona fide* resides for the greater part of the year, for which the tax may or shall be levied, and not elsewhere, except goods and chattels permanently located, which shall be taxed in the city or county where they are so located."[2]

The inevitable inequality of property assessment in Baltimore was greatly aggravated by the long intervals, varying from eight to twenty years, between the valuations of property. The Appeal Tax Court possessed nominal authority for the periodic revision of assessed valuations; but in the absence of any adequate assessing force its activities were limited in the main to abatements for sale and transfer, and to the assessment of newly erected buildings. From time to time the Court made sporadic effort to raise assessments in certain districts where the existing valuations were conspicuously incorrect, but such "raids," even when successful, simply contributed to the glaring inequalities in the assessed valuation of property in general. With the growth of the city and the shifting of the residential and mercantile centres, the discrepancy between the assessed and the actual value of real property often became marked. Gross injustice was suffered by the owners of property, which for one reason or another had undergone depreciation in real value, from the inability to secure a revision of the assessed valuation. The committee on municipal taxation of the Baltimore Reform League described and interpreted this condition of affairs with conservatism in 1895 in stating "so widespread is the belief that the Appeal Tax Court will not accept the usual tests of value, nor admit evidence rele-

[1] "Laws of Maryland," 1862, ch. 251; 1865, ch. 119.
[2] "Baltimore City Code," 1879, pp. 1059-1060, note 1.

vantly bearing on it, when it is a question of reducing assessments, that over-taxed owners usually take no steps to obtain relief. The disinclination to abate assessments, in the face of the strongest evidence of actual worth, probably results from the well-grounded belief that a large amount of property in this city is assessed considerably beyond its actual value, and from the recognition of the fact that the tax rate is near the danger point. This produces a feeling that any concessions to the owners of overvalued properties might be taken as a precedent, and result in a widespread demand on the part of others for similar treatment, which if accorded, would result in a still higher rate of taxation."

While under the most favorable conditions, personal injustice and fiscal inefficiency must have resulted from the local system, or rather complete lack of system, of assessment in Baltimore, evidence is not wanting that these evil consequences were further accented by the methods of administration in vogue. Offices in the Appeal Tax Court were always regarded as political appointments pure and simple, for which no technical qualification was requisite. Property assessments were sometimes manipulated for political reward and punishment. Finally abatements could at times be secured or increased assessments averted by the employment of the "legal services" of well-known city politicians or ward workers.[1]

[1] The remedy ordinarily proposed for the evils of the existing method of property valuation in Baltimore was the annual or biennial revision of assessments by a permanent assessing body (Mayors' Messages of January 23, 1871; January 1, 1881; January 1, 1884; Report of Appeal Tax Court, January 1, 1880).

In 1885 a formal commission of three persons was appointed to examine the local system of taxation and to suggest changes and additions. The report of the commission, presented in the same year, recommended (1) municipal control of local tax assessment and collection, (2) appointment of a permanent board of sixteen city assessors, (3) taxation of all personalty within the city, unless *bona fide* residence for more than six months elsewhere was proved, (4) triennial valuation of real and leasehold estates and annual

(Exemption). Certain classes of property were released from the payment of local as well as state taxes in the reassessments authorized by the state legislature. No exemptions were indeed permitted by the reassessment acts of 1852 and 1866, nor by the ordinance of 1858;[1] but a supplementary statute of 1869 released all property of literary, charitable and religious institutions, wearing apparel, farming utensils, crops, tools, personal property not exceeding $100 in value, mortgages for purchase money, securities of corporations already taxed, cash on hand and non-interest bearing deposits.[2] In the reassessment act of 1876, all property used exclusively for religious, charitable and benevolent purposes was exempt from state, county and municipal taxation, as were also crops in the hands of the producer, wearing apparel and mechanics' working tools. The important exemptions of the act of 1896 were the necessary plant and equipment of religious, charitable, benevolent, educational and literary institutions; crops in the hands of the producer; wearing apparel, except jewelry not habitually worn; the first $300 in value of the agricultural implements of farmers; property belonging to corporations taxed upon their capital stock, and the capital stock of railroads taxed upon gross receipts and property; book accounts and bills receivable of merchants taxed upon the average value of stock on hand. Mortgages were taxed as forms of personalty until 1870, when they were specifically exempted.[3] In 1896 they were subjected to a special tax

valuation of all other property, (5) sworn return of personalty in minutely detailed schedules with heavy penalties for neglect or false return, (6) final revision of assessments, upon appeal, by the Appeal Tax Court, (7) payment of taxes in quarterly installments, discontinuance of discounts for early payment, and increase of penalties for delinquencies.

[1] The ordinance of 1858 (sect. 42) did release from local taxation persons not owning property to the amount of $50.

[2] "Laws of Maryland," 1868, ch. 341.

[3] *Ibid.*, 1870, ch. 394.

of eight per cent. upon the gross amount of interest covenanted to be paid.[1] Stock of Baltimore City was exempt from all municipal taxation, and the regular state tax imposed thereon was paid by the city as in the case of any other corporation. No corresponding deduction was however made from the stockholder.[2]

The only distinctly local exemption of property from taxation was authorized by the General Assembly in 1880 "to encourage the development of manufactures and manufacturing industry in the city of Baltimore." Under this authority, the Appeal Tax Court was vested with power to abate municipal taxes upon manufacturing plants and machinery, not properly taxable as real estate.[3]

The spirit of the measure was early abused by the exemption of establishments which could only be described as manufacturing plants by an extravagant use of language, and which were peculiarly proper objects of local taxation. The aggregate plant exemption on January 1, 1888, was $2,085,571 of which $602,780 was on account of two gas companies alone.[4] This state of affairs was partly corrected in 1893 by the enactment of a revised ordinance, excepting gas, electric lighting companies and newspaper establishments from the operation of the measure and requiring annual renewal of the exemption privilege.[5] It is doubtful whether the exemption of plans stimulated industrial development to anything like the degree anticipated. On January 31, 1887, Mayor James Hodges declared: "There has been no material increase in the number of factories

[1] *Ibid.*, 1896, ch. 146 A-F. [2] Cf. below, p. 349.

[3] "Laws of Maryland," 1880, ch. 187; Ordinance of February 8, 1881, No. 7. The measure owed its existence largely to the efforts of Mayor F. C. Latrobe, by whom it was repeatedly recommended. See Mayors' Messages of January 8, 1877; January 1, 1879; January 1, 1880. The exemption of property under this ordinance increased from $514,867 in 1882, to $1,574,503 in 1884, to $1,983,522 in 1886, to $2,100,745 in 1890, to $3,405,055 in 1896. In 1898 the total exemptions had increased to $4,829,912.

[4] Mayor's Message of January 1, 1888.

[5] Ordinance of April 5, 1893, No. 71.

here to justify these large and increasing exemptions." This conclusion was confirmed by later experience. Manufacturing establishments were attracted to the city because of larger economic considerations. It is possible that tax exemption may have been the determining consideration with a limited number of enterprises; but the advantages thus accruing to the city were probably more than counterbalanced by the increased burden of property taxation due to the steadily increasing exemption.

The law of 1888 consolidating an adjoining portion of Baltimore County with the city provided that until the year 1900 the rate of municipal taxation upon this "annex" should not exceed the tax rate of Baltimore County for 1887 (60 cents on $100), and that until 1900 there should be no increase in existing assessments of property there located for purposes of municipal taxation. Faithful compliance was had with this statutory provision.

(Limitation and Rate). No effective limitation was put upon the taxing power of the corporation within the period here considered. In 1858 the maximum amount which the city might raise by the "Direct Levy" was fixed at $800,000.[1] In 1864 this was increased to $1,200,000,[2] and in 1874 all limitation was removed and the corporation, in response to its own petition, vested with power to fix the rate of the levy as municipal expenditure might require.[3] As a matter of fact even before 1874, the entire absence of any limitation upon the amount of the several municipal levies other than the Direct Levy, enabled the corporation to raise by direct taxation whatever sum was needed.[4] The

[1] "Laws of Maryland," 1858, ch. 68. [2] *Ibid.*, 1864, ch. 69.

[3] *Ibid.*, 1874, ch. 180; Resolution of Mayor and City Council of February 11, 1874, No. 39.

[4] Thus the statute of 1858, limiting the yield of the "direct levy" to $800,000, provided that "said tax shall be levied for the purpose of defraying the expenses of said corporation that may be over, above and exclusive of all expenses, charges and costs, that they now are empowered by law to defray by means of any tax they have or might heretofore have levied and collected." Similar provisions were contained in the statutes of 1864 and 1874, noted above.

only attempt to limit the rate of the aggregate tax levy was a declaratory ordinance of 1859, that the taxes thereafter levied upon the taxable property within the city limits should not exceed 90 cents on $100.[1] But a similar ordinance in the very next year raised this maximum to $1.00,[2] and the rate actually levied in 1861 was $1.09.

The Highway and Bridge Levy was imposed at a varying rate, in lieu of the Direct Levy, on property located without the limits of direct taxation. Until 1861 the rate appears to have been levied upon the aggregate assessed valuation, although nominally imposed only upon "houses and lands."[3] The separate return of realty and personalty, made after 1861 to facilitate the collection of taxes on personalty, permitted the imposition of the rate on the class of property which it was designed to reach.[4] In 1874 the corporation was unconditionally empowered to extend "the limits of direct taxation" from time to time as it might deem expedient.[5] But in 1874 the exempted area appears to have been merged completely with the city proper, for the Highway and Bridge Levy was imposed for the last time in that year. After 1876 the Direct Levy was formally imposed upon "assessable property in the city of Baltimore," instead of upon that located "within the limits of direct taxation."

The system of separate tax levies continued in vogue throughout the entire period under consideration. The seven levies already described[6] were supplemented in 1860 by a Police Levy, made necessary by the introduction of a metropolitan police system. The growth of the funded debt compelled the levy of an Interest on Funded Debt Levy in 1867 and the earlier Internal Improvements Levy was merged with this in 1877. The participation of the city in the cost of street reconstruction resulted in a special levy

[1] Ordinance of May 4, 1859, No. 73.

[2] Ordinance of May 16, 1860, No. 35.

[3] See above, p. 150.

[4] See below, p. 270.

[5] "Laws of Maryland," 1874, ch. 39.

[6] See above, pp. 148-150.

for this purpose after 1868. The irregular course of the sinking fund levies, authorized by successive loan ordinances, is described in another connection.[1] On the other hand, the Court Levy was discontinued in 1876 and the Highway and Bridge Levy ceased in 1874 with the abolition of the limits of direct taxation. The order of importance of the several levies was, for the greater part of the period, as follows: Direct Levy, Highway and Bridge Levy, Interest on Funded Debt Levy, Police Levy, School Levy, Certain Expenses Levy, Poor Levy, Internal Improvements Levy, Street Reconstruction Levy, Court Levy, and the various sinking fund levies.[2]

In actual practice, the system of distinct levies had lost all real significance before 1856, and its subsequent retention, as has already been stated, can only be described as a budgetary archaism. The aggregate tax levy was ordinarily a convenient rate, determined with reference to the aggregate estimated expenditures of the city and then apportioned among the several distinct levies. The result was a rough correspondence between departmental expenditure and the proceeds of the corresponding levy; but the levies were imposed in the form of a single tax rate, and the gross proceeds were covered into the municipal treasury and were appropriated entirely at the discretion of the corporation. An important exception to this resulted from the fiscal independence of the Board of Police Commissioners.[3]

Despite the heavy expenditures entailed by the development of municipal activity at the outset of the period here discussed, the aggregate tax rate remained for several years below the rate imposed in 1855 ($1.18¼). This was largely in consequence of the reassessment of 1858. The reckless financiering of the War and Reconstruction periods was reflected in an appreciable rise in the tax rate, but the more

[1] See below, p. 335. A water levy was imposed from 1885 to 1894; see below, p. 293. For the special water tax in force from 1862 to 1869, see below, p. 292.

[2] See Appendix E.

[3] See above, p. 223.

serious results were averted by the notable increase in the taxable basis brought about by the reassessment act of 1868. Similarly the upward course of the tax-rate was partially checked by the reassessment of 1876. After 1880, the deliberate restraint of municipal expenditure, the periodic accumulation and funding of floating indebtedness, the neglect of the sinking funds, and the use of funded loans for purposes theretofore the objects of current expenditure, combined to prevent any considerable increase in the tax rate. At the close of the period all of these resources had been more or less fully exploited, and the inevitable results appeared in a tax rate of $2.00 in 1896 and 1897, and $2.25 in 1898. In conjunction with the conditions of property assessment in Baltimore, the first rate was oppressive and the second was intolerable.

(Collection). The essential features of the system of tax collection underwent little change after 1856. Taxes were gathered by the City Collector,[1] graduated discounts were allowed for prompt payment, and interest penalties and legal processes were employed in the case of delinquents. The accumulation and persistence of large tax arrearages continued the serious problem of the collection department. The percentage of the general property tax collected within the year in which it was levied is shown, for the period from 1859 to 1897, in the following table:

Year.	Per Centum.	Year.	Per Centum.
1859	59.08	1868	68.90
1860	56.43	1869	72.60
1861	58.50	1870	72.44
1862	68.14	1871	58.42
1863	71.23	1872	55.33
1864	77.44	1873	50.71
1865	77.43	1874	54.50
1866	76.36	1875	55.46
1867	74.72	1876	54.46

[1] The City Collector also collected the State taxes levied in the city and received a percentage of the proceeds as a special remuneration therefor.

Year.	Per Centum.	Year.	Per Centum.
1877	63.23	1887	73.71
1878	60.97	1888	71.22
1879	65.61	1889	71.45
1880	70.21	1890	70.31
1881	74.79	1891	72.44
1882	72.93	1892	72.79
1883	71.43	1893	69.38
1884	71.73	1894	72.17
1885	72.95	1895	71.84
1886	73.33	1896	71.26

With the creation of the office of City Comptroller in 1857, the office of City Auditor was abolished and the actual incumbent was retained in office only long enough to complete the unfinished collection of arrearages. At the end of the designated period, a large number of accounts still remained open and the office was continued with its separate clerks and bailiffs.[1] In 1859 the Auditor's duties were transferred to the Comptroller, and although in 1860 the office of Auditor was revived, a single person acted both as Comptroller and as Auditor.[2] Soon after 1862 the appointment of an Auditor was discontinued, and thereafter the collection of arrearages devolved upon the City Collector. In 1861 the assessment of real and personal property was separated; larger discounts were offered for the prompt payment of taxes on personal than on real property; taxes on personal property were made collectible by distraint within five months after the levy of the tax, while taxes on real property became in arrears and liable to interest penalties and legal processes only after the close of the fiscal year.[3] The effect of these changes was imme-

[1] Ordinance of February 26, 1858, No. 3; Report of City Collector, January 1, 1862.

[2] Ordinances of September 1, 1859, No. 102; March 14, 1860, No. 7; July 14, 1860, No. 54. In 1861 the Collector was appointed Auditor for a year; see Ordinance of February 28, 1861, No. 6.

[3] Reports of City Collector, January 1, 1861, and January 1, 1862; Ordinances of April 1, 1861, No. 9; April 27, 1861, No. 33; June 2, 1862, No. 46; November 17, 1863, No. 68.

diately apparent in increased tax collections. Between 1863 and 1871 the percentage of taxes collected within the year of the levy fell below 72 per cent. upon but one occasion, and tax arrearages, although considerable, were not serious enough to embarrass municipal finances. The succeeding decade, with its long-continued industrial depression and its earlier termination of the fiscal year,[1] showed far less favorable results. In 1873 a little more than one-half of the taxes levied in that year were collected, and at no time before 1880 were arrearages less than 34 per cent. This large amount of delinquency, the evil effects of which are discussed in another connection,[2] was variously explained as due to the inadequate force of the collector's office, to the imperfections of the laws and ordinances relating to the sales of property for taxes in arrears, to the lateness of the levy and the shortness of the discount period, and to the laxity of the city in enforcing collections.[3] Probably the last factor was the most important, and the decline in tax arrears after 1879 was largely due to a more rigid enforcement of tax levies. The rate of municipal taxation and general economic conditions exerted important influence upon tax collections; but other things being equal, the percentage received in any given year was dependent upon the capacity and industry of the City Collector.

The system of graduated discounts for the early payment of taxes remained in vogue during the entire period considered. The results in Baltimore confirm the unfavorable experience of American states and cities in the use of this fiscal device. The allowance of discounts was unnecessary, since

[1] See above, p. 205. [2] See below, p. 329.

[3] "So much indulgence has been given in the past to delinquent tax-payers that many of them have come to believe that the payment of taxes in arrears cannot be enforced until after the expiration of three years from the time they fall due," after which they were barred by limitation. Report of City Collector, January 10, 1880. The existing practise and the need of new methods are clearly set forth in this well-written report.

the prompt payment of taxes could be compelled by legal process. It wrought marked inequality between citizens who could afford to avail themselves of the maximum discounts and the poorer tax-payers who could not. It was a most expensive method of supplying the municipal treasury with funds for current expenditure, since the discounts allowed were far in excess of the rate at which the city could borrow money. Finally it encouraged the mischievous attitude that the prompt payment of taxes was an unusual act entitled to reward instead of mere compliance with civic duty.[1] The entire repeal of the discount system was recommended by the Baltimore Tax Commission of 1885, and public sentiment rapidly tended in that direction thereafter.[2]

License Taxes.

The relative importance of license taxes in the financial system of Baltimore declined with the growth of the municipal budget and the larger recourse to direct property taxation. The appropriation of traders' licenses or privilege taxes by the state tended, probably more than other circumstances, to prevent a larger local use of this fiscal device. During the greater part of the period here considered local license taxes continued to be used primarily for regulative rather than for financial purposes. Many of the charges were in the nature of license fees "imposed to cover the cost of regulation or to meet the outlay incurred," rather than license taxes, designed "to bring in a distinct net revenue to the government above the cost of regulation."[3] Yet the fiscal consideration was never entirely absent, and after 1890 it became at least a co-ordinate

[1] "Report of Massachusetts Tax Commission," 1875, pp. 71-79.

[2] The discount system was greatly modified but not entirely abolished in the new city charter.

[3] Seligman, "Essays in Taxation," p. 279. It has been found necessary to sacrifice the distinction which Professor Seligman has drawn with characteristic acuteness, and to conform to local usage in aggregating all such receipts, as "license taxes."

influence in the new license taxes actually imposed, as well as the chief impulse to a further extension of the system.

Little or no qualitative change was made in the license taxes in vogue before 1856. Vehicles, market traders, public amusements, pawnbrokers, dogs were the important categories.[1] The earlier charges were changed in amount from time to time and new ones were occasionally imposed. Thus, upon the introduction of street railways in 1859, a license tax of $20 per annum was imposed upon street-cars, and reduced in 1873 to $5.[2] In 1864 a permit from the City Commissioner, approved by the Mayor, was required for the construction of private sewers, and a specific charge of twenty cents for each lineal foot of ground covered was imposed upon the owner but was commonly avoided.[3] In 1881 a nominal license tax was imposed upon retail dealers in petroleum, and in 1890 a heavier annual charge was put upon street sales of fruits and vegetables. In 1891 the ordinances of the city relating to the inspection of buildings were revised, and additional license charges were imposed for the erection of certain structures.[4]

License taxes were imposed and collected annually by the Comptroller. The only exception was the license charges upon market dealers which, during the greater part of the period, were collected by the market clerks, and then paid, together with stall rentals, to the Comptroller in quarterly account. The practise encouraged laxity and irregularity and was finally discontinued for direct payment to the Comptroller.[5] In point of annual yield, the license taxes on vehicles were the most important of these earlier charges; this was largely because of the incorporation of

[1] See above, p. 158.
[2] Ordinance of March 28, 1859, No. 44, and April 30, 1873, No. 77.
[3] See above, p. 213.
[4] Ordinance of October 23, 1891, No. 146. In 1892 the legislature authorized the Mayor to issue permits to poor persons to peddle small wares within the corporate limits; in lieu of paying the ordinary trader's license tax to the state, such persons paid the sum of $7 to the city (Laws of Maryland, 1892, ch. 90).
[5] Cf. below, pp. 296-297.

the old specific taxes therewith. The market licenses came next in order; but the proceeds were ordinarily merged with the rentals and other receipts of the market clerks. Of the remaining taxes, only those imposed on public amusements yielded an appreciable revenue.[1]

Within the last few years of the period here considered, two of the most important license taxes in the fiscal system of Baltimore were imposed. As a result of long-continued agitation the General Assembly in 1890 authorized a high license tax on retail liquor sales in Baltimore. Distinct administrative machinery was provided by the creation of a bi-partisan Board of Liquor License Commissioners, composed of three members biennially appointed by the Governor. Licenses were granted by the Board under moderately stringent regulation and subject to an annual tax of $250. Payment was made to the Clerk of the Court of Common Pleas and transferred in quarterly account to the state treasury. One-fourth of the proceeds was retained by the state and the remainder paid over to the city. The salaries of the Board of Liquor License Commissioners and all attendant expenses were charged to the city.[2] The large proportion of the tax withheld from the city was nominally a compensation for the loss of revenue from the abandonment of the old state license tax. As a matter of fact it was much in excess of this amount, and was to that extent a tribute levied by the legislature, overwhelmingly controlled by the counties, upon the city for the passage of a purely local measure. It was one of the infrequent in-

[1] In 1898 the license tax on dogs was reimposed with penalties for non-compliance. In connection therewith, a contract was made with the Maryland Society for the Prevention of Cruelty to Animals for the impounding of stray and unlicensed dogs. The Society received a certain specified amount and also such part of the dog licenses and fines as might be necessary to defray the expenses incurred (Ordinance No. 96 of June 15, 1898). The measure resulted in an astonishing increase in the proceeds of the tax, no part of which could, however, be used for ordinary municipal purposes. The legality of the ordinance was attacked, and the case is now pending.

[2] "Laws of Maryland," 1890, ch. 343.

stances in the financial history of Baltimore of that mischievous interference of a state legislature in city affairs, to which many of the gravest abuses in American municipal government are due. Despite the large quota retained by the state, the net proceeds of the liquor license tax at once became next to the general property tax the most important source of revenue in the municipal budget. It was from its very nature inelastic; but in every other respect it was found to be as fiscally sound as socially expedient.[1]

A license tax of $2 per annum was imposed in 1893 upon every telegraph, telephone, electric light or other pole belonging to any person or corporation. The poles used exclusively for stringing trolley wires of street railways were specifically exempted from the tax. Owners made return of the number of poles and paid the tax imposed thereon to the Comptroller, who issued a numbered tin plate to be affixed to each pole.[2] The tax served important fiscal and regulative purposes. The proceeds of the charge exceeded the receipts from any of the license taxes except those imposed on liquor sales and on vehicles. It placed some check upon the duplication of poles, and discouraged the further extension of overhead wire service. Both of these results emphasized the error of exempting the trolley poles of street railways from the tax.[3]

Franchise Taxes.

The experience of Baltimore with respect to its public franchises, save in one notable particular, has been that of the ordinary American city. The sagacity and far-sightedness of Mayor Thomas Swann early introduced the principle of a franchise tax upon the gross receipts of street railways, and this in more or less modified form remained

[1] The income of the city from liquor licenses was as follows: 1891, $384,012.17; 1892, $380,315.14; 1893, $390,137.89; 1894, $403,-985.78; 1895, $405,891.95; 1896, $400,181.53.

[2] Ordinance of April 20, 1893, No. 86.

[3] It has been said that the exemption was absolutely necessary to secure the passage of the measure.

the subsequent course of the municipality. In the case of other industries of service—gas supply, electric lighting, telegraphs, telephones—a policy of wasteful prodigality was pursued. The use of the city streets, involving public inconvenience and private gain, were conferred again and again for no consideration whatever. To this end both the blind negligence of the municipal administration and the unwarranted interference of the state legislature contributed. Not until the closing years of the period here examined was any evidence afforded of a saner municipal policy with respect to municipal franchises. This was inadequately indicated in the imposition of a franchise tax on telephone conduits in 1889 and fully expressed in the franchise provisions of the new charter.[1]

Street Railways. The introduction of street railways in Baltimore, although proposed several years earlier, was first actively agitated in 1858. Efforts were then made to secure the necessary articles of incorporation and franchise grants from the General Assembly and from the City Council, but without success. In March, 1859, after a sharp struggle, a voluntary association, the nucleus of the Baltimore City Passenger Railway Company, succeeded in obtaining the passage of a municipal ordinance authorizing the laying of tracks and the operation of street railways in the most important thoroughfares of the city.[2]

Through the far-sighted wisdom of Mayor Thomas Swann, the franchise granted by the city was made subject to important limitations. The projectors of the railway were required to purchase the property of the existing omnibus lines; the passenger fare was limited to a maximum of five cents with free transfers; an annual license tax of twenty

[1] An important influence was doubtless exerted by the decision of the Maryland Court of Appeals (77 Md. 354) and the United States Supreme Court (166 U. S. 673) in the "Lake Roland Elevated Railway Company Case," that a franchise granted by the city is in the nature of a license, subject to reasonable modification, rather than an inviolable contract.

[2] Ordinance of March 28, 1859, No. 44.

dollars was imposed on cars, and the Company was required to keep in repair the portion of the street covered by the tracks, including two feet from the outer limits. The city reserved the right to purchase at intervals of fifteen years the entire stock and equipment of the Company, the value thereof to be determined by arbitration, if necessary.[1] Most important of all, a franchise tax was imposed of one-fifth of the gross receipts "accruing from the passenger travel upon said roads located within the city limits under this ordinance, or any extension of said limits which may be determined upon hereafter." The proceeds of the franchise tax were appropriated exclusively to the establishment and improvement of the new boundary avenue, then contemplated, and to the purchase and improvement of public parks for the city. The city reserved the right to reduce the rate of passenger fare within the range of the gross receipts tax, relinquishing after such reduction a corresponding proportion of the tax.

[1] This provision, in the practically unchanged form in which it was inserted in the act of incorporation granted by the General Assembly in 1862 ("Laws of Maryland," 1862, ch. 71), is interesting and important enough to warrant citation in full:

"The said Mayor and City Council shall have the privilege, within two years after the expiration of fifteen years from the date of the passage of said ordinance, to purchase and buy out the said corporation, and all its property and franchises, whether originally conceded by the ordinance aforesaid, or granted by this act, for and at a fair and equitable consideration, or value, and in case of a disagreement, as to the said value and consideration, the Mayor and City Council aforesaid, shall appoint one referee, and the corporation hereby created shall appoint another referee, who, in event of disagreement, shall appoint an umpire, the decision of whom shall be final as to the price to be paid as aforesaid; and provided further, that if the said Mayor and City Council shall decline or neglect to give notice to the said corporation of their intention to make said purchase within the aforesaid two years, then the grants and privileges held and enjoyed by the corporation shall continue to belong to it for fifteen years longer from the expiration of said original fifteen years, subject to all the terms and conditions imposed and recognized by this act, and continuable thereafter in like manner from time to time as aforesaid, upon the said terms and conditions."

The municipal franchise was conferred in March, 1859, making the purchase periods 1874-76, 1889-91, 1904-1906, etc.

Within less than three weeks after this franchise had been granted, the grantees disposed of their interest therein to a Philadelphia syndicate for a consideration reported to have been $100,000.[1] This transaction excited popular rage and bitterness. It not only demonstrated that the city had conferred the franchise at much less than its real value; but prevented a popular subscription to the stock of the association and precluded the conduct of the enterprise by local interests which the original ordinance had contemplated.

Popular animosity took the form of intense opposition to the incorporation of the association and to the confirmation of the municipal grant by the state legislature, then deemed necessary. A rival association offering reduced fare was endorsed; a legislative inquiry was instituted into the circumstances under which the original franchise had been secured and assigned, and a substitute enterprise controlled by local interests was urged. As a result of this combined opposition, articles of incorporation were denied by the legislature for several years, and not until February, 1862, were the requisite confirmatory grant and corporate privilege secured.

The original attitude of the municipality to street railways was thus intelligent and far-sighted. Municipal ownership seems to have been seriously considered and, but for the extent to which the city was then involved with the Baltimore and Ohio Railroad, might have perhaps been realized. It was certainly entertained as an ultimate policy of the city. This was evident not only in the insertion of the fifteen years purchase clause in the municipal franchise, but in the repeated expressions of willingness and ability to enter upon municipal construction made while the incorporation of the voluntary association was under discussion. Even thereafter, in 1865, a proposition of the street railway company (made under stress of financial embarrassment) to sell franchise and property to the city at actual cost, or if preferred, at a valuation to be ascertained by arbitration,

[1] Scharf, "History of Baltimore City and County," p. 363.

was seriously considered.[1] In lieu of the profits of municipal ownership and operation, a franchise tax was imposed on the gross receipts of the street railway company. The value of the streets and the profits likely to be realized from local transportation were clearly recognized. The alternatives presented were: should the city's share be realized in the form of reduced passenger fare or in the form of a tax on gross receipts! The eagerness of Mayor Thomas Swann to secure funds for the purchase and support of municipal parks was probably responsible for the adoption of the franchise tax, and this sagacious choice determined subsequent municipal policy.[2]

In the forty years succeeding the projection of the first street railway in Baltimore, an elaborate system of local transportation was evolved. During the greater part of this period, transit service was slowly extended by the creation of new companies and the grant of independent franchises. Beginning with 1888 rapid transit was introduced, the numerous independent companies were consolidated into a few great systems, and service was extended by grants supplementary to the original franchises.[3] The essential features of the first street railway franchise were reproduced in the successive grants made thereafter. An important exception to this was the fifteen-year purchase clause which was unfortunately omitted from all later franchises.[4] The tax on gross receipts, the license tax on cars, the fixture of a maximum passenger fare, and the requirement to keep in repair the portion of the street bed occupied, figured in the specific franchises and were incorporated in general statute law.

[1] Scharf, "History of Baltimore City and County," p. 365.

[2] In the one instance in which a franchise was conferred without the gross receipts tax, the maximum fare was limited to three cents (Ordinance of Dec. 7, 1859, No. 6).

[3] As these pages are passing through the press, the inevitable tendency to combination has resulted in the complete consolidation of the street railways into a single system.

[4] It did, however, appear in a second minor franchise granted in 1859 (see Ordinance of Dec. 7, 1859, No. 6).

The financial relations of the municipality and the street railways however underwent important modifications within the period considered. This resulted from the reduction of franchise payments, (1) by legislative enactment; (2) by judicial interpretation.

(1) During the Civil War, the Baltimore City Passenger Railway Company was permitted to make a charge for transfer tickets and to increase the rate of fare from five to six and later to seven cents—the latter increase as a compensation for the war tax on gross receipts. Application was made to the legislature for a reduction of the franchise tax, but without success. In 1870 the federal statute permitting common carriers to recoup themselves for the internal revenue tax was repealed and the fare of the local street railways was reduced to six cents. In 1873 ex-Governor Oden Bowie was elected president of the Baltimore City Passenger Railway Company, and remained in that office until his death in 1894.[1] A strong personal influence and a wide political experience were thus enlisted in the interest of the local street railways, with most effective results. In April, 1873, the City Council reduced the license tax on street cars from $20 to $5 per annum, and specifically exempted the capital stock and property of the companies from all other local taxes as long as this license tax and the twenty per cent. franchise tax should be paid.[2] But still further "economies" were in view, and at the session of 1874 a memorial was presented to the General Assembly asking for a reduction of the franchise tax from twenty to ten per cent. of gross receipts. The legislature declined to act in the matter, and recourse was had to the City Council. This body proved more tractable, and in June, 1874, the franchise tax upon the gross receipts of the street railways was reduced from twenty to twelve per cent.[3] The only

[1] It is probably something more than a mere coincidence that the vacancy created by ex-Gov. Bowie's death was filled by the election of an ex-Governor of Maryland.

[2] Ordinance of April 30, 1873, No. 77.

[3] Ordinance of June 9, 1874, No. 48.

concession received by the city in return for this extraordinary gift was the substitution of conductors for fare boxes upon certain lines, and the limitation of children's fares to four cents. For the next eight years the integrity of the franchise tax, although on several occasions assailed, was not affected. A strenuous effort in 1882 was finally successful, and in return for a reduction of passenger fares from six and four to five and three cents, respectively, and the sale of transfer tickets at three cents, the General Assembly authorized the reduction of the franchise tax from twelve to nine per cent. of gross receipts.[1]

No further change was made in the rate of the franchise tax. By the legislation of 1882 all control over the matter was practically taken from the City Council and vested in the General Assembly. Almost every subsequent legislative session witnessed a more or less persistent effort on the part of the street railway companies to secure some further abatement; but the intensity of public sentiment in Baltimore and the increasing importance of the proceeds of the tax in the municipal budget were able to prevent any reduction.

(2) Although the rate of the "park tax" remained unchanged after the reduction to nine per cent. by the General Assembly in 1882, the revenue of the city from this source was seriously affected thereafter by judicial interpretation. In 1887 the Baltimore Union Passenger Railway Company, operating a railway of which ½ mile lay without the city limits, refused to pay the franchise tax on more than fifty per cent. of its gross receipts. This refusal was justified on the ground that the franchise tax was imposed only upon gross receipts within the city and that fifty per cent. represented a reasonable proportion of the total receipts collected within the taxable area.

The city declined to accept such an arbitrary apportion-

[1] Laws of Maryland, 1882, ch. 229. The reduction in fare was the actual rather than the statutory consideration for the lower franchise tax.

ment and the matter was brought up for judicial determination. In a decision, which from the standpoint of the city's interest can only be regarded as most unfortunate, the Court of Appeals sustained the opinion of the lower court that the part of the track located outside of the city limit was not subject to the franchise tax. Since no means existed of determining how far each passenger travelled, "the only way to approximate a fair basis of settlement was to act on the assumption that each part of each line carries as many as any other part." This theory had been applied by the legislature in the taxation of the gross receipts of railroads, located partly within and partly without Maryland.[1] Accordingly the rule of apportionment laid down was that, that amount of the gross receipts of the street railway was liable to the franchise tax which stood in the same proportion to the aggregate gross receipts, as did the car mileage of the railway within the city bear to the total car mileage.[2]

Unfortunate enough in itself, the decision led to far more serious consequences. In 1888 a large belt of suburban territory was annexed to the corporate limits, subject to the provision that property there located should not be subject to additional local taxation until 1900.[3] The introduction of rapid transit a few years later led to a general extension of the street railways into the annexed territory, for the most part over private property or turnpike roads acquired by the railways by purchase or condemnation. On that proportion of gross receipts credited to the "Annex," in accordance with the rule of apportionment before laid

[1] Public General Laws, Art. 81, sect. 153 (vol. II, p. 1264). The rule was pronounced "fair and reasonable" by the Maryland Court of Appeals (45 Md. 384), and was approved by the United States Supreme Court (92 U. S. 608-611; 125 U. S. 530-552).

[2] Baltimore Union Passenger Railway Company *vs.* Mayor and City Council of Baltimore, 71 Md. 405. The circumstance that certain tracks were employed in common by several lines of the same company suggested the use of car mileage instead of track mileage in the apportionment of the gross receipts.

[3] Cf. above, p. 266.

down, the street railways refused to pay the franchise tax. This action was based on the grounds (1) that the annexation act offered exemption from additional local taxation, and (2) that in any event the franchise tax could not be imposed upon the receipts from travel over private property.

The Court of Appeals in 1896 explicitly accepted the narrow interpretation intimated in the earlier decision, and defined the nine per cent. tax as "a franchise tax exacted in exchange for the privilege given to the companies to run their cars upon streets subject to the control of the city." Accordingly, gross receipts accruing from tracks upon property acquired by the railways without municipal grant or concession were exempted from the franchise tax.[1] As to the liability of the street railways for the franchise tax upon receipts accruing from the use of public highways in the "Annex," the court made no ruling.

The limitation of the franchise tax to the proceeds of travel over the city's streets, and the apportionment of gross receipts according to car mileage combined to make serious inroads upon the municipal income from this source. The practice of the street railways in making return only of the amount and not of the proportion of the gross receipts liable to the franchise tax renders it impossible to determine the full effect to which the city has suffered.[2] It is probable that since 1890 an increasing proportion of gross receipts have escaped the franchise tax, and that the premium thus put upon otherwise unprofitable suburban extension will effect further reductions in the taxable proportion.

Wire Conduits. In 1889 the local telephone company secured from the city an important franchise to construct a

[1] "The Park Tax Case," 84 Md. 1.

[2] The city might properly exercise the authority conferred by the legislature in 1894 to examine the accounts of the street railways (Acts of Assembly, ch. 550), and require, instead of the bare statement now made, full details of gross receipts, aggregate car mileage, proportion liable to taxation, etc.

system of underground conduits for the reception of wires used in connection with a new telephone exchange. The preamble of the ordinance conferring the franchise emphasized the altruistic impulse of the corporation in desiring to reduce the concentration of overhead wires. Nothing was said of the economies attending a sub-way, as compared with an overhead system, nor of the incidental escape from the license tax on poles.[1] Some appreciation of these latter considerations, as well as of the public nuisance involved in tearing up the streets of the city for the construction of the conduits, induced the municipal administration to confer the grant subject to a franchise tax, inadequate in amount but none the less significant as the first effort since Mayor Swann's time to secure some direct return for the franchise privileges enjoyed by local industries of service. The telephone company was required to pay annually to the city thirty cents for each lineal yard of the first four miles in aggregate length of wire conduits constructed under the franchise, and twenty cents per lineal yard for each succeeding mile or fraction of a mile; the aggregate tax was however fixed at a minimum of $3000 per annum. The company was also required to provide space, free of cost or rent, in every underground conduit for a cable, to be laid by the Board of Fire Commissioners, for the exclusive and official use of the municipal police patrol and fire alarm telegraph wires.[2] The plan, location and construction of the conduits was subject to the approval and superintendence of the City Commissioner.[3] Between 1889 and 1897 thirteen miles of conduits were constructed in the streets of the city under this grant, and the franchise tax regularly imposed thereupon.[4]

In the light of the subsequent policy of municipal construction of wire conduits, the grant of this independent

[1] See above, p. 275. [2] See below, p. 297.

[3] Ordinance of May 9, 1889, No. 41.

[4] The receipts from the tax was as follows: 1889, $1,500; 1890, $1,500; 1891, $4,150 50; 1892, $6,953.10; 1893, $4,635.80; 1894, $4,635.80; 1895, $4,635.80; 1896, $4,635.80.

franchise was short-sighted and unfortunate.[1] The charge was moreover hardly more than nominal and certainly not an adequate return for the privileges conferred. The real significance of the measure was the assertion of the principle of public compensation for public franchises, and of the advisability of conferring franchises subject to an annual tax rather than of selling them for a definite amount.

Special Assessments.

The special assessment, although an appreciable source of municipal revenue in the period from 1857 to 1897, was of relatively less importance than in the earlier history of the city. It continued to be levied primarily in aid of the cost of street paving and repaving, and of street reconstruction; but an increasing proportion of the cost of such improvements was defrayed by direct municipal appropriation. The acquisition of a municipal water plant rendered unnecessary the further provision of public pumps and wells, and the new and important occasion for the use of the special assessment, offered by the construction of storm-water sewers, was not embraced. The restricted use of the special assessment was due not to any dissatisfaction with it as a fiscal device, but to the growing burden of direct taxation upon real property. Any attempt to assess upon the property presumably benefited the whole or a considerable part of the large expenditures required for the repaving and reconstruction of important thoroughfares or the con-

[1] This was vividly realized in 1898 after the city had practically determined to construct a system of municipal conduits. While the enabling ordinance was awaiting the Mayor's approval, the telephone company secured a "blanket" permit from a pliant City Commissioner and proceeded hurriedly to extend its own conduits along certain of the most important streets of the city. This high-handed procedure was aggravated by the fact that the size and capacity of the new conduits were stated to be far in excess of the actual requirements of the company. Public sentiment was aroused to a high pitch and the "blanket" permit was revoked, with the intention of subordinating the further extension of the company's conduits to the proposed municipal sub-ways. See below, p. 297.

struction of permanent sewers would have probably delayed the improvements; or if successful, it would have involved the practical confiscation of much of the property involved.

Street Paving and Repaving. For some years no change whatever was made in the form of the special assessment levied for street paving and repaving. Upon the application of the owners of a major part of the ground bordering upon any unpaved street or upon the passage of a special enabling ordinance, the City Commissioner gave public notice of a designated day for determining upon the petition. If the decision was favorable, proposals for the work were invited and a contract awarded. The total cost of the improvement, including expenses of collection but omitting the cost of paving cross-streets and sidewalks, was assessed upon the owners of abutting property, in proportion to frontage. The amount so assessed constituted a lien upon the property for the benfit of the contractor, and a clause was inserted in all contracts releasing the city from responsibility for the expenditure involved. The assessments were collected by the City Collector, paid over to the Register, and thence transferred to the contractor upon the warrant of the City Commissioner. Delinquents were sued by the Collector upon the petition and in behalf of the contractor, in the name of the Mayor and City Council of Baltimore.[1]

In 1870 modifications of some importance were introduced. A right of appeal from the awards of the City Commissioner to the Baltimore City Court was conferred.[2] Streets in process of reconstruction were exempted from the provision requiring the assent of the owners of a major part of abutting property as a preliminary requisite for the levy of a special assessment for paving and repaving.[3] The City Collector was required to enforce the collection of assessments upon his own initiative, but the city still declined

[1] Revised Ordinances of 1858, No. 13; Baltimore City Code, 1869, Art. 43.

[2] "Laws of Maryland," 1870, ch. 322.

[3] *Ibid.*, 1870, ch. 282; Ordinance of June 3, 1870, No. 74.

responsibility for any part of the contract expenditure. Four years later this doubtful practise was discontinued and the modern procedure introduced of treating the cost of paving as a direct municipal liability and the special assessment as a form of compulsory municipal revenue.[1] In actual practise the number of unpaved streets was reduced so rapidly with the growth of residential areas that the levy of the special assessment for initial paving was limited largely to that made necessary by street reconstruction.

In the case of repaving identically the same procedure was prescribed as in the case of paving, except that one-third of the aggregate cost was defrayed by the city.[2] The general replacement of cobblestones with modern pavements began in 1880 and the large expenditures required for this purpose were defrayed, as already described, entirely by the city from out the proceeds of funded loans, instead of by the city and the benefited property owners, jointly.[3]

Street Reconstruction. For some years the special assessment to defray the cost of street reconstruction was levied in the manner defined in 1841. The transfer of the functions of the Commissioners for Opening Streets to the Appeal Tax Court in 1861 involved no essential change in procedure. But the revival of the former board in 1866 was accompanied by important modification. Theretofore

[1] "Laws of Maryland," 1874, ch. 218; Ordinance of June 4, 1874, No. 44.

[2] Ordinance of June 4, 1874, No. 44.

[3] Cf. above, page 212. The city suffered serious loss from time to time because of the defective wording of paving ordinances. Thus by the decision of the Court of Appeals in the "Light Street Paving Case" (Burns *vs.* Mayor, 48 Md. 198), the cost of a number of improvements for which a special assessment might properly have been levied was thrown upon the municipal treasury, because the ordinances referred to the improvements as required by "public convenience" (cf. Report of City Solicitor, January 1, 1879). In 1885 a preliminary opinion as to the validity of any paving or repaving ordinance was required of the law officers of the city before the improvement could be actually undertaken (Ordinance of April 17, 1885, No. 37).

the practise had prevailed of assessing the entire cost of the improvement, including the aggregate damages awarded, upon the property benefited—regardless of the fact whether or not the cost so assessed exceeded the benefit actually derived. In 1866 the modern principle was recognized of levying the assessment only to the amount of the accruing benefit, and of defraying the balance from out the general treasury.[1] As long as it was necessary to provide the amount "assessed against the city" from out of current municipal revenues, care was taken to assess property owners to the full amount of the benefit conferred and the major cost of the improvement was defrayed by the special assessment so levied. With the use of funded loans instead of current revenues for this purpose, the municipality assumed a more generous attitude and the relative importance of the contributions of city and property owners was reversed.[2]

Sewers. The provision made in 1868 for the construction of a system of storm-water sewers or drains involved the levy of a special assessment in part payment of the cost thereof. Whenever directed by municipal ordinance to construct or extend any sewer, the Commissioners for Opening Streets and the City Commissioner, acting as a single board, met after due public notice for the determination of damages and benefits. The special assessment was levied upon "all the ground and improvements within and adjacent to the city, the owners of which, as such, the said commissioners shall decide and deem to be directly benefited by accomplishing the object authorized." The rule of apportionment was to be "as far as practicable . . . the number of superficial feet drained." In the event of the aggregate benefits assessed not equalling the damages awarded and the expenses incurred, the balance was to be paid by the City Register from out the municipal treasury.

[1] Cf. Rosewater, "Special Assessments," p. 96.

[2] See above, page 219. For details of procedure in the levy of the special assessment for street reconstruction and for the decisions of the Maryland courts in reference thereto, see Poe, "Pleading and Practice," II., 799.

The valuations of the commissioners were published and were subject to correction; final right of appeal lay to the Baltimore City Court. The assessed benefits constituted a lien upon the property and were collected by the City Collector in the manner of other city taxes.[1]

As a matter of fact, few storm-water sewers were constructed before 1881 and those for the most part of a primitive character. The cost of the important sewers built after the introduction of the Gunpowder Water Supply in 1881, was defrayed by the issue of funded loans and not by the levy of a special assessment.[2]

FEES.

As a source of municipal revenue, fees were of trivial importance in the later history of the city. A rigidly precise classification would probably include under this category a portion of the revenue derived from the issue of "permits." Conforming to local usage, receipts of this character have been treated under the head of license taxes. The nominal charge for text-books in the public schools of the city yielded an appreciable income; but this ceased in great part in 1884 when the schools were made entirely free to residents of Baltimore. A small revenue continued to accrue from the attendance of non-resident pupils.

Quarantine attendance, the maintenance of delinquents and dependents chargeable to the counties and to the federal government, the residence of medical students in the city almshouse, the trial of cases removed from the counties to the city courts, the inspection of gas meters, the issue of health certificates and the fixture of the city seal yielded slight revenues which may properly be described as fees.[3]

[1] "Laws of Maryland," 1868, ch. 1; Ordinance of May 7, 1868, No. 55.

[2] Cf. above, p. 216.

[3] The five Inspectors of Weights and Measures and the single Inspector of Long and Dry Measures were remnants of the old body of inspection officers, whose services were paid by fees and correspondingly unsatisfactory.

Fines.

Receipts from fines, penalties and forfeitures formed an insignificant item in the municipal budget during the entire period under consideration. This resulted naturally from the state control of the local police force and from the incorporation of the local courts with the state judiciary. Fines, forfeitures and penalties imposed under the laws of the state were paid over in quarterly account to the Clerk of the Court of Common Pleas. If imposed under the ordinances of the corporation, they were paid similarly to the Register for the benefit of the city; but the city received only one-half of the fines accruing in the Criminal Court of Baltimore for the violation of municipal ordinances.[1]

Quasi-Private Receipts.

Water Supply. Municipal control of water supply in Baltimore was from the outset characterized by the policy of "cost service," that is, of supplying water for private consumption at the minimum rate necessary for defraying the gross cost of operation, including interest upon the funded water debt. During certain periods the revenues of the department were inadequate for this purpose and the deficit was provided by municipal appropriation or by direct taxation. At other times receipts were in excess of all expenditures charged to the department, and an annual surplus reverted to the municipal treasury. This imperfect adjustment between income and expenditure, notable in successive terms of years, was due in large part to the anomaly existing in the financial administration of the department. The Water Board enjoyed virtual independence in fiscal matters, to the extent that all revenues of the department were expended at the discretion of the Board for cost of operation and for interest upon the water debt. On the other hand, water rentals were fixed by the City Council and were not always determined in accordance with the

[1] Thus see "Laws of Maryland," 1876, ch. 28.

fiscal policy of the department. In the main, however, there was never any sustained endeavor to conduct the water works either at a definite profit nor at an actual loss, and water rentals approximated the rates necessary to make both ends meet.

The financial importance of the water department may be conveniently dated from 1857, when the reorganized Water Board was directed to prepare a schedule of water rates with the consent of the City Council. Rental charges were gathered by collectors appointed by the Mayor; the proceeds were transferred to the Water Register, appointed biennially by the Water Board, and finally paid over in daily settlement to the City Register. The distinct fund so formed was disbursed upon the drafts of the Water Board for current expenses of operation and maintenance, and for the interest upon a part of the funded water debt.[1] For some years the income from the works was insufficient to entirely defray these charges, and on January 4, 1862, the accumulated deficit was one hundred and eight thousand dollars, which sum had been advanced by the city and was charged against the department.[2] In 1862 the financial affairs of the department underwent important modification. A new tariff of rental charges was established by municipal ordinance, and upon the recommendation of the Water Board a specific water tax, varying according to frontage and designated as the "water and fire-plug rate," was imposed on all buildings within three hundred feet of a water main even though water had not been introduced on the premises. Discounts varying from ten to four per cent. were allowed for the prompt payment of all water rentals and rates. All moneys received by the Water Department were kept in distinct account and distributed as before, with the added provision that any remaining surplus should be applied annually to the sinking fund for the redemption of

[1] Ordinance of April 14, 1857, No. 28.
[2] Report of Water Department, January 4, 1862.

the water debt.[1] The specific water tax remained in existence until 1869. Originally imposed as a means of distributing the cost of water used for public purposes, notably for fire protection, the tax was later defended as a measure to compel house owners to introduce water service. During the entire period that it was in force, the tax was the subject of controversy and a most unreliable source of revenue.[2] Its yield increased from $13,507.82 in 1862, to $22,309.01 in 1863, to $26,276.10 in 1864, declining thereafter to $16,806.32 in 1866, and to $14,672.54 in 1868. In 1869 the Water Board expressed the opinion that "an equal amount of revenue might be raised under the general levy in a way to avoid every appearance of injustice to any particular property owner,"[3] and the tax was actually repealed in that year.

The net receipts of the department steadily increased in the decade following 1862. Losses were suffered from the administrative laxity of the Reconstruction period, and current revenues were diverted in considerable amount to the extension of mains in the city and to the plant proper. To prevent the extravagant waste of water, it became necessary in 1870 to introduce water-meters in large manufacturing establishments and to charge according to the amount consumed. But in 1871, in addition to paying all expenses of the department, the Water Board assumed charge of the interest upon the entire existing water debt of $5,000,000, of which only $3,650,000 had theretofore been borne. Interest upon the Gunpowder loan, authorized in 1874 and gradually issued thereafter, was at first paid from out the city treasury, and the increasing annual surplus of

[1] "Laws of Maryland," 1862, ch. 83; Ordinance of March 27, 1862, No. 10. Buildings assessed for a sum not exceeding $200 were exempt from the water rate by Ordinance of May 23, 1862, No. 41.

[2] "Certain large property owners resisted its collection on the ground of the unconstitutionality of the ordinance, and thus far no part of the tax has been collected from these parties" (Report of Water Department, January 25, 1869, p. 417).

[3] *Ibid.*, January 25, 1869.

the water department from 1872 to 1878 was devoted to the maintenance and improvement of the existing plant or carried forward from year to year as a department balance. In 1878, aided by a refunding at five per cent. of the six per cent. $5,000,000 loan, the Water Board assumed the interest charge upon $2,000,000 of the new debt. A year later the department undertook the interest payment upon all of the older water stock then outstanding and expressed the intention of pursuing the same course with regard to the remaining portion of the Gunpowder loan, in advance of any return from the new supply.

This assumption of interest payment upon the aggregate water debt delayed the reduction of water rentals that would probably otherwise have taken place with the introduction of the Gunpowder supply.[1] In 1880 the Water Board was vested with power to fix the charges for water supplied by meter measurement to manufacturing establishments. Upon the recommendation of Mayor F. C. Latrobe, an appreciable reduction was made in the existing rates, with a view to encouraging the industrial development of the city.[2] In 1884 occurred the anticipated reduction in general water rentals. The revenues of the department had been before barely adequate for meeting the aggregate charges imposed upon it; with the reduction in rates, it became necessary to supply the deficit by direct taxation. A water levy of three cents appeared in the municipal tax rate in 1884, and of two cents in that from 1885 to 1894. Nominally this was imposed not to supply any deficit in the finances of the department, but in payment for water supplied free of direct charge for all municipal purposes.[3]

[1] Reports of Water Department, January 7, 1878; January 1, 1879; January 1, 1880.

[2] Ordinance of May 25, 1880, No. 117; Mayor's Message of January 1, 1881.

[3] Report of Water Department, January 2, 1886. In 1878 the Water Board had been specifically forbidden to charge municipal boards and institutions for water consumed for public purposes (Ordinance of May 14, 1878, No. 55).

A further reduction of water rentals in 1888 necessitated the retention of this tax for some years longer than would otherwise have been the case, and not until 1895 was it finally discontinued. The favorable turn in the finances of the water department was aided by the redemption in 1894 of $4,000,000 of the funded water debt from out the municipal sinking fund and the consequent saving of interest thereon to the department. This was reflected in a surplus aggregating $348,840 in 1895 and 1896, derived from the operations of the department and paid over to the Department of Finance for the benefit of the water sinking fund.[1] The fiscal independence of the Water Board was emphasized in 1896 by the complete segregation of the revenues of the department from the ordinary funds of the municipality.[2]

An important element in the financial history of the water works was the provision of inadequate sinking funds and the partial redemption of maturing water loans from out the proceeds of general municipal taxation instead of from out any funds or revenues of the water department. Originally the surplus receipts of the department were expected to provide the sinking funds necessary for the redemption of maturing loans.[3] For the reasons indicated above, no continuous surplus resulted from the operations of the department, and in the absence of any other provision for the amortization of the water debt, the redemption of successive water loans was thrown upon the municipal treasury, or simply deferred by refunding operations. Sinking fund levies for water loans were included in the general tax rate from 1857 to 1870 and a special water sinking fund was maintained until 1879 in which year it was incorporated with the general sinking fund of the city. The $5,000,000 six per cent. "water stock" matured in 1875 and was refunded at five per cent. to mature in 1916. The sinking fund levy authorized by this loan was neglected until 1896,

[1] "Report of Water Department," January 1, 1897. For the surplus of 1897, see below, p. 352.

[2] Mayor's Message of January 25, 1897. [3] See above, p. 194.

in which year the levy for the water loan of 1882 was also for the first time imposed. A sinking fund levy for the loan of 1886 was imposed from the first. Finally in 1894-95 the matured $4,000,000 water debt was redeemed from the general sinking fund.

With what rapidity a municipal debt represented by a productive asset, such as water works, should be extinguished, and whether provision for the amortization of such a debt should be made by taxation of the community whose property it ultimately becomes or by a slightly higher charge to the consumers of the service rendered, are moot questions of municipal finance. In Baltimore the policy was pursued, more or less unconsciously, of distant amortization and direct taxation. In any consideration of the financial status of the water department and of what really constitutes "water at cost," it is necessary to bear in mind that to the extent to which water loans were redeemed from out sinking funds created by direct taxation, the department was relieved from paying bare interest upon the gross cost of the plant. To really supply water at cost, the net revenue of the water works must be adequate for paying interest not only upon outstanding loans, but upon the total amount expended in construction.[1]

Wharves. Municipal income from the wharves and docks of the city remained practically fixed in amount during the entire forty years under review. The primary sources of revenue were dockage rates and wharfage charges. The dockage rates were imposed *per diem* upon all vessels lying at any city wharf or dock, and varied with the tonnage of the vessel. The wharfage charges were specific amounts

[1] The policy of "free water," that is, of maintaining the water department by general taxation instead of by the levy of water rentals, was recommended from time to time, notably by Mayor Wm. Pinkney Whyte (Mayor's Message of January 23, 1882). A more common proposition was the transfer of the duties of the Water Register to the City Collector (Cf. "Report of Baltimore Tax Commission," 1885, p. 31).

imposed on all goods and merchandise landed upon and shipped from any public wharf, and were re-imposed for each succeeding day that the wares remained upon the wharves. Both rates and charges were occasionally varied; but the aggregate yield was not seriously affected. Certain of the public wharves were leased from time to time to private persons upon terms proposed by the Mayor and nominally approved by the Department of Finance. Revenue from this source was covered into the general treasury, instead of being devoted to the sinking fund as was the case with the income from ordinary municipal property.

The number of Harbor Masters was increased to six, annually appointed by the Mayor[1] and serving within a designated territory. All charges were collected by the Harbor Masters within their respective districts and paid over in monthly account to the Register. The obsolete practise of remuneration by fees was still retained in the case of these officials.

Markets. Municipal growth was accompanied by the periodic extension of market facilities and the gradual increase of revenue from this source. No essential change was made in the procedure already described.[3] Upon the erection or extension of a market house, public sale was made of leasehold interest in the additional stalls provided. The annual charge upon stalls thus sold as well as upon those leased from year to year was fixed by municipal ordinance and varied from time to time as well as from market to market. In addition to the rental payment and to the annual license tax, a nominal per diem charge was imposed upon the occupants of all market stalls. Market

[1] Ordinances of February 18, 1859, No. 18, and May 5, 1877, No. 32.

[2] The first five Harbor Masters each received four per cent. of their total collections; the sixth Harbor Master received twenty per cent. of his collections.

[3] See above, p. 171.

revenues were collected by the market clerks, and paid in quarterly account to the Comptroller.[1]

Wire Conduits. A provision of the franchise granted the local telephone company in 1889 to construct underground conduits was that space be afforded therein, free of cost, for the wires of the police patrol and fire alarm telegraph system of the city.[2] To supply the city with additional facilities an item of $225,000 for the construction of conduits was included in the composite $6,000,000 loan of 1892. In 1893 the Board of Fire Commissioners and the Superintendent of Police and Fire Alarm Telegraph were authorized to contract for the construction of such sub-ways as were necessary, together with the telephone company's conduits, for the reception of the public wires.[3] In 1894 the construction commission was reconstituted and made to consist of the Mayor, the City Register and the President of the Board of Fire Commissioners.[4] A plan of construction was determined upon, and the necessary contracts awarded.

The multiplication of overhead wires, incident to the general introduction of electricity for lighting and transit purposes, resulted in popular demands for regulative legislation. In 1892 the General Assembly authorized the city to construct a series of municipal conduits, to compel all overhead wires to be placed therein, and to prescribe proper rental charges. Three years later the municipality prepared to exercise the power thus conferred by the creation of an Electrical Commission, consisting of the Mayor, the City Register and the President of the Board of Fire Commissioners. In 1896 a special "conduit loan" of $1,000,-

[1] With the direct payment of market license taxes to the Comptroller the practise developed of requiring the payment of the first quarterly rental in conjunction with the issue of the license. The *per diem* charges continued to be collected by the market clerks, and it was currently believed that this practise resulted in appreciable leakage.

[2] Cf. above, p. 284.

[3] Ordinance of May 1, 1893, No. 106.

[4] Ordinance of April 16, 1894, No. 49.

000 was authorized; but no further steps were taken until after the close of the period here considered.[1]

Originally the city entertained no intention of using the police patrol and fire alarm telegraph conduits for other than public purposes. In 1896 a "competing" telephone company however secured the right to use unoccupied portions of the conduits at an annual rental of seven cents per linear foot of duct occupied,[2] and provision was added that surplus space might be rented to other persons or corporations upon the same terms.

Municipal Property. No important additions were made after 1856 to the productive real estate belonging to the city. By the removal of municipal buildings, by discontinued use for public purposes, by processes of street reconstruction, the city came from time to time into possession of small scattered areas of income-bearing property. These were leased for short periods upon terms fixed by the Department of Finance, and the accruing income was devoted to the sinking fund. The unintelligent policy was pursued throughout of disposing by sale of such property, upon the theory that the resulting increase of the taxable basis more than compensated for the loss of direct municipal income. The administration of whatever productive property remained in the possession of the city was, as a merely incidental duty of the Department of Finance, lax and careless, and it is not improbable that certain losses were suffered from sheer neglect of ownership.

In 1876 the General Assembly provided that the Commissioners of Finance, whenever authorized by city ordinance, might invest moneys belonging to the sinking fund in the purchase of annuities or ground rents reserved out of lands

[1] In 1898, after a long, bitter struggle between corporate interests and public expediency, the policy of constructing municipal conduits was definitely confirmed; a new enabling ordinance was passed, and the work of construction actually begun.

[2] Ordinance of July 1, 1896, No. 110. The grant was made subject to the provision that the charges for telephone service should never exceed prescribed rates.

leased by the city, and that after such purchase the rents should continue to be paid by the city to the Commissioners of Finance and applied in the manner of other investments of the sinking fund.[1] Discretionary power to exercise this authority was conferred upon the Commissioners of Finance by municipal ordinance in 1881, and thereafter efforts were made by the Commissioners to counteract in some measure the effects of the expensive policy of acquiring a mere leasehold interest in property needed for municipal purposes.[2] On December 31, 1896 the aggregate amount expended by the Commissioners of Finance in the purchase of ground-rents was $336,485.27 and the income received thereon from the general municipal treasury in the fiscal year then ended was $19,246.12. By far the largest part of this sum represented purchases made in years immediately following the passage of the ordinance of 1881.

Of the city's large investments in internal improvement projects, the subscriptions to the stock of the Baltimore and Ohio Railroad Company alone proved productive. In 1856 the city held $4,550,000 B. & O. stock, of which $500,000 represented the original subscription, $3,000,000 the additional subscription of 1836, and $1,050,000 scrip dividends. Upon this entire amount annual dividends, varying from six to ten per cent., were received, and the proceeds devoted to paying the interest upon the internal improvement debt. In 1864 the city sold $550,000 of the dividend stock, realizing $619,837.49; in 1865-66 the remaining $500,000 brought $611,641.13; in 1867 $250,000 of the original holding was sold for $319,612.88, leaving the city thereafter in possession of $3,250,000.

The suspension of dividends in 1888 was the forerunner of the disastrous turn in the affairs of the Baltimore and Ohio Railroad Company a few years later. Thanks to the sagacious insistence of a few far-sighted men, the city disposed at par of its $3,250,000 in 1890 and escaped the sharp

[1] Laws of Maryland," 1876, ch. 167.
[2] Ordinance of May 17, 1881, No. 81.

loss that would have come thereafter.[1] The proceeds were turned into the general sinking fund and promptly employed in the redemption of maturing loans.

The experience of the city with the Western Maryland Railroad Company was very different. From the original extension of municipal aid in 1861, the city, by a series of subscriptions, loans and guarantees—each made in the hope of avoiding the loss of what had been given before—became more and more seriously involved. As a result of this consistent policy the aggregate indebtedness of the Company to the city on January 1, 1897, was $8,099,725.27, secured by a complicated series of mortgages and covenants.[2] At no time in the history of the Western Maryland Railroad Company was its relation to the city other than that of a debtor in default, and the most sanguine prospect afforded at the close of the period here considered was that the Gompany would ultimately be able to assume all of its interest obligations. Thus, the only return which the city received for large and burdensome investments was an unrecorded dividend of economic stimulus and industrial

[1] See below, p. 172. The net income of the city from its holdings of B. & O. stock from 1856 to 1887 was as follows:

Year	Amount	Year	Amount
1856	$210,000	1872	$292,500
1857	105,000	1873	128,389
1858	——	1874	325,000
1859	210,000	1875	325,000
1860	430,500	1876	325,000
1861	105,000	1877	422,500
1862	268,450	1878	215,500
1863	405,405	1879	253,662
1864	342,517	1880	292,500
1865	300,437	1881	325,000
1866	280,000	1882	325,000
1867	276,052	1883	303,588
1868	260,256	1884	325,000
1869	260,000	1885	325,000
1870	260,000	1886	300,000
1871	130,000	1887	130,000

The city also received a trivial income ($2,519.16 in 1896) from small holdings of the stock of two turnpike companies.

[2] Report of Department of Finance, January 1, 1897.

development, due to the possibility that the railroad might not have been built by unaided private capital, or if at all, only at a later period. It is impossible to estimate this return quantitatively, or to determine in how far it was counteracted by the ill effects of heavier municipal taxation. Certainly the considerations which might have warranted the construction of the railroad by means of municipal credit could not justify its continued operation at the partial expense of the city. The railroad was destined to take its place in the transportation system of the country and the hope of operating it for any length of time "in the interest of the city" was fanciful and remote. Consequently agitation for a sale of the city's interest in the railroad was continuous. That this result was not actually attained is a striking illustration of the danger of intimate association of public and private interests in municipal affairs. Probably a large majority of the citizens of Baltimore have long been of the opinion that the city should seize the first favorable opportunity to dispose of its interest in the Western Maryland Railroad Company. Against this general, and therefore languid, opinion has been arrayed a strong continuous pressure from persons practically interested in the continuance of the existing state of affairs. The result of such a conflict has been, as in ordinary municipal experience, the sacrifice of public expediency to private gain.[1]

[1] In 1893 a competent commission was appointed "to investigate the affairs of the Western Maryland Railroad Company and the interest of the city therein." An exhaustive inquiry was made with the aid of expert service, and a noteworthy report submitted. The ultimate sale of the city's interest was therein assumed; but an interval of two years, in the course of which the value and earning capacity of the road might be demonstrated, was recommended before definite measures should be taken. Attention was also called to the crude and misleading accounting of the Western Maryland Railroad Company, and to the necessity of radical changes for the protection of the city's interest. Failing to effect these, an immediate disposition of the city's interest was recommended.

Gifts and Subsidies.

The municipal budget included few forms of revenue properly described as gratuitous. An insignificant income accrued from intestacies and was appropriated exclusively to the support of the public schools. The state tax on auction sales reverted to the city treasury, to the maximum amount of $20,000 per annum; but the actual receipts were ordinarily less than a third of that sum. Street beds, open areas, building sites continued to be ceded at intervals to the city, but yielded no direct income.

In 1882 Enoch Pratt, a wealthy citizen of Baltimore, proposed to establish a free circulating library. His plan involved the construction of a central and four branch buildings at a cost of $300,000 together with an endowment gift to the city of $833,333.33 in city stock. The condition attached was that the city should create a perpetual annuity of $50,000 for the maintenance of the library, payable to a self-perpetuating board of trustees selected in the first instance by the donor. The proposition was accepted by the city and confirmed by popular vote. The endowment gift was put under the control of the Department of Finance who were required to invest the increments until the fund yielded an annual income of $50,000. In the interim the annuity was paid by direct taxation. The annual income from the fund amounted in 1892 to $50,341, and direct taxation for the purpose mentioned ceased. Somewhat later the redemption of maturing five and six per cent. stock contained in the fund and a reinvestment in three and a half per cent. stock reduced the income slightly below the amount of the annuity ($49,502.50), and necessitated a small municipal appropriation to supply the deficiency in annual income.[1]

[1] In 1888 a bequest of $10,000, of which the income was to be devoted to benevolent purposes, was made to the city ("Horwitz Benevolent Fund"); in 1897 a smaller bequest of $400 was made, of which the interest was to be devoted to awarding two prizes in public educational institutions ("Frederick Raine Fund"). Both funds are in the custody of the Department of Finance.

A general state system of public schools was established in Maryland in 1865. A state tax for school purposes was imposed and the proceeds apportioned among the counties and Baltimore City according to population of school age (between five and twenty years). Important changes were subsequently made in the administration and organization of the system; but the essential principles of taxation by the state and apportionment among the local bodies were retained. The rate of the state tax remained practically fixed and the varying shares of the local bodies resulted from increase in the aggregate taxable basis and changes in school population.

The income accruing to the "school fund" of Baltimore City from this source was large and increased from $145,-690.70 in 1870, to $193,596.48 in 1880, to $182,619.24 in 1890, to $209,176.14 in 1896. No item in the municipal budget was, however, the occasion of more pronounced dissatisfaction than this revenue. The explanation lay in the fact that while Baltimore, owing to greater relative wealth, contributed more than one-half of the proceeds of the state school tax, the share of the city, by the method of apportionment employed, was less than a third. In the six years from 1885 to 1890, the city contributed $743,821.00 more than it received and the annual excess was about $100,000.[1] This condition of affairs became more pronounced in 1896 when the legislature imposed an additional state tax for the supply of free school books and provided that the proceeds should be apportioned in the manner of the school levy.

It has been repeatedly proposed that the mode of apportioning the state school taxes should be so changed as to give the local bodies the respective amounts collected therefrom; but there appears little likelihood of such a modification. Viewed in a larger aspect, it seems entirely proper that the metropolis of the state should contribute to some extent to the educational development of the counties.

[1] Report of Board of Commissioners of Public Schools, January 1, 1891.

CHAPTER IV

MUNICIPAL INDEBTEDNESS.

The modern era of the municipal debt of Baltimore, with its burdens and its problems, may be conveniently dated from the expansion and reorganization of municipal functions during Mayor Thomas Swann's administration (1856-1858). The dividing line stands out, it is true, with less distinctness in the history of city indebtedness than in the development of administrative organization and fiscal life. The extension of municipal credit in aid of works of internal improvement, which formed the primary cause of municipal indebtedness prior to 1856, continued in some degree thereafter, and came to form in the relation of the city to the Western Maryland Railroad one of the serious problems of the later debt. Similarly, the utilization of public credit in large amount for direct municipal improvements, constituting the characteristic features of the funded debt since 1856, really began with the purchase of the plant of the Baltimore Water Company in 1854, and was in a measure coincident with the very inception of the debt. But the uninterrupted growth of funded indebtedness, the periodic recurrence and funding of floating indebtedness, the importance and varying treatment of the sinking funds, the application of funded loans to purposes more properly the objects of current municipal expenditure—in short the significant elements of recent municipal indebtedness may be said with reasonable correctness to date from the last forty years, and to distinguish that period from the forty years preceding.

FUNDED DEBT.[1]

The growth of the funded debt since 1856, although thus separated by common characteristics from the period pre-

[1] See Appendix G.

ceding, reveals upon examination at least three successive phases: The first, from 1856 to 1868, was marked by a relatively large and rapid increase in aggregate indebtedness, culminating in 1867 in a constitutional limitation upon the borrowing power of the corporation; the second, from 1868 to 1888, was distinguished by the repeated funding of floating indebtedness and by the neglect and diversion of the various sinking funds; the third, from 1888 to 1897, had as its striking features the issue of large composite loans for miscellaneous municipal purposes, and the remarkable decline in the interest rate upon municipal securities. The increase of the funded debt during these periods and the occasion therefor are summarized in the following table, and will be considered in detail:

	1857–1867.	1868–1888.	1889–1897.
Water	$3,000,359.65	$5,496,668.06	$2,600,000.00
Defence and Bounties	2,784,243.61	......	......
Municipal Buildings	720,716.11	2,569,576.48	2,900,000.00
Parks	741,320.05	400,000.00	1,250,000.00
Internal Improvement,	1,269,000.00	4,403,300.00	......
Floating Debt,	145,000.00	5,635,500.00	1,453,300.00
Miscellaneous	76,096.33	236,013.56	......
Street Paving	......	500,000.00	2,600,000.00
Jones' Falls	......	2,336,700.00	28,000.00
Sewers	......	600,000.00	2,750,000.00
Bridges	.....	......	850,000.00
School Buildings	......	......	800,000.00
Street Reconstruction	......	......	1,500,000.00
Wire Conduits	......	......	1,225,000.00
Topographical Survey	......	......	125,000.00
Total	$8,826,735.75	$22,177,758.10	[1] $18,081,300.00
Redemption	485,787.92	6,476,865.70	14,379,160.75
Net Increase[2]	$8,340,947.83	$15,700,892.40	$3,702,139.25

1856–1868. The extravagance and waste which characterized local administration during much of the period from

[1] Of this amount, $4,295,100 was, on December 31, 1897, still unissued.

[2] Exclusive of sinking funds.

1856 to the close of the Civil War were reflected in the accumulation of floating, rather than in the growth of funded indebtedness. The funded debt of the city underwent relatively large increase, rising from $11,996,675.90 in 1856 to $20,337,622.73 in 1868, or about 70 per cent. But of this increase of nearly $8,500,000, more than a third was incurred in the extension of the water supply; another third was expended in the defence of the city and in the payment of bounties to volunteers for local quotas during the military operations of the Civil War, while the acquisition of Druid Hill Park and the erection of various municipal buildings (Almshouse, Jail and City Hall) were responsible for the largest part of the remainder. There was probably no actual or deliberate misuse of the corporate borrowing power. With the feverish conditions of the War and Reconstruction periods, with the easy processes of debt contraction and with high municipal credit, municipal indebtedness threatened to outrun municipal resources. A healthy conservatism in this respect together with a recollection, made vivid by the pressure of tax levies, of the reckless participation of Baltimore in the projection of works of internal improvement, led the Constitutional Convention of 1867 to impose radical limitation upon the corporate borrowing power.

(Water Loans). The original provision made for the acquisition and extension of a municipal water supply empowered the issue of city stock to an amount not exceeding $2,000,000. As has already been stated, three-fourths of the total amount authorized was issued by the end of 1856.[1] In 1858 and 1861 further issues of $1,000,000 and $500,000, respectively, were authorized.[2] In 1862 the aggregate issue of "Water Stock" was limited to $3,500,000, and in 1866 this maximum was changed to $4,500,000.[3] Several loans were also made prior to the adoption of the Consti-

[1] See above, p. 193.
[2] "Laws of Maryland," 1858, ch. 38; 1861, ch. 20.
[3] *Ibid.*, 1862, ch. 83; 1866, ch. 38.

tution of 1867, by virtue of the power possessed by the corporation to issue stock for "any great or permanent improvement" to an amount not exceeding $1,000,000, exclusive of all debts authorized by special acts of the General Assembly.[1]

These statutes were mere enabling acts, empowering the city to emit certificates of indebtedness, to be designated as the "Baltimore Water Stock," and "to provide for the redemption of the same at times and under such provision as the Mayor and City Council may deem expedient and proper." A series of ordinances provided for the actual issue of the stock as the work of construction and extension progressed. The water loans bore interest at six per cent., and were redeemable at the pleasure of the corporation after 1875. The proceeds of the loans were deposited with the City Register, subject to the order of the Water Commissioners, and any premium resulting from the sale of the stock was transferred to the sinking fund created by the original act. Between 1856 and 1868, $3,090,359.65 of this stock was issued, making the aggregate water loans outstanding on December 31, 1868, $4,631,146.38.

(Defence and Bounty Loans). The events of the Civil War left an enduring impress upon the municipal debt of Baltimore. Geographical position exposed the city to attack and occupation, while a strong local sympathy with the South heightened the difficulty of securing the city's quotas for the successive calls for troops. Beginning in 1862 with the payment of a bounty of $100 to volunteers for three years service, it became necessary in 1865 to offer a cash bounty of $300 to one year recruits. Between 1856 and 1868, a debt of $2,784,243.61 was contracted in the defence of the city and in the payment of bounties.

The first "defence loan" was authorized in April, 1861, when the legislature empowered the Mayor and City Council to raise whatever funds might be necessary for the

[1] "Baltimore City Code," 1879, p. 1137, note.

protection of the city, and to provide for repayment by taxation or otherwise.[1] The sum of $500,000—to be secured by the issue of promissory notes, and to be expended under the direction of the Mayor—had already been appropriated by the city for purposes of defence.[2] This action of the municipality was promptly confirmed by the General Assembly, and its legality was upheld by the Court of Appeals.[3] The amount actually expended within the next twelve months was only some $80,000. This was borrowed on short time, and in April, 1862, was funded in six per cent., twenty-year bonds, together with $145,000 of floating indebtedness. A second appropriation of $100,000, to be taken from unexpended parts of the "bounty loan" of June, 1863, was made in 1863 for strengthening local defences. This sum was to be expended by a Defence Committee composed of the Mayor, and the President and one member from each branch of the City Council.[4]

The various "bounty loans" authorized by the corporation were as follows: (a) $350,000 in August, 1862; (b) $350,000 in September, 1862; (c) $400,000 in June, 1863; (d) $600,000 in February, 1864; (e) $400,000 in May, 1864; (f) $100,000 in June, 1864; (g) $750,000 in July, 1864; (h) $750,000 in January, 1865.[5]

The funds provided by the last two loans were administered by a Bounty Board, composed of the Comptroller and two other citizens appointed by the Mayor. Disbursements under earlier loans were made by the City Register upon the certificate of regimental officers. In 1862 the unexpended part of the $700,000 bounty loan issued in that year was appropriated as a Relief Fund for the benefit of the families of all local volunteers, and distributed by a board of commissioners, composed of the Mayor, City

[1] "Laws of Maryland," 1861, ch. 1.

[2] Ordinance of April 20, 1861, No. 22.

[3] "Laws of Maryland," 1861, ch. 2; Mayor *vs.* Poultney, 25 Md. 19.

[4] Ordinances of June 24 and 27, 1863, Nos. 51 and 52.

[5] "Baltimore City Code," 1879, Art. XLVI, sect. 32.

Register and the City Comptroller.[1] Two years later, the General Assembly authorized the city to raise an amount not exceeding $300,000 in any one year for the relief of the families of those enlisted or drafted into the military service of the United States as a part of local quotas.[2] The corresponding ordinance however provided for the issue of only $100,000, for the continuation of relief to the families of soldiers then in receipt thereof.

The city stock issued under the several bounty and defence loans bore interest at six per cent., and was ordinarily redeemable at the pleasure of the city after thirty years. Provision was commonly made for the accumulation of a sinking fund for the redemption of the loans at maturity, but the details of this are more conveniently examined in another connection.[3]

(Municipal Buildings Loans). Two important municipal buildings, the Almshouse and the Jail, were practically completed, while the erection of a third, the City Hall, was at least begun, in the period from 1856 to 1868. The entire expenditure involved was defrayed by a series of loans, resulting in increased funded indebtedness to the amount of $720,716.11.

The General Assembly in 1858 authorized the Mayor and City Council to issue six per cent. stock, to be redeemed in fifteen years from date of issue, to an amount not exceeding $250,000 for the purpose of discharging the indebtedness incurred in the construction of a new Jail, and for defraying the cost of completing the structure. In 1858 and 1859, stock was gradually issued with the progress of the work to the maximum amount authorized.[4] Three successive issues of six per cent. stock, redeemable after 1890, were authorized for the erection of the City Almshouse, or Bay View Asylum: (a) $100,000 in 1862, (b) $300,000 in

[1] Ordinance of September 27, 1862, No. 66.

[2] "Laws of Maryland," 1864, ch. 132. [3] See below, p. 335.

[4] "Laws of Maryland," 1858, ch. 294; Ordinances of April 20, 1858, No. 20; May 31, 1858, No. 28.

1865, (c) $50,000 in 1866.[1] The indebtedness actually incurred for this purpose aggregated $438,716.11. Bonds to the amount of $32,000 were issued in 1867 for the construction of a City Hall; but they formed an integral part of the important loans described below.[2]

(Park Loans). The newly-created Public Park Commission was authorized in 1860 to purchase a suitable site for a public park and to make payment therefor in corporate stock, bearing interest at six per cent. and redeemable at the end of thirty years.[3] Under the terms of this ordinance there were issued during 1861 the sum of $553,966.25 in "public park stock," of which $511,323.75 was for the purchase of Druid Hill Park and $42,642.50, of an addition to Patterson Park. The validity of the issue was questioned and the acquisition of Druid Hill Park was only accomplished by the public-spirited action of certain citizens who agreed to buy definite amounts of the stock in order that one-fourth of the purchase money might be paid in cash. To remove every vestige of doubt, confirmatory legislation was immediately secured from the General Assembly.[4] For the special improvement of the parks, additional stock to the amount of $170,000, bearing interest at six per cent. and redeemable in 1895 was authorized, of which $150,000 was appropriated to Druid Hill Park, and $20,000 to Patterson Park. A reservation of ten per cent. for the creation of a sinking fund was made in each case.[5] During 1864 and 1865, the entire amount authorized was issued. By the close of 1868, the total amount of stock issued for the purchase and improvement of the parks was $741,320.05.

The park loans, like the water loans, were to a certain extent independent, both in administration and in security,

[1] Ordinances of May 20, 1862, No. 40; June 7, 1865, No. 35; February 16, 1866, No. 3.

[2] See below, p. 318.

[3] Ordinance of July 21, 1860, No. 60.

[4] "Laws of Maryland," 1862, ch. 29, repealing *ibid.*, 1861, ch. 41.

[5] Ordinance of May 2, 1863, No. 37. Cf. also Reports of Public Park Commission, December 24, 1860; January 2, 1862.

of general municipal indebtedness. The franchise charge on street railways, the so-called "park tax," was originally imposed for the purchase and maintenance of public parks, and any municipal indebtedness incurred for this purpose was made chargeable both as to interest and ultimate redemption upon the proceeds of the franchise tax.[1]

(Various Loans). The debt of the city was also increased during this period by the issue, from 1857 to 1859, of $1,069,000—the remaining portion of the $5,000,000 loan to the Baltimore and Ohio Railroad Company;[2] by the funding in 1862 of a floating debt of $145,000 probably incurred in emergency preparations at the outbreak of hostilities; by a subscription in 1866-67 of $200,000 to the capital stock of the Western Maryland Railroad Company,[3] and by the issue of $76,096.33 for miscellaneous purposes.

1868–1888. The failure of the constitutional limitation of 1867 to act as a formidable check upon local borrowing was realized in the period from 1868 to 1888. The total funded indebtedness of the city increased from $20,337,622.73 in 1868 to $36,038,516.15 in 1888. Redemptions took place from out the slowly accumulating sinking funds to the amount of $6,476,865.70, making the gross issue of municipal securities within these twenty years, $22,177,758.10. The periodic funding of floating indebtedness, the completion of a metropolitan water system, the repeated extension of municipal aid to the Western Maryland Railroad, the erection of a City Hall, and the improvement of Jones' Falls were the constituent elements, enumerated in order of importance, of the increase in indebtedness.

(Floating Indebtedness Loans.) The causes of the periodic accumulation of floating indebtedness are considered in detail in a later connection.[4] It is here only necessary to notice that upon five successive occasions, unpaid existing claims against the city were accepted as a permanent deficit and funded in municipal stock.

[1] See above, p. 277.
[2] See above, p. 192.
[3] Ordinance of March 15, 1866, No. 16.
[4] See below, p. 326.

In 1868, the issue of $1,700,000 in six per cent. stock redeemable in 1890 was authorized for funding the then existing floating debt.[1] The entire amount authorized was issued within the year. In 1869-70 two similar loans of $300,000 and $800,000, respectively, were authorized, of which amounts only $800,200 was actually issued.[2] In 1874 a loan of $2,000,000 in six per cent. stock, redeemable in 1894, was authorized and actually issued for funding the floating debt "as it existed on October 31, 1873."[3] Finally in 1878, an issue of $1,500,000 in five per cent. stock, redeemable in 1916, was authorized for funding the floating debt of the city, as it existed on December 31, 1877; of this loan, $1,035,300 was issued.[4] It thus appears that of loans authorized to the amount of $6,300,00, the sum of $5,635,500 was actually issued, and that this entire indebtedness was contracted within a single decade.

(Water Loans). In 1868 the city effected a temporary loan on behalf of the Board of Water Commissioners to the amount of $175,000 for the completion of a High Service Reservoir in Druid Hill Park.[5] The loan was repaid and additional funds provided by the issue in 1870 of $368,-854.62 of Water Stock, thus increasing the aggregate amount then outstanding to precisely $5,000,000, all bearing interest at six per cent. and redeemable in 1875.[6] In 1877 this $5,000,000 was refunded in five per cent. stock redeemable in 1916.[7] The project of securing a permanent

[1] Ordinance of February 7, 1868, No. 1.

[2] "Laws of Maryland," 1870, ch. 143; Ordinances of November 13, 1869 (No. 3), and January 31, 1870 (No. 14). The $300,000 loan was for the purpose of funding the floating debt of the city as it existed at the time of the adoption of the Constitution of 1867.

[3] "Laws of Maryland," 1874, ch. 185; Ordinance of February 12, 1874, No. 6. Of this debt $900,000 had been incurred in the extension of the water supply, and $400,000 in the improvement of the ship channel.

[4] "Laws of Maryland," 1878, ch. 328; Ordinance of October 8, 1878, No. 93.

[5] Resolution of November 7, 1868, No. 467.

[6] Ordinance of April 15, 1870, No. 32.

[7] "Laws of Maryland," 1876, ch. 237; Ordinance of June 30, 1877, No. 65.

supply of water from the Gunpowder River was definitely undertaken by the city in 1874, and the issue of an additional loan of $4,000,000 was then authorized. Between 1875 and 1880 the entire amount was issued in six per cent. bonds, redeemable after July 1, 1894.[1] A loan of $500,000 in five per cent. bonds redeemable after 1922 was made in 1883 for the construction of Lake Clifton,[2] and in 1886 a further loan of $1,000,000 in four per cent. bonds redeemable in 1926 was authorized for the completion of the same work.[3] Of this latter loan, only $400,000 was issued during 1888.

(Internal Improvement Loans). The same municipal policy of substantial aid to works of internal improvement, identified with the early growth of the funded debt of Baltimore, was responsible for an important addition thereto in the period from 1868 to 1888. It took the form of successive loans to the Western Maryland Railroad Company to the amount of $3,388,000[4]—virtually making possible the completion of the road, and leaving the city at the close of the period here considered its practical owner. In addition the municipality subscribed for $1,000,000 of the capital stock of the Valley Railroad Company of Virginia and issued corporate stock to that amount.

The early financial relations of the municipality and the Western Maryland Railroad are associated with the development of the "guaranteed debt" of the city, and are discussed in another connection.[5] In 1869 to avert the im-

[1] "Laws of Maryland," 1874, ch. 209; Ordinance of February 12, 1874, No. 5.

[2] Ordinance of May 25, 1882, No. 91. The entire loan was taken by the Department of Finance for the "Enoch Pratt Free Library Sinking Fund"; see Ordinance of May 14, 1883, No. 64.

[3] Ordinance of June 3, 1886, No. 82.

[4] $500,000 of this amount represented the conversion of guaranteed into funded indebtedness.

[5] See below, page 321. For the entire history of the Western Maryland Railroad Company, see "Report of the Commission to investigate the affairs of the Western Maryland Railroad Company and the interest of the City therein" (1893).

pending financial embarrassment of the railroad, the city undertook to raise one million dollars, for investment in its unsold bonds. The plan proposed was to hypothecate a sufficient amount of the Baltimore and Ohio stock held by the city, until consent should have been secured from the General Assembly of Maryland for a municipal endorsement of Western Maryland bonds of equivalent amount.[1]

The proposed procedure was stopped by legal injunction; and it became necessary to seek enabling legislation. This was promptly obtained in 1870, and the city was authorized to guarantee additional bonds of the railroad to an amount not exceeding $1,400,000, secured by a third mortgage.[2] Difficulty was experienced in the sale of these "guaranteed third mortgage bonds," while it appeared that the proceeds would in any event be insufficient for the completion and equipment of the road from Baltimore to Williamsport. Accordingly in 1872, upon the surrender by the railroad of endorsed but unsold bonds to the amount of $275,000 and the release to the city of all rights in an additional $250,000 endorsed but not yet issued, the city agreed to loan to the railroad $1,000,000 in six per cent. bonds, secured by an obligation of the railroad to pay the interest and principal of the stock as it should fall due.[3] This instrument was known as the fourth mortgage, and the six per cent. bonds secured by it, as the "fourth mortgage bonds."[4] As a result of the transaction, the "third mortgage guaranteed bonds" were reduced to $875,000, and "fourth mortgage bonds" to the amount of $1,000,000 were issued. At the close of 1873 the Western Maryland

[1] Ordinance No. 42 of June 12, 1869.

[2] "Laws of Maryland," 1870, ch. 48; Ordinance of January 21, 1870, No. 11.

[3] Ordinance of January 17, 1872, No. 10.

[4] This obligation is a somewhat curious instrument in the nature of a mortgage, dated and recorded but not duly acknowledged, in which all the property, owned or to be owned by the railroad, was pledged to the city to secure the payment of the interest and principal of the stock mentioned.

Railroad was formally opened from Fulton Station, Baltimore, to Williamsport.

From 1875 to 1882, the railroad was enabled to provide terminal facilities, and to avert threatened danger from certain of its defaulted securities by the exploitation of the municipal sinking fund. This mischievous policy, however, involved no direct increase in funded indebtedness and is considered in detail elsewhere.[1] By 1882 the need for improved and additional equipment had once more become imperative, and recourse was again had to municipal aid. Generous response was made in a loan, authorized in 1882, of $684,000 of city stock, bearing four per cent. interest and redeemable in July, 1925. Between 1882 and 1886 the entire amount so authorized was issued in specific installments.[2] The loan was secured by "a memorandum in writing, signed by its president, and sealed with its corporate seal, accepting the terms of this ordinance"; with the further provision that such acceptance should import an obligation on the part of the Company and bind it to pay interest and principal of the municipal loan as it should fall due.

The final and most important extension of municipal aid to the Western Maryland Railroad, within the period here considered, occurred in 1886.[3] The railroad had then outstanding $1,800,000 of its own bonds, redeemable at pleasure, but under liens secured by mortgages of prior date to the third and fourth mortgages securing the city's interests. There were, however, large and increasing accumulations of unpaid interest coupons of such of these prior bonds as were not guaranteed by Baltimore City and by the Commissioners of Washington County. Upon representation that its own holdings were threatened by the railroad's default, the city was induced to authorize a new municipal loan to the amount of $1,800,000, bearing interest at three and one-half per cent., and redeemable at the end

[1] See below, p. 339. [2] Ordinance of May 10, 1882, No. 71.
[3] Ordinance of March 10, 1886, No. 11.

of forty years, for funding these various obligations. During 1887 $1,704,coo of such bonds were issued. Out of this amount the city retained $100,000 as a sinking fund. The residue of $1,604,000, together with $294,320.25 realized from the sale of securities in the Western Maryland sinking funds, and $55.75 in cash then drawn from the treasury of the Western Maryland Railroad Company, or $1,898,376 in all, was used for the cancellation and retirement of the following of the railroad's securities:[1]

First Mortgage Unendorsed Bonds.....	$400,000
First Mortgage Endorsed Bonds.......	156,500
Second Mortgage Endorsed (by Washington County) Bonds...............	300,000
Second Mortgage Endorsed Bonds......	300,000
Preferred Second Mortgage Bonds......	421,500
Funded Coupon Certificates (held by the public)	320,376
Total...............	$1,898,376

As a result of these complicated transactions, the aggregate indebtedness incurred by the city in aid of the Western Maryland Railroad Company, between 1868 and 1888, was $3,388,000—exclusive of an increase in guaranteed debt, for this purpose of $275,000.

One of the most remarkable incidents in the history of municipal aid to works of internal improvement was a subscription of $1,000,000 to the capital stock of the Valley Railroad Company of Virginia made by Baltimore in 1872. The project involved the construction of a railroad, entirely within the state of Virginia, extending from Harrisonburg in Rockingham County to a point at or near Salem in Roanoke County, on the line of the Virginia and Tennessee Railroad. The road from Harrisonburg to Harper's Ferry,

[1] "Report of Stephen Little on the Financial Condition of the Western Maryland Railroad Company," p. 28. Also Report of City Register, January 3, 1887.

on the Baltimore and Ohio Railroad, being already completed, it was expected that the proposed one hundred and thirteen miles of new road through the Virginia counties would connect Baltimore "by the most direct and favorable route, with the cotton and sugar-growing states, and [would] materially aid in securing an important share of the traffic of those sections, in addition to that to be obtained by a connection with the most fertile regions of Virginia, North Carolina and Tennessee, via Staunton and Salem, as well as via Lynchburg."[1]

Lured by this roseate vista, the municipality in September, 1869, authorized a direct subscription of $1,000,000 to the capital stock of the Valley Railroad Company, to be paid by the issue of six per cent. fifteen-year bonds, subject to the following conditions: (1) that the subscription should be confirmed by act of the General Assembly and by popular vote; (2) that the further sum of $2,200,000 should be subscribed by individuals and by the counties and towns of the Virginia Valley; (3) that of this $2,200,000, at least $1,000,000 should be subscribed by the Virginia counties and towns, or by corporations or persons resident therein; (4) that at least thirty per cent. of all subscriptions, other than those of the Virginia counties, should be actually paid in cash; (5) that the Commissioners of Finance of Baltimore should be satisfied that the Valley Railroad Company was in possession of sufficient funds to construct the entire line proposed.[2]

The contemplated loan was confirmed by legislative statute and by popular vote in 1870-71, and the Commissioners of Finance being satisfied that the other conditions had been complied with, the formal subscription of $1,000,000 was made by the city in October, 1871, and the corresponding municipal loan was negotiated in 1873-74.[3]

[1] Mayor's Message of January 15, 1872, p. 48.

[2] Ordinance of September 14, 1869, No. 59.

[3] The financial results of this reckless subscription were precisely what might have been expected. The investment was unproductive

(Municipal Buildings Loans). In 1865 a special commission was appointed for the erection of a new City Hall, and empowered to issue bonds to the amount of $500,000, subject to the ratification of the General Assembly.[1] An independent enabling act was passed in the following year, containing no confirmation of the borrowing clause of the ordinance.[2] Construction was, however, begun in 1867 in the manner provided by the ordinance, and bonds to the amount of $32,000 were issued. At this point, the legality of such issue, in the absence of any explicit confirmation by the General Assembly, was raised and submitted to judicial determination. In 1868 the Court of Appeals, reversing the ruling of the lower court, decided that specific confirmation was vital, and that in its absence, the appointment of the building committee was unauthorized, and its action nugatory. Before this decision had been rendered, the legislature had authorized a new municipal loan for the construction of a City Hall, and an ordinance conformable thereto was promptly passed. An amicable adjustment was effected with respect to the building contracts already made, and apparently also in regard to bonds already issued.[3] Three successive loans were authorized for the construction of the new building: $1,000,000 in 1868; $1,000,000 in 1870, and $500,000 in 1873.[4] All three loans bore interest at six per cent.; the first was redeemable after fifteen years, the second and third after thirty years. Between 1868 and 1875, $2,468,000 were issued, which, with the $32,000 issued in 1867, aggregated the maximum amount authorized.

from the first, and in 1898 the authoritative statement was made that the city's holding could not be sold "for any reasonable price in cash"; see letter from Receiver John K. Cowen of the Baltimore and Ohio Railroad Company, in Report of City Register, January 3, 1899.

[1] Ordinance of September 25, 1865, No. 58.

[2] "Laws of Maryland," 1866, ch. 1.

[3] Scharf, "History of Baltimore City and County," p. 177.

[4] "Laws of Maryland," 1868, ch. 391; 1870, ch. 303; 1872, ch. 37. Ordinances of June 24, 1868, No. 62; April 15, 1870, No. 37; February 8, 1872, No. 15.

In 1873, additional Jail Stock to the amount of $101,-576.48 was issued.

(Jones' Falls Loans). The destruction wrought to public and private property by successive freshets in Jones' Falls in 1868 led to the adoption of radical measures for the improvement of this troublesome water course. In 1870 a municipal loan of $2,500,000 was authorized for carrying out a plan of improvement recommended by a specially appointed commission.[1] Between 1872 and 1888, bonds to the amount of $2,336,700, bearing interest at from six to three per cent. and redeemable in 1900, were issued. A second loan of $1,500,000 was authorized in 1874 by state and municipal legislation, but failed of confirmation by popular vote.[2]

(Various Loans). Municipal loans were also issued for the following purposes: $250,000 in 1880-81 and $350,000 in 1885-88 for the construction of the Harford Run Sewer;[3] $500,000 in 1881-84 for repaving certain streets of the city with improved materials, the first of an important series of similar measures noted below;[4] $200,000 in 1873 and the same amount in 1883 for the extension of Patterson Park, the interest upon which, as upon other park loans, was defrayed by the Park Board from out the franchise tax upon street railways.[5] Finally, $236,013.56 was issued for miscellaneous purposes.

1889–1898. The distinctive feature in the growth of municipal indebtedness in the decade from 1889 to 1898 was the issue of large composite loans for various municipal

[1] "Laws of Maryland, 1870, ch. 113; Ordinance of January 31, 1870, No. 12. For amendatory and supplementary legislation, see "Baltimore City Code," 1879, pp. 553-554, note.

[2] "Laws of Maryland," 1874, ch. 179. Ordinance of February 12, 1874, No. 4.

[3] Ordinances of October 11, 1879 (No. 86), and May 29, 1884 (No. 115).

[4] "Laws of Maryland," 1880, ch. 116; Ordinance of October 4, 1880, No. 140. See below, p. 320.

[5] Ordinances of June 23, 1871 (No. 116), and October 19, 1882 (No. 120).

improvements. The need of additional school-houses, parks, bridges, municipal buildings, improved paving, street reconstruction was urgently felt, and, with a burdensome tax rate and inelastic revenues, there was a growing tendency to provide for these wants by borrowing, instead of by further direct taxation. It was found that legislative sanction and popular ratification could be obtained as easily for a large as for a small use of municipal credit, and the several loans actually made were considerable in amount and composite in kind. As in the case of an omnibus appropriation bill, the desirable items were often able to secure popular confirmation for a composite loan of which certain elements were objectionable. The actual increase in the funded indebtedness of the city during the decade was $3,702,139.25; redemptions took place from out the sinking funds and by the sale of the city's productive assets to the amount of $14,379,160.75—making the total increase of debt authorized $18,081,300. Of this amount, $4,295,100 was, on December 31, 1897, still unissued. Of the loans authorized, $15,000,000, was made in three composite loans, for various municipal improvements. The remaining amount was for the construction of wire conduits, for funding floating indebtedness, and for miscellaneous purposes.

(Municipal Improvement Loans). The three composite loans authorized for municipal improvements were as follows:

(a). $5,000,000, authorized in 1888, in the form of bonds bearing interest at from three to four per cent. (as issued, three and a half per cent.), redeemable in 1928, and devoted to the following purposes: water sewers, $1,750,000; street reconstruction, $1,200,000; street paving, $1,000,000; school houses, $400,000; parks, $250,000; bridges, $250,000; municipal buildings, $150,000.[1]

(b). $6,000,000 authorized in 1892 in the form of bonds bearing interest at not more than four per cent. (as issued,

[1] "Laws of Maryland," 1888, ch. 131; Ordinance of September 26, 1888, No. 98.

three and a half per cent.), redeemable in 1940, and devoted to the following purposes: court house $1,750,000; street paving, $1,600,000; water sewers, $1,000,000; bridges, $600,000; school houses, $400,000; street opening, $300,000; wire conduits, $225,000; topographical survey, $125,000.[1]

(c). $4,000,000 authorized in 1894 in the form of bonds bearing interest at not more than four per cent. (as issued, three and a half per cent.), redeemable in 1945, and devoted to the following purposes: court house, $1,000,000; water extension, $2,000,000; parks, $1,000,000.[2]

(Floating Debt Loan). The floating debt of the city, as it existed on January 1, 1896, was funded by virtue of legislation authorizing a loan to the amount of $1,600,000.[3] Of this maximum, the sum of $1,453,000, in three and a half per cent. stock redeemable in 1936, was issued during 1897.

(Various Loans). The remaining $600,000 of the Lake Clifton Water Loan of 1886 was issued in 1889-91, and $28,000 of the Jones' Falls loan was issued in 1892. In 1896 the General Assembly authorized the issue of $1,000,000 of city stock, bearing interest at not more than four per cent. and redeemable in 1922, to provide a system of municipal conduits for the reception of telegraph, telephone, electric light and other wires under the streets of Baltimore. The corresponding ordinance was passed and the necessary popular ratification secured, but no actual issue took place within the period considered.[4]

GUARANTEED DEBT.

The development of the guaranteed debt of Baltimore is entirely identified with the extension of municipal aid to

[1] "Laws of Maryland," 1892, ch. 138; Ordinance of October 7, 1892, No. 100.

[2] "Laws of Maryland," 1894, ch. 149; Ordinance of October 5, 1894, No. 137.

[3] "Laws of Maryland," 1896, ch. 370; Ordinance of July 2, 1896, No. 112.

[4] "Laws of Maryland," 1896, ch. 350; Ordinance of July 25, 1896, No. 120; cf. above, pp. 297-298.

works of internal improvement. Mention has already been made of the circumstances under which the city in 1852 became liable by municipal endorsement for the interest and principal of the bonds of the Northwestern Railroad Company, the York and Cumberland Railroad Company, and the Pittsburg and Connellsville Railroad Company, to the maximum amounts of $1,500,000, $500,000 and $1,000,000, respectively.[1] In the case of the Pittsburg and Connellsville Railroad Company, the municipal guarantee was subsequently replaced by a direct municipal loan. Endorsed bonds of the other two corporations were issued to the amounts proposed, and the city's interest was protected in each case by a mortgage lien upon the railroad and its equipment. In 1867 the city consented to guarantee the bonds of the Union Railroad Company—organized for the construction of a short line connecting certain local roads with tidewater—to the maximum amount of $500,000; but only $117,000 of the sum authorized was issued. Finally, three distinct issues of Western Maryland Railroad Company bonds were endorsed by the city between 1861 and 1870.

The increase and reduction of the guaranteed debt are shown in the following table:

Year.	Northwestern Virginia Railroad Company.	York and Cumberland Railroad Company.	Western Maryland Railroad Company.	Union Railroad Company.	Total.
1861....	$1,500,000	$500,000	$100,000	....	$1,600,000
1862....	1,500,000	500,000	175,000	....	1,675,000
1863–67.	1,500,000	500,000	200,000	....	1,700,000
1868....	1,500,000	500,000	350,000	75,000	2,425,000
1869....	836,500	500,000	500,000	112,000	1,948,500
1870....	773,500	500,000	500,000	117,000	1,890,500
1871....	748,000	500,000	1,000,000	117,000	2,365,000
1872....	724,500	500,000	1,650,000	117,000	2,991,500
1873....	656,500	500,000	1,375,000	117,000	2,648,500
1874....	3,000	500,000	1,375,000	117,000	1,995,000
1875–77.	....	500,000	1,375,000	117,000	1,992,000
1878–87.	....	....	1,375,000	117,000	1,492,000
1888–95.	....	....	875,000	117,000	982,000
1896–97.	....	....	875,000	....	875,000

[1] See above, p. 191.

The results of the policy of municipal endorsement were hardly more favorable than the consequences of direct municipal loans to works of internal improvement. Of the four projects which received aid of this kind, only the York and Cumberland Railroad Company met its interest obligation faithfully from the time of issue until the redemption of the $500,000 endorsed securities, in 1877. The Union Railroad Company was in default from 1867 until 1870, after which time until the maturity of the bonds no further lapse occurred. The Northwestern Virginia Railroad Company paid the interest obligation upon its guaranteed securities for some years after their issue, and Baltimore suffered no loss from the endorsement.[1] In 1861 the Company, then under the control of the Baltimore and Ohio Railroad Company, defaulted upon the semi-annual interest payment, and thenceforth the burden of the guaranteed bonds was thrown upon the city. On January 1, 1864, the total default in interest was $360,000, with a semi-annual payment then due. Ridiculous offers for the purchase of the city's interest were rejected, and a foreclosure of the city's first mortgage upon the road was agitated. This resulted in a proposition from the Baltimore and Ohio Railroad Company to purchase the city's entire claim for $1,200,000, and in the course of 1864 this offer was accepted.

[1] In 1859 the city assented to a remarkable proposition for a direct loan to the railroad, nominally for the purpose of permanently arching the tunnels of the line. Thirty-five per cent for the first year and twenty-five per cent. for three succeeding years of all cash dividends upon the city's holding of the capital stock of the Baltimore and Ohio Railroad Company were to be lent to the railroad. The amount advanced was not to exceed $73,000 in the first year and $53,000 in any succeeding year, and was to be secured by a five-year bond of the Company, pledging "the net earnings of their railroad after the payment of all previous obligations then accrued, to the discharge of such bond" (Ordinance of July 16, 1859, No. 100). Several loans were made under the authority thus conferred (Register's Report of January 16, 1862); and when, in 1862, the enabling ordinance was repealed (Ordinance of February 18, 1862, No. 1), the amount due the city, exclusive of interest, was nearly $80,000.

The funds so obtained were transferred to the Commissioners of Finance, allowed to accumulate as a sinking fund, and ultimately utilized, in part for the cancellation, in part for the redemption of the guaranteed bonds. After 1873 this endorsement ceased to figure as any part of the guaranteed debt of the city.

The repeated endorsement of Western Maryland Railroad Company securities formed the most important feature in the history of the guaranteed debt. The Baltimore, Carroll and Frederick Railroad Company was incorporated by the legislature of Maryland in 1852 for the construction of a railroad from Baltimore or from a suitable point on the Baltimore and Susquehanna Railroad, to Westminster, and thence westwardly to some point on the Monacacy River in the direction of Hagerstown. The total capital stock was limited to $1,000,000, and authority was given to borrow not more than $200,000. In the following year, the corporate name was changed to the Western Maryland Railroad Company, and power given to issue additional bonds to an amount of $1,000,000.[1] The total sum of bonds authorized ($1,200,000) was arranged in two series of equal amount, and in 1858 the railroad executed its first mortgage to secure $600,000 thereof. A portion of these bonds were sold at a considerable discount, and the proceeds enabled the road to be opened in August, 1859, from the Relay to Owings Mills. Further sales were found impossible save at ruinous sacrifice.

The city's aid was for the first time extended to the Company in 1861-62 by an endorsement of bonds in successive installments to the amount of $200,000, secured by a first mortgage upon the road and its equipment.[1] By means of the funds so provided, the road was extended to Union Bridge where its further progress was for some years ar-

[1] "Laws of Maryland," 1860, ch. 20; Ordinance of July 23, 1860, No. 68. Twenty per cent. of the proceeds of the sale of the bonds was reserved and invested by the City Register as a sinking fund for their ultimate payment.

rested. The city became more directly interested in 1866 by a direct municipal subscription of $200,000, paid in six per cent. stock, redeemable after July 1, 1890. During 1867-68 occurred a further municipal endorsement of the Company's bonds to the amount of $300,000, secured by a second mortgage.[1] The priority of the city's lien under this second mortgage was waived in 1868 in favor of a loan issued by the Company to the amount of $600,000, known as the "preferred second mortgage bonds," to which the city did not itself subscribe. In 1870 the road was again in financial straits, and the city agreed to endorse the six per cent. bonds of the Western Maryland Railroad Company, redeemable on January 1, 1900, to an amount of $1,400,000. During 1870, $500,000 of these endorsed "third mortgage bonds" were issued, and during 1871, $650,000; but $275,000 were surrendered and cancelled in connection with the direct municipal loan of 1872. The first two issues of endorsed bonds, aggregating $500,000, were retired in 1886 from out the proceeds of the large direct loan of that year.[2] The liability of the city was thus reduced to endorsement of the $875,000 "third mortgage bonds."[3]

The history of the guaranteed securities of the Western Maryland Railroad Company is largely a record of continuous default. As a burden upon the municipal treasury, there was practically no difference between municipal endorsement and direct municipal loan. On January 1, 1879, the city had paid $720,000 in interest upon the first, second

[1] "Laws of Maryland," 1864, ch. 298; Ordinance of May 18, 1864, No. 73. The same sinking fund reservation was required as in the first endorsement; by Ordinance of August 9, 1867, No. 58, the reservation was reduced from twenty to ten per cent.

[2] See above, page 316; $43,500 of the first issue remained in the possession of the Commissioners of Finance.

[3] These bonds mature on January 1, 1900. In 1898 a municipal loan was authorized to the amount of $1,875,000, of which $875,000 is to be applied in due course to the retirement of the "third mortgage bonds." This will result in the extinction of the guaranteed debt of the city, and the increase of the funded debt by a corresponding amount.

and third endorsed mortgage bonds—practically the entire amount for which the Western Maryland was liable with respect to these securities. In 1879 the municipal sinking fund, instead of the general city treasury, was charged with the payment of interest upon the Western Maryland indebtedness. Thereafter the road paid interest upon the first, but continued in default upon the second mortgage bonds, until both classes of securities were retired by the issue of the loan of 1887. The third endorsed mortgage bonds ($875,000) remained an uninterrupted charge upon the sinking fund accumulations, and the debt due the city by the road from the default of interest thereon was on January 1, 1897, $1,365,000.[1]

Floating Debt.

The periodic accumulation of floating indebtedness, with the consequent necessity of funding existing claims against the city by the repeated issue of formal loans, formed a characteristic feature of the later financial history of Baltimore. Between 1856 and 1897 six loans were authorized for this purpose, resulting in an increase of funded indebtedness to the amount of $7,233,800. Of this sum, $7,088,-800 was incurred after 1867, and $5,635,500 between 1867 and 1878 alone. The floating indebtedness at the beginning of each fiscal year from 1856 to 1897 is shown in the following table:

Year	Amount	Year	Amount
1857	$ 142,189.98	1862	$ 587,820.72
1858	111,333.00	1863	108,219.51
1859	419,017.78	1864	91,500.00
1860	458,745.59	1865	183,000.00
1861	235,106.87	1866	199,224.00

[1] Mention should be made of the continued default upon $43,500 of the "first mortgage endorsed bonds," held by the Commissioners of Finance, and upon the certificate of matured coupons, funded in 1879 (cf. below, page 339).

For the aggregate indebtedness of the Western Maryland Railroad Company to the city, see above, p. 300.

1867	$ 280,800.00	1884	$ 258,237.31
1868	1,929,866.94[1]	1885	55,379.53
1869	930,260.80	1886	38,480.47[5]
1870	617,355.20	1887	57,278.61[5]
1871	749,585.29[2]	1888	158,171.40
1872	610,531.46	1889	347,512.33
1873	875,415.90	1890	433,318.88
1874	142,576.03[3]	1891	148,394.54
1875	702,310.63	1892	82,935.97
1876	1,103,716.49	1893	473,490.43
1878	1,342,721.19[4]	1894	1,121,122.43
1879	622,649.18	1895	1,321,223.47
1880	296,370.28	1896	1,385,503.79
1881	155,776.37	1897	1,368,260.96
1882	29,774.48	1898	239,902.45[6]
1883	261,344.15		

Floating indebtedness played no important part in the city's finances prior to 1862. The City Register was commonly authorized to make temporary loans during the course of the year, of specified amount or to the amount of uncollected taxes, for the purposes of meeting the city's maturing obligations.[7] These loans were renewed at short intervals, and were reduced or extinguished with a favorable turn in the city's finances. The Register's estimate of expenditures for the ensuing twelvemonth, submitted to the City Council at the beginning of each fiscal year, ordinarily revealed "existing claims" against the city of considerable amount; but these represented temporary rather than permanent deficits. The only exception to this was a floating debt of $145,000, caused by extraordinary expendi-

[1] $1,700,000 funded during 1868.
[2] $800,200 funded during 1871-73.
[3] $2,000,000 funded during 1874-75.
[4] $1,035,300 funded during 1878-79.
[5] Surplus. [6] $1,453,000 funded during 1897.
[7] Ordinances of June 12, 1858 (No. 37); May 30, 1859 (No. 87); July 23, 1860 (No. 69).

tures at the outbreak of the Civil War; this was funded in 1862, together with a defence debt of $80,000.[1]

The first serious accumulation of floating indebtedness occurred in the years from 1862 to 1867. It is virtually impossible to trace the precise course of this deficit. The existence of any large floating indebtedness was at no time intimated in the financial reports of the city published during this period. Yet in the first formal financial statement made after the accession of Mayor Robert T. Banks to office in 1867, it appeared that unpaid claims were then outstanding against the city to the amount of $1,929,866.94.[2] A part of this was undoubtedly incurred in the reckless spirit born of military exigencies. The city was borrowing freely for its defence and for the payment of bounties, and was spending in all directions with lavish hand. In addition to this incidental waste, it seems likely, however, that some considerable portion of the debt was the direct outcome of municipal corruption. The city treasury was never actually looted as in New York under the Tweed regime; but public funds were undoubtedly squandered and freely diverted to improper persons and purposes. In February, 1868 a municipal loan to the amount of $1,700,000 was authorized for funding the then existing floating indebtedness, and this entire amount was issued within the year.[3]

In the decade following 1868, year after year found the municipal treasury embarrassed by large accumulations of unpaid claims. Upon three occasions the burden of floating indebtedness became intolerable and special funding loans were authorized—$800,000 in 1870, $2,000,000 in 1874, and $1,500,000 in 1878. The resulting addition to the funded debt of the city was $3,835,500.

The explanation of this chronic deficit is to be found in certain reprehensible practises in municipal financiering,

[1] Ordinance of April 19, 1862, No. 17.
[2] Mayor's Message of January 21, 1868.
[3] Ordinance of April 24, 1873, No. 45.

present to some extent in every period of municipal history, but peculiarly in vogue during these years. These were: (1) adoption of an inadequate tax-levy; (2) overestimate of municipal receipts; (3) appropriations for specific purposes made after the adoption of the tax-levy.

(1). After the close of the Civil War a low tax rate may be said to have become, to an increasing degree, a central issue in municipal campaigns. The tax-levy was ordinarily determined less with reference to sound budgetary principles than to its probable effect upon the unthinking voter. This was especially the case in election years. A low tax rate in the present with a possible floating debt in the future invariably proved more attractive than a higher tax rate and a clear balance. Accordingly either by the partial neglect of existing claims, or by taking the most favorable estimate of variable conditions, the tax-levy was fixed at an attractive rate, and a new or an increased floating debt incurred.

(2). The same result was attained, with what appeared to be some greater justification, by the deliberate or unintelligent overestimate of the amount of revenues likely to accrue to the municipal treasury within the fiscal year. Thus in the formation of the budget, miscellaneous receipts were often overestimated, and account taken of income from the city's investments, the receipt of which was highly uncertain. More serious and more reprehensible was the practise of assuming year after year a larger proportion of taxes collectible within the current year than repeated experience and sound fiscal judgment warranted. Thus in 1871 the fiscal year was made to end on October 31 instead of December 31, as theretofore, without any corresponding advance in the time of making up the budget and reporting the tax-levy. The period within which tax collections could be made was in consequence reduced precisely two months. Despite this reduction, the budget was formed and the tax-levy was determined upon the assumption that practically the same proportion of taxes would be collected within the shorter as in the longer term. Between the years 1871 and 1876 the tax rate was based on the estimate that seventy per cent. of the whole tax levied was collectible within the current year, whereas in actual fact the gross receipts averaged about fifty-five per cent.[1]

(3). As has been noted in the consideration of the municipal budget, the tax-levy ordinances and the general appropriation bill were presented to the City Council at the same time, commonly in the latter part of April. Any addition to the general appropriation bill made without a corresponding increase in the tax-levy, and any special appropriation made in the considerable interval between the adoption of the tax-levy and the close of the fiscal year, were under ordinary circumstances entirely unprovided for. The latter practise of making special appropriations to be paid from "unappropriated funds" in the city treasury, or by some other form of providential intervention, was especially in vogue, and was responsible in considerable part for the recurring floating indebtedness of the period.

The ordinary course by which a floating debt was accumulated is well illustrated in the financial history of 1876.[2] The municipal budget reported by the joint Ways and Means Committee to the City Council in April of that year, contained appropriations aggregating the sum of $6,284,061.36, wherein was included the then existing floating debt of $702,311.03. Receipts from sources other than taxation were estimated at $2,944,878.76, leaving to be provided by taxation, $3,339,182.60. The tax rate actually reported was $1.80 (on $100), upon a taxable basis of $231,503,129, with estimated collection of seventy per cent. within the fiscal year. Had the entire amount estimated been collected, the proceeds would have been only $2,868,323.75 or $470,758.85 less than the amount required, showing that, even under the conditions assumed, a tax-levy of something more than $2.00 instead of $1.80 was necessary. This inevitable float-

[1] See table on pp. 269-270, above.

[2] See Report of City Comptroller, November 1, 1876.

ing debt of $470,758.85 was more than doubled by the failure of tax-collections to reach the proportion estimated. During the five years preceding 1876 the collections had never in any one year reached fifty-nine per cent. of the amount levied, and averaged less than fifty-five per cent. Every member of the Ways and Means Committee was familiar with this fact, yet in the budget of 1876 a seventy per cent. collection was coolly counted upon. The actual collection was something less than fifty-five and a half per cent. of the amount levied, leaving a further deficiency of $636,767.87. Finally in the interval between the adoption of the budget proper and the close of the fiscal year, special appropriation bills were passed to the total amount of $379,717.98, for the payment of which in the current year no provision whatever was made. The gross deficiency arising from the inadequate levy, the overestimate of collection and the special appropriations aggregated $1,487,244.70. Appropriations to the amount of $428,352.12 however remained in the treasury undrawn at the close of the fiscal year, thus reducing the deficiency to $1,058,892.58. Adding to this amount the overestimates of revenue derived from sources other than taxation, the enormous floating debt of $1,103,716.49, in existence on November 1, 1876, is virtually explained.

Although emphatic protest was made by successive municipal officers against the mischief and danger of such financial practises, the credit of clearly exposing the procedure and of effecting some degree of reform is to be attributed to Joshua Vansant. Mr. Vansant had already served for four years as Mayor, when in 1875 he became Comptroller—an office which he held without interruption for a decade. His first report as City Comptroller, dated November 1, 1876, contained a conclusive indictment of the fiscal practises then in vogue, and is worthy of citation in some fullness. After tracing the growth of the existing floating debt, the report continued:

"It cannot be said that the financial *system* which brings

about such results is erroneous, because *system* has had no part or lot in it. System is an arrangement founded, through all its parts on some one principle. There was doubtless method in the practice, so far as was convenient; but it was based upon an arbitrary rule—not a principle in government. The remedy for the evil is simple, practicable and just—*Harmonize the tax-levy and appropriation bills.* Make the necessary appropriations for the administration of the city government, then adopt a tax-levy ample for the payment of them, allowing in addition thereto, a liberal specified margin for unforeseen contingencies. If, upon adding up the column of appropriations, it should require a greater levy to provide for the payment of the same than is just and proper to the tax-payers, strike from the list such items as can be dispensed with, or may be postponed without prejudice to the public interest, and thus bring down the appropriations to the minimum point that will subserve effectively the ends of the municipal government. No well-regulated government will deliberately incur a debt without providing the means for its liquidation. If considerations of great public interest or necessity demand large appropriations, it is much better to exhibit the same to the public on the face of a tax bill than to permit them to accumulate uncancelled, and in the end to swell the stealthy and oppressive incubus of a funded debt."

This wholesome advice exercised a salutary effect upon the subsequent financial policy of the city. It was reiterated in Mayors' messages and Comptrollers' reports,[1] and doubtless influenced the formation of sounder municipal budgets for more than a decade thereafter. The large floating debt still remaining after the funding operations of 1878 was gradually reduced, and on January 1, 1886, for the first time in many years, the municipal treasury revealed an actual surplus.

[1] Thus see Messages of January 1, 1879 (p. 57) and January 23, 1882 (p. 12).

One more painful experience was, however, necessary before the lesson taught by the financial history of the city in the period just considered was definitely and, it is to be hoped, finally accepted. On January 1, 1892, the floating debt of the city was $82,935.97; on January 1, 1893, it had increased to $473,490.43; on January 1, 1894, it had risen to $1,121,122.43, and on January 1, 1896, it aggregated $1,385,503.79. The alternatives presented were, funding or a succession of burdensome tax levies. The latter course was as usual recommended by the Mayor; the former was promptly adopted by the Council. During 1896 a funding loan of $1,600,000 was authorized, of which amount $1,453,000 was issued in the course of 1897.

The accumulation of this debt was due to precisely the same causes that had operated in the seventies. The tax-levy was reduced from $1.80 in 1889 and 1890, to $1.55 in 1891, 1892 and 1893, and increased only to $1.70 in 1894. The increase in the assessed valuation of property in the city, exclusive of that located in the annexed district, during this same period was from $280,158,527 in 1890, to $294,089,810 in 1893. The estimates made of taxes collectible within the current year exceeded the actual amounts collected by $287,779.73 in 1892 and by $428,000 in 1893. Finally, appropriations were made by the City Council after the fixture of the tax-levy to the amount of $102,774.73 in 1892, and of a somewhat larger sum in 1893.[1]

Sinking Fund.[2]

The systematic amortization of the funded indebtedness of Baltimore is practically identical in point of time with the modern period of the city government. Before 1856 two sinking funds had been established. The first, or "gen-

[1] See Mayor's Message of January 1, 1894 (p. 11); January 1, 1895 (p. 21). A hacknied explanation of the floating indebtedness incurred after 1888 was the excess of expenditures over receipts in the "Annex." As a matter of fact, the excess formed only a small part of the floating debt; but even were this not the case, it afforded no justification whatever for a chronic budgetary deficit.

[2] See Appendix H.

eral sinking fund," designed for the redemption of the original internal improvement and miscellaneous debt, was in charge of the Commissioners of Finance, and received the rentals of city property, and, ordinarily, the premiums accruing from the sale of city stock. The second, known as the "Baltimore and Ohio" or "Five Million" sinking fund, consisted of a reservation of ten per cent. of the $5,000,000 loaned to the Baltimore and Ohio Railroad in 1853, invested by the City Register and ultimately employed by the railroad in the repayment of this particular loan. For the amortization of the $1,000,000 loaned the Pittsburg and Connellsville Railroad, of the large indebtedness incurred in the purchase of the water plant, and of certain minor loans, no actual provision had been made, although in some cases specifically authorized.

In 1855 an ordinance requiring an annual appropriation of $6000 to the general sinking fund, enacted five years earlier, was for the first time enforced. Mayor Swann called attention to this fact in his first annual message of January 19, 1857, and announced his intention of securing strict compliance with the law thenceforth. In 1856 a sinking fund for the Pittsburg and Connellsville $1,000,000 loan was created by the appropriation of $6000 for this purpose, to be renewed annually thereafter.[1] The authorized tax of one-half cent for the amortization of the water debt was first included in the levy of 1857, and a fourth sinking fund thus created. Finally in 1860, a long-neglected provision for the creation of a sinking fund for the court-house stock, issued some years before, was enforced, and a tax of one cent, to be devoted to this purpose, was included in the levy of 1860.

Of greater importance than the enforcement of existing sinking fund requirements was the specific provision contained in practically every municipal loan authorized be-

[1] This appropriation seems to have been made only twice and the fund was left thereafter to grow slowly by its own accumulation. The default of the railroad in its interest payment was indirectly responsible for this neglect.

tween 1856 and 1870 for the creation of a special redemption fund and for the levy of a sinking fund tax, designated in amount and conceived to be adequate for the discharge at maturity of the particular loan authorized. Distinct sinking funds were thus in turn created and maintained for the Jail Loan, the Park Loan, the Floating Debt Loan, the Bounty and Defence Loans, the Almshouse Loan, the Park Improvement Loan, the Water Loans, and the Western Maryland Railroad Guaranteed Loan.[1] These sinking funds were in the charge of the Department of Finance, with the exception of the Baltimore and Ohio and Western Maryland funds, which were under the care of the City Register. Investments were limited to city stock, but each fund was not necessarily restricted to the particular securities for the redemption of which it was ultimately designed. Rentals of city property and premiums from the sale of city stock, unless otherwise appropriated, continued to accrue to the general sinking fund.

The aggregate tax levies authorized for sinking fund purposes were probably imposed in no single year. In some cases, the tax was simply omitted. Oftener, it was imposed irregularly or reduced below the point prescribed by ordinances and required by sound principles of municipal amortization. On the whole, however, the sinking funds prospered in the decade following 1856. A distinct fund was created for each successive loan, and augmented by the proceeds of a special tax-levy. The high interest rate of municipal securities permitted rapid accumulation, and the accretions of the funds were not permanently diverted to purposes other than those for which they had been designed.

In the loose administration and municipal misrule of the

[1] The Western Maryland Railroad Sinking Fund was created by a reservation of twenty and ten per cent., respectively, of the first and second guaranteed loans (cf. above, p. 325); it increased simply by the accumulation of interest. The Park Sinking Fund was established in 1861 and was maintained by the appropriation of one-fifth of the excess of the "park fund" over the interest upon the park debt.

early post-bellum period arose the dangerous practise of securing temporary loans for ordinary municipal purposes from the sinking funds instead of from the local banks. The City Register reported on January 27, 1868, that the city was using the redemption funds for its common expenditures to the amount of $780,000. It is probable that any unpaid portion of this advance was returned from out the proceeds of the refunding loan of 1868. To avert any repetition of the same dangerous practise, the sinking funds which had hitherto been merged with the general funds of the city, were segregated by the Commissioners of Finance in March, 1868.

The first retrogade movement in the care of the sinking funds began with the close of the Civil War and culminated a few years later. It consisted in the tacit abandonment of special tax levies authorized and hitherto imposed for the amortization of existing loans, and in the failure to make any adequate provision for the ultimate redemption of the new loans issued.[1] By 1868 the sinking fund levies for the Jail, Court-house, Floating Debt, Bounty and Defence Loans had been abandoned, leaving only the levies for the two Water Loans in force. Two years later these also were discontinued. This action was entirely without legislative authority, and like the accumulation of floating indebtedness was largely due to the injudicious reduction of the tax-levy. In face of rapidly increasing expenditure and a slowly increasing asessable basis, the levy was cut from $1.40 in 1867 to $1.20 in 1868, and from $1.60 in 1869 to $1.50 in 1870.

The nearest approach to any justification of the abandonment of the sinking fund levies appeared in a roseate report of the City Register of December 31, 1868. The amount of indebtedness which the city would ultimately be called upon to discharge was therein stated to be $16,869,724.69. The invested sinking funds aggregated $4,384,985.93, which would on January 1, 1895, with their accumulations amount

[1] See Appendix E.

to $19,150,017. This would allow a discharge of the entire indebtedness and leave a balance of $2,280,292.31. This estimate was held to warrant the conclusion that "the sinking fund and its resources, as it now is, is ample to discharge the whole debt at its maturity." The repeal of the various ordinances requiring sinking fund levies was accordingly recommended.[1]

There seems to have been no outright repeal of the existing ordinances as recommended in 1869; but the amortization provisions were tacitly neglected. After 1870 no direct tax was levied for the benefit of the earlier sinking funds, and their growth was due solely to interest accretions, to the rentals of city property and to occasional extraordinary items of revenue.

More serious in its consequences than the discontinuance of sinking fund levies for the older loans was the utter failure to make provision for the amortization of the additional indebtedness contracted after 1870. For the important Western Maryland loans of 1882 ($684,000) and 1886 ($1,704,000), inadequate sinking funds were provided—for the former, by the appropriation of the premiums accruing from the sale of stock so issued; for the latter, by the appropriation of $100,000 from out the proceeds of the loan, together with premium accruing from its sale. Both funds were to accumulate solely by their own interest accretions.

Sinking fund levies were prescribed in conjunction with other important loans issued between 1868 and 1888, but

[1] Similarly in 1871 the Commissioners of Finance reported "That the available assets and productive property of the corporation are nearly equivalent, at fair valuation, to the total amount of its existing liabilities." A sufficient answer as to the soundness of this conclusion is contained in the succeeding report of the Commissioners of Finance (November, 1871). Previous city administrations were therein sharply criticised for their failure to impose the prescribed sinking fund levies for the water loans, whereby the city then found itself upon the eve of the maturity of a loan of five million dollars, a portion of which had existed nearly twenty years, with a redemption fund of less than seven and a half per cent. of the amount to be redeemed.

in practise these levics were either entirely omitted or imposed for a few years and then discontinued. A comparative statement of the important sinking fund levies prescribed by ordinancc and of the amounts actually imposed is here appended:

Title of Loan.	Amount.	Authorized Sinking Fund Levies.	Actual Sinking Fund Levies.
Floating Debt Loan of 1868.	$1,700,000	3 cents.	1 cent, 1874–77.
" " " " 1870.	800,000	1 cent.	....
" " " " 1874.	2,000,000	2 cents.	2 cents, 1874; 1 cent, 1875.
City Hall " " 1868.	1,000,000	2 cents.	2 cents, 1869–72; 3 cents, 1873–74; 2 cents, 1875–78.
" " " " 1870.	1,000,000	2 cents.	
" " " " 1873.	500,000	1 cent.	
Jones' Falls " " 1870.	2,500,000	2 cents.	2 cents, 1874; 1 cent, 1875.
" " " " 1874.	1,500,000	2 cents.	
Water " " 1874.	4,000,000	4 cents.	3½ cents, 1868–70.
" " " 1877.	5,000,000	2 cents.	
" " " 1882.	500,000	½ cent.	
" " " 1886.	1,000,000	1 cent.	
Paving " " 1880.	500,000	½ cent.	....
Harford Run " " 1879.	250,000	¼ cent.	....
" " " " 1884.	350,000	½ cent.	....

The abandonment of sinking fund levies has been described as the first retrograde movement in the history of local amortization. A second and even more reprehensible procedure was the diversion of sinking fund accumulations to purposes other than the redemption of municipal indebtedness. In other words, having first been deprived of the most important source of revenue from without, the funds were further reduced by the appropriation of their own accretions. This procedure is directly connected with the relation of the city to the Western Maryland Railroad, and is one of the most unfortunate results of that association. The methods of exploitation were two-fold: (1) a portion of the sinking funds was employed in the provision of terminal facilities for the Western Maryland Railroad Company, and in the purchase of certain of the same Company's securities; (2) the sinking fund was charged with the annual interest payment upon certain municipal indebtedness, contracted for the most part in aid of the Western Maryland Railroad Company.

(1). The first inroad upon the sinking fund seems to have been made in 1873, when the Commissioners of Finance were instructed to purchase for the sinking fund, with any funds in their possession, $178,000 of the Western Maryland Railroad's second preferred bonds and also the railroad's interest in $200,000 of its third mortgage bonds in the possession of the City Register.[1] The latter securities were endorsed by the city, and formed a legitimate investment for the redemption funds. The former purchase was simply a successful attempt on the part of the railroad to obtain an excellent market for otherwise unmarketable securities.

In 1874 the Commissioners of Finance were vested with discretion to purchase as investments for the redemption funds detached coupons of the Western Maryland Railroad's first mortgage bonds,[2] and purchase was made of these securities in the next few years to the amount of $71,742. Similarly in 1879 the Commissioners of Finance were authorized to fund in six per cent. certificates issued by the Western Maryland Railroad, all of the coupons of the railroad's first mortgage endorsed bonds paid by the city and also of the preferred second mortgage bonds held by the city.[3] Under this authority funding certificates to the amount of $226,530 were issued to the city and were transferred to the sinking fund. Both coupons and funding certificates have likewise remained in the redemption funds up to the present time, an utterly unproductive investment.

In 1875 efforts were made by the Western Maryland Railroad Company to secure a city depot. A desirable site was secured, but the requisite funds were lacking. The

[1] Ordinance of April 10, 1873, No. 23. These second preferred bonds have remained in the general sinking fund to the present time, an unproductive investment.

[2] Ordinance of June 2, 1874, No. 41.

[3] Ordinance of April 3, 1879, No. 22.

line of least resistance was eventually followed, or as the president of the Western Maryland Railroad Company with a certain genial frankness, stated: "The plan of applying to the city for aid, though not remarkable with the company for novelty, nor the last to suggest itself, was acted upon." The Commissioners of Finance were directed to use redemption funds in their possession to the amount of $200,000 to provide terminal facilities, to be leased to the railroad at an annual rental of $16,000. One-eighth of the rental was to be set apart annually as a sinking fund, on which the railroad was allowed six per cent. interest and which fund might be applied at any time to the purchase for the railroad of the reversion in the property.[1] The maximum amount authorized was expended between 1875 and 1879, and a lease made as directed. Enlarged depot facilities were provided in the same manner in 1882-83 by an investment of $131,163.81 of the sinking funds, upon which the railroad contracted to pay as rental seven per cent. upon the amount invested. Of this rental one per cent. was set apart for the ultimate acquisition of the property by the railroad.[2]

The Western Maryland Railroad paid the stipulated rentals for both the original and the enlarged terminals, with promptness and regularity, and the investments yielding seven and six per cent. respectively, proved eminently profitable to the sinking fund. The funds segregated for the ultimate purchase by the railroad of the reversion of the leases amounted on December 31, 1897, to $66,-910.66 and $24,937.76, respectively, and the ultimate disassociation of city and railroad in this particular seems likely. Whatever advantage may have accrued to the city, the procedure was none the less reprehensible and in violation of fundamental principles of debt amortization.

(2). The heaviest handicap imposed upon the growth of the sinking funds after the discontinuance of the tax levies

[1] Ordinance of May 24, 1875, No. 97.
[2] Ordinance of May 25, 1882, No. 92.

was the enforced assumption of the annual interest payment upon certain municipal loans. In 1879, with the plausible preamble that the city's real estate and investments were a part of the funds provided for the redemption of the funded debt, the sinking fund was charged with the annual interest payment upon the $1,000,000 Pittsburg and Connellsville loan and upon such part of the $2,375,000 of Western Maryland indebtedness as the city might be called upon to assume.[1] The annual interest charge of $60,000 upon the one million Pittsburg and Connellsville loan was borne by the sinking fund from 1880 until 1886 when the principal was paid by the city. There was unfortunately no such release from the burden of Western Maryland indebtedness. The $2,375,000 for the interest payment upon which the sinking funds were made responsible, consisted of $200,000 first mortgage endorsed bonds; $300,000 second mortgage endorsed bonds; $875,000 third mortgage guaranteed bonds, and a direct municipal loan of $1,000,000. All of these securities bore six per cent. interest. The Company paid the interest upon its first mortgage bonds, but defaulted upon its second series, and the resulting interest charge was defrayed from out the sinking fund until 1887, when both of these earlier issues were replaced by the fifth mortgage loan, described above.[2] Upon the $875,000 third mortgage bonds and the $1,000,000 direct loan, the Company defaulted practically from the outset, and from 1879 the aggregate interest charge of $112,500 per annum was borne by the sinking fund.

The effect of this exploitation policy upon the growth of the sinking fund can best be illustrated by a typical example. During 1888 the sinking funds received $281,660.95 from the interest upon investments; $29,765 from premium on sales of stock; $26,915.10 from rental of real estate; $21,-869.88 from rental of Western Maryland terminals, and miscellaneous items swelling the aggregate to $379,412.39. Owing to the payment of $112,400 interest upon Western

[1] Ordinance of April 17, 1879, No. 33. [2] See page 316.

Maryland loans, the net increment of the funds was only $254,713.13, or $26,947.82 less than the mere interest accumulation upon the amount already invested. In some years the loss was even greater. Thus during 1880 the increase of the funds was $436,030.07; but $196,290.91 of this was from the sale of city property, reducing the increment from ordinary sources to $239,739.76. The interest accretions of the funds within the same period should have been $397,447.14. The comment of the Commissioners of Finance upon this result is inexplicable: "This gratifying result justifies and strengthens our confidence in the efficiency of the redemption system, and in the sufficiency of the means provided for the payment of the public debt at maturity."[1] The extent to which the general sinking fund has been mulcted since the inauguration of the policy of utilizing its accretions in interest payments is shown in the appended table:

Year	Amount	Year	Amount
1880	$189,420	1889	$112,605
1881	189,885	1890	112,380
1882	192,150	1891	112,725
1883	190,215	1892	112,320
1884	190,785	1893	112,380
1885	190,710	1894	112,380
1886	160,005	1895	112,275
1887	122,145	1896	112,275
1888	112,440	1897	112,500

The neglect of the sinking funds may be said to have culminated in 1878-85, in which years no tax levies whatever were imposed for this purpose, and considerable amounts were withdrawn from the accretions of the funds for the payment of interest upon municipal indebtedness.[2] The

[1] Report of the Department of Finance, December 31, 1880.

[2] It was sometimes stated that the high price of municipal securities was responsible for the slow growth of the sinking funds. In his message of January 1, 1885, Mayor F. C. Latrobe undertook to show that "the city would annually pay $150,000 for the privilege of paying-off annually $600,000 of its debt." This was, however, surely not the explanation of the discontinuance of sinking fund levies.

stationary condition and threatened exhaustion of the funds in the face of maturing loans and the incurring of additional funded indebtedness compelled the resumption of sinking fund levies. In 1889 a tax of one-half cent was imposed for the general sinking fund. It was omitted in 1890 but increased to five cents in 1891 and continued thereafter. The sinking fund levies provided by the water loan of 1886 (1 cent), and the municipal improvement loans of 1888 (3 cents) and 1892 (2 cents) were imposed with the issue of the respective loans and were maintained thereafter.[1] A further impulse in the right direction was given by the vigorous administration of Mayor Alcaeus Hooper (1895-97). In his first budget, the levy for the general sinking fund was increased to 8¼ cents and other levies were continued at the rates prescribed. Provision was also made for the creation of sinking funds for the water loans of 1877 and 1882, authorized at the time of the issue of the stock but hitherto neglected. The sinking fund levies imposed in 1896 aggregated 17¼ cents.

A partial consolidation of the sinking funds was recommended by the Commissioners of Finance in 1871 as conducing to greater simplicitiy in account and larger effectiveness in operation, and was authorized by ordinance in 1872.[2] In 1874 the general sinking fund absorbed the smaller funds, reducing the total number of accounts from sixteen to nine. A further consolidation took place in 1879, whereby the number of funds was reduced to five of which two, the Baltimore and Ohio and the Western Maryland funds, were in the custody of the City Register. The process of consolidation by veiling the growth of specific accounts undoubtedly contributed to the neglect of the sinking funds. After 1879 by the operation of new and the revival of neglected redemption provisions, additional sinking funds were created until on January 1, 1897, the total number in existence was thirteen.

[1] The resumption of sinking fund levies was strongly recommended by Mayor Robert C. Davidson in his message of January 26, 1891.

[2] Ordinance of February 18, 1872, No. 18.

The rentals of city property accrued to the sinking fund during the entire period here considered. Premiums from the sale of city stock were commonly appropriated in the same manner, and in some cases new issues of city stock were secured for the funds at par although commanding a considerable premium in the open market.[1] In 1880 a general ordinance provided that premiums upon subsequent loans should be invested in the particular securities issued and should be added to the sinking fund created for the redemption of that particular loan. If no such special sinking fund had been created, the premium was to be placed to the credit of the general sinking fund.[2]

The condition of the sinking funds permitted no appreciable redemption of city securities during the first half of the period here considered. In 1863 the early issues of "court house stock" and "miscellaneous stock" were reduced by the amount of $363,173.87, and in 1866 "defense stock" to the amount of $109,613.95 was cancelled. $5,000,000 six per cent. "water stock" matured in 1875, and in consequence of the depletion of the sinking funds, the entire loan was refunded in 1877 at five per cent. In 1878 the $2,000,000 "floating debt loan," issued in 1874, and the $200,000 "Patterson Park extension loan," issued in 1873—the full amount of both of which were contained in the sinking funds—were cancelled. Four maturing loans were redeemed from the general sinking fund in 1884-86, to the aggregate amount of $4,029,061.54.[3] No other municipal obligations matured until 1890, when important redemptions and funding operations occurred. The "Baltimore and

[1] Ordinance of March 22, 1882, No. 28.

[2] Ordinance of February 20, 1880, No. 5. Certain designated loans were excepted from the operation of this ordinance.

[3] $1,000,000 City Hall Loan; $1,000,000 Valley Railroad Company Loan; $1,000,000 Pittsburg and Connellsville Railroad Company Loan; and $1,029,061.54 Consolidated Loan.

Small portions of the loans were not presented for redemption at maturity, even though no further interest was paid thereon. This fact will explain the discrepancy between the above figures and those presented in Appendix G.

Ohio $5,000,000 loan" was discharged by the receipt of $2,570,754.26 from its special sinking fund and the payment of $2,429,267.29 by the Baltimore and Ohio Railroad Company. A consolidated six per cent. loan of $7,306,546.22 was redeemed to the amount of $2,306,546.22 from out the proceeds of the city's holding of Baltimore and Ohio Railroad Company stock; the remaining $5,000,000 in the absence of an adequate sinking fund was refunded at three and a half per cent. Finally $555,566.25 of the original park indebtedness was paid from out the special sinking fund maintained by the Park Commission. Consolidated loans aggregating $2,621,421.92 and $4,000,000 of the water debt were redeemed upon maturity in 1894 from out the sinking funds. No other loans matured within the period examined.[1]

ADMINISTRATION AND LIMITATION.

The administration of the municipal debt, including the negotiation of loans, the payment of interest and the discharge of principal at maturity was vested in the Commissioners of Finance.

The statutory limitation of the general borrowing power of the city to $1,000,000[2] was modified in 1861 by the grant of authority to increase the municipal debt by an amount not exceeding $1,500,000. Certain miscellaneous loans appear to have been issued under this general power, but the essential increase in municipal indebtedness continued to be based upon special enabling acts of the General Assembly and the statutory limitation exercised a merely indirect influence.

The lavish extension of municipal aid to works of internal improvement, the reckless contraction of indebtedness during and immediately after the Civil War, and the general

[1] $4,300,000 in various issues mature in 1900. In 1898 it became evident that the sinking funds would be unable to meet the obligation and preparatory measures were taken to refund the loans when redeemable.

[2] See above, page 195.

discredit cast upon local administration by the financial operations of that period, combined to induce the Maryland Constitutional Convention of 1867 to insert in the fundamental instrument then drafted a radical restriction upon local borrowing power. The city was prohibited from thereafter creating any debt or giving or lending its credit for any purpose whatsoever, unless such debt or credit were authorized by a special act of the General Assembly, and by an ordinance of the City Council submitted to the legal voters of the city and approved by a majority of the votes then cast. From these limitations were excepted temporary loans to meet any deficiency in the city treasury, to maintain the police, safety and sanitary condition of the city and to provide for municipal indebtedness incurred before the adoption of the Constitution.[1]

Every municipal loan issued after 1867 thus involved an enabling act of the legislature, an ordinance of the municipality and a ratification by popular vote. The restrictive effect of this procedure was probably less than the framers of the Constitution of 1867 anticipated. The initiative with respect to any proposed municipal loan was taken by the City Council and an enabling ordinance passed on the eve of a session of the legislature. The General Assembly ordinarily viewed the proposal as entirely a matter of local concern and yielded to the preference of the city delegation. To an electorate, of whom considerably less than fifty per cent. were taxpayers, municipal borrowing was peculiarly "an agreeable process," and the referendum served as a potential rather than as an actual check. The natural predisposition of the general body of voters to ratify a long term funded loan for costly public improvements, offering large opportunities for local employment and expenditure, was strengthened after 1888 by the use of composite loans, wherein, as in an omnibus appropriation, several desirable items were able to carry through one or more unworthy ones. As a matter of fact not until the adoption of the

[1] Constitution of Maryland, 1867, Art. XI, sect. 7.

Australian ballot system in 1890, with its incident of a single ballot, did the referendum elicit any large proportion of the municipal vote.

However short the restraining influence of the constitutional limitation may have fallen of the views originally entertained in regard thereto, its effect was none the less important. Leaving out of account its potential influence, on at least two occasions within the period here considered, large improvement loans were defeated at the polls, and it seems likely that with the dawn of a new municipal spirit popular endorsement of any proposed increase of municipal indebtedness will become a much less assured fact than has hitherto been the case.

The actual vote upon certain important funded loans is presented in the following table:[1]

Year.	Purpose of Loan.	Amount.	Votes for.	Votes against.
1870	Jones' Falls.	$2,000,000	8,989	7,393
1874	Jones' Falls.	1,500,000	11,270	16,832
1874	Water Supply.	4,000,000	13,131	6,202
1874	Funding Floating Debt.	2,000,000	18,027	9,405
1876	Water Supply.	5,000,000	16,507	6,513
1880	Street Paving.	500,000	13,639	4,769
1882	Western Maryland Railroad.	684,000	17,374	5,732
1882	Water Supply.	500,000	13,363	2,560
1886	Western Maryland Railroad.	1,800,000	12,098	2,588
1886	Water Supply.	1,000,000	11,443	1,907
1888	Municipal Improvements.	5,000,000	30,102	9,703
1892	Municipal Improvements.	6,000,000	30,797	5,863
1894	Municipal Improvements.	4,000,000	24,875	10,859
1896	Wire Conduits.	1,000,000	21,599	13,507
1898	Western Maryland Railroad.	1,875,000	31,500	15,955
1898	Refunding.	4,300,000	28,021	16,124
1898	Municipal Improvements.	4,500,000	21,589	23,243

Municipal Credit.

The status of municipal credit at the beginning of the period under review is strikingly indicated by the circum-

[1] For many of the data I am indebted to a memorandum furnished me by Dr. Fabian Franklin of Baltimore.

The defeated loans were a Jones' Falls Improvement issue of $1,500,000 in 1874 and a Municipal Improvements issue of $4,500,000 in 1898.

stances attending the purchase of Druid Hill Park in 1860.[1] Under ordinary conditions, however, the city was able, as in the preceding decade, to negotiate at par a six per cent. bond running for a period of thirty or forty years. The quick succession of large funded loans, the urgent need of ready money for bounty payments and public defence, and the reckless character of municipal financiering during and immediately after the Civil War brought local credit to probably the lowest point in the history of the city. A six per cent. long term bond remained in use, but in actual negotiation and in open sale it was subject to large and fluctuating discounts. With municipal reorganization in 1867, municipal credit revived. In 1870 the Commissioners of Finance bought six per cent. city stock for the sinking funds at 93.79 and in 1871 at 95.94. Municipal credit suffered keenly in the panic of 1873; but before the close of 1874 the six per cent. securities of the city were selling practically at par. In 1877 a $5,000,000 five per cent. refunding loan was negotiated at slightly better than par, and three years later further issues of similar securities were overbid four and five times and netted premiums ranging from nine to nearly fifteen per cent.[2] The use of a four and a half per cent. par bond had been suggested by Mayor F. C. Latrobe in his message of January 1, 1880; but succeeding loans were actually issued at four, three and sixty-five hundredths, and three and a half per cent. In 1882 four per cent. bonds were sold at something better than 103, and in 1885 the ability of the city to float a three and sixty-five hundredths per cent. bond at par had become established. In 1887 the last named securities were negotiated at 104½, and thereafter a three and a half per cent. bond was employed by the city. The terms upon which the important loans of the succeeding decade were negotiated revealed the same continuous improvement. Three

[1] Cf. above, p. 310.
[2] Report of Department of Finance, December 31, 1880.

and a half per cent. bonds, running forty and fifty years, realized 103.25 in 1890, and 105.23 in 1896.[1]

One of the most important influences responsible for the extraordinary decline in the net rate at which the city was able to fund its later loans was the peculiarly attractive character of such securities, as a form of investment, to Maryland corporations. This arose from the facts (1) that the city did not tax its own stock and furthermore paid the state tax imposed thereon; (2) that the taxable basis of corporations was determined by deducting from their capital stock the value of their investments. In consequence to the extent which a corporation owned city stock, it was released from both state and municipal taxation. The terms actually realized by the city in the negotiation of its later loans was thus not an entirely accurate gauge of municipal credit.[2]

[1] In 1898 the same securities were sold by the city at the phenomenal rates of 110.27 ($250,000) and 116.27 ($250,000).

[2] The later loans were taken upon prohibitive terms almost exclusively by the financial corporations of Baltimore, and "One of the most noticeable features of the daily transfers of city stock is the fact that individual holders are steadily disposing of their stock, which is being absorbed by the banks, trust companies and other corporations" (Report of City Register, January 3, 1899).

PART V

THE PRESENT FINANCIAL CONDITION OF BALTIMORE

CHAPTER I

MUNICIPAL FINANCES IN 1897.

The year 1897 represented the last period in the financial history of Baltimore under the old municipal organization. The new city charter was granted in March, 1898, and certain of its most important features went into effect immediately thereafter. The bitter struggle between Mayor and City Council, referred to below,[1] affected administrative activity rather than financial procedure during 1897, and the financial experience of the year can be regarded as fairly typical of the period which it was destined to terminate.

The municipal budget was prepared by the joint Ways and Means Committee and presented to the City Council in the early summer, in the usual form of a general appropriation bill and a series of tax levy ordinances. Few changes were made by the Council and the ordinances were approved on July 2, 1897.

The appropriation bill contained 270 items, arranged in 21 departmental groups and aggregating $7,429,149.57. Estimates for the "Annex" were in every case distinguished from those designed for the city proper. The greater part

[1] Page 356.

of the appropriation to the Inspector of Buildings was for the construction of school buildings. With this exception the bill provided for the mere "operating expenses" of the city government, and left extraordinary disbursements to be met from out the proceeds of funded loans.

The levy ordinances were fifteen in number and imposed a total tax on general property of $2.00 on every $100. The estimated taxable basis was $278,500,000 and the estimated proportion of taxes collectable, 73 per cent.—making the assumed yield within the year $4,066,100. The statutory rates established by the reassessment act of 1896 were levied upon bonds and securities and upon mortgages;[1] the estimated receipts from these two sources were $129,000 and $10,000, respectively. The estimated receipts from sources other than property taxation were $3,343,090.30, making the total estimated revenues for the year $7,548,190.30.

A distinctive feature of the finances of 1897—due in part to the vigilance of the city executive, in part to the differences between the two branches of the city government—was the practical absence of special appropriation bills. The budget included, under the head of General Expenditures, an item of $36,100 subject to disbursement by special ordinances and resolutions; no other appropriation was made, after the passage of the budget, save from out this fund. Expenditures and receipts, estimated and actual, for the fiscal year are shown in the following statements:

EXPENDITURES.

	Budget Appropriation.	Actual Expenditures.
Inspector of Buildings	$266,531.56	$223,148.76
Street Cleaning	389,392.05	374,475.90
General Superintendent of Lamps	411,807.50	401,676.87
Harbor Commission	76,362.79	70,540.34
Health Department	80,000.00	89,154.59
Fire Department	460,650.00	469,696.29
City Commissioner	221,557.13	224,805.21
City Collector	58,700.00	59,088.14

[1] See above, p. 258.

	Budget Appropriation.	Actual Expenditures.
Commissioners for Opening Streets.....	10,100.00	9,979.61
Liquor License Commissioners	15,000.00	14,608.44
Supervisors of Elections	81,800.00	77,183.98
General Expenditures	464,208.20	421,236.26
City Library	8,299.54	8,212.94
Superintendent of Public Buildings	41,900.00	41,870.54
Schools	1,273,998.00	1,253,274.67
Police Department	837,270.00	837,270.00
City Poor	383,250.00	374,581.42
Certain Expenses	226,800.00	237,020.81
Interest on Stock Debt	1,447,287.00	1,447,287.00
Opening Streets	163,910.43	163,910.43
Sinking Funds	510,325.37	467,470.31
Total	$7,429,149.57	$7,266,492.51
Excess of budget appropriations over actual expenditures	166,457.06	

REVENUES.

	Estimated Receipts.	Actual Receipts.
Tax on General Property (in City)......	$4,066,100.00	$3,672,089.04
Tax on General Property (in Annex)...	147,400.00	189,502.58
Tax on Bonds and Securities..........	129,000.00	142,907.82
Tax on Income from Mortgages.......	10,000.00	4,717.06
Taxes in Arrears	1,753,000.00	1,644,526.05
Share of State School Tax.............	210,635.00	214,618.29
Special Income for Interest on Funded Debt[1]	554,051.04	554,051.04
License Taxes:		
Liquor	400,000.00	410,239.93
General	65,000.00	65,831.83
Markets	45,000.00	53,215.66
Wharves	20,000.00	24,910.57
Fees	23,700.00	27,002.34
Surplus from Previous Year	84,968.46	84,968.46
Miscellaneous	39,335.80	46,772.16
Total	$7,548,190.30	$7,139,412.74
Excess of estimated over actual receipts.	408,777.56	

The excess of estimated over actual receipts was $408,-777.56, increased by minor items to $410,052.90. Against

[1] Derived as follows: Water Board, $313,984.75; Park Board, $33,287.50; Western Maryland Railroad Company, $82,740.00; Commissioners of Finance (from sinking funds), $124,038.79.

this potential deficit were credited the excess of estimated receipts over appropriations, $115,240.73; the excess of appropriations over actual payments, $166,457.06, and balances from closed accounts $9,238.55. The actual treasury deficit for the year was thus $119,116.56.[1]

The budget made no provision for the maintenance of the water works and the public parks, and assumed no income from water rentals and the franchise tax on street railways—the sources of income devoted to the support of these fiscally independent branches of municipal service. Similarly, imperfect account was taken of expenditure and revenue on account of street paving or street reconstruction, the costs of which were partially defrayed by the levy of special assessments.

The total net collections of the water department were $800,706.16, out of which were paid $313,984.75 as interest on outstanding "water bonds"; $189,994.40 as the operating expenses of the department; $140,000 as a surplus to the Commissioners of Finance, and the remaining $156,727.01, for the extension of water supply and for minor outlays. The total receipts of the Park Commission were $271,834.81, of which $263,040.47 was derived from the franchise tax on street railways. Of this aggregate, $33,287.50 was paid to the Commissioners of Finance for interest upon the "park debt," and the remaining amount, with the exception of a small balance of $4,243.91, was devoted to the maintenance of the public parks and squares. Expenditures for street reconstruction for the year were $245,263.16, of which $163,910.43 was "assessed upon the city"; and $85,865.61 was obtained by special assessment. The expenditures for street paving were $39,447.26 and the receipts from the special assessment, $45,638.08. In both cases unexpended balances were left to the credit of particular accounts.

[1] The "floating debt" for which provision was made in the City Register's estimate of expenditures for 1898 was $239,902.45. The discrepancy is traceable to certain existing claims against the city of which no account was taken in the budget of 1897.

Extraordinary expenditures to the amount of $1,329,786.89 were made from out the proceeds of the three composite loans of 1888, 1892 and 1894, as follows: Enlargement of water supply, $717,021.26; court house, $463,177.11; water sewers, $84,250.61; paving streets, $29,298.62; bridges, $26,459.32; school houses and lots, $9,579.97.

The increase of the funded and guaranteed debt during the year was from $33,502,018.43 to $36,170,576.95, or $2,668,558.52. This increase is accounted for by the issue of $1,453,300 of the funding loan of 1896 and $1,219,800 of the municipal improvement loans of 1892 and 1894, and by redemptions to the amount of $4,541.48. Temporary loans were made and repaid to the amount of $3,938,000. The net increment of the sinking funds during the year was $858,559.64. The condition of municipal credit was indicated by the sale by public advertisement of $1,453,000 of three and a half, forty-year bonds at 105.77.

The funded and guaranteed debt bore interest at rates varying from six to three per cent., distributed as follows: $4,975,000 at 6 per cent.; $7,237,000 at 5 per cent.; $3,484,000 at 4 per cent.; $18,168,200 at 3½ per cent.; $483,000 at $3\frac{65}{100}$ per cent.; $1,704,000 at 3¼ per cent.; $100,000 at 3 per cent.; on $19,376.95 overdue, no interest was allowed. Of the total debt, $5,175,000 matures in 1900; $1,850,000 in 1902-1904; $6,280,000 in 1916; $9,688,000 in 1920-1928; $6,453,300 in 1936; $5,284,400 in 1940; $1,420,500 in 1945.

CHAPTER II

THE NEW CHARTER.

The completion of a century of corporate existence was practically coincident, in the municipal history of Baltimore, with the beginning of agitation for the revision of the obsolete instrument of government under which the greater part of that hundred years had been spent. The immediate cause of dissatisfaction was the high-handed action of the City Council in 1896 in attempting to take away the entire appointing power of a non-partisan Mayor and vesting it in the legislative branch of the city government.[1] This revolutionary procedure—made possible by the features of the city charter permitting the corporation to pass ordinances regulating the manner of appointing its officials, and allowing the City Council by a three-fourths vote to pass ordinances over the Mayor's veto—was ultimately defeated by the decisions of the Court of Appeals.[2] But the incidental revelation of the possibilities for evil inherent in the old municipal organization, as well as the actual loss and embarrassment occasioned to city affairs left a deep impress upon public sentiment.

Intelligent discussion as to the desirability and form of municipal reorganization culminated in the passage of an ordinance in November, 1896, authorizing the newly elected city executive, Mayor William T. Malster, to appoint an unpaid commission of eight persons to draft a new charter for the city of Baltimore, to be submitted to the General Assembly for enactment at the current session.[3] Mayor

[1] For details of this remarkable incident, see a statement by the writer in "Notes on Municipal Government" in *Annals of American Academy of Political and Social Science*, May, 1896.

[2] Creager *vs.* Hooper, 83 Md. 490; Hooper *vs.* Creager, 84 Md. 195.

[3] Ordinance of November 24, 1897.

Malster at once appointed a model "New Charter Commission," incidentally arousing by the excellence of his selections widespread anticipation of a reform administration. The personnel of the commission was as follows: Hon. William Pinkney Whyte, who had served acceptably as Mayor of Baltimore and as Governor of Maryland; Hon. Ferdinand C. Latrobe, who enjoyed the distinction of having been seven times elected to the mayoralty and was in intimate acquaintance with every phase of municipal development; Dr. Daniel C. Gilman, President of the Johns Hopkins University; Mr. Samuel D. Schmucker, and Mr. George R. Gaither, Jr., skilled members of the bar; City Solicitor Thomas I. Elliott; City Councillor Thomas G. Hayes, and City Attorney Lewis Putzel.[1]

It is within bounds to state that difficulty would be experienced in attempting to select eight other citizens of Baltimore as familiar with the defects of the local political framework, or better fitted to suggest measures of improvement. Both political parties were represented, but the commission was non-partisan rather than bi-partisan. It at once commanded public confidence and respect and the course of subsequent events in no wise modified this attitude. No serious charge was at any time made that partisan interest or unworthy motive determined any feature of the new instrument.

The time available for the completion of the work was little more than three months; but by intelligent division of labor, harmonious co-operation, and extraordinary industry and application, a new charter was drafted within that period. It was submitted to the General Assembly for enactment in the closing weeks of the legislative session, together with a codification of existing laws. The whole formed a volume of 350 printed octavo pages, and the mere bulk of the proposed legislation served as its most effective guard against mutilation. An effort of the City Council to "revise" the work of the charter commission

[1] Mr. Frederick T. Dorton served as secretary of the commission.

was defeated, and on March 24, 1898, the charter was enacted into statute law in practically unchanged form.[1]

The new charter represents a conservative adaptation of accepted principles of municipal reform to local requirements and established usages. In few respects has there been any complete or radical departure from the administrative forms to which the citizens of Baltimore have been accustomed for a century. On the other hand, recognized elements of municipal improvement have been boldly incorporated, and the influence of modern municipal reorganization in the United States, notably in New York City, has been decided. The fundamental principles which consciously governed the commission in the preparation of the charter were:

1. Association of related branches of municipal service into single departments.

2. Concentration of powers of appointment and removal in the hands of the Mayor, with location of definite responsibility upon all public officials.

3. Minority representation in all departmental boards.

4. Separation of municipal from state and federal elections.

5. Appointment of experts in all departments requiring professional knowledge and skill.

6. Grant of public franchises to the highest bidder, for a limited term, subject to municipal regulation and control.

7. Check upon municipal expenditure and prevention of floating indebtedness.

8. Removal of the public school system from all possible political influence.

9. Public supervision of the indigent sick and poor while subjects of municipal aid.

[1] Accompanying the charter and recommended by the charter commission were two supplementary bills, limiting the bonded indebtedness of the city to seven per cent. of its taxable basis and providing for the receipt by the city of the entire proceeds of the liquor license taxes imposed in the city. Neither of these measures passed. The formal reference to the new charter is "Laws of Maryland," 1898, ch. 123.

The charter retains the traditional corporate framework —a Mayor and a bicameral Council. The term of the Mayor is extended from two to four years, and his salary is also increased to $6000. He possesses a veto power over all ordinances of the City Council, which can be overridden by a vote of three-fourths of all members of each Branch.

The City Council consists, as before, of two chambers, designated as the First Branch and the Second Branch, respectively. The lower chamber, or First Branch, remains constituted of one member from each of the twenty-four wards of the city; but the term has been extended from one to two years. The upper chamber, or Second Branch, heretofore composed of one member elected for two years from every two contiguous wards, has undergone important modification. The city is now divided into four "councilmanic districts,"—consisting of six contiguous wards in numerical succession—from each of which two Councilmen are elected to the Second Branch. Their term of office is increased from two to four years, so arranged that one-half of the entire body retires every second year. The President of the Second Branch of the City Council is made an independent official with the same property qualification as the Mayor ($2000). He receives a salary of $3,000 per annum and is elected for a term of four years. The property qualifications of the Councilmen remain unchanged at $300 for the First Branch and $500 for the Second Branch; but these provisions are made effective by the requirement that taxes must have been paid thereon for one and two years, respectively, prior to election. Municipal elections are fixed, distinct from federal and state elections, on the Tuesday next after the first Monday in May, and are preceded by a supplementary registration of voters.[1]

[1] The first election under the new charter occurs on May 2, 1899. The new Mayor will not, however, enter into office until November 15, 1899, when the full term for which the present Mayor was elected expires. This involves an awkward "hold-over" of some six months.

All administrative branches of the city government are arranged into departments and sub-divided into sub-departments; the heads of both departments and sub-departments are appointed by the Mayor. Regard for local conservatism unfortunately prevented the commission from vesting the power of absolute appointment in the Mayor; but the right of confirmation is transferred from the joint convention of the two chambers to the Second Branch of the City Council. The Mayor can remove any of his appointees without cause within the first six months of their term of office; thereafter only by preferring charges and after trial. The heads of departments and sub-departments are given absolute power of appointing and removing subordinates. The heads of departments are also given the privilege of the floor of the First Branch of the City Council, with the right to participate in the discussion of matters relating to their respective departments, but without power to vote.

The administrative branches of the city government are organized into eight departments: (1) Finance, (2) Law, (3) Public Safety, (4) Public Improvements, (5) Public Parks and Squares, (6) Education, (7) Charities and Corrections, (8) Review and Assessments. Under these are logically arranged as sub-departments the essential agencies of municipal service. In control of each department is a board, composed of the heads of its sub-departments. These boards are ordinarily designed for consultation and advice and possess no power to direct or control the duties or work of the sub-departments.

The sub-departments represent, with one or two noteworthy exceptions, existing municipal departments. Complexity has been reduced and contradictions and duplications eliminated; but the purpose of the charter is throughout to effect maximum improvement with a minimum wrench.

(1). The Department of Finance is composed of six sub-departments: (a) Comptroller, (b) City Register, (c) City Collector, (d) Collector of Water Rents and Licenses, (e)

Commissioners of Finance, (f) Board of Estimates. The first four officials and the presidents of the remaining boards constitute a Board of Finance, in nominal control of the department. No changes are made in the appointment and duties of the Register, the Collector and the Commissioners of Finance. The Comptroller is to be elected by popular vote for a term of four years, but may be removed upon charges preferred by the Mayor by a majority vote of the Second Branch of the City Council. The Board of Estimates is an entirely new institution and is described below.[1] The Collector of Water Rents and Licenses is charged with the duties indicated by his title, before vested in the Water Department and the Comptroller, respectively.

(2). The Department of Law is under the direction of a City Solicitor who receives a salary of $4000 per annum. He is appointed by the Mayor, and in turn appoints a First, Second, and Third Assistant City Solicitor. Provision is made for the permanent organization of the department.

(3). The Department of Public Safety includes four sub-departments: (a) Board of Fire Commissioners, (b) Commissioner of Health, (c) Inspector of Buildings, (d) Commissioner of Street Cleaning. The last three officials, the President of the Board of Fire Commissioners, and *ex-officio* the President of the Board of Police Commissioners constitute the Board of Public Safety, whose functions are nominal. No change is made in the Board of Fire Commissioners, the Inspector of Buildings and the Commissioner of Street Cleaning, other than vesting all subordinate appointments in the heads of the respective sub-departments. The Commissioner of Health absorbs the duties of the old Board of Health and is placed in full charge of the sanitary care of the city.

(4). The Department of Public Improvements consists of four sub-departments: (a) City Engineer, (b) Inspector of Buildings, (c) Water Board, (d) Harbor Board. At the head of the department is a Board of Public Improvements

[1] Page 363.

composed of the first two officials and the presidents of the two boards. The important duties of this board are described in connection with budgetary procedure.[1] The City Engineer replaces the old City Commissioner in the care of public streets and roadways. The Water Board and the Harbor Board are each composed of five members of whom four are unsalaried; the fifth, a skilled engineer, receives a salary of $4000 per annum and serves as president.

(5). The Department of Public Parks and Squares is under the control of a Board of Park Commissioners, composed of five unsalaried members, in whom are vested the duties both of the old park commission and of the independent commissioners of squares.

(6). The administration of the public school system undergoes wholesome reconstruction. The existing board of twenty-two ward commissioners, appointed by the City Council, is replaced by a smaller body of nine commissioners, appointed at large by the Mayor for a term of six years; one-third of the new board retires every two years. This body in turn appoints a Superintendent of Public Instruction, six or more Assistant Superintendents, and a number of unpaid School Visitors.

(7). The Department of Charities and Corrections consists of the Supervisors of City Charities and the Visitors to the City Jail. The president and one other member of each body, together with the Mayor *ex-officio* constitute the Board of Charities and Corrections, with mere consulting and advisory powers. The Supervisors of City Charities replace the Trustees of the Poor and form an unsalaried board of nine members appointed for a term of six years; three members of the board retire every second year. The Supervisors are vested with broad powers relative to the municipal care of dependent and defective classes. In lieu of the system of municipal subsidies to private institutions the city hereafter pays a contract price for public charges placed in such institutions, and the Supervisors are given

[1] See below, p. 364.

full control over such persons while in receipt of public aid. The conduct of the city jail is vested in an unsalaried board of nine Visitors to the Jail.

(8). The Department of Review and Assessment is composed of the Appeal Tax Court and the Commissioners for Opening Streets. The corresponding departmental board consists of the presidents of the two sub-departments and the Mayor *ex-officio*. The term of office of the three Judges of the Appeal Tax Court is extended to three years, one member retiring every year. The Court is authorized to appoint such number of assessors as the city by ordinance may direct. A similar change is made in the tenure of the three Commissioners for Opening Streets.

(9). Certain unclassified administrative departments are left essentially unchanged, save as affected by the general principles of departmental responsibility already noted. These minor independent departments are: (a) City Librarian, (b) Art Commission, (c) Superintendent of Lamps and Lighting, (d) Surveyor, (e) Constables, (f) Superintendent of Public Buildings, (g) Public Printer.

Radical change has been made in the financial procedure of the municipality, largely in line with the corresponding features of the charter of Greater New York. The municipal budget was formerly prepared and submitted to the City Council, it will be remembered, by a joint Ways and Means Committee of the two chambers. The new charter provides for the creation of a Board of Estimates, composed of the Mayor, the City Solicitor, representing the Department of Law; the Comptroller, representing the Department of Finance; the President of the Second Branch of the City Council, representing the legislative department, and the City Engineer, representing the Department of Public Improvements. The Board of Estimates is required to prepare and submit to the City Council in October of each year a precise estimate of the necessary appropriations for the next ensuing fiscal year, arranged in three distinct lists: (a) "departmental estimates," or the amounts required for conducting the several branches of ordinary municipal service during the ensuing fiscal year; (b) "estimates for new improvements," or the amounts required during the year for new improvements recommended by the heads of various departments and sub-departments; (c) "estimates for annual appropriations," or the amounts required, in accordance with existing legislation, for charitable, educational and other purposes.[1]

The City Council may reduce but not increase the several amounts fixed by the Board of Estimates, and may not insert any new items, nor subsequently divert any appropriation from the purpose for which it was originally designed. In the same manner, the Board of Estimates is required to submit to the City Council an estimate of the annual tax levy, which may be increased but not reduced by that body.[2] Any ordinance authorizing a public improvement, to exceed in cost the sum of $2000 and not included in the annual estimates submitted by the Board of Estimates, must be referred after its first reading in either branch of the City Council, to the Board of Public Improvements, for report as to its desirability, and to the Board of Estimates, for report as to the ability of the municipal treasury to meet the expenditure, and no ordinance can become valid until both of these reports have been received. Contracts for municipal work and for the purchase of municipal supplies, involving an expenditure of $500 or more, can only be made after public advertisement and award to the lowest bidder by a board composed of the Mayor, the Comptroller, the City Register, the City Solicitor, and the President of the Second Branch of the City Council.

The danger of floating indebtedness is reduced by the provision that no temporary loans shall be authorized save in anticipation of the receipts of taxes levied for the cur-

[1] The sum of $50,000 is annually included as a contingent fund.

[2] Municipal taxes are payable within the first six months of each year and become subject to interest penalties thereafter.

rent year. In case municipal revenue is insufficient in any year, there must be a *pro rata* abatement of all appropriations, except those fixed by statute, and any surplus accruing must be credited to the general sinking fund.

A salutary provision of the new charter relates to the disposition of municipal franchises. Grants of specific franchises or rights in or relating to public property are limited to a term of twenty-five years, subject upon revaluation to successive renewals for a not longer period. The compensation to be paid for all public franchises is determined after public advertisement by the Board of Estimates, and the City Council may not change the terms so fixed. In all grants the municipality may reserve the right to resume control of the plant, with or without further compensation, upon the termination of the franchise period.

Viewed in its entirety, the new charter is an efficient instrument of government, eminently creditable to the intelligence and discretion of its authors. In retaining a bicameral City Council and in requiring the assent of the Second Branch to the appointments of the Mayor, unnecessary concessions have perhaps been made to local conservatism. These are the only instances of signal neglect of accepted principles of municipal reform, and even here—bearing in mind existing local conditions—the results may be very different from those naturally to be anticipated. The new charter may not effect immediate reformation in local administration; but it can hardly fail, in the reasonable phrase of the charter commission, to remedy " many of the faults of the old law, and to provide such a law as will naturally contribute to the future development and prosperity of the great metropolis of Maryland."

CHAPTER III

THE FINANCIAL OUTLOOK.

The characteristic feature of the present financial condition of Baltimore is the pressure of increasing expenditure upon inelastic revenue. The growth of the city has added to the cost of municipal activity, and the rise in social consciousness has created a demand for better service. Not only has it become more expensive to perform accustomed functions over a wider area and for a larger population, but it has been necessary to perform them in a more costly manner. The municipal budget must provide both for lighting and paving more streets, and for substituting asphalt blocks for cobble stones and electric lighting for oil lamps.

On the other hand, there has been no corresponding increase in the financial resources of the city. Municipal development has brought with it a less than proportionate growth in original forms of revenue, and relatively few and unimportant new sources have been made available. In consequence the municipal economy discloses a reversal of the normal rule of public finance, and the expenditures of the city, instead of determining, are determined by its revenues.

Not only the increase of current expenditure, but the incurring of further funded indebtedness is checked by the rigidity of municipal revenue. Under existing conditions the municipal budget can tolerate scanty addition to the present burdensome interest charge. The future decades hold out no promise of a fall in the rate of interest upon municipal securities corresponding to the extraordinary decline since 1875. A sounder amortization policy will permit the regular redemption of maturing loans, but the decline in the interest rate and the rise in market value of municipal securities necessarily involves a slower accumulation of the sinking funds.

The phenomenal improvement in municipal credit in recent years in no wise affects this forecast. As long as the ownership of city securities carries with it exemption to that extent from state and municipal taxation, the competition of financial corporations will maintain city bonds at a fictitious valuation. The artificial demand thus created is strictly limited in amount, and whenever municipal securities are issued in excess of requirements for exemption purposes, the relapse in municipal credit will be sharp and immediate.

The insufficiency of municipal revenue is made the dominant element in the financial outlook of Baltimore by the urgent need of larger municipal expenditure in the near future. If the city is to become of increasing attractiveness as an industrial and residential centre, or even to keep pace with the general march of urban improvement in the United State, it must within the coming years spend and spend largely for municipal improvements.

The displacement of surface drainage by a comprehensive sewerage system, the protection and improvement of the municipal water supply, the erection of additional school buildings of modern arrangement, the extension of improved street paving throughout the greater part of the city—are all occasions for large municipal disbursements which even the most conservative sentiment recognizes as imperative and incapable of long delay.

To those who believe that the industrial city is destined to become a determining element in social development and that the conditions of urban residence in this generation will shape the moral and physical status of a large social class in the next—it is no less desirable that Baltimore be provided with additional parks and public squares, with municipal baths and play-grounds, and that slum districts be wiped out by the reconstruction of congested streets and the provision of open areas.

In the past decade Baltimore has supplied certain of its most pressing needs by the issue of long-time funded loans. The cost of transient improvements, properly chargeable to current income, has thus been thrown upon those who are to come hereafter. This vicious policy of discounting the future can not continue indefinitely and the defeat by popular vote of the "municipal improvement" loan of 1898 indicates popular apprehension of its danger.

Assuming, then, that the future development of Baltimore is dependent upon the possibility of progressive expenditure, a wise municipal policy will seek relief in three fiscal devices: (1) economy in municipal administration, (2) more productive use of existing sources of revenue, (3) discovery and appropriation of new forms of local income.

(1) The administrative history of Baltimore has been free from any one great scandal or palpable corruption, such as distinguishes the municipal experience of New York or Philadelphia. The affairs of the city have simply been conducted upon a dull level of expensive mediocrity. Reasonably sound business principles have prevailed in certain departments, such as the public parks and the water works, and at rare and brief intervals the whole standard of local administration has been appreciably raised. On the other hand, important branches of municipal service, such as the City Commissioner's Office and the street-cleaning and lamp-lighting departments, have been managed throughout upon notoriously cheap political methods; while at time it has been morally if not demonstrably certain that improper influences were shaping the whole course of municipal affairs.

It is doubtful whether in the long run an outright looting of the municipal treasury is more costly than continued maladministration. The consequence of the first course is popular reaction; of the second, popular acquiescence. Any quantitative estimation of how much Baltimore has annually suffered in this respect is impossible. The same end is attained by the deliberate statement, that the city has been administered during the greater part of its later history with a wastefulness and inefficiency that no individual or corporation would permit in the conduct of private affairs. In recent years the need of increased revenue has been felt; but at no time in the history of the city have the services rendered been commensurate with the resources actually available.

The grant of a new city charter and the birth of a new municipal spirit afford the possibility of marked change in this direction. Instead of a cumbrous and costly organization, permitting laxity and waste in every direction, opportunity is now given for a skilled and economical conduct of municipal affairs. In so far the financial future of Baltimore is completely identified with its administrative policy. With the city government in the hands of proper men, the important features of the new charter—centralization of power in the city executive and departmental responsibility—make it possible to appreciably reduce the cost of municipal service. If the contrary condition prevail, the same factors become instruments of oppression and a vista is afforded of extravagant administration such as Baltimore in a century of corporate existence has never known.

(2) An efficient municipal administration can, under the new charter, not only reduce the cost of present municipal service but render existing sources of revenue more productive. Conducted on economical principles the water department can be made to yield a large annual surplus. A wiser policy with respect to municipal real estate would appreciably increase income from this source. The method in vogue with respect to the audit of the franchise tax on street railways encourages carelessness and laxity. It is more than likely that stricter supervision would result in larger revenue from municipal markets and wharves.

It is, however, with respect to property taxation that the largest gains can be effected. The methods employed in the assessment of property for municipal taxation have been crude and primitive. At long and irregular intervals revaluations of local property have occurred, in conjunction with general state reassessments. In the intervening periods—the last of which endured twenty years—valuations remained unchanged save as modified by the spasmodic descent of an inadequate assessing force upon the realty of particular localities. The legislation of 1896 was designed to correct the most conspicuous of these evils by providing for periodic local revaluation and for the taxation of intangible wealth at a minimum rate. That the resulting gain has been far less than that anticipated is directly attributable to the methods of administration employed. As long as the local assessors are selected solely with reference to political qualifications, will their work, if not characterized by inefficiency and neglect, be at least very different in results from that which expert service would secure.

Municipal policy is here again of peculiar importance at the present time. Failing to attain appreciable results, it is probable that the periodic revision of assessments authorized by the act of 1896 will be allowed to lapse, and dependence had, as before, upon widely separated state revaluations. An important area of the city, the "Annex," becomes subject, for the first time, in 1900 to municipal assessment and taxation, and the methods of valuation there pursued will largely determine to what extent the burden of municipal taxation is to be lightened by this addition. Finally there is every likelihood that, with the aid of the penalty clauses and the limited tax rate of the act of 1896, securities could be reached to a reasonable degree by an efficient assessing force; on the other hand, unless a favorable turn in municipal finances dispels the growing fear that the full local rate will ultimately be imposed thereon, intangible wealth will tend more and more to escape assessment.

(3) Important economies may be effected in the administration of the city and larger receipts derived from existing forms of income. Yet sooner or later the necessity will arise for additional sources of local revenue, if, indeed,

the occasion therefor has not already come. Public sentiment has long favored two devices: (a) apportionment of the proceeds of the state school taxes so that the city may receive the full amount which it contributes, and (b) receipt by the city of the entire amount instead of three-fourths of the revenue from license taxes on local liquor-dealers. Both measures involve the diversion into the municipal treasury of revenue now accruing to the state and the counties, and require enabling acts of the General Assembly. The attitude of the legislature to the municipality has not been such as to afford reasonable likelihood that the mere equity of such measures will secure their passage.

In at least three directions the city treasury has suffered from an indirect loss of local revenue and corrective measures are desirable and feasible. Legislative amendment or new adjudication should devise a more equitable method than that now in vogue for determining the proportion of the gross receipts of local street railways liable to the franchise tax. The exemption of manufacturing plants from municipal taxation should be discontinued as a form of local protectionism for which there is little theoretical justification and less practical advantage. Finally, measures should be taken by a modification or outright disposition of the city's interest in the Western Maryland Railroad Company to realize a net income from what has long been a burdensome and unproductive asset.

Similar in importance but more novel in character is the possibility of a series of local license taxes, graduated in amount and designed particularly to reach industries which derive especial advantage from urban growth, or which are able by virtue of existing methods of assessment and exemption to escape a proper share of local taxation. The large retail department stores are a type of the first class, and an increasing number of financial corporations, whose capital stock is largely invested in tax-exempt securities, represent the second class. Agitation of such a tax would probably summon forth the bogey of threatened removal, but public sentiment in Baltimore can fairly be counted upon to appraise this argument at its proper valuation. An increase in the amount of the license tax on liquor sales—the entire increment to accrue to the city treasury—would probably result in increased revenue from this source, and would, in any event, better serve the regulative purpose contemplated but not satisfactorily attained by the original measure.

An immediate source of local revenue is made available by the franchise provisions of the new charter. Henceforth no rights in or relating to any public place or property can be granted by the city save upon competitive award and for a term not exceeding twenty-five years, subject to renewal and revaluation. The Board of Estimates is vested with absolute power to determine the amount and kind of compensation to be paid for the grant of all franchises. The consolidation of the important local industries of service—street railways and electric lighting companies—has in great part nullified the provision for competitive award and added in corresponding degree to the responsibility of the Board of Estimates.

It is of high importance that in all future franchise grants the principle of a definite "lump sum" payment be abandoned, and that provision be made for the receipt of an annual income, either in the form of a progressive charge or a percentage upon gross receipts. In this way alone can there be any permanent adequate addition to the productive resources of the city from franchise grants. A specific payment is ordinarily frittered away within the current year or employed in the discharge of an improperly incurred existing claim. In any event the "lump sum" principle fails to provide for the increment in the value of the franchise which comes in the interval between grant and renewal. The citizens of Baltimore have a striking object-lesson in the operation of the "park tax" of the salutary effects of deriving an annual revenue from municipal franchises, and in all subsequent grants the same principle should prevail.

The city has already conferred certain of its most valuable franchises, as the right of way to gas, electric lighting and telephone companies, for no consideration whatever. Radical legislation having in view the correction of the consequences of this reckless prodigality is at the present time unlikely. A more feasible suggestion is that the municipality should recognize the existing condition of affairs and derive some profit from the situation. It is notorious that large amounts are periodically expended by these industries of service to avert hostile legislation—proposed solely with this end in view—by the General Assembly, and to a very much less degree by the City Council. Some part of what is thus levied as legislative blackmail, by methods technically known as "bell-ringing" and "corporation-plugging," would in all probability be willingly paid to the city for undisturbed possession of reasonable privileges. Municipal finances, corporate dividends and political morality would alike be benefited by such an arrangement.

Whatever be the fiscal programme of Baltimore in the coming years, its effectiveness will continue dependent upon the character of local administration. Mechanism has been provided for an efficient municipal organization, rendering improving service at diminishing cost. But this apparatus constitutes no panacea, and popular will must, in the last resort, determine whether the old conditions shall endure—unwise, yet compulsory retrenchment in expenditure, friction and distress in taxation, ominous accumulation of indebtedness—or whether Baltimore in the twentieth century shall be a wholesome, healthful area, well lighted and paved, with excellent schools and abundant comforts and conveniences, where residence will have become a delight and a blessing.

BIBLIOGRAPHICAL NOTE.[1]

ADAMS, THOMAS S. Taxation in Maryland. Chapter I of "Studies in State Taxation." Baltimore, 1899. In *Johns Hopkins University Studies in Historical and Political Science*, Extra Volume XXI.

ALLEN, WILLIAM, and JOHNSON, JOHN. Life and Work of John McDonogh and Sketch of the McDonogh School. Baltimore, 1886.

BALTIMORE. Records of the Commissioners of Baltimore Town, 1729-1796 (MS).

—— Mayor's Annual Message and Annual Reports of City Officers. Baltimore, 1797-1897.

—— Ordinances and Resolutions of the Mayor and City Council. Baltimore, 1797-1897.

—— Baltimore City Code. Baltimore, 1858, 1869, 1879, 1892, 1893.

—— Report of the Tax Commission of Baltimore, appointed under Ordinance No. 61, of May 9, 1885. Baltimore, 1885.

—— Report of the Commission to investigate the affairs of the Western Maryland Railroad Company and the interest of the City therein; together with the reports of Stephen Little, Expert Accountant, and H. T. Douglas, Expert Engineer. Baltimore, 1893.

—— Report of the Sewerage Commission of the City of Baltimore. Baltimore, 1897.

BALTIMORE AND OHIO RAILROAD COMPANY. Annual Report of the President and Board of Directors to the Stockholders. Baltimore, 1827-1856.

DILLON, JOHN F. Commentaries on the Law of Municipal Corporations. Boston, 1890.

GRIFFITH, THOMAS W. Annals of Baltimore. Baltimore, 1824.

HADLEY, ARTHUR T. Railroad Transportation: its History and its Laws. New York, 1893.

[1] General treatises on finance and municipal government, newspaper files and legal reports are not herein included.

MARYLAND. Laws of Maryland: 1637-1763, edited by Thomas Bacon, n. p. n. d. 1763-1898, published in annual and biennial volumes by the General Assembly. Annapolis and Baltimore, 1763-1898. Constitutions of 1776, 1851, 1864 and 1867.

—— The Maryland Code: Public General Laws. Baltimore, 1888. Public Local Laws. Baltimore, 1888.

—— Report of the Maryland Tax Commission to the General Assembly, January, 1888. Baltimore, 1888.

MASSACHUSETTS. Report of the Commissioners appointed to inquire into the expediency of revising and amending the Laws relating to Taxation and exemption therefrom. Boston, 1875.

REIZENSTEIN, MILTON. The Economic History of the Baltimore and Ohio Railroad, 1827-1853. Baltimore, 1897. In *Johns Hopkins University Studies in Historical and Political Science*, Fifteenth Series, Nos. VII-VIII.

ROSEWATER, VICTOR. Special Assessments: a Study in Municipal Finance. New York, 1893. In *Columbia College Studies in History, Economics and Public Law*, Vol. II, No. 3.

SCHARF, J. THOMAS. The Chronicles of Baltimore; being a complete history of "Baltimore Town" and Baltimore City from the earliest period to the present time. Baltimore, 1874.

—— History of Baltimore City and County from the earliest period to the present day: including biographical sketches of the representative men. Philadelphia, 1881.

SCHMECKEBIER, L. F. The History of the Know-Nothing Party in Maryland. Baltimore, 1899. In *Johns Hopkins University Studies in Historical and Political Science*, Seventeenth Series, Nos. III-IV.

SELIGMAN, EDWIN R. A. Essays in Taxation. New York, 1895.

THOMAS, THADDEUS P. The City Government of Baltimore. Baltimore, 1896. In *Johns Hopkins University Studies in Historical and Political Science*, Fourteenth Series, No. II.

WARNER, AMOS G. American Charities: a Study in Philanthropy and Economics. New York [1894].

WILHELM, L. W. Maryland Local Institutions. Baltimore, 1895. In *Johns Hopkins University Studies in Historical and Political Science*, Third Series, Nos. V-VI-VII.

WOODBRIDGE, S. HOMER. Report on the Sanitary Condition of the Primary Schools of Baltimore. Baltimore, 1898.

WYNNE, JAMES. Sanitary Condition of Baltimore. Baltimore, 1850. [Extract from the First Report of the Committee on Public Hygiene of the American Medical Association; reprinted in Municipal Reports of Baltimore City, 1850.]

APPENDIX A.—Summary of Annual Balance Sheets of the Special Commissioners of Baltimore Town, 1783–1796.[1]

Dr.	1783. £ s. d.	1784. £ s. d.	1787. £ s. d.	1788. £ s. d.	1789. £. s. d.	1790. £ s. d.	1793. £ s. d.	1794. £ s. d.	1795. £ s. d.	1796.
1. Obligations incurred	9393 6 7	4213 10 10	1945 19 11½[1]	2799 18 1	1396 8 4	....	5771 12 7½	3132 16 0¼	6396 8 1¾	$5641 48
2. Existing claims	....	....	1191 5 7½	....	535 19 5	1123 9 9½	....	1088 0 11¾	1597 9 7½	8286 95
3. Taxes remitted and collectors' commissions.	....	....	257 15 7	511 2 2	450 8 0	365 0 5	364 13 7½	135 4 4	201 6 7	160 25
4. Taxes in arrears	....	....	1515 1 10	814 4 7	538 5 8½	683 10 7	186 6 4½	277 4 1¾	284 4 6	1665 59
5. Per diem allowance of special commissioners.	149 10 0	232 0 0	....	....	(58 0 0)	(43 10 0)	(92 10 0)	(97 17 6)	(108 0 0)	
Total	9542 16 7	4345 10 10	4910 3 0	4125 4 10	2921 1 5½	2172 0 9½	6322 12 6¾	4633 5 5¾	8479 8 10	$15,850 24
Cr.	**1783.**	**1784.**	**1787.**	**1788.**	**1789.**	**1790.**	**1793.**	**1794.**	**1795.**	**1796.**
1. Fines and forfeitures.	....	....	66 3 6	49 3 3	26 0 0	83 10 3	129 15 2½	112 0 3¾	167 9 4	$328 27
2. Lotteries	....	....	....	....	....	....	....	519 6 0½	522 1 1½	1500 00
3. Special assessments	5491 12 0	1178 5 4	1247 10 2	980 0 0	578 2 6	....	2723 2 10	766 9 2	2507 17 2	....
4. General Property Tax	642 7 6	490 7 0	....	....	....	629 0 6	277 8 3½	350 12 4	348 17 5	....
5. Auction Receipts Tax	2490 7 5	1804 12 6	....	688 16 0	190 16 5	....	....	....	....	....
6. Special Taxes:										
(a) Taverns.				385 16 3	365 0 0	365 0 0	332 10 0	476 0 10	577 11 3	1629 98
(b) Horses and carriages.	703 17 7 [(a)–(d)]	740 6 0 [(a)–(d)]	625 10 0 [(a)–(b)]	339 15 0	342 4 1	351 5 0	213 15 0	255 5 0	320 10 0	1051 42
(c) Billiard Tables.			150 0 0	150 0 9	135 0 0	135 0 0	167 10 0	158 15 0	133 15 0	685 51
(d) Exhibitions.			63 0 0	16 12 6	25 12 7	57 10 0	47 8 8	52 8 9	35 2 6	136 33
7. Unpaid taxes	(1111 17 1)	(368 18 11)	2353 19 0	1515 1 10	1050 13 9	550 15 0½	1295 10 4¾	186 6 4½	277 3 9½	498 11
8. Miscellaneous	....	....	404 0 4	....	....	....	47 11 2½	158 11 13	40 13 9	....
9. Bills due but unpaid	214 12 1	132 0 0	....	....	207 12 1½	....	1088 0 11¾	1597 9 7½	3503 7 8½	9981 15
Total	9542 16 7	4345 10 10	4910 3 0	4125 4 10	2921 1 5½	2172 0 9½	6322 12 6¾	4633 5 5¾	8479 8 10	$15,850 24

[1] Neither manuscript nor printed reports of the fiscal operations of any of the administrative bodies of Baltimore Town have been preserved. The above table as well as B and C following have been compiled from the annual balance sheets published in the local newspapers. Careful search has failed to reveal any published accounts in certain years.

APPENDIX B.—Summary of Annual Balance Sheets of Port Wardens of Baltimore Town, 1783–1795.

	1783-86.			1787.			1788.			1789.		
EXPENDITURES.	£	s.	d.	£	s.	d.	£	s.	d.	£	s.	d.
1. Obligations incurred ..	295	18	3	55	15	0	77	8	7	101	6	7
2. Commission on expend..				1	7	10⅓	4	14	10⅓	11	19	3
3. Salaries	44	15	0	......			104	8	5⅓	63	0	10
4. Balance on hand	122	0	10	120	0	4½	188	4	8½	126	18	2
5. Miscellaneous	......			......			7	17	6	2	15	0
Total..............	462	14	1	177	3	3	382	14	1⅓	305	19	10
RECEIPTS.	1783-86.			1787.			1788.			1789.		
1. Tonnage duty..........	462	14	1	54	14	11	256	17	8	102	12	0
2. Arrears	......			122	0	10	120	0	4	188	4	8
3. Fines	......			0	7	6	5	16	1	15	3	2
4. Wharfage on firewood..	......			......			......			......		
5. Wharfage on vessels....	......			......			......			......		
6. Auction tax	......			......			......			......		
Total..............	462	14	1	177	3	3	382	14	1⅓	305	19	10

	1790.			1791.			1792.			1793.			1795.		
EXPENDITURES.	£	s.	d.	£	s.	d.	£	s.	d.	£	s.	d.	£	s.	d.
1. Obligations incurred ..	14	6	10½	277	2	3½	476	16	5⅓	379	11	9	2959	2	11
2. Commission on expend..	13	6	4⅓	44	8	0½	57	12	3⅓	53	3	6	72	3	3
3. Salaries	54	12	6	72	5	0	66	17	1	87	0	0	153	17	6
4. Balance on hand	126	3	6	354	1	0	468	7	11	1595	3	8½	2325	12	6
5. Miscellaneous	7	8	7	2	7	6	7	10	0	12	1	3	23	10	0
Total..............	215	17	10	760	3	10	1077	2	9	2127	0	2½	5533	5	2
RECEIPTS.	1790.			1791.			1792.			1793.			1795.		
1. Tonnage duty..........	......			438	13	2	477	10	8	539	8	0	480	18	9
2. Arrears	126	18	2	126	3	6	354	1	0	468	7	11	2646	16	2
3. Fines	5	11	7	5	12	9	14	13	3	2	2	1½	6	4	9
4. Wharfage on firewood..	50	8	1	55	7	4	58	12	7	103	19	0	45	18	11
5. Wharfage on vessels....	33	0	0	42	0	0	57	0	0	56	17	5	140	9	1
6. Auction tax	......			92	7	1	115	5	3	956	5	9	2212	18	4
Total..............	215	17	10	760	3	10	1077	2	9	2127	0	2½	5533	6	0

APPENDIX C.—Summary of Annual Balance Sheets of Baltimore County Court, in account with Baltimore Town, 1790–1795.

	1790.			1791.			1792.			1793.			1794.			1795.			1796.		
Dr.	£	s.	d.	£	s.	d.	£	s.	d.	£	s.	d.	£	s.	d.	£	s.	d.	£	s.	d.
1. Watching and lighting......	846	3	7	1096	7	9	546	7	6	1251	2	6	1554	13	7	1324	18	5	3707	10	4
2. Balance on hand	280	13	10	105	9	9	24	11	10	358	11	4	384	0	2	672	12	11	597	3	10
3. Total............	1126	17	5	1201	17	6	570	19	4	1609	13	10	1938	13	9	1996	11	4	4204	14	2
Cr.																					
1. Balance b't forward	223	4	9	280	13	10	105	9	9	24	11	10	358	11	4	386	0	2	671	12	11
2. Liquor license tax..........	630	4	7	626	8	1	420	9	7	712	1	7	776	8	9	836	6	0	1209	7	2
3. Direct tax	133	18	7	150	0	0	45	0	0	187	10	0	189	8	9	200	0	0	....	..	..
4. Dog tax	139	9	6	87	1	8	......			......			......			......			......		
5. House tax	......			......			......			637	10	0	226	13	10	576	5	2	2143	14	1
6. Taxes in arrears...........	......			57	13	11	......			48	0	5	387	11	1	200	0	0	180	0	0
Total................	1126	17	5	1201	17	6	570	19	4	1609	13	10	1938	13	9	1996	11	4	4204	14	2

APPENDIX D.—Annual Expenditures and Receipts of Baltimore City, 1797–1897.

EXPENDITURES.	1797.	1798.	1799.	1800.	1801.	1802.	1803.	1804.	1805.	1806.
Street paving and repairing	12,335 13	13,336 66	19,308 73	16,300 43	34,057 36	27,875 55	30,759 18	25,316 52	23,109 77	22,122 09
Sewers	....	....	....	....	....	....	....	142 14	1,462 56	1,017 98
Bridges	....	3,998 78	2,200 00	310 43	918 58	853 70	562 11	246 15	802 96	480 35
Street reconstruction	....	....	....	....	....	....	....	....	....	....
Street cleaning	....	....	1,326 97	2,498 47	11,393 42	3,378 19	2,024 88¼	2,966 49	2,877 80	3,180 98
Watching and lighting	2,970 31	11,362 30	10,713 81	9,237 40	10,680 41	11,895 33	12,417 24	10,486 95	11,066 38	11,459 31
Fire	....	....	43 08	375 00	75 00	1,300 00	1,200 00	1,605 25	2,124 25	1,800 00
Water	780 96	3,255 51	5,099 85	2,082 16	2,018 59	3,462 85	2,386 00	1,006 07	2,091 14	3,882 50
Health	2,762 63	3,813 68	3,080 00	3,519 42	2,802 92	4,685 73	2,567 47¼	3,024 73	2,909 08	2,635 02
Markets	113 00	887 00	5,680 65	1,042 50	....	....	1,532 35	687 24	112 76	11,590 70
Wharves	98 49	....	323 00	471 92	1,886 73	2,045 61	4,955 14	3,117 38	5,009 66	4,548 64
Harbor	2,000 40	3,932 35	2,124 63	2,601 83	5,144 44	6,796 48	6,009 05	5,978 12	5,535 90	9,853 38
Courts	....	....	....	....	....	....	....	....	....	....
Municipal buildings	....	....	....	2,665 29	409 66	845 18	27 25	302,43	216 75	....
Schools	....	....	....	....	....	....	....	....	....	....
Charities	....	....	....	6,373 40	1,082 99	....	....	....	435 10	41 07
Administration	5,184 91	10,046 62	7,452 28	7,444 49	11,492 58	12,081 12	14,106 97	8,730 63	13,548 77	14,533 76
Internal improvements	....	....	....	....	....	....	....	....	....	....
Interest on debt	....	....	....	....	....	....	....	....	....	....
Principal of debt	....	6,133 78	4,672 15	....	....	2,034 10	....	....	....	....
Sinking fund	....	....	....	....	....	....	....	....	....	....
Miscellaneous	....	896 77	1,013 30	1,693 19	449 49	535 33	140 50	1,058 50	829 25	900 97
Balance	8,772 77	6,732 63	11,708 29	10,346 60	6,865 04	2,101 49	5,141 97	7,258 76	12,064 58	2,068 68
Total	35,078 65	64,381 08	76,106 72	67,574 62	80,277 21	80,490 66	84,724 12	72,544 16	85,456 66	91,170 29

RECEIPTS.	1797.	1798.	1799.	1800.	1801.	1802.	1803.	1804.	1805.	1806.
Gifts and Subsidies	....	....	....	....	....	....	....	....	....	....
Markets	1,120 30	1,508 97	2,310 00	1,547 78	1,900 10	1,021 96	1,808 56	1,079 22	1,654 45	1,694 58
Wharves	2,787 59	4,390 10	4,857 24	4,094 06	4,099 27	5,880 35	5,866 16¼	5,807 05	6,666 94	7,368 17
City property	....	....	....	....	....	....	....	....	....	....
Lotteries	....	3,153 00	....	3,981 70	....	....	450 00	720 00	....	....
Fines	....	3,445 85	4,058 82	2,502 73	3,078 01	3,108 53	3,451 76¼	1,390 78	2,161 00	1,448 07
Fees	....	21 33	154 25	76 15	811 17	1,109 62	1,440 84	1,480 77	1,702 31	1,822 75
Special Assessments:										
Pumps	....	969 41	2,553 48	3,000 00	2,000 00	2,800 00	2,105 19	760 62	1,208 64	2,259 22
Opening streets	....	....	....	....	....	....	....	....	....	....
Paving streets	5,813 68	9,189 63	13,106 41	9,201 35	21,985 52	16,368 24	25,706 41	12,089 09	16,100 47	13,458 06
Taxes:										
License	6,104 75	14,127 58	16,822 95	10,107 65	17,492 04	16,140 37	17,425 19	18,068 33	20,203 97	14,951 30
Auction receipts	2,918 81	4,134 95	12,512 04	8,708 10	9,453 47	7,538 76	6,929 19	10,434 44	12,767 67	12,438 31
Specific	1,481 41	821 51	719 37	871 10	1,116 79	1,311 87	1,357 13	1,227 98	1,157 17	1,609 86
Direct	8,270 28	8,398 72	6,806 12	3,874 87	11,261 73	11,787 27	12,014 10	10,901 22	10,214 09	12,880 61
Taxes in arrears	1,498 21	5,195 51	5,347 41	6,888 58	4,112 24	2,967 92	2,949 47	2,304 10	3,882 73	6,075 56
Loans	....	....	....	....	....	....	....	....	....	2,742 62
Miscellaneous	280 80	249 50	132 00	927 70	1,578 27	2,184 31	46 46	648 59	418 35	347 60
Balance	4,802 87	8,781 02	6,732 63	11,708 29	9,488 60	6,865 04	2,101 49	5,141 97	7,258 76	12,064 58
Total	35,078 65	64,381 08	76,106 70	67,574 62	80,277 21	80,490 66	84,724 12	72,544 16	85,456 66	91,170 29

APPENDIX D (continued).—ANNUAL EXPENDITURES AND RECEIPTS OF BALTIMORE CITY, 1797-1897.

EXPENDITURES.	1807.	1808.	1809.	1810.	1811.	1812.	1813.	1814.	1815.	1816.
Street paving and repairing	19.753 93	17,467 73	20,848 84	19,834 63	21,902 34	27,624 79	24,440 48	6,987 34	14,799 89	21,233 20
Sewers	339 21	292 72	100 00	264 80	100 00	....	....	....	....	500 00
Bridges	943 09	1,862 78	15,698 55	8,278 67	16,479 25	15,103 73	3,468 50	829 42	2,000 70	623 03
Street reconstruction	....	....	....	....	....	....	....	....	1,324 35	17 00
Street cleaning	3,164 43	3,584 70	4,418 12	4,739 92	5,365 98	5,371 56	5,872 50	5,647 87	5,672 14	6,361 52
Watching and lighting	9,718 99	11,056 33	10,994 15	11,168 88	12,792 53	14,122 13	20,114 40	13,410 78	15,340 51	16,108 54
Fire	2,086 90	1,680 33	1,150 91	3,137 00	4,023 16	4,484 38	3,594 08	1,982 35	2,598 53	6,304 24
Water	4,122 06	1,707 98	3,507 92	7,378 37	4,279 30	1,596 16	971 56	2,440 18	1,787 44	3,870 61
Health	1,207 71	992 42½	1,622 78	1,413 33	498 33	1,638 79	1,376 31	892 78	1,444 73	1,764 44
Markets	1,616 03	240 92	....	....	2,336 44	3,735 00	348 52	89 50	....	3,314 44
Wharves	164 44	107 69	1,577 47	4,101 12	4,370 64	1,219 50	1,070 63	....	....	350 00
Harbor	4,350 96	5,010 72	4,716 08	4,510 46	4,172 99	5,019 02	7,707 90	8,529 63	22,827 65	24,908 49
Courts	....	....	....	....	....	....	....	....	....	....
Municipal buildings	....	3,488 79	22,282 22	634 53	454 00	7,618 82	6,672 01	535 45	3,671 82	3,556 87
Schools	....	....	....	....	....	....	....	....	....	....
Charities	....	2,500 00	1,500 00	....	....	....	....	....	....	1,650 00
Administration	15,974 48	12,331 22½	11,244 54	11,846 87	12,370 54	14,200 11	14,390 04	14,072 61	13,844 26	18,125 71
Internal improvements	....	....	....	....	....	....	....	....	....	....
Interest on debt	122 69	....	117 52	616 72	1,501 25	1,774 09	2,208 45	2,119 42	2,014 41	4,862 00
Principal of debt	3,000 00	....	....	....	....	....	....	....	17,000 00	....
Sinking fund	....	....	....	....	....	....	....	....	....	....
Miscellaneous	848 75	403 68	126 39	75 00	75 00	119 30	1,075 00	3,360 32	1,076 24	3,808 58
Balance	7,433 09	11,005 17	4,156 72	774 41	1,782 00	1,780 00	958 02	1,447 70	2,053 84	2,408 63
Total	74,957 04	74,446 42	84,082 71	78,768 21	93,104 15	105.426 38	94.263 80	62,354 27	107,456 51	119,739 40

RECEIPTS.	1807.	1808.	1809.	1810.	1811.	1812.	1813.	1814.	1815.	1816.
Gifts and Subsidies	....	....	....	....	....	....	....	....	....	....
Markets	1,614 79	2,492 93	2,431 05	2,182 69	1,928 10	2,460 03	2,671 67	2,475 42	2.413 98	3,856 23
Wharves	8,610 64	6,946 36	7,783 10	8,662,03	10,058 78	8,496 20	4,253 84	2,301 54	7,091 94	9,226 17
City property	....	....	....	....	....	....	260 75	212 50	325 00	775 66
Lotteries	....	....	....	....	....	....	....	....	....	....
Fines	1,245 38	1,056 95	508 34	2,730 94	1,299 41	1,865 29	903 47	582 10	1,679 52	902 95
Fees	1,160 96	1,615 53	1,811 10	1,575 88	1,215 52	912 05	2,052 39	776 00	....	1,602 73
Special Assessments:										
Pumps	2,412 57	1,275 80	264 17	300 00	100 00	....	10 34	1,021 66½	849 94	1,718 52
Opening streets	....	....	....	....	....	....	....	690 20	1,257 51	313 58
Paving streets	9,639 03	12,078 36	14,313 94	13,848 76	12,328 26	16,210 05	18,490 40	2,524 30	2,591 82	7,188 02
Taxes:										
License	15,969 90	14,561 70	14,454 77	15,218 83	10,590 25	18,053 47	17,167 54	13,505 05	16,480 68	21,574 99
Auction receipts	14,064 79	10,544 68	16,032 20	17,605 32	18,121 77	38,342 84	28,401 77	11,707 53	45,048 84	36,073 95
Specific	1,327 02	1,476 81	1,005 90	904 03	604 58	642 63	537 71	1,521 89	1,171 28	1,361 36
Direct	12,421 37	12,410 71	11,241 96	9,221 86	10,282 57	9,919 72	10,240 09	19,430 18½	17,976 18	19,644 38
Taxes in arrears	2,302 04	2,408 36	2,822 82	2,795 98	3.488 00	7,437 50	1,875 98	249 87	2,025 60	12,434 22
Loans	....	....	....	....	10,000 00	4,000 00	5,000 00	4,000 00	....	....
Miscellaneous	729 98	145 00	388 19	56 17	50 00	104 00	617 85	298 00	1,618 55	722 80
Balance	2,068 63	7,438 09	11,005 17	4,156 72	774 41	1,782 60	1,780 00	958 02	1,447 70	2,053 84
Total	74,957 04	74,446 42	84,082 71	78,768 21	93,104 15	105,426 38	94,263 80	62,354 27	107,456 51	119,739 40

APPENDIX D (continued).—ANNUAL EXPENDITURES AND RECEIPTS OF BALTIMORE CITY, 1797–1897.

EXPENDITURES.	1817.	1818.	1819.	1820.	1821.	1822.	1823.	1824.	1825.	1826.	1827.	1828.	1829.	1830.
Street paving and repair	43,987 43	40,246 61	11,253 52	17,428 24	19,145 06	13,543 39	15,125 11	10,128 68	6,458 00	7,026 64	7,298 69	11,440 15	11,543 41	10,385 09
Sewers	142 53	108 06	....	....	641 60	1,019 61	609 67	378 21	150 82	251 00	90 07	444 61	194 47	391 09
Bridges	10,505 52	18,626 23	1,660 96	4,408 55	19,992 95	10,426 38	2,757 46	1,356 96	594 43	708 01	541 03	1,998 22	3,123 92	1,046 30
Street reconstruction	60 42	192,880 03	20,340 07	9,930 45	3,286 75	2,013 58	15,234 04	10,552 78	9,785 94	180 16	286 73	1,000 80	42,442 66	3,140 21
Street cleaning	8,173 81	7,693 68	7,452 92	7,112 34	5,498 40	4,724 72	3,870 82	3,198 17	3,067 28	2,979 88	3,731 08	3,600 00	3,562 74	4,437 26
Watching and lighting	18,160 39	17,781 95	20,548 33	24,578 80	22,865 74	25,202 85	23,375 71	23,994 43	28,093 26	26,004 25	26,076 65	25,374 86	27,018 42	28,901 20
Fire	6,143 49	3,015 43	4,812 67	4,058 80	3,932 18	6,089 37	4,271 66	4,295 82	5,560 34	6,300 00	7,600 00	7,390 00	5,000 00	4,400 00
Water	8,826 42	7,957 04	7,013 52	4,341 13	3,927 02	6,142 12	4,688 23	4,429 27	4,277 36	5,769 65	7,411 96	6,508 84	5,707 57	560 30
Health	3,435 86	2,902 82	5,446 61	8,231 59	4,929 85	5,721 34	3,833 36	4,165 55	3,300 80	2,908 15	4,002 11	2,615 12	3,743 88	3,187 63
Markets	6,073 05	2,822 62	4,968 18	2,560 53	1,404 32	681 69	809 17	3,223 56	3,080 84	3,158 50	1,057 08	1,738 00	1,113 10	555 80
Wharves	....	....	734 69	1,119 76	1,115 72	1,808 00	1,064 32	900 82	152 97	433 28	629 13	1,292 20	4,839 20	500 00
Harbor	25,739 06	28,768 94	19,872 26	15,015 10	20,306 24	31,065 63	23,683 02	19,339 82	20,927 18	23,823 17	29,805 51	27,155 01	26,290 97	22,565 20
Courts	....	9,561 08	15,366 62	13,438 00	11,642 69	16,374 93	14,289 18	15,470 39	14,806 82	9,284 59	15,742 47	20,998 74	20,255 76	25,004 35
Municipal buildings	1,042 88	3,047 60	3,210 12	1,039 91	4,000 87	10,238 24	9,959 14	3,018 74	1,184 42	1,067 89	1,201 77	824 96	3,000 53	8,414 79
Schools	....	....	....	....	....	....	....	....	....	....	....	....	....	3,915 76
Charities	....	1,500 00	300 00	12,550 00	14,725 00	19,686 00	21,647 00	24,609 69	20,325 00	18,855 00	19,345 00	20,650 00	17,875 00	18,205 00
Administration	22,208 85	24,134 67	27,348 85	25,557 84	23,436 17	27,007 38	23,085 50	23,600 77	22,006 08	25,098 65	24,331 47	24,981 12	24,948 12	25,222 00
Internal improvements	....	....	....	....	....	....	....	....	5,000 00	7,000 00	6,000 00	5,000 00	75,000 00	62,000 00
Interest on debt	8,729 15	15,246 88	23,739 14	24,067 14	23,880 24	27,534 50	25,698 05	24,676 52	23,192 12	23,910 49	19,895 63	20,734 47	22,323 89	24,723 74
Principal of debt	5.126 29	4,557 04	6,000 00	1,312 68	14,448 42	....	41,000 00	340,155 64	5,400 00	....	....	....	....	....
Sinking fund	....	18,010 00	....	12,000 00	....	....	....	2,027 82	12,402 18	26,732 18	....	1,079 38	16,798 32	16,509 74
Miscellaneous	5,989 44	10,223 66	2,580 70	4,145 56	5,819 85	3,819 61	5,025 15	3,588 28	5,281 61	15,342 57	4,543 15	4,534 67	1,877 01	2,341 78
Balance	2,801 03	2,390 04	2,090 01	6,114 46	4,159 47	2,735 20	1,617 01	7,328 37	14,435 46	7,764 00	16,018 32	15,055 00	9,925 20	15,092 17
Total	177,775 52	411,080 53	189,619 81	199,014 98	220,387 94	217,385 25	241,449 10	533,929 87	205,531 97	214,718 19	196,248 68	211,193 04	320,337 90	331,302 22

RECEIPTS.	1817.	1818.	1819.	1820.	1821.	1822.	1823.	1824.	1825.	1826.	1827.	1828.	1829.	1830.
Gifts and subsidies	....	15,000 00	....	....	15,000 00	....	....	....	....	21,710 25	....	10,691 84	9,392 89	15,165 86
Markets	4,380 91	4,740 85	6,125 25	6,389 90	6,582 33	6,346 28	6,115 17	5,906 31	6,833 75	7,735 11	8,617 95	8,012 17	8,020 50	9,364 16
Wharves	6,028 40	4,148 55	8,702 37	9,340 56	9,451 37	9,258 78	9,283 06	9,294 12	10,231 00	10,584 41	10,017 37	10,078 60	8,296 93	9,806 00
City property	275 00	2,038 67	485 00	612 89	1,108 12	1,045 20	570 00	953 76	706 20	2,061 98	629 30	1,270 41	1,735 08	1,006 45
Lotteries	....	....	....	....	....	....	....	....	....	....	....	....	....	....
Fines	501 91	545 13	529 21	705 86	540 99	1,911 85	647 38	505 46	1,281 69	668 92	557 16	690 28	389 30	302 66
Fees	1,573 37	1,789 96	3,461 45	4,847 57	2,846 89	2,579 19	4,746 73	3,740 14	3,043 49	2,501 20	2,795 26	2,300 26	3,530 16	3,077 39
Special Assessments:														
Pumps	7,232 81	7,406 46	4,011 08	2,090 94	2,502 91	2,245 33	946 01	485 16	176 71	544 63	880 01	1,081 74	1,086 17	354 62
Opening streets	1,300 00	139,706 59	5,509 43	6,629 76	1,650 00	456 98	7,488 49	6,682 32	11,432 46	1,423 27	4 73	643 00	42,216 82	5,811 74
Paving streets	14,986 95	24,309 73	6,540 18	12,816 94	10,054 40	4,649 05	4,103 06	2,739 50	2,441 46	350 65	2,806 02	3,145 20	4,862 82	8,420 38
Taxes:														
License	23,097 77	22,669 33	25,470 89	25,341 30	25,698 09	24,333 63	26,641 91	27,542 70	31,244 30	25,088 98	24,239 28	23,040 42	7,567 69	21,223 55
Auction receipts	34,061 31	25,634 17	20,779 20	18,948 06	16,514 99	18,572 04	22,054 43	22,731 08	25,984 54	31,286 77	25,970 11	28,001 14	18,898 86	39,251 99
Specific	1,650 54	2,104 98	1,757 00	1,225 93	1,519 18	1,943 22	824 92	761 13	914 31	950 00	993 27	941 38	989 58	805 38
Direct	20,480 57	47,905 09	70,098 20	82,083 14	84,997 88	79,473 71	84,811 82	78,781 70	63,607 69	58,616 63	59,780 48	58,706 91	60,820 17	72,323 82
Taxes in arrears	5,001 74	2,517 71	11,781 67	20,112 32	22,065 93	28,854 46	27,767 26	27,077 89	38,688 00	30,546 90	48,473 00	41,553 41	62,138 82	49,183 91
Loans	53,250 67	100,619 10	19,998 90	3,000 00	13,000 00	31,000 00	43,321 80	341,841 89	....	....	....	....	98,000 00	82,115 00
Miscellaneous	504 98	6,352 58	1,984 64	2,329 11	....	506 00	481 07	3,224 75	1,657 50	317 02	2,504 66	1,378 36	446 98	2,503 41
Balance	2,408 63	2,801 03	2,390 04	2,090 01	6,114 46	4,159 47	2,736 20	1,617 01	7,328 37	14,435 46	7,764 00	16,918 32	15,055 00	9,925 20
Total	177,775 52	411,080 53	189,610 81	199,014 98	220,337 94	217,335 25	241,449 10	533,929 87	205,531 97	214,718 19	196,248 08	211,193 04	320,337 90	331,302 22

APPENDIX D (continued).—ANNUAL EXPENDITURES AND RECEIPTS OF BALTIMORE CITY, 1797-1897.[1]

EXPENDITURES.	1835.	1840.	1845.	1850.	1855.	1860.	1865.	1870.	1875.	1880.	1885.	1890.	1895.
St. paving and repair	78,094 91	26,004 51	49,024 16	35,346 34	111,147 95	56,937 75	101,841 52	115,965 97	316,517 28	298,247 62	129,568 31	150,529 88	173,072 86
Sewers	335 04	1,042 64	529 84	10,368 30	9,981 34	4,082 82	7,943 80	18,614 37	......	......	77,048 57	290,461 84	8,132 48
Bridges	4,557 48	527 12	1,742 53	20,082 49	7,570 75	1,003 11	16,085 81	131,677 64	......	......	11,800 23	181,928 05	99,286 58
Street reconstruction	52,290 22	4,055 45	2,786 09	31,002 37	142,393 52	44,910 18	16,843 40	199,375 33	416,103 46	280,334 10	176,802 93	584,331 90	64,129 37
Street cleaning	12,420 63	17,450 82	10,852 81	8,970 27	51,608 02	46,845 74	72,466 50	144,827 30	......[4]	......[4]	254,984 60	283,502 08	306,576 17
Police	87,543 48	54,935 02	70,238 48	110,102 29	232,620 57	259,962 33	308,791 57	568,500 90	590,500 00	589,382 45	622,000 00	780,199 03	808,995 00
Lighting	......	......	......	......	......	67,854 38	142,098 71	206,640 32	230,851 71	180,175 24	263,942 34	294,010 84	380,580 06
Fire protection	15,893 36	8,580 35	13,290 73	15,492 69	30,331 21	137,090 35	91,043 61	137,854 30	170,664 06	188,369 30	205,161 76	316,506 05	458,298 20
Water supply[2]	9,805 77	7,488 91	6,234 77	18,136 80	78,920 98	704,094 06	534,818 31	727,526 12	536,984 84	929,188 78	642,015 14	909,561 22	610,423 47
Health	7,925 08	8,759 40	5,125 22	9,483 37	16,214 21	12,707 23	24,820 58	56,113 22	281,913 05	245,580 81	74,522 25	95,356 45	110,872 73
Markets	14,099 35	3,011 24	6,191 37	7,198 88	33,485 78	8,093 12	37,282 12	138,104 12	9,980 91	6,139 27	15,969 57	14,360 22	5,397 74
Wharves	906 60	......	......	12,630 34	15,325 89	......	......	......	......	......	......	......	......
Harbors	26,872 17	18,407 64	25,180 40	28,497 38	50,802 00	54,941 59	80,627 24	241,559 30	241,738 32	122,813 40	119,086 23	76,016 09	87,087 79
Courts	36,055 44	27,889 39	33,804 94	44,422 23	74,432 08	127,753 07	126,142 10	192,450 06	249,532 52	187,318 20	162,947 44	149,529 64	207,702 78
Schools	6,000 00	18,000 00	29,400 00	46,082 88	88,821 59	165,162 71	232,601 82	589,909 21	568,788 11	617,152 64	748,233 41	1,109,066 58	1,222,745 84
Charities and corrections	25,727 60	23,823 63	28,001 82	35,137 42	50,179 44	107,680 36	147,725 08	194,718 87	157,107 46	204,195 43	280,288 01	345,675 48	398,947 75
Parks and squares[3]	......	1,749 99	2,398 29	8,238 41	6,703 05	57,764 45	152,825 55	170,921 62	132,760 87	167,910 30	156,700 75	219,906 08	275,421 54
Art and science	......	......	......	......	......	......	......	......	......	......	53,000 00	58,000 00	9,000 00
Municipal buildings	15,601 49	2,028 80	3,706 17	......	38,178 77	61,922 40	11,012 47	12,962 21	195,544 59	98,105 31	468,357 02	48,095 12	104,545 93
Administration	16,001 85	16,529 10	23,716 25	26,539 00	34,023 79	65,226 78	103,239 84	161,585 98	193,839 19	193,805 89	214,334 74	263,085 87	250,182 22
Interest on debt	51,780 77	214,301 81	316,742 37	315,377 24	583,112 12	713,802 55	814,451 92	1,256,786 72	1,571,882 30	1,439,781 10	1,403,797 16	1,222,302 30	1,166,082 40
Sinking fund	......	......	......	......	......	34,530 97	118,316 51	114,609 36	......	220,075 08	15,238 02	40,921 07	317,251 48
Temporary loans (net)	7,000 00	......	32 62	5,030 81	69,459 33	87,265 00	541,388 97	......	80,000 00	50,000 00	......	......	......
Miscellaneous	5,365 67	7,420 08	27,694 10	16,974 49	37,680 38	55,308 35	46,797 43	96,128 38	209,613 42	52,601 52	27,288 26	89,578 51	111,107 29
Total	422,406 00	442,006 70	687,972 96	806,504 06	1,072,140 02	2,875,774 39	3,724,198 86	5,270,621 86	6,213,912 99	6,081,171 22	6,179,708 04	7,509,571 31	7,235,793 68

RECEIPTS.	1835.	1840.	1845.	1850.	1855.	1860.	1865.	1870.	1875.	1880.	1885.	1890.	1895.
Taxes:													
General property	203,180 70	272,389 06	393,442 61	608,708 69	1,061,380 01	1,209,593 36	1,033,002 83	2,944,059 88	3,811,586 20	3,583,310 23	4,145,002 20	5,080,322 40	5,143,599 30
Interest on arrears	......	......	6,479 61	7,781 76	15,509 26	10,411 35	68,430 33	107,208 52	......	82,092 38	35,961 49	30,608 18	32,764 63
Specific taxes	2,248 81	1,639 48	......	......	......	......	......	......	......	......	......	......	......
Auction receipts tax	......	......	......	......	......	......	......	......	12,958 76	......	......	......	......
St. railway franchise tax	......	......	......	......	......	30,326 06	181,290 60	125,769 63	103,562 33	123,106 84	120,140 08	105,280 12	276,280 73
Licenses	24,535 75	33,024 21	41,700 47	51,935 17	59,985 33	48,316 16	32,756 54	43,112 60	35,724 84	51,256 44	49,283 37	442,634 19	473,293 58
Special assessment:	15,410 05												
Street paving	22,701 52	16,023 11	7,341 72	......	493 38	2,806 14	5,641 67	1,053 75	64,309 86	69,046 58	175,352 74	106,177 57	56,402 06
Street reconstruction	52,396 79	3,950 90	2,897 59	31,000 89	140,357 94	54,709 63	42,058 10	265,653 94	202,400 07	180,012 37	78,651 23	47,836 56	63,239 44
Wells and pumps	1,258 39	1,416 08	1,547 36	5,352 30	5,619 00	238 92	......	......	......	......	......	......	......
Fees	4,695 39	7,572 92	5,472 16	8,687 63	8,168 87	5,247 16	4,881 78	8,923 45	57,440 32	75,096 70	33,061 69	45,226 26	34,949 40
Fines	183 71	512 08	956 43	1,325 10	2,846 33	6,725 01	7,939 41	325 30	......	2,002 30	2,845 87	4,180 35	3,607 06
Quasi-private receipts:													
Wharves	11,915 23	21,008 51	23,022 55	26,840 36	27,007 15	30,637 55	28,977 76	58,157 50	29,015 00	25,989 03	32,204 67	28,788 44	28,375 07
Markets	22,115 21	15,893 06	18,687 28	21,974 04	21,991 02	37,453 09	92,784 16	50,435 74	57,703 00	55,573 45	64,763 05	55,231 60	44,020 75
Municipal property including interest on investments	13,502 92	12,690 36	107,354 28	3,907 67	358,409 97	738,871 09	1,109,520 40	581,086 94	641,969 86	812,144 36	651,358 65	155,873 48	161,190 60
Water department	......	......	......	......	86,326 73	668,795 14	587,223 00	735,428 42	526,609 00	632,377 93	602,786 43	865,685 38	759,500 32
Gifts and state grants	20,676 54	4,951 60	5,502 43	5,525 53	24,863 63	......	......	......	147,147 76	147,303 99	157,126 56	182,619 24	215,424 92
Temporary loans (net)	......	21,500 00	......	......	......	......	......	515,265 01	......	......	......	......	15,000 00
Miscellaneous	13,174 81	6,468 08	20,311 13	1,980 01	23,058 15	20,112 80	22,939 84	42,447 81	828,210 25	40,308 28	16,871 94	42,767 56	27,267 73
Total	407,909 82	419,728 96	634,775 67	773,294 65	1,837,576 47	2,859,304 06	3,817,452 44	5,580,888 49	6,518,676 42	5,880,224 94	6,165,470 87	7,381,235 33	7,340,651 69

[1] This table can be used for comparative purposes only. Owing to the multiplicity of items in the Comptrollers' Reports, and the absence of descriptive detail, it has been impossible to compile an accurate balance sheet, and in certain years the discrepancy is large. Extraordinary receipts and expenditures have been eliminated as far as possible. [2] Including interest on the water debt. [3] Including interest on the park debt. [4] Included in health expenditure.

APPENDIX E[1].—Annual Tax Levies of Baltimore City, 1797-1898 (in Cents, upon $100 of Assessed Property).

Year.	Direct.	Court.	Poor.	Certain expenses.	School.	Internal improvements.	Police.	Interest on debt.	Opening streets.	Public water.	Sinking Fund Levies.																			Highways and bridges.
											Jail.	Court House.	Water No. 1.	Water No. 2.	Floating debt.	Defence and bounty.	City Hall.	Floating debt of 1868.	Jones' Falls.	Floating debt of 1874.	Water (1926).	Internal improvements, 1928.	General.	Public improvements (1940).	Municipal improvements (1945).	Water (1916).	Water (1928).	Floating debt (1930).	
1797-1817	75	...	...	...	...	...	...	...	...	...	...	...	...	...	...	...	...	...	...	...	...	...	...	...	...	...	...	...	...	...
1818	150	...	...	...	...	...	...	...	...	...	...	...	...	...	...	...	...	...	...	...	...	...	...	...	...	...	...	...	...	...
1819	200	45	...	...	...	...	...	...	...	...	...	...	...	...	...	...	...	...	...	...	...	...	...	...	...	...	...	...	...	...
1820	200	40	40	...	...	...	...	...	...	...	...	...	...	...	...	...	...	...	...	...	...	...	...	...	...	...	...	...	...	...
1821	200	25	35	...	...	...	...	...	...	...	...	...	...	...	...	...	...	...	...	...	...	...	...	...	...	...	...	...	...	...
1822	200	20	45	...	...	...	...	...	...	...	...	...	...	...	...	...	...	...	...	...	...	...	...	...	...	...	...	...	...	...
1823	200	30	60	...	...	...	...	...	...	...	...	...	...	...	...	...	...	...	...	...	...	...	...	...	...	...	...	...	...	...
1824	200	45	60	...	...	...	...	...	...	...	...	...	...	...	...	...	...	...	...	...	...	...	...	...	...	...	...	...	...	35
1825	250	45	75	...	...	...	...	...	...	...	...	...	...	...	...	...	...	...	...	...	...	...	...	...	...	...	...	...	...	35
1826	250	40	60	...	...	...	...	...	...	...	...	...	...	...	...	...	...	...	...	...	...	...	...	...	...	...	...	...	...	35
1827	250	35	65	...	...	...	...	...	...	...	...	...	...	...	...	...	...	...	...	...	...	...	...	...	...	...	...	...	...	35
1828	250	65	65	45	...	...	...	...	...	...	...	...	...	...	...	...	...	...	...	...	...	...	...	...	...	...	...	...	...	35
1829	250	40	60	25	...	...	...	...	...	...	...	...	...	...	...	...	...	...	...	...	...	...	...	...	...	...	...	...	...	35
1830	300	40	60	25	12½	...	...	...	...	...	...	...	...	...	...	...	...	...	...	...	...	...	...	...	...	...	...	...	...	35
1831	237½	40	60	25	12½	...	...	...	...	...	...	...	...	...	...	...	...	...	...	...	...	...	...	...	...	...	...	...	...	35
1832	300	40	50	90	12½	...	...	...	...	...	...	...	...	...	...	...	...	...	...	...	...	...	...	...	...	...	...	...	...	50
1833	300	33	50	40	12½	...	...	...	...	...	...	...	...	...	...	...	...	...	...	...	...	...	...	...	...	...	...	...	...	50
1834	333⅓	37½	47	40	12½	...	...	...	...	...	...	...	...	...	...	...	...	...	...	...	...	...	...	...	...	...	...	...	...	50
1835	333⅓	35	47	50	12½	...	...	...	...	...	...	...	...	...	...	...	...	...	...	...	...	...	...	...	...	...	...	...	...	50
1836	50	4	5¼	6¼	1⅓	...	...	...	...	...	...	...	...	...	...	...	...	...	...	...	...	...	...	...	...	...	...	...	...	4½
1837	50	3⅓	6⅓	5⅔	1⅓	...	...	...	...	...	...	...	...	...	...	...	...	...	...	...	...	...	...	...	...	...	...	...	...	4½
1838	50	4½	7	4⅔	1⅔	...	...	...	...	...	...	...	...	...	...	...	...	...	...	...	...	...	...	...	...	...	...	...	...	4½
1839	39⅓	2⅔	5	3⅓	1⅓	10⅓	...	...	...	...	...	...	...	...	...	...	...	...	...	...	...	...	...	...	...	...	...	...	...	3½
1840	36	2¼	5	4	1⅓	30	...	...	...	...	...	...	...	...	...	...	...	...	...	...	...	...	...	...	...	...	...	...	...	3⅓
1841	32	3	4⅓	4	1⅓	40	...	...	...	...	...	...	...	...	...	...	...	...	...	...	...	...	...	...	...	...	...	...	...	2
1842	6	3⅓	1⅔	5	2	63	...	...	...	...	...	...	...	...	...	...	...	...	...	...	...	...	...	...	...	...	...	...	...	2
1843	25	4	3½	3⅓	5	36	...	...	...	...	...	...	...	...	...	...	...	...	...	...	...	...	...	...	...	...	...	...	...	9
1844	28	1⅔	2¼	3⅓	5	30	...	...	...	...	...	...	...	...	...	...	...	...	...	...	...	...	...	...	...	...	...	...	...	5
1845	25	2⅓	3⅓	4	4	31	...	...	...	...	...	...	...	...	...	...	...	...	...	...	...	...	...	...	...	...	...	...	...	5
1846	30	3	3⅓	2½	3	28	...	...	...	...	...	...	...	...	...	...	...	...	...	...	...	...	...	...	...	...	...	...	...	8
1847	30	3	2¼	3	5	26⅓	...	...	...	...	...	...	...	...	...	...	...	...	...	...	...	...	...	...	...	...	...	...	...	6½
1848	30	2⅓	1¼	3¼	5	58	...	...	...	...	...	...	...	...	...	...	...	...	...	...	...	...	...	...	...	...	...	...	...	10
1849	46	3	3	3	4	34	...	...	...	...	...	...	...	...	...	...	...	...	...	...	...	...	...	...	...	...	...	...	...	8
1850	27¼	3	2⅓	3⅓	5⅔	40	...	...	...	...	...	...	...	...	...	...	...	...	...	...	...	...	...	...	...	...	...	...	...	16
1851	47	3	2	[illegible]	[illegible]	[illegible]	[illegible]	[illegible]	[illegible]	[illegible]	[illegible]	[illegible]	[illegible]	[illegible]	[illegible]	[illegible]	[illegible]	[illegible]	[illegible]	[illegible]	[illegible]	[illegible]	[illegible]	[illegible]	[illegible]	[illegible]	[illegible]	[illegible]	[illegible]	6

1853	55½	2½	1½	3	11½	3																							[illegible]
1854	53¾	4½	3	6½	14½	21																							11
1855	40	1¾	1¾	6	4¾	64																							26
1856	48	3	2	5	8	25																							8
1857	51	5	6	11	20½	6							½																30
1858	60½	3½	5	2½	11	30					2		½																50
1859	50	3½	5	8½	10½	10					2		½																30
1860	50	3	4	5	12½		22				2	1	½																30
1861	47	5	7	15	12		19½				2	1	½																20
1862	33½	1½	5½	9	9½	24	3½				2	1	½		2														15
1863	27½	4	7	1	15½	1½	25				2	1	½		2	5													
1864	39	2¼	5¾	10¼	12¼	1½	13½					1	½	3	2	9													25
1865	45	3	7	6½	18	1½	22½					1	½	3	2	15													35
1866	45	3	6½	7	15	5	25					1	½	3	2	12													25
1867	50	4	6	8	18½	7	29	5				1	½	3		8													15
1868	34	3	6	7	16½	4½	28½	17					½	3															34
1869	57	3	4½	6	23	4	23	16	18				½	3			2												50
1870	54	3½	7	7	20	6	32	15					½	3			2												34
1871	50	4	6½	9	13	5	28½	25	7								2												25
1872	78	3	5	8	18	10	21	18									2												50
1873	77	3	5	6	17	4	22	20	6								2												50
1874	69	3	6	8	21	10	23	29	3								3	1	2	2									50
1875	75	3	5	8	21	6	21	27	9								3	1	1	1									cease
1876	86	3	5	6	19	7	21	27	3								2	1											
1877	71		6	11	19	7	22	30	6								2	1											
1878	67		7	10	17		26	52	11																				
1879	69		5	8	18		23	23	4																				
1880	53		6	9	14		20	31	4																				
1881	55		9	10	17		22	24																					
1882	53		6	8	16		24	30																					
1883	58		8	8	18		24	30	4																				
1884	64		7	9	19		26	31	1	3																			
1885	61		9	9	23		24	27	5	2																			
1886	69		8	9	23		28	27	4	2																			
1887	56		9	8	23		27	27	8	2																			
1888	66		9	9	24		27	40	13	2																			
1889	79		8	10	23		27	35	5	2											½		½						
1890	70		10	8	26		29	33	6	2											½	½							
1891	46		10	9	23		28	24	4	2											1	3	5						
1892	43		10	8	25		25	30	3	2											1	3	5						
1893	29		11	7	32		31	30	4	2											1	3	5						
1894	52		10	8	32		25	23	7	2											1	3	5	2					
1885	53		12	8	31½		28	30	1												1	3	5	2	½				
1896	66½		11	9	37½		27	27	4¾												1	3	8½	2	½	2	½		
1897	52		13	7½	36¾		30	32½	10												1	3	8½	2	½	2	½	1	
1898	64½		14	10	45¾		33½	37½	1½												1	3	8½	2	½	2	½	1	

[1] Compiled from the Ordinances of Baltimore City and from the Reports of the City Collector.

APPENDIX F.—Taxation of General Property in Baltimore City, 1831-1898.[1]

Year.	Tax rate (per $100.)	Assessment of Real Property.	Assessment of Personal Property.	Total assessed valuation.	Collected within year.	Discount for prompt payment.	Year.	Tax rate (per $100.)	Assessment of Real Property.	Assessment of Personal Property.	Total assessed valuation.	Collected within year.	Discount for prompt payment.
1831	$3 75	....	....	$3,469,403	$68,999	....	1865	$1 25	....	....	$143,840,022	$1,320,326	$92,170
1832	4 92½	....	....	3,504,904	95,524	....	1866	1 25	....	....	144,920,217	1,318,496	55,889
1833	4 35¼	....	....	3,641,626	82,083	....	1867	1 40	....	....	147,078,105	1,457,864	64,008
1834	4 70¼	....	....	3,733,194	79,312	....	1868	1 20	....	....	206,136,248	1,648,009	57,942
1835	4 77½	....	....	3,787,702	101,509	....	1869	1 60	....	....	203,730,804	....	....
1836	66¾	....	....	42,931,960	152,114	....	1870	1 50	....	....	202,756,140	2,103,867	90,661
1837	60¾	....	....	41,544,062	146,952	....	1871	1 50	....	....	210,310,965	1,746,053	88,803
1838	67½	....	....	41,104,860	139,854	....	1872	1 63	....	....	217,102,970	1,851,690	96,238
1839	58½	....	....	55,793,370	91,903	....	1873	1 63	....	....	222,498,305	1,743,035	91,951
1840	78½	....	....	56,641,010	100,633	....	1874	1 80	....	....	228,571,316	2,030,024	108,181
1841	85	....	....	54,584,845	....	....	1875	1 80	....	....	231,365,863	2,192,209	117,384
1842	81¼	....	....	63,619,093	295,414	$13,922	1876	1 80	....	....	228,816,110	2,128,089	115,047
1843	77	....	....	60,103,537	275,882	12,788	1877	1 75	$178,572,032	$77,533,309	256,105,341	2,641,231	192,844
1844	70½	....	....	61,494,632	254,394	10,413	1878	1 90	178,958,592	70,308,003	249,266,595	2,768,992	118,682
1845	69	....	....	60,113,492	245,423	10,763	1879	1 50	183,580,023	60,463,158	244,043,181	2,279,949	121,983
1846	70	....	....	64,832,151	258,903	11,052	1880	1 37	183,051,396	58,929,242	241,980,638	2,237,874	89,708
1847	69½	....	....	74,921,145	327,715	13,808	1881	1 37	185,197,157	62,033,032	247,230,189	2,417,005	116,147
1848	1 00	....	....	76,509,611	430,062	22,331	1882	1 37	187,636,451	58,597,605	246,234,056	2,382,401	77,762
1849	93	....	....	78,252,588	415,357	21,706	1883	1 50	189,913,494	58,889,738	248,803,232	2,580,406	84,615
1850	82	....	....	80,166,992	380,240	15,898	1884	1 60	191,516,113	58,135,586	249,651,699	2,774,073	90,907
1851	65	....	....	81,418,924	270,503	10,854	1885	1 60	194,416,894	59,496,377	253,913,271	2,869,904	93,775
1852	90	....	....	84,804,454	392,038	15,896	1886	1 70	197,730,574	58,510,081	256,240,655	3,080,719	101,121
1853	77	....	....	98,831,487	388,039	14,794	1887	1 60	200,775,614	64,784,338	265,559,952	3,091,670	102,942
1854	1 03	....	....	102,424,915	487,714	19,362	1888	1 90	203,752,853	63,763,871	267,516,724	3,509,844	104,201
1855	1 18½	....	....	....	634,090	28,049	1889	1 90	206,892,526	65,878,357	272,770,883	3,558,823	109,347
1856	91	....	....	108,284,323	504,476	24,085	1890	1 85	209,553,077	68,696,614	278,249,691	3,484,609	102,740
1857	1 00	....	....	108,021,516	578,769	21,724	1891	1 55	211,289,901	69,577,168	280,867,069	3,081,842	98,925
1858	1 15	....	....	107,716,423	752,847	24,917	1892	1 55	212,662,237	70,058,583	282,720,820[2]	3,093,821	96,113
1859	90	....	....	135,499,873	692,652	21,727	1893	1 55	216,478,601	73,830,512	290,309,113	3,028,815	93,400
1860	1 00	....	....	138,505,765	750,206	24,469	1894	1 70	221,505,067	70,585,879	292,090,946	3,475,181	108,400
1861	1 09	....	....	138,199,900	847,044	26,910	1895	1 75	223,915,304	71,149,917	295,065,321	3,596,768	112,572
1862	92	....	....	134,532,804	809,014	33,423	1896	2 00	227,237,412	66,997,153	294,234,565	4,009,782	125,694
1863	92	....	....	135,091,035	847,787	38,413	1897	2 00	205,443,487	61,614,103	267,057,590[3]	3,800,679[4]	80,264
1864	1 00	....	....	139,417,797	1,023,831	49,567	1898	2 25	200,169,019	62,082,448	262,251,467[5]	4,412,613[4]	106,742

[1] From 1831 to 1865 the above figures are derived from the "Report of the Baltimore Tax Commission" (1885); thereafter, from the Reports of the City Collector and the Appeal Tax Court. Prior to 1877 the reports of the Appeal Tax Court fail to distinguish real and personal property.

[2] In the City Collector's Report this aggregate is $280,041,260.

[3] Exclusive of $55,386,511 in securities, subject to municipal taxation at the rate of 30 cents on $100.

[4] Including collections from tax on securities.

[5] Exclusive of $51,399,406 in securities.

APPENDIX G.—GROWTH OF FUNDED DEBT OF BALTIMORE CITY, 1857-1897.

FUNDED DEBT.	1857.	1858.	1859	1860.	1861.	1862.	1863.	1864.	1865.	1866.	1867.
Amount of Debt on January 1:	11,996,675 90	12,743,074 02	13,731,411 87	14,577,295 11	15,013,590 09	15,728,855 32	16,146,755 32	16,830,681 45	17,960,681 45	18,940,378 29	19,728,656 47
Water Loans..........	121,427 62	430,987 55	700,254 04	436,295 08	161,299 98	100,000 00	300,000 00	....	100,000 00	435,033 71	296,111 67
Jail "	....	154,455 88	95,544 12	....	....	....	....	....	....	....	....
Almshouse Loans....	....	....	....	....	....	....	100,000 00	....	300,000 00	38,716 11	....
Park "	....	....	....	....	553,966 25	....	....	61,000 00	109,030 00	....	17,323 80
Defence and Bounty Loans....	....	....	....	....	....	172,900 00	647,100 00	1,070,000 00	491,666 84	397,536 77	5,040 00
Funding Floating Debt Loans.......	....	....	....	....	....	145,000 00	....	....	....	....	....
Internal Improvement Loans.......	624,970 50	402,944 42	41,085 08	....	....	....	....	....	....	....	....
City Hall Loans......	....	....	....	....	....	....	....	....	....	....	32,000 00
Jones' Falls Loans...	....	....	....	....	....	....	....	....	....	....	....
Western Maryland Railroad Company Loans..............	....	....	....	....	....	....	....	....	....	....	200,000 00
Harford Sewer Loans	....	....	....	....	....	....	....	....	....	....	....
Paving Loans.........	....	....	....	....	....	....	....	....	....	....	....
Municipal Improvement Loans. (composite)...	....	....	....	....	....	....	....	....	....	....	....
Miscellaneous Loans.	....	....	....	....	....	....	....	....	....	17,005 54	58,490 79
Redemptions...........	....	....	....	....	....	....	303,173 87	1,000 00	12,000 00	109,613 95	....
Amount of Debt on December 31: ...	12,743,074 02	13,731,411 87	14,577,295 11	15,013,590 09	15,728,855 32	16,146,755 32	16,880,681 45	17,960,681 45	18,940,378 29	19,728,656 47	20,837,622 73

FUNDED DEBT.	1868.	1869.	1870.	1871.	1872.	1873.	1874.	1875.	1876.	1877.	1878.
Amount of Debt on January 1:	20,837,622 73	22,009,224 69	23,254,970 85	24,399,125 47	24,691,525 47	25,964,425 47	27,108,925 77	30,103,725 77	30,951,425 77	31,351,251 73	32,600,965 17
Water Loans..........	....	....	368,854 62	....	....	....	....	263,000 00	400,000 00	1,114,413 44	1,230,100 00
Jail "	....	101,576 48	....	....	....	....	....	....	....	....	....
Almshouse Loans....	....	....	....	....	....	....	....	....	....	....	146,700 00
Park "	....	....	....	....	....	200,000 00	....	....	....	....	....
Defence and Bounty Loans....	29,377 10	....	....	....	....	....	....	....	....	....	....
Funding Floating Debt Loans.......	1,700,000 00	....	699,900 00	74,000 00	....	26,300 00	1,740,500 00	259,500 00	....	135,300 00	910,000 00
Internal Improvement Loans.......	....	....	....	....	387,800 00	....	612,200 00	15,300 00	....	....	....
City Hall Loans......	4,000 00	885,800 00	78,200 00	218,400 00	225,800 00	345,700 00	502,700 00	207,400 00	....	....	....
Jones' Falls Loans...	....	....	....	....	47,800 00	184,700 00	139,400 00	102,500 00	....	....	....
Western Maryland Railroad Company Loans....	....	....	....	....	1,000,000 00	....	....	....	....	....	....
Harford Sewer Loans	....	....	....	....	....	....	....	....	....	....	....
Paving Loans.........	....	....	....	....	....	....	....	....	....	....	....
Municipal Improvement Loans. (composite)....	....	....	....	....	....	....	....	....	....	....	....
Miscellaneous Loans.		199,159,68	3,003 30	....	4,000 00	413 48	....	....	....	....	....
Redemptions...........	1,775 14	790 00	5,863 30	....	4,200 00	413 18	....	....	174 04	....	2,411,467 11
Amount of Debt on December 31:	22,009,224 69	23,254,970 85	24,399,125 47	24,691,525 47	25,964,425 47	27,108,925 77	30,103,725 77	30,951,425 77	31,351,251 73	32,600,965 17	32,476,298 06

APPENDIX G (continued).—GROWTH OF FUNDED DEBT OF BALTIMORE CITY, 1857-1897.

FUNDED DEBT.	1879.	1880.	1881.	1882.	1883.	1884.	1885.	1886.	1887.	1888.	1889.
Amount of Debt on January 1:	32,476,298 06	33,531,798 06	34,600,298 06	34,894,191 73	35,453,691 73	36,029,991 73	36,051,591 73	35,241,247 59	33,468,289 64	35,377,176 15	36,088,516 15
Water Loans	841,500 00	378,800 00	....	....	500,000 00	....	....	....	....	400,000 00	200,000 00
Jail "	....	....	....	....	....	....	....	....	....	...	....
Almshouse Loans	133,700 00	650,000 00	....	....	....	....	....	....	....	....	....
Park "	....	....	....	....	200,000 00	....	....	....	....	....	....
Defence and Bounty Loans	....	40,000, 00	....	....	....	....	....	....	....	....	....
Funding Floating Debt Loans	90,000 00	....	....	....	....	....	....	....	....	....	....
Internal Improvement Loans	....	....	....	371,000 00	131,000 00	115,000 00	67,000 00	....	1,704,000 00	....	....
City Hall Loans	....	....	....	....	....	....	....	....	....	....	....
Jones' Falls Loans	....	....	40,400 00	88,500 00	88,500 00	200,000 00	100,000 00	120,000 00	135,000 00	100,000 00	....
Western Maryland Railroad Company Loans	....	....	....	....	....	....	....	....	....	....	....
Harford Sewer Loans	....	....	210,000 00	....	....	....	1,700 00	155,000 00	90,000 00	103,300 00	....
Paving Loans	....	....	45,000 00	100,000 00	259,800 00	95,200 00	....	....	....	....	....
Municipal Improvement Loans. (composite)	....	....	....	....	....	....	....	....	....	....	500,000 00
Miscellaneous Loans	....	....	....	....	....	....	....	....	....	....	....
Redemptions	9,700 00	300 00	1,506 33	....	3000 00	988,600 00	979,045 16	2,052,957 95	15,113 49	1,060 00	430 00
Amount of Debt on December 31:	33,531,798 06	34,600,298 06	34,894.191 73	35,453,691 73	36,629,991 73	36,051,591 73	35,241,247 59	33,463,289 64	35,377,176 15	36,088,516 15	36,738,107 70

FUNDED DEBT.	1890.	1891.	1892.	1893.	1894.	1895.	1896.	1897.
Amount of Debt on January 1:	36,738,107 70	30,091,787 06	31,784,050 95	33,671,297 48	33,108,475 56	30,134,625 57	31,562,818 43	32,627,018 43
Water Loans	200,000 00	200,000 00	....	....	....	....	....	....
Jail "	....	....	....	....	....	....	....	....
Almshouse Loans	....	....	....	....	....	....	....	....
Park "	....	....	....	....	....	....	....	....
Defence and Bounty Loans	....	....	....	....	....	....	....	....
Funding Floating Debt Loans	....	....	....	....	....	....	....	1,453,300 00
Internal Improvement "	....	....	....	....	....	....	...	....
City Hall Loans	....	....	....	....	....	....	....	....
Jones' Falls Loans	....	....	28,000 00	....	....	....	....	....
Western Maryland Railroad Company Loans	....	....	....	....	.. ..	....	....	....
Harford Sewer Loans	....	....	....	....	....	....	....	....
Paving Loans	....	....	....	....	....	....	....	....
Municipal Improvement Loans. (composite)	800,000 00	1,669,300 00	1,880,700 00	1,759,500 00	972,900 00	1,672,500 00	1,080,200 00	1,219,800 00
Miscellaneous Loans	....	....	....	....	....	....	...	....
Redemptions	7,646,320 64	177,036 11	21,458 47	2,322,321 02	3,946,749 99	244,307 14	16,000 00	4,541 48
Amount of Debt on December 31:	30,091,787 06	31,784,050 95	33,671,297 48	33,108,475 56	30,134,625 57	31,562,818,43	32,627,018 43	35,295,576 95

APPENDIX II.—Growth of Sinking Funds of Baltimore City, 1856–1898.

	1856.	1857.	1858.	1859.	1860.	1861.	1862.	1863.	1864.	1865.	1866.
General	143,279 11	202,327 39	229,308 17	269,053 53	260,334 69	309,496 28	373,534 78	480,090 84	254,792 26	877,879 28	1,575,675 63
Pittsburg and Connellsville R. R. Co.	....	6,000 00	12,587 56	13,370 10	14,188 67	15,008 08	15,856 16	1,727 45	9,857 45	17,857 45	20,065 75
Water	....	....	....	7,145 57	11,769 73	15,200 52	15,200 52	85,332 77	41,932 77	91,932 77	124,273 06
Jail	....	....	....	12,974 05	33,965 78	55,519 13	89,888 80	128,909 96	176,125 89	197,084 42	210,062 12
Court House	....	....	....	....	....	4,115 00	4,115 00	32,936 74	22,630 50	42,589 50	53,590 50
Park	....	....	....	....	....	....	2,825 00	4,708 38	7,560 00	13,700 00	89,441 20
Floating Debt	....	....	....	....	....	....	....	16,000 00	37,000 00	72,000 00	105,000 00
Defence and Bounties	....	....	....	....	....	....	....	2,000 00	28,000 00	28,300 00	30,300 00
Almshouse	....	....	....	....	....	....	....	....	3,500 00	3,500 00	5,200 00
City Hall	....	....	....	....	....	....	....	....	....	....	....
N. W. Va. R. R.	....	....	....	....	....	....	....	....	....	....	....
Funding 1900	....	....	....	....	....	....	....	....	....	....	....
Funding 1894	....	....	....	....	....	....	....	....	....	....	....
Jones' Falls 1900	....	....	....	....	....	....	....	....	....	....	....
Hillen Station	....	....	....	....	....	....	....	....	....	....	....
Western Maryland of 1925	....	....	....	....	....	....	....	....	....	....	....
Four Million of 1945	....	....	....	....	....	....	....	....	....	....	....
Western Maryland Terminal Co.	....	....	....	....	....	....	....	....	....	....	....
Western Maryland of 1927	....	....	....	....	....	....	....	....	....	....	....
Water of 1926	....	....	....	....	....	....	....	....	....	....	....
Five Million of 1928	....	....	....	....	....	....	....	....	....	....	....
Clifton Park	....	....	....	....	....	....	....	....	....	....	....
Six Million of 1940	....	....	....	....	....	....	....	....	....	....	....
Water of 1916	....	....	....	....	....	....	....	....	....	....	....
Water of 1922	....	....	....	....	....	....	....	....	....	....	....
Funding of 1936	....	....	....	....	....	....	....	....	....	....	....
Total	143,279 11	208,327 39	241,895 73	303,443 25	320,258 87	390,339 01	501,420 26	701,706 14	580,907 87	1,344,903 42	2,164,508 26

APPENDIX H (continued).—GROWTH OF SINKING FUNDS OF BALTIMORE CITY, 1856-1898.

	1867.	1868.	1869.	1870.	1871.	1872.	1873.	1874	1875.	1876.	1877.
General	2,285,687 09	2,429,116 05	2,600,462 32	2,877,311 93	3,088,353 52	3,305,084 84	3,548,241 44	3,881,366 46	4,959,434 35[1]	5,288,465 34	6,692,647 70
Pittsburg and Connellsville R. R. Co.	22,179 55	23,510 29	24,908 40	26,508 20	28,357 84	30,080 70	31,951 70	34,108 60	....	....	....
Water	143,212 00	155,176 00	164,422 18	235,476 52	325,086 35	368,297 15	398,186 65	417,442 04	443,667 77	470,412 61	497,451 90
Jail	228,711 52	238,308 23	252,558 89	267,136 59	285,616 79	301,007 79	317,050 00	334,244 80	....	....	....
Court House	72,382 05	80,288 14	94,501 23	103,175 34	100,950 52	117,224 37	123,674 13	130,128 89	....	....	....
Park	57,241 73	65,462 08	60,266 01	80,269 70	122,618 33	150,691 86	174,100 91	218,790 14	196,071 07	220,720 91	244,370 34
Floating Debt	130,176 65	152,615 53	161,558 71	169,561 31	181,243 42	185,104 29	201,707 97	212,311 65	....	....	....
Defence and Bounties	33,518 50	35,529 60	37,641 72	39,774 07	42,510 65	44,982 90	47,515 58	50,097 67	....	....	....
Almshouse	5,574 42	5,880 88	6,117 88	6,464 34	6,909 97	7,283 43	7,686 89	8,084 35	....	....	....
City Hall	....	....	....	20,003 54	61,924 05	106,648 82	151,250 30	206,275 01	276,125 36	342,147 36	405,543 97
N. W. Va. R. R.	1,301,318 15	1,489,770 65	973,408 00	851,857 50	845,608 85	853,116 65	834,821 05	808,247 61	....	....	....
Funding 1900	....	....	....	....	....	....	....	....	11,853 54	32,081 36	52,569 08
Funding 1894	....	....	....	....	....	....	....	....	23,707 07	52,016 77	62,465 51
Jones' Falls 1900	....	....	....	....	....	....	....	....	23,707 07	52,016 77	62,465 51
Hillen Station	....	....	....	....	....	....	....	....	....	....	1,383 34
Western Maryland of 1925	....	....	....	....	....	....	....	....	....	....	....
Four Million of 1945	....	....	....	....	....	....	....	....	....	....	....
Western Maryland Terminal Co.	....	....	....	....	....	....	....	....	....	....	....
Western Maryland of 1927	....	....	....	....	....	....	....	....	....	....	....
Water of 1926	....	....	....	....	....	....	....	....	....	....	....
Five Million of 1928	....	....	....	....	....	....	....	....	....	....	....
Clifton Park	....	....	....	....	....	....	....	....	....	....	....
Six Million of 1940	....	....	....	....	....	....	....	....	....	....	....
Water of 1916	....	....	....	....	....	....	....	....	....	....	....
Water of 1922	....	....	....	....	....	....	....	....	....	....	....
Funding of 1936	....	....	....	....	....	....	....	....	....	....	....
Total	4,365,001 76	4,684,697 49	4,384,985 93	4,686,539 13	5,098,240 89	5,469,432 49	5,831,886 46	6,296,086 81	5,936,506 28	6,457,861 12	8,018,847 35

[1] In 1874, the Court House, Floating Debt, Pittsburg and Connellsville, Jail, Almshouse, Defence and Bounties, N. W. Va. R. R. Co. Sinking Funds were consolidated with the General Sinking Fund.

APPENDIX H (continued).—GROWTH OF SINKING FUNDS OF BALTIMORE CITY, 1856-1898.

	1878.	1879.	1880.	1881.	1882.	1883.	1884.	1885.	1886.	1887.	1888.
General	7,136,965 20	5,427,511 70	7,091,719 96[1]	7,491,518 38	7,747,181 51	7,974,218 64	8,190,296 33	7,605,621 03	6,837,362 08	5,108,827 54	5,251,696 77
Pittsburg and Connellsville R. R. Co.	....	....	....	....	....	....	....	....	....	....	....
Water	527,888 83	560,546 83	....	....	....	....	....	....	....	....	....
Jail	....	....	....	....	....	....	....	....	....	....	....
Court House	....	....	....	....	....	....	....	....	....	....	....
Park	296,708 87	296,220 17	323,906 49	357,753 79	390,271 28	426,123 98	458,678 72	497,665 89	536,056 06	563,116 43	605,942 67
Floating Debt	....	....	....	....	....	....	....	....	....	....	....
Defence and Bounties	803,247 61	....	....	....	....	....	....	....	....	....	....
Almshouse	....	....	....	....	....	....	....	....	....	....	....
City Hall	482,477 36	523,234 02	....	....	....	....	....	....	....	....	....
N. W. Va. R. R. Co.	....	....	....	....	....	....	....	....	....	....	....
Funding 1900	80,582 19	90,914 45	....	....	....	....	....	....	....	....	....
Funding 1894	69,523 79	....	....	....	....	....	....	....	....	....	....
Jones' Falls 1900	69,523 79	74,621 37	....	....	....	....	....	....	....	....	....
Hillen Station	3,741 66	5,916 66	8,100 66	10,485 66	12,830 66	15,460 66	17,785 66	20,415 16	22,822 66	25,423 91	28,141 41
Western Maryland of 1925	....	....	....	....	....	11,283 15	22,179 95	36,659 85	42,484 15	44,248 90	46,015 90
Four Million of 1945	....	....	....	....	....	....	....	....	....	....	....
Western Maryland Terminal Co.	....	....	....	....	....	....	1,507 75	2,168 59	3,579 69	4,808 29	6,127 64
Western Maryland of 1927	....	....	....	....	....	....	....	....	....	....	101,317 00
Water of 1926	....	....	....	....	....	....	....	....	....	....	....
Five Million of 1928	....	....	....	....	....	....	....	....	....	....	....
Clifton Park	....	....	....	....	....	....	....	....	....	....	....
Six Million of 1940	....	....	....	....	....	....	....	....	....	....	....
Water of 1916	....	....	....	....	....	....	....	....	....	....	....
Water of 1922	....	....	....	....	....	....	....	....	....	....	....
Funding of 1936	....	....	....	....	....	....	....	....	....	....	....
Total	8,640,411 69	6,978,965 20	7,423,727 11	7,859,757 78	8,150,286 45	8,427,086 43	8,690,448 41	8,162,530 52	7,442,304 64	5,743,425 07	6,039,241 39

[1] In 1879 all sinking funds except those for the Park and Hillen Station Loans were merged with the General Sinking Fund.

APPENDIX II (continued).—GROWTH OF SINKING FUNDS OF BALTIMORE CITY, 1856-1898.

	1889.	1890.	1891.	1892.	1893.	1894.	1895.	1896.	1897.	1898.
General	5,418,236 47	5,567,213 19	6,767,499 52	6,921,969 92	7,279,010 93	5,330,623 50	1,606,099 67	1,542,710 96	1,716,415 68	1,906,255 80
Pittsburg and Connellsville R. R. Co.	....	....	....	....	....	....	....	....	....	....
Water	....	....	....	....	....	....	....	....	....	....
Jail	....	....	....	....	....	....	....	....	....	....
Court House	....	....	....	....	....	....	....	....	....	....
Park	656,442 62	710,538 44	200,307 90	121,462 92	107,905 47	65,315 60	24,499 48	24,499 48	9,499 80	9,831 98
Floating Debt	....	....	....	....	....	....	....	....	....	....
Defence and Bounties	....	....	....	....	....	....	....	....	....	....
Almshouse	....	....	....	....	....	....	....	....	....	....
City Hall	....	....	....	....	....	....	....	....	....	....
N. W. Va. R. R.	....	....	....	....	....	....	....	....	....	....
Funding 1900	....	....	....	....	....	....	....	....	....	....
Funding 1894	....	....	....	....	....	....	....	....	....	....
Jones' Falls, 1900	....	....	....	....	....	....	....	....	....	....
Hillen Station	31,250 03	34,464 28	37,484 29	40,906 53	44,402 04	48,546 87	52,577 51	56,975 81	62,215 61	66,910 66
Western Maryland of 1925	48,197 15	50,828 40	51,233 65	53,562 15	55,680 85	58,034 55	60,543 92	63,177 12	66,398 82	70,449 99
Four Million of 1945	....	....	....	....	....	....	....	57,251 85	72,508 74	110,124 98
Western Maryland Terminal Co.	7,687 86	9,124 21	10,616 81	12,319 78	14,028 97	15,939 66	17,950 44	20,074 63	22,709 57	24,967 78
Western Maryland of 1927	104,347 00	107,213 25	110,662 25	113,715 63	117,139 13	121,318 62	125,690 52	130,131 70	135,587 00	140,909 12
Water of 1926	27,793 89	52,763 70	66,516 12	91,388 08	117,929 31	149,737 85	184,813 73	220,579 57	254,821 49	287,782 85
Five Million of 1928	....	20,846 12	50,302 55	120,807 30	204,910 78	293,155 04	393,596 48	494,094 62	604,366 91	801,810 24
Clifton Park	....	....	....	....	....	....	....	3,222 38	15,477 89	28,578 67
Six Million of 1940	....	....	....	....	....	....	57,920 59	131,333 60	217,843 15	272,178 35
Water of 1916	....	....	....	....	....	....	....	....	335,834 80	397,361 22
Water of 1922	....	....	....	....	....	....	....	....	10,174 43	162,395 72
Funding of 1936	....	....	....	....	....	....	....	....	....	96,971 16
Total	6,293,954 52	6,552,491 59	7,303,623 08	7,476,126 31	7,941,007 48	6,082,671 69	2,583,641 33	2,744,051 23	3,528,871 57	4,876,398 48

INDEX

JOHNS HOPKINS UNIVERSITY STUDIES

IN

Historical and Political Science.

HERBERT B. ADAMS, Editor.

FIRST SERIES.—Local Institutions.—$4.00.

I. **An Introduction to American Institutional History.** By E. A. FREEMAN. 25 *cents.*
II. **The Germanic Origin of New England Towns.** By H. B. ADAMS. 50 *cents.*
III. **Local Government in Illinois.** By ALBERT SHAW.—**Local Government in Pennsylvania.** By E. R. L. GOULD. 30 *cents.*
IV. **Saxon Tithingmen in America.** By H. B. ADAMS. 50 *cents.*
V. **Local Government in Michigan, and the Northwest.** By E. W. BEMIS. 25 *cents.*
VI. **Parish Institutions of Maryland.** By EDWARD INGLE. 40 *cents.*
VII. **Old Maryland Manors.** By JOHN HEMSLEY JOHNSON. 30 *cents.*
VIII. **Norman Constables in America.** By H. B. ADAMS. 50 *cents.*
IX-X. **Village Communities of Cape Ann and Salem.** By H. B. ADAMS. 50 *cents.*
XI. **The Genesis of a New England State.** By A. JOHNSTON. 30 *cents.*
XII. **Local Government and Schools in South Carolina.** By B. J. RAMAGE. 40 *cents.*

SECOND SERIES.—Institutions and Economics.—$4.00.

I-II. **Methods of Historical Study.** By H. B. ADAMS. 50 *cents.*
III. **The Past and the Present of Political Economy.** By R. T. ELY. 35 *cents.*
IV. **Samuel Adams, The Man of the Town Meeting.** By JAMES K. HOSMER. 35 *cents.*
V-VI. **Taxation in the United States.** By HENRY CARTER ADAMS. 50 *cents.*
VII. **Institutional Beginnings in a Western State.** By JESSE MACY. 25 *cents.*
VIII-IX. **Indian Money in New England, etc.** By WILLIAM B. WEEDEN. 50 *cents.*
X. **Town and County Government in the Colonies.** By E. CHANNING. 50 *cents.*
XI. **Rudimentary Society among Boys.** By J. HEMSLEY JOHNSON. 50 *cents.*
XII. **Land Laws of Mining Districts.** By C. H. SHINN. 50 *cents.*

THIRD SERIES.—Maryland, Virginia and Washington.—$4.00.

I. **Maryland's Influence upon Land Cessions to the U. S.** By H. B. ADAMS. 75 *cents.*
II-III. **Virginia Local Institutions.** By E. INGLE. 75 *cents.*
IV. **Recent American Socialism.** By RICHARD T. ELY. 50 *cents.*
V-VI-VII. **Maryland Local Institutions.** By LEWIS W. WILHELM. $1.00.
VIII. **The Influence of the Proprietors in Founding New Jersey.** By A. SCOTT. 25 *cents.*
IX-X. **American Constitutions.** By HORACE DAVIS. 50 *cents.*
XI-XII. **The City of Washington.** By J. A. PORTER. 50 *cents.*

FOURTH SERIES—Municipal Government and Land Tenure.—$3.50.

I. **Dutch Village Communities on the Hudson River.** By I. ELTING. 50 *cents.*
II-III. **Town Government in Rhode Island.** By W. E. FOSTER.—**The Narragansett Planters.** By EDWARD CHANNING. 50 *cents.*
IV. **Pennsylvania Boroughs.** By WILLIAM P. HOLCOMB. 50 *cents.*
V. **Introduction to the Constitutional and Political History of the States.** By J. F. JAMESON. 50 *cents.*
VI. **The Puritan Colony at Annapolis, Maryland.** By D. R. RANDALL. 50 *cents.*
VII-VIII-IX. **The Land Question in the United States.** By S. SATO. $1.00.
X. **Town and City Government of New Haven.** By C. H. LEVERMORE. 50 *cents.*
XI-XII. **Land System of the New England Colonies.** By M. EGLESTON. 50 *cents*

FIFTH SERIES.—Municipal Government, History and Politics.—$3.50.

I-II. **City Government of Philadelphia.** By E. P. ALLINSON and B. PENROSE. 50 *cents.*

III. **City Government of Boston.** By JAMES M. BUGBEE. 25 *cents.*

IV. **City Government of St. Louis.** By MARSHALL S. SNOW. 25 *cents.*

V-VI. **Local Government in Canada.** By JOHN GEORGE BOURINOT. 50 *cents.*

VII. **Influence of War of 1812 upon the American Union.** By N. M. BUTLER. 25 *cents.*

VIII. **Notes on the Literature of Charities.** By HERBERT B. ADAMS. 25 *cents.*

IX. **Predictions of Hamilton and De Tocqueville.** By JAMES BRYCE. 25 *cents.*

X. **The Study of History in England and Scotland.** By P. FRÉDÉRICQ. 25 *cents.*

XI. **Seminary Libraries and University Extension.** By H. B. ADAMS. 25 *cents.*

XII. **European Schools of History and Politics.** By A. D. WHITE. 25 *cents.*

SIXTH SERIES.—The History of Co-operation in the United States.—$3.50.

SEVENTH SERIES.—Social Science, Education, Government.—$3.50.

I. **Arnold Toynbee.** By F. C. MONTAGUE. 50 *cents.*

II-III. **Municipal Government in San Francisco.** By BERNARD MOSES. 50 *cents.*

IV. **The City Government of New Orleans.** By WM. W. HOWE. 25 *cents.*

V-VI. **English Culture in Virginia.** By WILLIAM P. TRENT. $1.00.

VII-VIII-IX. **The River Towns of Connecticut.** By CHARLES M. ANDREWS. $1.00.

X-XI-XII. **Federal Government in Canada.** By JOHN G. BOURINOT. $1.00.

EIGHTH SERIES.—History, Politics and Education.—$3.50.

I-II. **The Beginnings of American Nationality.** By A. W. SMALL. $1.00.

III. **Local Government in Wisconsin.** By D. E. SPENCER. 25 *cents.*

IV. **Spanish Colonization in the Southwest.** By F. W. BLACKMAR. 50 *cents.*

V-VI. **The Study of History in Germany and France.** By P. FRÉDÉRICQ. $1.00.

VII-VIII-IX. **Progress of the Colored People of Maryland.** By J. R. BRACKETT. $1.00.

X. **The Study of History in Belgium and Holland.** By P. FRÉDÉRICQ. 50 *cents.*

XI-XII. **Seminary Notes on Recent Historical Literature.** By H. B. ADAMS, J. M. VINCENT, W. B. SCAIFE, and others. 50 *cents.*

NINTH SERIES.—Education, History, Politics, Social Science.—$3.50.

I-II. **Government and Administration of the United States.** By W. W. WILLOUGHBY and W. F. WILLOUGHBY. 75 *cents.*

III-IV. **University Education in Maryland.** By B. C. STEINER. **The Johns Hopkins University (1876-1891).** By D. C. GILMAN. 50 *cents.*

V-VI. **Development of Municipal Unity in the Lombard Communes.** By WILLIAM K. WILLIAMS. 50 *cents.*

VII-VIII. **Public Lands of the Roman Republic.** By A. STEPHENSON. 75 *cents.*

IX. **Constitutional Development of Japan.** By T. IYENAGA. 50 *cents.*

X. **A History of Liberia.** By J. H. T. MCPHERSON. 50 *cents.*

XI-XII. **The Indian Trade in Wisconsin.** By F. J. TURNER. 50 *cents.*

TENTH SERIES.—Church and State: Columbus and America.—$3.50.

I. **The Bishop Hill Colony.** By MICHAEL A. MIKKELSEN. 50 *cents.*

II-III. **Church and State in New England.** By PAUL E. LAUER. 50 *cents.*

IV. **Church and State in Maryland.** By GEORGE PETRIE. 50 *cents.*

V-VI. **The Religious Development in the Province of North Carolina.** By STEPHEN B. WEEKS. 50 *cents.*

VII. **Maryland's Attitude in the Struggle for Canada.** By JOHN W. BLACK. 50 *cents.*

VIII-IX. **The Quakers in Pennsylvania.** By A. C. APPLEGARTH. 75 *cents.*

X-XI. **Columbus and his Discovery of America.** By H. B. ADAMS and H. WOOD. 50 *cents.*

XII. **Causes of the American Revolution.** By J. A. WOODBURN. 50 *cents.*

ELEVENTH SERIES.—Labor, Slavery, and Self-Government.—$3.50.

I. **The Social Condition of Labor.** By E. R. L. GOULD. 50 *cents.*

II. **The World's Representative Assemblies of To-Day.** By E. K. ALDEN. 50 *cents.*

III-IV. **The Negro in the District of Columbia.** By EDWARD INGLE. $1.00.

V-VI. **Church and State in North Carolina.** By STEPHEN B. WEEKS. 50 *cents.*

VII-VIII. **The Condition of the Western Farmer as illustrated by the economic history of a Nebraska township.** By A. F. BENTLEY. $1.00.

IX-X. **History of Slavery in Connecticut.** By BERNARD C. STEINER. 75 *cents.*

XI-XII. **Local Government in the South and Southwest.** By EDWARD W. BEMIS and others. $1.00.

TWELFTH SERIES.—Institutional and Economic History.—$3.50.

I-II. The Cincinnati Southern Railway. By J. H. HOLLANDER. $1.00.
III. Constitutional Beginnings of North Carolina. By J. S. BASSETT. *50 cents.*
IV. The Struggle of Protestant Dissenters for Religious Toleration in Virginia. By H. R. MCILWAINE. *50 cents.*
V-VI-VII. The Carolina Pirates and Colonial Commerce. By S. C. HUGHSON. $1.00.
VIII-IX. History of Representation and Suffrage in Mass. By G. H. HAYNES. *50 cents.*
X. English Institutions and the American Indian. By J. A. JAMES. *25 cents.*
XI-XII. The International Beginnings of the Congo Free State. By J. S. REEVES. *50 cents.*

THIRTEENTH SERIES.—South Carolina, Maryland, Virginia.—$3.50.

I-II. Government of the Colony of South Carolina. By E. L. WHITNEY. *75 cents.*
III-IV. Early Relations of Maryland and Virginia. By J. H. LATANÉ. *50 cents.*
V. The Rise of the Bicameral System in America. By T. F. MORAN. *50 cents.*
VI-VII. White Servitude in the Colony of Virginia. By J. C. BALLAGH. *50 cents.*
VIII. The Genesis of California's First Constitution. By R. D. HUNT. *50 cents.*
IX. Benjamin Franklin as an Economist. By W. A. WETZEL. *50 cents.*
X. The Provisional Government of Maryland. By J. A. SILVER. *50 cents.*
XI-XII. Government and Religion of the Va. Indians. By S. R. HENDREN. *50 cents.*

FOURTEENTH SERIES.—Baltimore, Slavery, Constitutional History.—$3.50.

I. Constitutional History of Hawaii. By HENRY E. CHAMBERS. *25 cents.*
II. City Government of Baltimore. By THADDEUS P. THOMAS. *25 cents.*
III. Colonial Origins of New England Senates. By F. L. RILEY. *50 cents.*
IV-V. Servitude in the Colony of North Carolina. By J. S. BASSETT. *50 cents.*
VI-VII. Representation in Virginia. By J. A. C. CHANDLER. *50 cents.*
VIII. History of Taxation in Connecticut (1636-1776). By F. R. JONES. *50 cents.*
IX-X. A Study of Slavery in New Jersey. By HENRY S. COOLEY. *50 cents.*
XI-XII. Causes of the Maryland Revolution of 1689. By F. E. SPARKS. *50 cents.*

FIFTEENTH SERIES.—American Economic History.—$3.00.

I-II. The Tobacco Industry in Virginia since 1860. By B. W. ARNOLD. *50 cents.*
III-IV-V. Street Railway System of Philadelphia. By F. W. SPEIRS. *Cloth*, $1.00.
VI. Daniel Raymond. By C. P. NEILL. *50 cents.*
VII-VIII. Economic History of Baltimore and Ohio R. R. By M. REIZENSTEIN. *50 cents.*
IX. The South American Trade of Baltimore. By F. R. RUTTER. *50 cents.*
X-XI. State Tax Commissions in the U. S. By J. W. CHAPMAN. *50 cents.*
XII. Tendencies in American Economic Thought. By S. SHERWOOD. *25 cents.*

SIXTEENTH SERIES.-Anglo-American Relations and Southern History.-$3.00.

I-IV. Neutrality of the American Lakes and Anglo-American Relations. By J. M. CALLAHAN. $1.50.
V. West Florida and its Relation to the Historical Cartography of the United States. By H. E. CHAMBERS. *25 cents.*
VI. Anti-Slavery Leaders of North Carolina. By J. S. BASSETT. *50 cents.*
VII. Life and Administration of Sir Robert Eden. By B. C. STEINER. $1.00.
VIII. The Transition of North Carolina from a Colony to a Commonwealth. By E. W. SIKES.
XII. Jared Sparks and Alexis De Tocqueville. By H. B. ADAMS. *25 cents.*

SEVENTEENTH SERIES.—1899—Subscription, $3.00.

I-II-III. History of State Banking in Maryland. By A. C. BRYAN. $1.00.
IV-V. History of the Know-Nothing Party in Maryland. By L. F. SCHMECKEBIER. *75 cents.*
History of Slavery in North Carolina. By J. S. BASSETT.
History of Slavery in Virginia. By J. C. BALLAGH.
The Labadist Colony in Maryland. By B. B. JAMES.
The Separatists of Zoar. By GEORGE B. LANDIS.
Early Development of Chesapeake & Ohio Canal Project. By GEORGE W. WARD.
The Admission of Iowa into the Union. By J. A. JAMES.
The Colonial Executive Prior to the Restoration. By P. L. KAYE.
The History of Suffrage in Virginia. By J. A. C. CHANDLER.

THE JOHNS HOPKINS PRESS,
BALTIMORE, MD.

www.ingramcontent.com/pod-product-compliance
Lightning Source LLC
Chambersburg PA
CBHW030602300426
44111CB00009B/1071

* 9 7 8 3 3 3 7 3 3 8 6 8 8 *